BIRDS IN THE ANCIENT WORLD

Jeremy Mynott is the author of *Birdscapes: Birds in Our Imagination and Experience* (2009), a book exploring the variety of human responses to birds, described by reviewers as 'the finest book ever written about why we watch birds' (*Guardian*) and 'a wonderful rumination on birds and birders through space and time for anyone interested in our relationship with nature' (THES). He has also published an edition and translation of Thucydides in the series 'Cambridge Texts in the History of Political Thought' and, more recently, *Knowing your Place*, an account of the wildlife in a tiny Suffolk hamlet. He has broadcast on radio and television, is a regular reviewer for the *TLS* and *Wildlife* magazines, a founder member of 'New Networks for Nature', and is the former Chief Executive of Cambridge University Press and an Emeritus Fellow of Wolfson College, Cambridge.

Praise for *Birds in the Ancient World*

'Jeremy Mynott's *Birds in the Ancient World* is an absolute joy, beautifully written and gloriously illustrated.'

Peter Thonemann, Books of the Year 2018, *The Times Literary Supplement*

'[A] superb book…Mynott quotes […] 120 authors in total, some translated into English for the first time. All the translations are Mynott's own. The period covered is approximately 700 BC to AD 300 and, since Mynott's approach is thematic, each chapter ranges pretty freely across those thousand years. It is, without doubt, a major achievement and a brilliantly sustained exercise in what Mynott […] calls "thinking with birds"…We are fortunate to have in Mynott, who is both an ornithologist and a classicist, the perfect guide for such explorations.'

Mathew Lyons, *History Today*

'An astonishing combination of knowledge and sheer readability…a copiously and richly illustrated review…I think we should be grateful to Jeremy Mynott for this wonderful book, which both illuminates that understanding and broadens our knowledge.'

Roger Riddington, *British Birds*

'[A] stunning new book…reading this splendid study, I experienced some of the excitement that humanists must have felt at entering into a lost world…Beautifully produced, informed by wonderful scholarship, *Birds in the Ancient World* embodies the Renaissance spirit, as a model of humane and civilised learning.'

Mike McCarthy, *Resurgence & Ecologist Magazine*

'It is […] thought-provoking, highly readable and exhaustive. Mynott has made an enormous effort to trawl the whole of the classics for bird references. The materials unearthed are far greater than anything previously considered and an appendix supplying potted biographies of the Greek and Roman authors discussed in the book includes more than 100 names…Perhaps the pre-eminent achievement of the book is not its fastidious examination of classical birds, but the way it pans backwards from the avian minutiae to give us a much broader vision of the two great civilisations.'

Mark Cocker, *The Spectator*

'This scholarly, yet readable and fascinating book presents a detailed account on how our current obsession with birds began…beautifully produced volume, illustrated throughout with striking colour images…Mynott's book brings to life the variety of ancient scholars and artists who were inspired by birds. The sheer volume of material must, one feels, have been daunting, yet Mynott has processed it in a sensitive and logical fashion…this definitive and original account of birds in the ancient world will serve as an invaluable reference for all subsequent historians of ornithology, and indeed, zoology as a whole.'

Tim Birkhead, *Archives of National History*

'A book the world has been waiting for, rich, scrupulously organised, imaginative, beautifully written, and driven by a double passion. On the one hand, for birds and human interactions with them. On the other, for the ancient world, especially those Greeks who "invented the concept of nature" and the scholarship which brings their thoughts and observations alive.'

Ruth Padel, Author of *Darwin—A Life in Poems, The Mara Crossing, and In and Out of the Mind*

'[An] excellent new book.'

Robin Lane Fox, *The Financial Times*

'A distinguished publisher and writer on both classics and bird-watching, Mynott has scoured thousands of pages on a literary nature trail…'

Peter Stothard, *The Times Literary Supplement*

'With a glorious array of references, vivid images, and his own astute philosophical commentary, Mynott deftly brings all this into sharp focus: are all these ancient associations, uses and abuses really so different from the way we see birds?'

Philip Hoare, *New Statesman*

'Mynott organises his elegant and thought-provoking book by theme and deploys a comprehensive range of quotes from throughout the classical period…His approach is nuanced and open-minded, and he writes with a light, often wry touch…The book is full of delightful titbits.'

Philip Womak, *Literary Review*

'Jeremy Mynott's masterful cultural and scientific history tours their [birds] roles as timepieces, soundscapes, pets, messaging services even intermediaries with the supernatural. The vivid artworks and literary passages give this wings…'

Barbara Kiser, *Nature*

'This is a wonderfully readable book, scholarly but fully accessible, continually thoughtful, properly sceptical, often amusing, and culled from knowledge of ancient literature that must be second to none…It is nicely illustrated in full colour. Whether you read the book straight through, or in a series of dips, it is full of revelation and insight into the ancient mind-set, which was once familiar and strange…Thanks to Jeremy Mynott, the birds of the ancient world have taken flight, and we can go birding in that magical lost world.'

Peter Marren, *British Wildlife*

'For Dr Mynott, "the significance of birds" is his binding theme in this illustrated cultural history with liberal quotations from some of humanity's greatest literature at this formative period of Western history.'

John McEwen, *Country Life*

'…provides a comprehensive introduction and overview of the role of birds within ancient society. The book is distinct from previous scholarship on birds in the ancient world with its approach to the material…Mynott's style will no doubt engage non-Classicists, particularly ornithologists and bird-watchers, through his intelligent use of modern comparisons and presentations of extracts of ancient texts. However, I also believe his book could work as a set-text for undergraduate students, particularly for modules that discuss the interaction between ancient societies and the natural world.'

Ben Greet, *The Classical Review*

'Jeremy Mynott's new book is by far the most erudite book on birds I have ever read. It is a compelling combination of the history of birds and the ancient world that throws both into new relief…this original guide comes highly recommended.'

Alexandra Henton, *The Field*

'*Birds in the Ancient World* is a welcome and important resource for the scholar working on any aspect of birds in all spheres of medieval life…Mynott's erudite discussions, though, will make an excellent companion for those wishing to explore the classical legacy in medieval "nature" paradigms.'

Michael Warren, *Medium Aevum*

'This publication can be considered an essential sourcebook for those who want to delve deeper into how birds were appreciated by the Greeks and Romans.'

Antiqvvs

'One of the most beautiful, most engaging and simply most delighful books I have read in a long time…Mynott has offered a masterclass in writing a work that popularizes Classics and explains the discipline's relevant authority, clearly and memorably to outsiders…Among many splendid features of this volume, I wish to highlight its illustrations…this is a splendidly learned and superbly interesting account of the manifold ways in which birds and humans interacted in antiquity, but it is more than that: this is a book which incites one to ponder upon fundamental ecological and environmental issues and to re-examine our own relationship to the natural world.'

Andrej Petrovic, *Greece & Rome*

'At a time when we need to be listening to the messages from birds from declining puffins losing their sand eels from warming seas, to Mediterranean Great White Egrets now breeding each year in Somerset this book offers brilliant insights into an earlier human culture's intimate relationship with another species.'

Terry Glifford, *Green Letters: Studies in Ecocriticism*

'The history lover inside me drew me to this title but I was pleased to find my ecologist's curiosity satisfied many times whilst reading this book…From the earliest images and writings that birds can be identified from, you will find yourself amazed at what can be discovered from sources well over 1000 years old that can be linked with present day species and their distributions. It is such a richly detailed book that you might not be able to read it from start to finish in one go, but the chaptering allows you to dip in and out and discover something new each time you pick it up.'

Katharine Bowgen, *British Trust for Ornithology (BTO)*

'Classical literature is a rich source of bird-related forteana, as this superb study reveals…a delightfully easy read, thanks to Mynott's stylistic panache: fluent, quasi-Herodotean, jargon-free, consistently witty…Not many writers can claim to have the last word on their subject. Mynott though, is that—have to say it—rare bird…For naturalists, scientists, social historians, twitchers, this superlative study will surely fly…'

Barry Baldwin, *The Fortean Times*

'A beautifully produced volume, with full-colour illustrations, acknowledgements, a bird index and a general index, a very full bibliography, detailed references, footnotes and lists of the bird species found in the sources. These academic accoutrements only add a flourish, though, to the approachable and enjoyable nature of the actual read.'

Liz Dexter, *Shiny New Books*

'Mynott provides a detailed picture of ancient understandings of birds-whether as food source or literary symbol—in the context of the literary passages and the social order of the time…He includes a time line of ancient writers and historical events as well as a biographies section, which summarizes the contributions of various ancient authors in documenting birds. Further scholarly apparatus include a general index, a bird index, and extensive endnotes. This title complements *Birds in the Ancient World A–Z* (2012) and belongs in robust classical studies collections and in ornithology departments.'

CHOICE

BIRDS *in the* ANCIENT WORLD

Winged Words

JEREMY MYNOTT

OXFORD
UNIVERSITY PRESS

OXFORD

UNIVERSITY PRESS

Great Clarendon Street, Oxford, OX2 6DP,
United Kingdom

Oxford University Press is a department of the University of Oxford.
It furthers the University's objective of excellence in research, scholarship,
and education by publishing worldwide. Oxford is a registered trade mark of
Oxford University Press in the UK and in certain other countries

© Jeremy Mynott 2018

The moral rights of the author have been asserted

First published 2018
First published in paperback 2020

Published in the United States of America by Oxford University Press
198 Madison Avenue, New York, NY 10016, United States of America

British Library Cataloguing in Publication Data
Data available

Library of Congress Cataloging in Publication Data
Data available

ISBN 978–0–19–871365–4 (Hbk.)
ISBN 978–0–19–885311–4 (Pbk.)

Printed in Great Britain by
Ashford Colour Press Ltd

PREFACE

Birds pervaded the ancient world. They populated the landscapes in an abundance and diversity scarcely imaginable in today's highly developed Western societies, and they would have impressed their physical presence on the daily experience of ordinary people in town and country alike. Nightingales could be heard singing in the suburbs of Athens and Rome; there were cuckoos, wrynecks, and hoopoes within city limits; and eagles and vultures would have been a common sight overhead in the countryside beyond. Not surprisingly, therefore, birds entered the popular imagination too, and figure prominently in the creative literature, art, and drama of the time. They were a fertile source of symbols and motifs for myth, folklore, and fable, and were central to the ancient practices of augury and divination.

The ambition of this book is to bring together as much as possible of this fascinating material in a connected and accessible way for the modern reader. I present a large selection of readings from the ancient sources, all of which I have translated freshly for the purpose. One hundred and twenty or so different authors are represented—an indication in itself of the ubiquity and variety of references to birds in classical literature—including all the most famous Greek and Latin authors, along with many less well-known ones, and some material not previously translated into English.

The book is organized thematically to illustrate the many different roles birds played in the thousand years between about 700 BC and AD 300: as markers of time, weather, and the seasons; as a resource for hunting, farming, eating, and medicine; as pets, entertainments, mimics, and domestic familiars; as scavengers and sentinels; as omens, auguries, and intermediaries between the gods and humankind. There are also selections from early scientific writing about the taxonomy, biology, and behaviour of birds—the first real works of ornithology in the Western tradition—as well as from more incidental but revealing observations in works of history, geography, and travel. The aim is to give as full a picture as the evidence allows. The translations are supplemented with numerous illustrations from ancient art—paintings, pottery, sculpture, coins, and seals, all of which are texts in their own right with related stories to tell.

There is a wealth of intriguing material to illustrate these themes. I revisit, and sometimes reinterpret, such cases as: the functions of official 'bird-watchers' as military consultants (Homer); the observation of crane migrations to calibrate the agricultural calendar (Hesiod); the 'crocodile bird' that supposedly acted as a toothpick to its fearsome host (Herodotus); the origins of expressions like 'cloud-cuckoo land' and 'jinxed'; the possible double entendres in 'waking the nightingale' and 'out with the cuckoo' (Aristophanes); the enigmatic last words of Socrates about paying the debt of a cockerel (Plato); the identity of Lesbia's pet 'sparrow' (Catullus); the sentinel geese on the Roman Capitol (Livy); the use of flamingoes in haute cuisine (Apicius); and the Aesop fables about the raven and the water jar (a feat of avian intelligence confirmed by modern experimentation), and the eagle and the tortoise (a warning to be wary of special offers by large airline operators).

I try to provide a strong line of narrative that gives a structure to these readings and explains their literary and historical context. I also make comparisons, where appropriate, with the roles birds have played in other cultures, including our own, and encourage readers to reflect for themselves on their significance. I see my task as that of a cultural and ornithological guide to some of these remarkable exhibits from the ancient world, using birds as a prism through which to explore both the similarities and the often surprising differences between early conceptions of the natural world and our own. My hope is that the work as a whole may in this way serve both as a contribution to the cultural history of birds and as an introduction for non-classicists to this formative period of Western history and some of its greatest literature.

As my references indicate, I am greatly indebted to many previous authors, and in particular to three classical scholars who did pioneering research in this area: the redoubtable D'Arcy Wentworth Thompson, who while a professor of biology at Dundee produced his *Glossary of Greek Birds* in 1895; John Pollard, who compiled an early thematic survey of the Greek material in 1977; and W. G. Arnott, whose comprehensive A–Z dictionary of ancient bird names appeared in 2007. These works were indispensable in gathering references to the key sources, but they are organized on quite different principles from the present book and provide few extended translations that would enable readers to engage more directly with the texts discussed. A closer model in that respect, though a model one can only aspire to, is Keith Thomas's study of a quite different period and place in his *Man and the Natural World: changing attitudes in England, 1500–1800* (1983)—a masterpiece of organization that deploys an astonishing range of sources in support of his narrative about how our current views evolved.

In reading the ancient classical authors on these themes we tend to move between experiences of happy recognition and deep puzzlement. We react just as they did to some of the familiar sights and sounds they describe and we share the same feelings of curiosity and wonderment. But one should never assume in advance that modern concepts or categories will coincide with those that would have seemed natural two and a half thousand years ago, and there are constant risks of anachronism and misunderstanding. There were, for example, no words in Greek or Latin meaning exactly what we mean by 'nature', 'weather', 'landscape', 'science', or 'the environment'; and conversely some words that do seem familiar sometimes had a different range of meanings then—even the word for 'bird'. Take this passage from a comedy by Aristophanes, where a chorus of birds is explaining to their human visitors the benefits they bestow on mankind:

> You don't start on anything without first consulting the birds,
> whether it's about business affairs, making a living, or getting married.
> Every prophecy that involves a decision you classify as a bird.
> To you, a significant remark is a bird; you call a sneeze a bird,
> a chance meeting is a bird, a sound, a servant, or a donkey—all birds.
> So clearly, we are your gods of prophecy.
>
> Aristophanes, *Birds* 716–24

What on earth does all that mean? At first sight, it looks as though the translator must have lost the plot somewhere. But it becomes clearer, or at least more interesting, when you realize that the Greek word for a bird, *ornis*, was also their word for an omen. The *significance* of birds—the 'winged words' of the subtitle—is the theme running through this book.

There are also some outright mysteries of a cultural as well as a linguistic kind. Why is there no account in the classical world of falconry as we now understand it? Why did no one before Aristotle mention butterflies in descriptions of the countryside? Why are singing nightingales almost always thought to be female? And how could such bizarre beliefs as those in 'halcyon [kingfisher] days' and 'swan songs' have originated and persisted? More generally, how could the peoples who pioneered (and gave us the modern names of) such subjects as biology, zoology, philosophy, logic, and mathematics have simultaneously entertained what now seems such a welter of superstitions and dubious folklore about birds?

But puzzlement, as Socrates always insisted, can be a necessary pre-condition to better understanding. I thank in the list of Acknowledgements (p. ix) many people who have helped me try to answer the various questions I have pursued in writing this book; but I want to mention in advance two particular mentors—one from long ago and one my contemporary—who much encouraged me in the habit of creative questioning and were both often in my mind throughout the writing.

The first was my old classics master at Colchester Royal Grammar School, Arthur Brown. Whenever I wrote him a callow essay on some topic from ancient history he would return the script to me with his spidery marginal annotations in the form, 'Yes, interesting, but how do we *know* that?' Arthur always sent us back to the sources—and away from textbooks, reference works, and secondhand opinions generally. He gave me my first inklings that everything has its context and has to be critically interpreted. The second, and much more recent, influence was my friend Geoffrey Hawthorn, the former professor of international politics at the University of Cambridge (though that title does little to convey the range and character of his interests, which extended deep into both ornithology and the classical world). Geoffrey would generously read in draft pretty much everything I wrote and would then send me, usually by return, a long list of gentle but probing suggestions and queries. His characteristic question was the complementary one, 'Yes, interesting, but does that *imply* ...?'. Geoffrey always made me think about what might be the larger significance or interest, if any, in what I was struggling to express. He read much of this book in draft and discussed it with me on many occasions (mostly 'in the field'), but to my great sadness died at the end of 2015.

These questions, 'How do we know this?', 'What does this actually mean?', and 'Why does this matter?' seem to me fundamental to most forms of enquiry. There are still more questions than answers in what follows, but I dedicate this book to the memory of these two inspirational mentors.

JEREMY MYNOTT

SHINGLE STREET, 31 OCTOBER 2016

ACKNOWLEDGEMENTS

I mention in my Preface two people to whom I owe special long-term debts: Arthur Brown and Geoffrey Hawthorn.

I am grateful to many other people for answering specific queries and making helpful comments: in particular, Armand D'Angour, Pat Bateson, Charles Bennett, David Butterfield, Paul Cartledge, Isabelle Charmentier, Mark Cocker, Pat Easterling, Stephen Edwards, Martin Hammond, Richard Hines, Geoffrey Lloyd, Peter Marren, Martin Nesbit, Bob Montgomerie, Ruth Padel, Geoff Sample, Quentin Skinner, Anne Thompson, Michael Warren, and Andrew Wilson. Special thanks are due to Tim Birkhead, Jonathan Elphick, Geoffrey Hawthorn, Mike McCarthy, William Shepherd, and Tony Wilson, each of whom read several (in some cases all) chapters in draft, proposed numerous improvements, and cheered me on generally. Their encouragement was more necessary and inspiring than they probably ever realized. Tony Wilson even went the extra mile and read the proofs, with meticulous attention, as ever. My wife, Diane Speakman, read the whole work in typescript, made many valuable suggestions, and, most importantly, believed in the project from the start— to her, thanks of every kind.

Pauline Hire generously edited the Endnotes for me and compiled the Bibliography. I have again benefited greatly from her friendship as well as from her professional experience and critical attention to detail.

For advice and assistance with the illustrations, my thanks to Lucilla Burn, J. R. Green, and Vanessa Lacey, and in particular to the picture researcher, Jane Smith.

Thanks to Caroline Dawnay of United Agents for advice and active support throughout.

I am grateful to Luciana O'Flaherty for her thoughtful editorial comments, to Jonathan Bargus for his creative work on the design, to Rosemary Roberts for her rigorous and searching copyediting, to Hannah Newport-Watson for managing the production process so efficiently and sympathetically, and to all their other colleagues at OUP who helped to bring this book to completion. It has been a very happy collaboration.

CONTENTS

NOTES FOR READERS

The volume is organized by thematic **parts** and **chapters** to explore the many different roles birds played in the ancient cultures of Greece and Rome, but these are not watertight divisions and there is a good deal of overlap and cross-referencing between them. Bird song, for example, crops up in several chapters, as do large topics like medicine, folklore, and omens. Readers who want to follow specific trails of this kind can do so through the indexes. Each part has an **introduction** to explain the progression of themes through the volume.

Brief explanatory notes on points of ornithology and historical background appear as numbered **footnotes** in the text. References and guides to further reading are collected in a section of **Endnotes** (pp. 389–415) and are indicated in the text by an asterisk.

Translations of **prose texts** are set off in the usual way in justified lines, while **poetry** is presented in shorter, unjustified lines. Many ancient authors wrote in verse on subjects that we might nowadays expect to be treated in prose. This was partly, no doubt, because the spread of literacy was still very limited over much of this period and verse is usually the more memorable form of expression; but it may also have been partly that modern distinctions between works of the imagination and works of description were then more blurred or differently drawn. At any rate, we find various authors choosing to present in verse long didactic works on such themes as the farming year (Hesiod), weather signs (Aratus), and the physical basis of the universe (Lucretius). My versions of these are therefore more like 'prose poems', poetic in language to some extent but not in formal structure, since the translations do not follow the lineation of the originals exactly nor do they seek to replicate their metrical systems.

To avoid repetition, the 120 or so authors quoted are introduced with minimal background information at the point of quotation, but there is a section of **Biographies of Authors Quoted** (pp. 369–88) that gives fuller details of their work and its literary context. The length of these entries is determined more by the relevance of the authors to the themes of this volume than by their larger historical importance or reputation—so Aratus gets a longer entry than Plato, for example. In the case of works whose authorship is uncertain or are now judged to have been falsely attributed in antiquity, square brackets are used around the name, as in [Aristotle], *On Plants*.

There is also a **Timeline** (pp. xviii–xix), listing principal authors and key events in historical sequence to give an overall chronological framework.

In the case of **bird names**, it should be remembered that in many cases it is impossible to identify the precise species intended, for the reason that some of our current distinctions were drawn differently in the ancient world and some not at all. I have therefore often used a generic term like 'eagle', 'vulture', 'crow', or 'bird of prey' rather than anything more specific that could be neatly matched against a modern list. I comment on some particular difficulties in the translation of ancient bird names in the text *passim* and in the **appendix** (pp. 363–7).

The **indexes** should help those who may wish to explore the translations in other ways than through the themes I have adopted as my basic structure. They should make it easy, for example, to locate all the Homer quotations or nightingale references.

LIST OF ILLUSTRATIONS

TIMELINE

Many of the dates are approximate or uncertain. For literary figures, see
'Biographies of Authors Quoted' (pp. 369–88) for fuller information.

GREEK   ROMAN

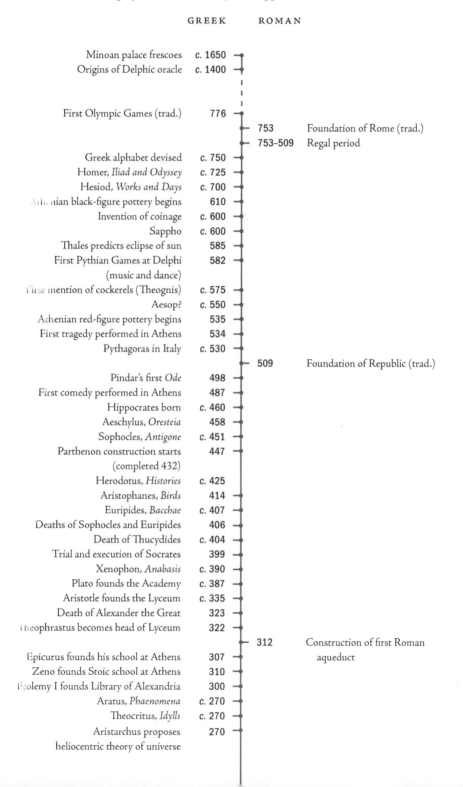

	GREEK	ROMAN	
Minoan palace frescoes	c. 1650		
Origins of Delphic oracle	c. 1400		
First Olympic Games (trad.)	776		
		753	Foundation of Rome (trad.)
		753–509	Regal period
Greek alphabet devised	c. 750		
Homer, *Iliad and Odyssey*	c. 725		
Hesiod, *Works and Days*	c. 700		
Athenian black-figure pottery begins	610		
Invention of coinage	c. 600		
Sappho	c. 600		
Thales predicts eclipse of sun	585		
First Pythian Games at Delphi	582		
(music and dance)			
First mention of cockerels (Theognis)	c. 575		
Aesop?	c. 550		
Athenian red-figure pottery begins	535		
First tragedy performed in Athens	534		
Pythagoras in Italy	c. 530		
		509	Foundation of Republic (trad.)
Pindar's first *Ode*	498		
First comedy performed in Athens	487		
Hippocrates born	c. 460		
Aeschylus, *Oresteia*	458		
Sophocles, *Antigone*	c. 451		
Parthenon construction starts	447		
(completed 432)			
Herodotus, *Histories*	c. 425		
Aristophanes, *Birds*	414		
Euripides, *Bacchae*	c. 407		
Deaths of Sophocles and Euripides	406		
Death of Thucydides	c. 404		
Trial and execution of Socrates	399		
Xenophon, *Anabasis*	c. 390		
Plato founds the Academy	c. 387		
Aristotle founds the Lyceum	c. 335		
Death of Alexander the Great	323		
Theophrastus becomes head of Lyceum	322		
		312	Construction of first Roman
Epicurus founds his school at Athens	307		aqueduct
Zeno founds Stoic school at Athens	310		
Ptolemy I founds Library of Alexandria	300		
Aratus, *Phaenomena*	c. 270		
Theocritus, *Idylls*	c. 270		
Aristarchus proposes	270		
heliocentric theory of universe			

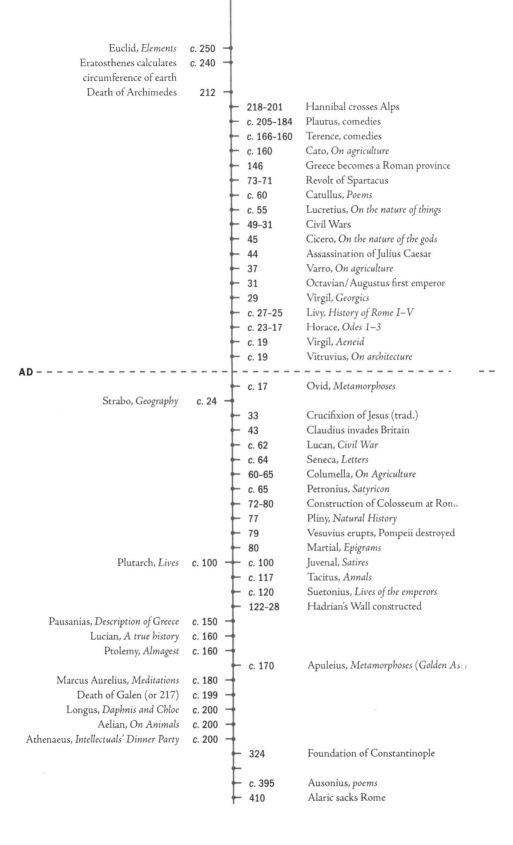

Euclid, *Elements*	c. 250	
Eratosthenes calculates circumference of earth	c. 240	
Death of Archimedes	212	
	218–201	Hannibal crosses Alps
	c. 205–184	Plautus, comedies
	c. 166–160	Terence, comedies
	c. 160	Cato, *On agriculture*
	146	Greece becomes a Roman province
	73–71	Revolt of Spartacus
	c. 60	Catullus, *Poems*
	c. 55	Lucretius, *On the nature of things*
	49–31	Civil Wars
	45	Cicero, *On the nature of the gods*
	44	Assassination of Julius Caesar
	37	Varro, *On agriculture*
	31	Octavian/Augustus first emperor
	29	Virgil, *Georgics*
	c. 27–25	Livy, *History of Rome I–V*
	c. 23–17	Horace, *Odes 1–3*
	c. 19	Virgil, *Aeneid*
	c. 19	Vitruvius, *On architecture*

AD –

	c. 17	Ovid, *Metamorphoses*
Strabo, *Geography* c. 24		
	33	Crucifixion of Jesus (trad.)
	43	Claudius invades Britain
	c. 62	Lucan, *Civil War*
	c. 64	Seneca, *Letters*
	60–65	Columella, *On Agriculture*
	c. 65	Petronius, *Satyricon*
	72–80	Construction of Colosseum at Rome
	77	Pliny, *Natural History*
	79	Vesuvius erupts, Pompeii destroyed
	80	Martial, *Epigrams*
Plutarch, *Lives* c. 100	c. 100	Juvenal, *Satires*
	c. 117	Tacitus, *Annals*
	c. 120	Suetonius, *Lives of the emperors*
	122–28	Hadrian's Wall constructed
Pausanias, *Description of Greece* c. 150		
Lucian, *A true history* c. 160		
Ptolemy, *Almagest* c. 160		
	c. 170	Apuleius, *Metamorphoses (Golden Ass)*
Marcus Aurelius, *Meditations* c. 180		
Death of Galen (or 217) c. 199		
Longus, *Daphnis and Chloe* c. 200		
Aelian, *On Animals* c. 200		
Athenaeus, *Intellectuals' Dinner Party* c. 200		
	324	Foundation of Constantinople
	c. 395	Ausonius, *poems*
	410	Alaric sacks Rome

MAPS OF THE CLASSICAL WORLD

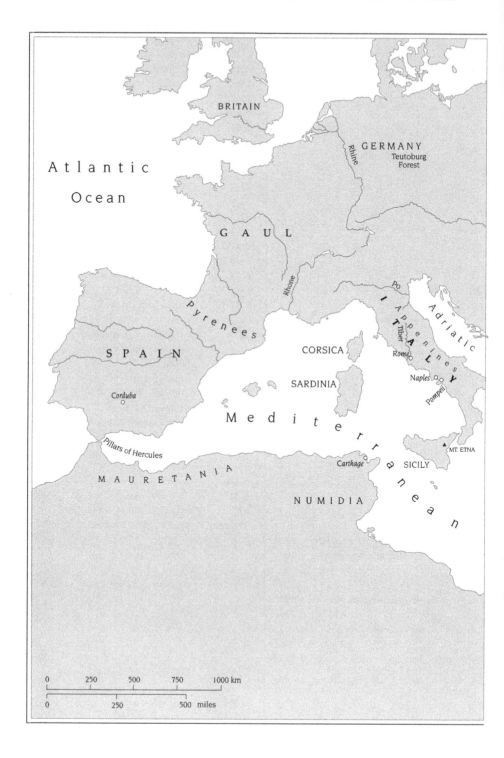

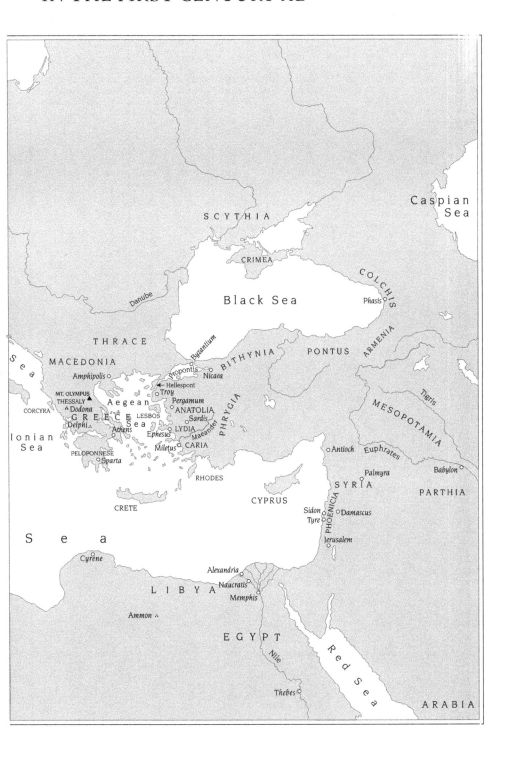

Caspian
Sea

SCYTHIA

CRIMEA

COLCHIS

Danube

Black Sea

Phasis

THRACE

Byzantium

BITHYNIA

PONTUS

ARMENIA

MACEDONIA

Propontis

Nicaea

S
e
a

Amphipolis

Hellespont

Troy

MT. OLYMPUS

Pergamum

PHRYGIA

MESOPOTAMIA

Tigris

THESSALY

Dodona

Aegean

ANATOLIA

CORCYRA

GREECE

LESBOS

Sardis

Delphi

Sea

LYDIA

Athens

Ephesus

Maeander

Ionian
Sea

Miletus

CARIA

Antioch

Euphrates

Babylon

PELOPONNESE

Palmyra

Sparta

RHODES

SYRIA

PARTHIA

CYPRUS

PHOENICIA

Sidon

Damascus

S   e   a

Tyre

Jerusalem

Cyrene

Alexandria

Naucratis

LIBYA

Memphis

Ammon

EGYPT

Nile

Red
Sea

Thebes

ARABIA

GREECE, ROME, AND THE AEGEAN

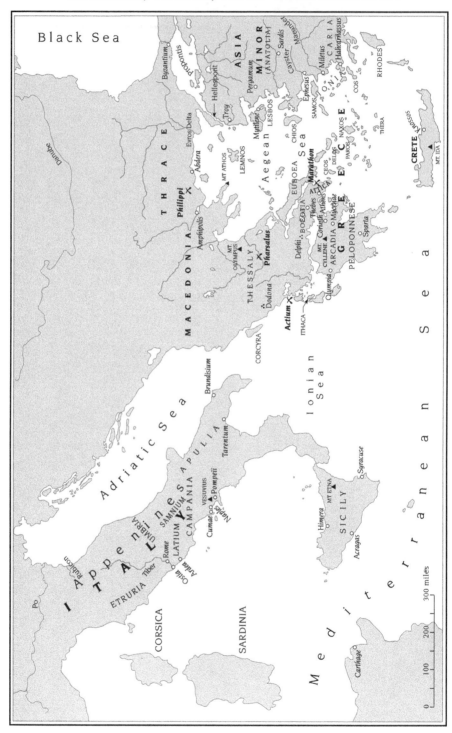

Black Sea

Danube

Byzantium

Propontis

Hellespont

Troy

ASIA MINOR
(ANATOLIA)

Pergamum

Cayster

Sardis

Maeander

CARIA

Halicarnassus

RHODES

Ephesus

IONIA

Mytilene

LESBOS

SAMOS

COS

THRACE

Euros Delta

Abdera

MT ATHOS

LEMNOS

CHIOS

NAXOS

Aegean Sea

THERA

DELOS

PAROS

CEOS

CRETE

Cnossos

MT. IDA

Philippi

Amphipolis

MT OLYMPUS

EUBOEA

MACEDONIA

Pharsalus

THESSALY

Dodona

Marathon

ATTICA

BOEOTIA

Thebes

Athens

Delphi

MT CYLLENE

Corinth

Mycenae

ARCADIA

Olympia

GREECE

Sparta

PELOPONNESE

Actium

ITHACA

CORCYRA

Ionian Sea

Adriatic Sea

Brundisium

Tarentum

APULIA

CAMPANIA

SAMNIUM

VESUVIUS

Pompeii

Nola

Cumae

Capua

UMBRIA

LATIUM

Rome

Ardea

Ostia

Tiber

Rubicon

Po

ETRURIA

Apennines

ITALY

CORSICA

SARDINIA

Mediterranean Sea

Himera

MT ETNA

SICILY

Syracuse

Acragas

Carthage

300 miles

200

100

0

It is no easy matter to give novelty to what is old, authority to what is new, freshness to the worn, light to the obscure, charm to the tedious and credibility to the uncertain—and indeed to give all things their nature and assign to nature all that is her own. So even if we do not succeed, it will have been a wholly fine and grand objective.

Pliny (AD 23–79), Preface to his *Natural History*

When you set out on the journey to Ithaca,
pray that the road be long,
full of adventures, full of knowledge ...

C. P. Cavafy, 'Ithaca' (1911), lines 1–3

The subject also has much to offer historians, for it is impossible to disentangle what the people of the past thought about plants and animals from what they thought about themselves.

Keith Thomas, *Man and the Natural World* (1983), 16

Winged words: highly significant or apposite words

Oxford English Dictionary

PART 1

Birds in the Natural World

Look up, lads, do you see it? It's a swallow! Spring is here.

Aristophanes, *Knights* 418–19

Hirundo domestica!!!*

Diary note by Gilbert White, 13 April 1768

If items of folklore, such as beliefs that certain birds foretell bad weather, were only the drifting scraps of information, true or false, that they have often been taken to be, they would merit no more than the anecdotal treatment they have usually received. But this is a superficial view. They are rather to be compared to the floating leaves and blossoms of water lilies springing from plants rooted far below.

Edward A. Armstrong, Preface to *The Folklore of Birds* (1958) p. xii

1.1 Spring fresco. Detail of swallows and lilies from the 'Spring fresco' in the Minoan palace at Akrotiri, Thera (Santorini), c.1650 BC. The settlement at Akrotiri was engulfed, following a cataclysmic volcanic eruption towards the end of the seventeenth century BC, comparable to the one that buried Pompeii in AD 79. As one of the earliest examples of Western art, the palace frescoes have long attracted attention for their remarkable freshness and evident delight in the natural world. The swallows pictured here are the familiar barn swallows (*Hirundo rustica*), probably the commonest spring markers, then as now. The swallow (Greek *chelidon*) also gave its name to the spring wind on which it arrives (*chelidonia*) and the greater celandine (*chelidonion*) that blooms at the same time.

Introduction

The Greeks invented the idea of nature. That is, they invented the concept. The natural world itself already existed before it was so described, of course, but it was in this phase of human history that it became a category that was used to describe something and contrast it with other things. It may come as a surprise, initially, to think that something so basic, something so apparently familiar and universal as nature, might not always have existed as part of the way humans understood the world and talked about it. But there will be various surprises of this kind in the chapters that follow.

We know in a general way, of course, that words and ideas all have *histories*. You don't need to have studied semantics to be aware that 'gay' has changed its meaning since the 1960s, that words like 'radical' and 'text' have acquired new connotations, and that what we now understand by 'democracy' will have developed from its original conception. People are, in fact, fascinated by etymologies. They take great pleasure in discovering the earlier meanings of such familiar words as 'nice', 'idiot', 'novice', and 'salary', or the derivations of their local place names and their personal names. But it can still be a cultural shock to learn that some of our most familiar concepts did not always exist in their present form— that the ancient Greeks, for example, had no terms meaning just what we mean by 'religion', 'weather', 'morality', 'conscience', 'science', or 'literature'; and that terms like 'human rights', 'landscape', and 'environment' are comparatively recent ones.

'Nature' itself is a particularly slippery term, which has a fascinating history and a huge range of different senses, which can be separated out but are often confused in arguments about what human nature is or ought to be and about our responsibilities for the non-human world. Are human beings a part of nature or somehow separate from it? What about the inanimate world of rocks, sky, and stars? If something is 'natural' is that a reason for approving of it? The nature of nature will be a theme running through this whole volume.

The very first use of the word in European literature comes in a famous passage in Homer's *Odyssey*, where the god Hermes is showing Odysseus a special plant that can save him from Circe's spells:

> So saying, Hermes, the slayer of Argus, gave me a herb
> he had pulled from the ground and showed me its nature.
> It was black at the root, but the flower was white as milk.
> *Molu* is the name the gods give it. It is difficult
> for mortal men to dig it up, but gods can do anything.
>> Homer, *Odyssey* x 302–06

Here the word seems to mean no more than the 'characteristics' of the plant, or possibly 'the way it grew', since the Greek word for 'nature', *phusis*,* is derived etymologically from the verb *phuo*, 'to grow'. That might suggest an early conceptual link between nature and the animate. This is an isolated reference, however, and can't bear the weight of too much interpretation. It was not until centuries later that medical writers and philosophers started using the word *phusis* in a more general sense to denote the whole domain of natural phenomena or, as we should say, 'the natural world'. The word went on to have a complex and changing history. One key distinction that came to be made was between the human attributes that were owed to nature (*phusis*) and those owed to culture and convention (*nomos*), and that led to serious philosophical controversies. Which category did morality fall into, for example? But the assumption always was that human life embraced both.

From *phusis* we ultimately get 'physics', 'physical', 'physiology', and so on; and from its usual Latin translation, *natura*, we get 'nature', 'natural', 'natural science', and 'natural history'. But these are tricky concepts in all languages and it can't be assumed, either, that they always meant the same thing in each or that they can be straightforwardly translated from one language to another. Think, for example, of the varying uses of the word 'natural' in English, as illustrated by some of its contraries: 'supernatural', 'deviant', 'abnormal', 'conventional', 'artificial', 'human'. Each of these assumes a very different sense of 'nature' or what is 'natural': some are purely descriptive, while others are loaded with moral or political implications about what 'human nature' might be like, or should be like, or even raise the issue of whether there is such a thing at all.

Both *phusis* and *natura* have interesting histories of their own and a range of different uses that don't always map exactly on to their English equivalents.*

But the main point to emphasize here is that the ancients would almost always have taken the natural world to include the human world and not as something to be contrasted with it, as we often do. The relations between the two were understood to be in the same sphere of activity, whatever form that relationship might take on different occasions. Indeed, in another famous passage Homer notes that human life is subject to just the same cycles of generation and death as other living creatures, like trees:

> The generations of men are just like those of leaves.
> The wind scatters one year's leaves on the ground, but the woods
> grow others as they burst into life at the coming of spring.
> So among men, one generation rises up and another passes away.
>   Homer, *Iliad* VI 145–49

Birds have the further connection with us of being not only animate but also mobile and active in a shared physical space. They have always been among the most prominent features of the natural world for humankind, readily visible and audible almost anywhere you happen to be, and so part of our daily experience. This was especially true of ancient Mediterranean societies, which were less urbanized than most modern ones, conducted much of their lives out of doors, and were therefore 'closer to nature' in all sorts of ways. With this intimacy went an interdependency. It was important to understand the natural world in order to interact in appropriate ways with it, protect oneself against it when necessary, and exploit its resources for human purposes.

In this first part we shall be looking in chapters 1–3 at the ways in which birds were used to interpret, forecast, or calibrate changes in the natural world and at the ways certain species thereby acquired a special status. Birds have always been important 'markers', associated with particular seasons, times, and places. This remains true today, even in our highly developed Western societies, where the annual spring arrival of birds like the swallow, cuckoo, and swift is still eagerly, if now ever more anxiously, awaited each year.* In the ancient world the forecasting of weather and of seasonal changes generally was often of more pressing practical importance—for the planning of agriculture, travel, trade, and military or political expeditions, and for the rounds and rituals of domestic life. Birds might be seen as powerful omens and intermediaries for interpreting the purposes of the gods in all this (see parts 5 and 6 below), but they might also, more prosaically, act as clocks and calendars in ways that were evident to everyone. Every culture has its own accumulated folklore about such things and there are many continuities and resemblances across time and place, both in the species taken to be especially significant and in the content of the particular beliefs and superstitions about them.

Chapter 4 goes on to consider the importance of sound in human responses to the natural world, and in particular to birds, its most vocal inhabitants. Does an oral culture have a different aural relationship to nature, and how do societies so permeated by music in their daily lives regard the music of bird song? Here, as elsewhere, we may need to make some imaginative leaps to understand how the ancients perceived their world.

1

The Seasons

The first reference to birds in the whole of European literature is Homer's comparison of the Greek forces mustering for the assault on Troy with the sight and sound of cranes and wildfowl on migration:

> Just as the many tribes of winged birds—
> geese or cranes or long-necked swans—gather
> on Asian meadows by the Caystrian streams,[1]
> flying this way and that, exulting in their wing-beats,
> settling and resettling with clangorous cries
> until the land resounds with their calls.
> Just so, the many tribes of men poured forth
> from their ships and huts into Scamander's plain,
> and the earth echoed with the dread sound
> of their pounding feet and horses' hooves.
> They took their stand there in the bright meadows,
> numberless as the leaves and flowers in spring.
>
> Homer, *Iliad* II 459–68

This is a vivid image, surely based on direct observation of such migratory gatherings. Birds were a standard point of reference in recording and calibrating the seasonal rhythms of the year.

The Mediterranean climate had an established pattern (which seems to have changed little since classical times). It was characterized by hot, dry summers and mild, wet winters. There was a certain degree of regional variation, the eastern

---

[1] The River Cayster in Turkey flows into the Aegean near Ephesus; it was famous in antiquity for its gatherings of wildfowl.

1.2 Massed cranes. Common cranes (*Grus grus*) congregating at dawn before migrating, on a frosty morning in Poland in October. The group on the left, which have cinnamon heads without any white on them, are young birds of the year.

parts tending to be drier and the western wetter, and a good deal more very local weather determined by the physical geography of mountains, valleys, and plains. There were annual variations too, of course, and some runs of good years and bad ones that could produce droughts and famines. There were also occasional extreme events like earthquakes, floods, and volcanic eruptions that caused other disruptions. But on the whole the pattern was regular and predictable, based on these two dominant seasons that largely determined the cycles of human activity by land and sea.*

Spring and autumn were the interludes, the periods of rapid transition between the two major seasons and the ones with the highest average rainfall. They were crucial to the agricultural calendar and also saw the seasonal changes most associated with the main migratory movements of birds.

Hesiod was a near contemporary of Homer (*c.*700 BC), a surly countryman who came from the small village of Askre in Boeotia (central Greece), which he describes as 'awful in winter, miserable in summer and no good at any time'. He wrote a handbook for farmers, in the form of a long didactic poem entitled *Works and Days*, in which he refers to the migrations of the crane, cuckoo, and swallow as timely reminders for different seasonal activities on the land. First, the crane:

Take note when you hear the clarion calls of the crane,
who yearly cries out from the clouds above.
He gives the signal for ploughing
and marks the season of rainy winter.[1]

Hesiod, *Works and Days* 448–51

This, it is worth noting, is a reference to *autumn* migration. For familiar psychological and cultural reasons, we tend to notice migrant birds more as the welcome signs of spring, but there were good practical reasons then for farmers to register the times of their autumnal movements too. In any case, in the autumn there are actually more migrant birds around, their numbers swelled by juvenile birds of the year. They tend to be more widely dispersed and to pause longer too, so they might have been more evident to rural communities.* Hesiod then goes on to his spring calendar for farmers, (from which I shall quote in the later sections on the cuckoo and the swallow).

Other authors pick up on the same themes—some in imitation, others in elaboration—and one sees the trail of borrowings and reworkings over subsequent centuries. In the third century BC Aratus wrote a hugely popular book called *Phaenomena* ('Appearances') about astronomy and weather signs, which is full of traditional folklore and doubtful stories. This work too was in verse form and, despite a withering academic review from the Roman critic Quintilian,[2] it is a salutary reminder of the mutability of literary reputations, since it seems to have been the most widely read poem in antiquity after Homer's *Iliad* and *Odyssey*. Like Hesiod, Aratus is very aware of the practical difficulties and uncertainties in the farmer's year. Summer brings its own problems and migrating flocks of birds may portend difficulties to come:

Nor does the farmer on the mainland rejoice
at the coming of summer, when flocks of birds
invade his land in hordes from the islands.
He fears terribly for his harvest, lest a drought
reduces it just to empty ears and chaff.
But goatherds quite welcome these same birds,
if they come in moderate numbers, hoping
they presage a year of overflowing pails of milk.

---

[1] The common crane *Grus grus* migrates south through the Mediterranean on its way to north Africa, usually in mid- to late October.

[2] 'His subject lacks movement—it has no variety, no emotion, no characters, no speeches—but Aratus is adequate for the task to which he believed he was equal', Quintilian, *Institutio oratoria* x 1.55.

So we poor insecure mortals find our livelihoods,
some this way, some that; but we are all ready
to heed the signs immediately before us
and act on them for the moment.

  Aratus, *Phaenomena* 1094–103

He adds his bit on the cranes' migration in autumn:

The punctual farmer is glad to see flocks of cranes
arriving on time; the tardy one prefers them later,
for the winters are in step with the cranes.
Winters are early when the cranes arrive early and in flocks;
but when the cranes appear later and are dispersed,
arriving in smaller groups over a longer period,
the delayed farm work benefits from winter's own delay.

  Aratus, *Phaenomena* 1075–81

And that in turn has its counterpart in Theophrastus (also third century BC),
though it is unclear which author is imitating which here:

If cranes fly early and all together it will be an early winter; if late and spread over
a long period it will be a late one. And if they wheel round in flight they are signal-
ling stormy weather.

  Theophrastus, *Weather Signs* III 38

These seasonal observations about cranes are common to many European cultures and reflect the cranes' well-known and conspicuous migratory patterns.
There was also a general understanding that different climates produce different
distributions and seasonal patterns, as the historian Herodotus remarked of the
lands through which the Nile passes:

Kites and swallows can live there the whole year round and cranes flee the bad
weather in Scythia to winter in these places.

  Herodotus, *Histories* II 22

Aelian, an encyclopedist writing in the first century AD, summarizes the popular
knowledge of his time about these crane migrations, with some nice observations about formation flying:

Cranes come from Thrace, which has the worst and coldest winters of any place I
know. They love the country of their birth but they also care about themselves, so

they devote themselves partly to their ancestral haunts and partly to their own preservation. They stay in their country for the summer, but in mid-autumn they depart for Egypt, Libya, and Ethiopia, as if they knew the map of the earth, the nature of the winds, and the variations in the seasons. And after spending a winter that is like a spring there, when the weather is more settled and the skies are calm, they head for home again. They appoint leaders for the flight from those who have experience of the route—these would most likely be the older birds; and they choose others of the same age to bring up the rear, while the younger birds are ranged in the middle. After waiting for a fair wind favourable to their journey to blow at their backs, they use that as an escort to push them forward and they adopt the formation of an acute-angled triangle to cut through the air in the most efficient way and so hold their course. This, then, is how cranes spend their summers and winters.

Aelian, *On Animals* III 13

But some material about the seasonal activity of birds was much more dubious or just plain false, as in the belief that there was a special period of 'halcyon days' at the time of the winter solstice, associated with the breeding season of the kingfisher (the *alcyon*). The lyric poet Simonides (sixth century BC) records this curious fallacy:[1]

As when in the month of winter
Zeus calms the fourteen days
and men on earth call it the windless season,
a holy one, when the many-hued kingfisher
rears her young.

Simonides fr. 508

We are back on firmer ground with the spring and summer migrants. Aristophanes' famous comic play *The Birds* is a fantasy about the citizens of Athens negotiating with the birds to establish a 'Cloud-Cuckoo Land' in their domain of the sky. The cuckoo would probably have been selected for the name of the new city partly because then, as now, to be 'a bit cuckoo' was to be given to foolish ideas and fancies[2] and the play (produced in 414 BC) would, at a deeper level, have been understood by the audience as a political satire on the Athenians' disastrous decision to invade Sicily, an act of national hubris that effectively lost

---

[1] A multiple fallacy, in fact: there are no such regularly calm days in mid-December; the kingfisher breeds from April to July not in December; and even the name *halcyon* is a corruption of *alcyon*, adapted to suggest the spurious etymology of *hals-kuon* 'sea-breeding'.*

[2] The association with 'cuckoldry', however, seems to be a Latin not a Greek extension of the meaning.*

1.3 Kingfisher. Detail from a mosaic in the House of Blandus, Pompeii (*c*.40 BC), depicting a common kingfisher (*Alcedo atthis*) perched on a rudder between a triton and a sea monster. Kingfishers are regular visitors to the Mediterranean seas and islands in winter, and Aristotle noted their habit of 'hovering around boats at anchor'.*

them the war against Sparta. The expression 'Cloud-Cuckoo Land' has entered the language of politics in English too, of course, though politicians need to be careful what they thereby dismiss as pure fantasy.[1] The cuckoo was, in any case, conveniently familiar as the iconic sound of spring and the wake-up call for farmers to look lively and get out into the fields:

> When the cuckoo is first heard from the spreading oak leaves
> and gladdens the hearts of men across the wide world,
> and the heavens rain two days later and do not stop
> until the rainfall is just about the depth of an ox's hoof,
> then the late ploughman will catch up with the early one.
> Keep all this well in mind and don't fail to observe
> the greening of grey spring and the season of rain.
> Hesiod, *Works and Days* 485–89

[1] Margaret Thatcher famously used this phrase in a speech in 1987: 'The ANC is a typical terrorist organisation…Anyone who thinks it is going to run the government in South Africa is living in cloud-cuckoo land.'

Aristophanes had a more ribald take on this cuckoo alert in a passage that might be very freely translated by the old army reveille, 'Off cocks and on socks.' The more literal version has it the other way round, with a few other double entendres thrown in for good measure:

PEISETAERUS Then again, the cuckoo was the king of all Egypt and Phoenicia,
And whenever the cuckoo cried 'cuckoo', then all the Phoenicians
would get down to harvesting the wheat and barley [cock]
in their fields [cunt].
EUELPIDES Ah, so that's the real meaning of the saying, 'Cuckoo! Cocks peeled back
and into the fields.'

Aristophanes, *Birds* 504–07

1.4 Cuckoo. The cuckoo (*Cuculus canorus*, shown here in a modern painting) makes its spring appearance in March in Greece, and the male bird's call was very familiar in the ancient world. Aristotle accurately described at least some of its unusual breeding strategies (see p. 239). There are, however, curiously few identifiable representations of the cuckoo in classical art, for such an 'iconic' bird.

In a later passage in the same play, various species of birds are proclaiming their value to humankind as a series of calendar reminders:

All the greatest blessings mankind enjoys come from us, the birds.
For a start, we reveal the seasons of spring, winter, and autumn.
The time to sow is when the crane flies off to Libya bugling:
that tells the ship-owner to hang up his rudder and take a lie-in,
and for you to weave a warm cloak for Orestes,

so he doesn't get cold and snatch them from other people.
Next it's the kite's[1] turn to appear and herald another season:
this is the time for the spring sheep-shearing.
Then it's the swallow—time to sell those winter woollens
and buy yourself something more summery.
    Aristophanes, *Birds* 708–15

The swallow is probably the commonest spring marker for the ancients. Sappho does also nominate the nightingale in one surviving fragment about 'the messenger of spring, sweet-voiced nightingale', but it was the swallow that gained proverbial status, and they had the same cautionary saying, 'One swallow doesn't make a summer,'* though, like us, they ignored its truth and welcomed spring along with the first swallow:

Next comes the swallow, voice of dawn and daughter of Pandion,[2]
returning to humankind in the light of spring.
And it's best to prune your vines before she arrives.
    Hesiod, *Works and Days* 568–70

Famed herald of sweet-scented spring,
blue swallow
    Simonides fr. 597

Let go my tales of war, my hymns of praise
for gods' marriages and men's feasts
and the merry-makings of the blessed.
Sing popular lays of the lovely-haired Graces,
composing a tender Phrygian tune—to celebrate
the swallow twittering loudly with the coming of spring.
    Stesichorus, *Oresteia* frs*

Yes, by god, I was up to all sorts of tricks as a boy;
I used to deceive the cooks by shouting out:
'Look up, lads, do you see it? It's a swallow! Spring is here.'
So up they looked, and meanwhile I stole some meat away.
    Aristophanes *Knights* 417–20

Am I mistaken, or has the herald of spring arrived, the swallow,
and is she not afraid that winter may turn and come again?

---

[1] Aristophanes must mean here the black kite, which is migratory, as its scientific name *Milvus migrans* suggests, though the red kite *Milvus milvus* is also found in Greece.
[2] For the myth of Tereus, Philomela (daughter of Pandion), and Procne, see p. 279.

Often you will complain, Procne, that you came too soon,
and your husband Tereus will be glad you are so cold.

Ovid, *Fasti* II 853–56

1.5 The first swallow of spring. Two men and a boy greeting the return of the swallow.
The speech bubbles (not visible here) say: 'Look, a swallow.''Good Lord, so it is.''There it
goes.''It's spring already!'* Attic red-figure vase, 515–505 BC.

Aelian also stresses the swallow's associations with humanity:

> The swallow is the sign that the best season of the year is coming to stay. It is a
> friend to humankind and is glad to share a roof with its fellow beings. It arrives
> uninvited and departs in its own good time when it chooses. And people welcome
> it according to Homer's laws of hospitality, which bid us cherish a visitor while he
> is with us and speed him on his way when he wishes to depart.
>
> Aelian, *On Animals* I 52

And a later writer, Athenaeus (third century AD), records a charming song
about the swallow from the island of Rhodes. A group of children are singing a

ritual chant about collecting food, rather like carol singers or trick-and-treaters demanding money:

> He's come, he's come, it's the swallow,
> bringing the good weather and good times,
> white on the belly and black on the back.[1]
> Roll out some fruit cake
> from your rich household,
> and a cup of wine
> and a basket of cheese.
> And the swallow won't say no
> to bread from wheat or pulse.
> Should we go or do we get some?
> If you give us some, we'll go.
> But if you don't, we won't let you be.
> We'll make off with your door or the lintel above,
> or your wife who is seated inside.
> She's tiny—it will be easy to carry her away.
> If you do bring something, make it big!
> Open up, open up, for a swallow,
> we are not old men but children.
>
> Athenaeus, *The Intellectuals' Dinner Party* 360c–d

Departures are usually more difficult to monitor than arrivals, but we are told that the philosopher Democritus (c.460–370 BC) produced a calendar of weather changes throughout the year, which included the entries:*

7 March. Cold winds. Bird migrations for nine days.

14 September. The weather changes and the swallow departs.

Seasons were associated with particular winds, which were important enough in their effect on daily life and work to be personified. The north wind was Boreas in Greek (Latin: Boreas or Aquilo), the east wind was Euros (Latin: Eurus), the south Notos (Latin: Auster) and the west Zephyrus (Latin: Favonius, 'the Cherisher').[2] This last was the soft, warm wind of spring:

---

[1] Poetic licence, perhaps, but this better describes the contrast in the house martin's appearance than the swallow's. The various hirundines were not always distinguished (see p. 233).

[2] Aristotle, ever analytical, goes further and identifies twelve different winds, including the *Ornithiai* ('bird winds') that blow two months after the winter solstice, presumably so named because they coincide with spring migration.*

Now spring brings back the warmth with milder days,
Now the fury of the equinoctial sky
Is quietened by the pleasant airs of Zephyr

> Catullus, *Poems* XLVI 1–3

*   *   *

I end this chapter with some jubilant celebrations of these regenerative powers of spring, in which birds, and in particular bird song, feature strongly. The first is from a Greek anthology of epigrams from the first century BC:

Now winter's winds have left the skies,
bright springtime smiles with blooming flowers.
Dark earth is clothed with grasses green
and dresses her plants with new-made gowns.
The meadows laugh to drink the dew
of nourishing dawn as roses open.
The goatherd on the hill pipes his clear notes
gladly and delights again in his white kids.
Now sailors voyage across the open seas,
sails billowing out in the gentle Zephyrs.
Now men sing of Dionysus, giver of wine,
and garland their hair with clusters of ivy.
Bees born of oxen[1] ply their busy trade,
constructing in hives the fresh, pale beauty
of their many-chambered honeycombs.
Every kind of bird sings with clear tuneful voice,
kingfishers over the waves, swallows around the eaves,
swans on the river bank, and nightingales in the grove.
When the leaves of plants rejoice and earth is reborn,
when the shepherd pipes and his woolly flocks sport,
when sailors ply the seas and Dionysus leads the dance,
and birds do sing and bees labour to create—
how then can we help but sing a song of spring?

> Meleager, 'Spring song', *Greek Anthology* IX 363

---

[1] A reference to the ancient belief in *bougonia* ('ox progeny'), the spontaneous generation of bees from animal carcasses, as in Samson's riddle in the Bible: 'Out of the strong came forth sweetness' (Judges 14:14) with reference to a dead lion (now celebrated in the image on Tate & Lyle Golden Syrup tins).

Virgil picks up this theme in his *Georgics*, an account of the farming year, ostensibly in the genre of Hesiod's *Works and Days*, but in fact a far more self-conscious and sophisticated literary creation:*

> The time to plant your vines is when in blushing spring
> the white bird[1] arrives, foe to the long snakes,
> or in late autumn, just before the cold comes and the sun's force
> first touches winter in its travels with the waning of summer.
> Spring it is that aids the foliage in our woods and forests;
> in spring the soil swells and begs for the seeds of life.
> Then the almighty father of Air descends in fecund showers
> into the lap of his fertile spouse and in their bodily union,
> mighty joined with mighty, nurtures all forms of growth.
> Then too the wild woods ring out with the songs of birds
> and in their due time the herds again seek sexual union.
> The bountiful land gives birth and under the warm west winds
> the fields loosen their bosoms. Soft moisture everywhere abounds,
> and the grasses dare to trust their safety to the new suns;
> the young vines no longer fear rising winds from the south
> or a storm driven from the sky by gusts of wind from the north,
> but thrust out their buds and unfold all their leaves.
> Such, I could believe, were the days that shone at the very birth
> of the growing world and such was the tenor of their course.
> Spring that was indeed; the great world observed its springtime
> and the east winds spared their wintry blasts, when the first cattle
> drank in the light of day and the iron race of men
> raised its head from the hard fields, and wild beasts
> were let loose into the forests and the stars into the heavens.
> Nor could such tender beings endure these trials,
> did not this calm respite come between the seasons' cold and heat
> and earth receive the blessing of a kindly sky.
>
>   Virgil, *Georgics* II 319–45

Ovid even suggests in his *Fasti*, a long poetic account of the Roman calendar, that the New Year might more fittingly be thought to start with spring:

> Come, tell me, why does the New Year start in the cold,
> when it would surely be better in the spring?
> Then it is that all things flower and a new age begins,
> And from the bursting vine the new bud swells,

---

[1] The white stork *Ciconia ciconia* was a common summer visitor, often commensal with man as now; its habit of feeding on snakes and amphibians was well known (Pliny, *Natural History* x 62).

The tree is clothed in fresh-formed leaves,
the first green shoots push through the earth,
the birds sweeten the warm air with their chorus
and the cattle frisk and revel in the fields.
Then the sun's rays soothe and the visiting swallow comes
and fixes his mud nest under the lofty beam.
Then the field yields to the farmer's plough and is renewed.
This is the time we should rightly call New Year.
Ovid, *Fasti* I 149–60

And finally Longus (second / third century AD), in his romantic novel *Daphnis and Chloe*, shows how all this activity by the birds and the bees can suggest some ideas to the two sexual innocents in his story:

It was the beginning of spring, and all the flowers were bursting into bloom—in the woods, the fields and on the mountain sides. Now there was a hum of bees, the air rang out with the song of birds, and newborn animals skipped about. Lambs gambolled on the hills, bees buzzed in the meadows, and the thickets were alive with bird song. With such spring beauty all around them this sensitive and impressionable young couple began to imitate what they heard and saw. Hearing the birds sing, they sang; seeing the lambs skipping about, they danced around lightly too; and in imitation of the bees they gathered flowers, tucking some inside their clothes and weaving others into garlands to present to the nymphs.
Longus, *Daphnis and Chloe* I 9

The next spring they try to progress things further, but unfortunately take goats as the model to imitate and end up more frustrated than fulfilled (III 12–14). It all turns out happily in the end, though, with some help from a friend.

2

Weather

As Dr Johnson observed, 'when two Englishmen meet, their first talk is of the weather'. But not only Englishmen. If you Google 'weather folklore' you will find in a trice more than a million references, from every time and place. Whoever and wherever you are in the world, the daily weather may affect your sense of well-being and also many of your daily decisions, if only about what to wear and how to travel, so it is not surprising that over the ages people accumulated observations, experiences and theories to help them understand likely changes in the weather. Even with the advances of modern technology and meteorological science we still look to the skies to interpret the local weather signs and we cling to some of the traditional beliefs to help us out. Folklore traditions of this kind seem not only to be universal and persistent, but they are also highly imitative, with the same stories and superstitions endlessly recycled, whatever their accuracy.*

And if we are tempted to think of ancient beliefs on the subject as quaint or absurd, it may be worth noting in advance some recorded English 'country sayings' which, as we shall see, turn out to be suspiciously similar:

'Seagulls in the field indicate a storm to come.'
'If swallows touch the water as they fly, rain approaches.'
'An owl hooting quietly in a storm indicates fair weather on the way.'
'When the finch chirps, rain follows.'
'If ducks or drakes shake and flutter their wings when they rise, it is a sign
    of ensuing weather.'
'If crows go to the water, beat it with their wings, throw it over themselves
    and scream, it foreshadows storms.'

'When ravens croak continuously, expect gales; but if their croaking is
interrupted or stifled, or comes at longer intervals, it signals rain.'

These are all taken from compilations of 'weather lore', one of the fullest of
which is by Paul Marriott, himself a professional meteorologist, who earnestly
gives each saying a 'veracity rating' on a scale of one to six.* Unsurprisingly, most
of them turn out to be either obvious or false. One suspects, in any case, that
most of these 'country sayings' are more easily encountered nowadays in such
works of reference than in the countryside itself.

The Greeks and Romans had no single words meaning what we mean by
'weather', though of course they had the full range of words denoting different
weather conditions like wind, rain, storm, snow, frost, and sun. But they were
probably even more aware of weather in general than we are, since they were more
vulnerable to it. The weather was crucial for practical activities like farming and
most kinds of travel, whether for trade or war, in particular sailing. The Greeks
were above all a seafaring people, whose communities around the Mediterranean
and the islands Plato described as living 'like frogs round a pond'.* But these are
rough and dangerous seas, as recent migrations have demonstrated all too clearly.
Hesiod was something of a landlubber, coming from central Boeotia, and is pessimistic about the risks. Late summer, he says, is the only time when the weather
is really settled enough to sail safely, and even spring is a gamble:

> Another time for sailing is the spring.
> As soon as the topmost shoot on a fig tree
> reaches the size of a crow's footprint,
> then you can put out to sea again,
> for this is the spring sailing season.
> I don't myself recommend it, since my heart
> isn't in it—a snatched voyage could well mean trouble.
> Men are driven even to that in their folly,
> for goods mean life to wretched mortals,
> but it's a terrible thing to die among the waves.
>   Hesiod, *Works and Days* 678–87

Hesiod also sympathizes with the farmers and sailors over the difficulties of weather forecasting. The 'will of Zeus' here stands for the vagaries of the climate:

> The will of Zeus the Almighty is subject to change
> and is hard for mortal men to interpret.
>   Hesiod, *Works and Days* 484–85

It is not surprising, then, that the winds and extreme weather events like earthquakes, storms, and floods attracted their own mythology and might be attributed to the interventions of the gods. Zeus (Latin: Jupiter) thundered, Poseidon (Neptune) shook the earth and Aiolos (Aeolus) loosed the winds. The gods hovered in this way behind many important events in both the natural and the cultural world; for most people they were powerful but ill-defined agents, perhaps something between metaphorical presences and natural causes.

*   *   *

The classical tradition of weather folklore runs through Hesiod, Aratus, Theophrastus, Virgil, Pliny, and Aelian, each referring to many of the same phenomena and with a large measure of overlap in their interpretations, though in Virgil at least these are more creatively deployed for literary purposes.

Aratus divides his 'weather signs' into celestial phenomena and terrestrial ones, and among the latter bird behaviour is one of the most conspicuous. First, a gale warning:

> Take as a sign of wind the swelling sea,
> and the roaring surf on a distant shore,
> the coastline resounding in calm weather,
> and the moaning of mountain tops.
> And when the heron flaps erratically landward[1]
> from the salt sea with many a harsh cry,
> he is moving ahead of a gale out at sea.
> At such times too the storm petrels,[2]
> fluttering in flight over calm waters,
> turn in flocks to face the rising wind;
> and often wild ducks and seafaring gulls
> beat and shake their wings on dry land,
> or a cloud lengthens over mountain ridges.
>
> Aratus, *Phaenomena* 909–21

[1] As in many horoscopes, these forecasts play it safe by having it both ways, and later (at line 972) the sign is said to be a heron flying *seaward*.

[2] Descriptions of these *kepphoi* (or *kemphoi*) in other sources, like Dionysius, seem to support this identification. The storm petrel *Hydrobates pelagicus* is now a very rare breeder in Greece, but may have been commoner then and would have been familiar to sailors from its habit of following ships and pattering over the water. As the English name suggests, it has been regarded as a portent of bad weather in our folklore, too.

Rain can be expected later when:

> Often birds of marsh or sea dive and splash
> themselves repeatedly, plunging in the water;
> or swallows keep darting over the lake,
> rippling the surface with their chests;
> or those wretched creatures, the fathers of tadpoles
> and a boon to water-snakes, croak loudly from the lake itself;
> or the lone songster[1] murmurs his morning tune;
> or on the jutting coast the raucous crow ducks
> into the coming wave from the shore,
> or dips his head and shoulders in the river,
> or dives in completely or stalks up and down
> beside the water, croaking harshly.
>
> Aratus, *Phaenomena* 942–53

Ravens and crows (which would here be hooded crows, *Corvus cornix*, the local species) do frequent shores in this way, but Aratus rather spoils what sounds like an interesting observation, since a crow would not actually dive in. He may here have conflated the behaviour and names of two other black maritime species, the cormorant and shag, which do dive but would not stalk the shore croaking. The usual Greek word for raven was *korax* and for crow *korone*, but neither the species nor the names were always clearly distinguished; nor were those of the cormorant and shag, which could also be called by either of these names.[2]

Theophrastus generalizes on this:

> When birds that do not live in the water bathe, they are signifying rain or storm.
>
> Theophrastus, *Weather Signs* 15

and he mentions some other signs of rain involving birds behaving uncharacteristically: 'if the raven, who usually makes many different sounds in succession, quickly repeats one of these twice over, and if he whirrs and shakes his wings'; 'if crows and jackdaws fly high and scream like hawks'; 'if a hawk perches on a tree and flies right inside it to look for insects'; 'if in summer birds that live on islands flock together in numbers'; 'if cocks and hens forage for insects and when they imitate the sound of falling rain'; 'if a domestic duck shelters under the eaves, and when jackdaws and cockerels flap their wings like a duck'; and 'if the heron calls as he flies out to sea, that is a sign of rain rather than of wind; and in general a heron's cries indicate wind' (*Weather Signs* 16–18).

---

[1] This *ololugon* ('moaner') is usually identified as a tree frog, but see p. 48 n. 1.

[2] The confusion is reflected in the current scientific name of the cormorant and shag genus, *Phalacrocorax*, meaning literally 'bald raven'.

1.6 The 'crow' (corvid) family, clockwise from top left: raven (*Corvus corax*), carrion crow (*Corvus corone*), hooded crow (*Corvus cornix*), and rook (*Corvus frugilegus*). These were often confused, as they still are. The raven and the hooded crow are common in the Mediterranean region, the rook much less so (see pp. 29–30). The carrion and hooded crows are closely related; the carrion crow is the common one in most of England and central and western Europe, the hooded crow in eastern, south-eastern, and northern Europe (including north-west Scotland and Ireland).

Aratus goes on to explain that an impending storm has many signs:

Geese hastening on to their feeding grounds cackling
are a sure sign; and the crow, nine generations old,[1]
croaking at night, and the jackdaws chattering late
or the finch[2] chirruping shrilly at dawn; and all kinds of birds
coming inland from the sea, the wren or the robin too,
ducking into nooks and crevices; and the tribes of jackdaws
returning late to roost from their rich pastures.
When a mighty storm threatens, the buzzing bees

[1] See 'Time' below, pp. 39–40.
[2] *Spinos* has a generic feel to it (goldfinch, greenfinch, serin, siskin, and chaffinch are all possible), but it may most often have represented the chaffinch, which is *spinos* in modern Greek too.

do not venture far afield to forage for their wax,
but hover round their honeycombs and hives.
Nor do the long lines of cranes up high in the sky
hold to a steady course, but wheel and turn back home.

Aratus, *Phaenomena* 1021–32

And better weather ahead has its indicators too:

Steady flames from the lamp and the nightly owl
hooting gently may be your signs of a storm abating;
as may the many-voiced crow, if in the evening time
he croaks gently with a varying tone; a sign too
when solitary ravens call first with a double note,
but then a succession of croaking calls,
and when there are more of them gathered together
and they seek out the roost, all in full voice.
One could imagine them glad the way they call—
now with shrill cries, now noisily round the branches,
now on the trees where they roost,
coming and going and clapping their wings.[1]
Cranes, too, may at times before a gentle calm

1.7 Migrating cranes. The flight patterns of cranes were sometimes (rather unconvincingly) compared to, or even thought to be the origin of, some Greek letter forms like capital lambda Λ and delta Δ (see p. 293).

---

[1] Again, it is hard to know which corvid (raven, crow, rook, or jackdaw) is intended here. From their behaviour these sound more like rooks, but see below pp. 29–30.

all stretch out as a flock on a straight course,
borne along steadily by the fair weather.

    Aratus, *Phaenomena* 997–1012

The Latin poet Lucretius wrote a hugely ambitious work entitled *De rerum natura* ('On the Nature of Things'), in which he sets out a fully rationalistic account of the evolution and workings of the universe without recourse to any mythological or religious explanations. In the course of this he offers a very interesting speculation about the origin of speech and language in the need to make distinctions. The point is generalized to include animals and birds, and here he is emphasizing the significance of changes in the vocal behaviour of birds in different situations:

Some birds change their raucous calls to match the weather,
like the ancient race of ravens or flocks of rooks,
when they are said to be calling for water and rain
and sometimes to be invoking winds and breezes.
So, if different kinds of feelings compel animals,
dumb though they are, to utter corresponding sounds,
how much more natural it must be for human beings
to mark different things with different expressions.

    Lucretius, *De rerum natura* v 1083–90

Ravens and crows crop up as omens of rain and bad weather in many cultural contexts from the Mesopotamian and biblical Flood narratives onwards,* and the association was almost a conventional literary trope in Latin poetry:

Tomorrow shall a tempest,
let loose from the East,
strew the grove with many leaves
and the shoreline with useless seaweed,
unless the ancient raven, prophet of rain,
shall this time prove false.

    Horace, *Odes* iii 17.9–12

I do not like these signs—the tossing of the trees,
the beat of waves upon the shore, or when
the restless dolphin challenges the seas,
or when the seabird prefers the dry land, and the heron
dares to fly aloft, trusting his storm-tossed feathers,
and the raven spraying his head with brine,
anticipates the rain and stalks the shore with unsteady gait.

    Lucan, *Pharsalia* v 551–56

Virgil was clearly familiar with all the earlier Greek material on weather signs, but radically reshapes it in Book 1 of the *Georgics*, so that the descriptions of weather disturbances prefigure the portents of Caesar's death and the storms of the civil wars that were to hit Rome:

> Never has rain brought men trouble without warning.
> Either the cranes flee skyward from the valley's depths
> as the showers sweep in; or the heifer casts an eye to the skies
> and with open nostrils snuffles the breeze;
> or the twittering swallow flits around the lake;
> and in the mud the frogs croak their ancient complaints.
> Often too, the ant, wearing out her narrow track,
> brings forth her eggs from their hidden cavities;
> a huge rainbow drinks up the water; and an army of crows,
> decamping from the field in a long column,
> fill the air with the sound of their serried wings.
> Various seabirds, too, and the waders who probe
> the Asian meadows in the sweet pools of Cayster—
> these you may see vying to drench their shoulders with spray,
> now ducking their heads in the sea, now dashing
> into the waves and idly enjoying the pleasures of a bath.
> Then the rogue raven calls down the rain with his deep bass,
> and stalks single and alone on the dry strand.
>
>   Virgil, *Georgics* I 373–89

In his description of how the birds react when the weather clears, Virgil makes some interesting comments about possible naturalistic explanations for their behaviour. We now know, in fact, that birds are sensitive to small changes in atmospheric pressure and so can anticipate weather systems.

> Then the rooks with narrowed throats give voice
> to a stream of three or four notes, and from their lofty nests,
> as if cheered by some unaccustomed pleasure, chatter
> noisily amongst themselves amid the leaves—glad after
> the rains to see again their little broods and sweet nests.
> Not, I think, that they have divine guidance from above
> or learn from Fate any larger knowledge of things to be;
> but when the storm and the fitful vapours of the sky
> change course and the heavens, humid with the south wind,
> condense what was just now thin and rarefy what was dense,
> then the constitutions of their minds change too and in their breasts
> they now feel different impulses from when the wind was chasing

the clouds away. Hence that chorus of birds in the fields
and the contented cattle and joyful cries of the rooks.

    Virgil, *Georgics* 1 410–23

1.8 Rooks at a rookery. The scientific name *Corvus frugilegus* means 'food-gathering
crow', and their principal diet consists of earthworms and larvae. Rooks are a colonial
species that build loose stick nests in the tops of clumps of trees, usually in close proxim-
ity to one another, so their rookeries tend to be noisy and highly interactive societies.
Crows are more solitary.

There are some translation issues in this Virgil passage and the earlier Greek
ones that may seem technical but that point to more general problems of
identification. We don't really know if these are rooks or crows. The Greek
korax or *korone* and the Latin *corvus* or *cornix* are not used consistently by
ancient authors and seem to refer in different places to ravens, crows, rooks, or
just generically to corvids (including jackdaws). It would seem surprising if
rooks were common in the region then and they are certainly rare there now.
They need soft, moist grassy pastures with lots of worms. On the other hand,
some of the descriptions of communal nesting and chorusing strongly suggest
rooks. It can't be proved definitively either way. There are, in any case, similar
confusions between these species in our own culture, exemplified by the mis-
nomer 'scarecrow', which could be effective only against rook flocks.* But in

England at least we have the excuse that rooks and carrion crows look very similar, while the 'crows' in the Mediterranean in the classical period would have been hooded crows, which have distinctive grey bodies with black heads and wings.[1]

Then there are two specific difficulties. Firstly, the phrase I have translated as a 'stream of ... notes' in the second line of this extract renders the phrase in the Latin *liquidas voces*. The *voces* are 'calls' or 'notes', but the Latin adjective *liquidus* can in context mean 'clear', 'flowing', or 'pure', and is even used by both classical and English linguists as a phonetic term describing the 'liquid consonants' like 'r' and 'l'. The translation makes a big difference to how you perceive these calls. C. Day Lewis in his popular version, for example, renders this as 'cool, clear note', Fairclough in the Loeb volume as 'soft cries'.* Secondly, Lewis translates *cubiles* ('nests') as 'cradles', which is misleading since *cubiles* can refer to any kind of resting-place and elsewhere in Latin literature it is used of bees, mice, dogs, moles, and even elk. I think he probably favoured 'cradles' as a more poetic idea, which suits his translation of *corvi* as 'rooks'.* A reminder that translation always involves interpretation.

In any case, it is unclear in most such examples, ancient or modern, whether the observed 'signs' are supposed to be predictive of the weather phenomena or just their accompaniments. But there is one passage in Aelian that if read literally seems to suggest that birds could actually *cause* changes to the weather by their behaviour, as well as producing some other surprising effects:

> The bugling calls of cranes call up showers of rain, while their brains cast some kind of magic spell on women to grant sexual favours, if we can believe the reports of those who first observed this.
>
> Aelian, *On Animals* 1 44

For the most part the later encyclopedists Pliny and Aelian just continue the folk-lore tradition inherited from Aratus and Theophrastus* with small variations:

> Animals also can presage changes in weather: for instance, dolphins sporting in a calm sea indicate wind from the quarter from which they come, and similarly when they splash about in disturbed water they are predicting a calm. Other signs

---

[1] The carrion crow *Corvus corone* and the hooded crow *Corvus cornix* have been regarded as separate species since 2002. In the British Isles the hooded crow is largely restricted to north-west Scotland and Ireland.

of a storm are: cuttlefish flitting about, shellfish sticking fast and sea urchins
either anchoring themselves or ballasting with the sand; likewise frogs making
more noise than usual and coots clamouring in the morning; also diving birds[1]
and ducks preening their feathers with their beaks—all these signify wind, as do
other water birds congregating together, cranes hastening inland, diving birds and
seagulls deserting the seas and lakes. Cranes flying high in the skies and in silence
foretell fine weather, as does the owl calling in the midst of a shower (just as it
forecasts a storm when it calls in fine weather); so too crows cawing with a sort of
gurgle and shaking themselves, if they do so continuously; but if they choke it
back and call intermittently, expect rain and wind. Jackdaws returning late from
feeding foretell stormy weather; and so do the white birds[2] when they flock
together; and land birds when they noisily approach a body of water and sprinkle
themselves (especially the raven); the swallow too, swooping so close to the water
that it keeps touching the surface with its wings; and the birds that live in trees
taking refuge in their nests; geese as well when they set up a continuous cackling
at an unusual time; and a heron when it stands forlorn in the middle of the beach.
It is no surprise that water birds or birds in general can perceive signs of change
in the atmosphere.

   Pliny, *Natural History* XVIII 360–64

Pliny also makes some very sensible and pragmatic points about weather forecasting in general: there are so many variables that there will always be exceptions to general rules, and both we and birds can easily be caught out by
unseasonal weather (XVIII 209); farmers may do better to rely on direct observation of their fields than on meteorological theory in making their decisions
about sowing and harvesting, since weather patterns will vary locally (XVIII
206); and farming work should be regulated by what the weather is actually like,
rather than what it should be like at any time of year (XVIII 238).

   Finally, a couple of passages that suggest humankind might have something
to learn from the birds in all this, either directly:

If a ship's captain in mid-ocean sees a flock of cranes turning round and flying
back to land he knows that they have refrained from going further because of the
impact of contrary winds. And becoming a pupil of the birds, as you might say, he
sails back home and saves his ship. So, what was first a lesson learnt by the birds
has been handed on to mankind.

   Aelian, *On Animals* III 14

---

[1] *Mergus*, possibly a grebe; not many of the diving ducks reach as far south as the Mediterranean, and
divers (the usual translation here) certainly don't.
[2] Possibly gulls (but egrets have also been suggested).

or by reaction and analogy:

> It's absurd to be giving such close attention to the croaking of crows and the
> clucking of hens and 'swine rampaging in their litter' (as Democritus* puts it), and
> constructing signs of winds and rain out of these, but to be taking no precautions
> to forestall the stirrings, motions, and warning symptoms in the human body and
> not to see these as the signs of a storm that is going to happen within oneself and
> is about to break.
>
>   Plutarch, 'Advice on keeping well' 14, *Moralia* 129a

*   *   *

Changes in the weather and the seasons were closely related, of course, and they
jointly represented the outward signs of dynamic change in the natural system
itself. Forecasting those changes involved interpreting the relevant vital signs in
a combination of astronomy, meteorology, and natural history, in the last of
which birds were the key markers. Behind all these were the unseen powers of
the gods, whether considered as convenient personifications or as actual motive
forces. Their wilful interventions helped explain some of the uncertainties in the
system and also gave rise to the further art of divination, in which birds again
were key intermediaries. That will be the topic of later chapters. Meanwhile,
there are two further dimensions of the natural world to investigate: time and
sound.

3

Time

We need to take a large conceptual leap to understand the very different perceptions of time people had in the ancient world. This isn't just a matter of their more primitive technology for measuring what we think of as the passage of time—the sundial and the *clepsydra* (water clock), which actually became quite sophisticated devices in due course.[1] It is more a difference in what is being measured and why. We live in a world where our days are subdivided precisely into hours, minutes, and seconds and our years into months, weeks, and days. The calculation of the years themselves can be extended forwards or backwards in an equally determinate way as far as we like. And at any one moment we can know precisely what position we occupy on this continuum, which in principle comprises the whole of past history and the whole of the future, all specifiable in the same terms and on whatever scale we choose. The ancients, by contrast, lived in a world where the changes that mattered were the changes in the day between dawn and nightfall and in the year between spring, summer, autumn, and winter. These and the associated natural phenomena were what regulated their daily lives and in a sense limited their imaginations. It was left to the first proper historians, Herodotus and Thucydides, to invent the notion of historical time and propose their own systems for measuring it.*

Time and weather were in fact closely connected concepts. In Greek the word *hora* (from which we get 'hour') can mean a time, a part of the day, a period, a day, an appropriate moment, a season, or the season of spring—all according to context. Similarly in Latin, the word *tempestas* can be equivalent to *tempus* ('time'), a

---

[1] And it is estimated that ancient astronomers could tell the time at night to an accuracy of within ten minutes.*

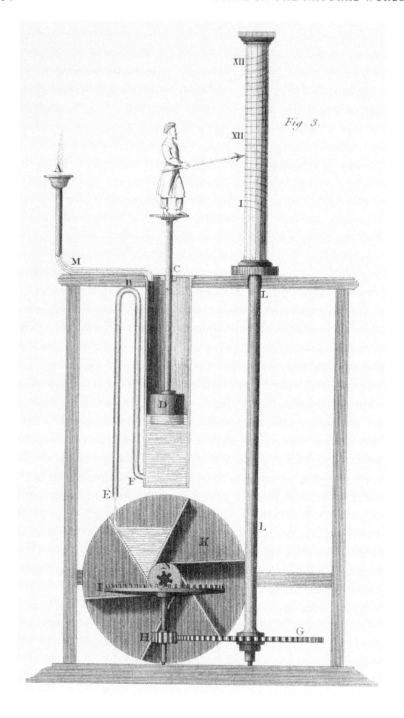

1.9 Water clock. Illustration of a *clepsydra* ('water thief') designed by Ctesibius (285–222 BC) from Abraham Rees's *Clocks, Watches and Chronometers* (1819), plate 1, fig. 3. This model incorporates an ascending hour indicator and gears to adjust for changing day lengths. Its recorded uses include: allotting time to speakers in courts of law; calculating the pulse rates of patients against a standard norm for their age group; and imposing time limits on clients at a brothel (this practice is attributed to a famous Athenian prostitute known in the trade as 'Mrs Clepsydra', who had one installed in her boudoir).

period, season, weather (good as well as bad), or a storm (and the French preserve something of this ambiguity in their idiom 'il fait mauvais temps').

The Greeks and Romans did have 'calendars', based approximately on lunar cycles and observed celestial phenomena, which were used to fix festivals and certain public events and appointments; but these were unsystematic and local, to a degree that made coordinated action between different places problematic.[1] For the most part they managed serious practical matters, like the times to rise and sleep or the times to plough and reap, by reference to what they could see and hear, not by what a clock or calendar might abstractly indicate, since those measurements would need to be checked and corrected by reference to the natural phenomena and not vice versa.

The passage of days was not in any case always thought of as an undifferentiated flow of identical units. Very early in the period dealt with in this book, Hesiod describes how different days of the month might have a distinct god-given character, and one that might need special interpretation and particular responses. Some of these now seem very odd, especially when set against the sensible practical advice to farmers elsewhere in the work, but a superstitious belief in favourable and unfavourable days is, of course, a widespread phenomenon and not one restricted to ancient societies, as the continuing popularity of horoscopes and astrology indicates. Rational and irrational beliefs can often coexist in a society quite comfortably, as anthropologists often remind us.* Hesiod, at any rate, lists the good and bad days for various activities in some detail and then summarizes:

> These [fortunate] days are a great blessing to men on earth,
> but the other ones are fickle, vapid, and offer nothing.
> Some praise one day, some another, but few understand them.
> Sometimes a day is a stepmother, sometimes a mother.

[1] The historian Thucydides reports a case where a covert joint military action failed because the two participants were using different diary dates and set off on different days (IV 89.1).

Happy and fortunate the man who knows all these things
and goes about his work without offending the immortals,
interpreting bird signs rightly and avoiding transgressions.

Hesiod, *Works and Days* 822–28

The connection of birds with particular times of day is more familiar and naturalistic. The start of the day, then as now, was especially associated with the dawn chorus of birds:

First, when the dawn sprinkles the earth with the new light of day
and the different kinds of birds, flitting through the trackless woods,
fill everywhere with the sound of their liquid notes
streaming through the soft air, then suddenly the rising sun
will at such a moment clothe and drench the whole world
with its light, to be clear and manifest for all to see.

Lucretius, *De rerum natura* II 145–49

When Aristophanes in his fantasy play has the citizens of Athens go 'bird-crazy', the first sign of their *ornithomania* is 'getting up with the birds at the crack of dawn' (*Birds* 1286–7). And being employed as a reaper in the fields, we learn from the pastoral poet Theocritus, means more specifically getting 'up with the lark' (*Idylls* x 50). But the single species of bird most associated with the dawn is not a wild one but that domestic alarm clock, the cockerel. This familiar species, descended from the red jungle fowl of Asia (*Gallus gallus*), is now the most numerous bird in the world.[1] It was probably introduced into the Mediterranean region from Persia some time in the seventh century BC. Interestingly, it does not feature at all in Homer, that repository of the Greeks' historical experience, or for that matter in the Old Testament, but it later became so widely distributed as a domesticated species that it was sometimes simply referred to as 'the bird'.* The earliest literary reference seems to be in the lyric poet Theognis (sixth century BC), where it has already acquired its iconic role:

My friends betray me and deny me anything
when men are about. So of my own accord
I leave in the evening and return at dawn,
when the cockerels awaken and crow.[2]

Theognis, *Elegies* 861–64

[1] Estimated at about 12 billion. Some 24 million chickens are killed for the table each day in the US alone.*

[2] The reference to the cockerel is clear enough, but no one is quite sure who the speaker (feminine) is, or what she is up to here. Among many inventive suggestions are an owl and a harlot's cat.

1.10 Cockerel coin. Silver didrachm (2 drachmas) from Himera in Sicily, *c.*480–470 BC, by which time the cockerel had evidently become a familiar feature of everyday life.

Plato records that Socrates was another who sometimes stayed up all night. Here he is after an all-night drinking-party, still talking philosophy as the cock crowed in the day:

> Aristodemus awoke towards dawn, as the cocks were crowing, and saw that all the rest of the party were either sleeping or had left, except for Agathon, Aristophanes, and Socrates, who were the only ones still awake. Socrates was arguing with them. Aristodemus could not remember most of the discussion, since he had missed the beginning and was also dropping off; but he said the essence was that Socrates was forcing them to admit that the same man could have the knowledge required for writing comedy and tragedy—that the skills were the same in both cases. While they were being driven to this conclusion and were struggling to follow the argument, they began to nod off: first Aristophanes fell asleep and then, as day began to dawn, Agathon too. When Socrates had seen them comfortably settled, he rose and went on his way.
>
> Plato, *Symposium* 223c–d

Various poets suggest that the cockerel's wake-up call may or may not be welcome:

> Sleep on, breathing in each other's love and longing,
> but don't forget to wake at dawn.
> We shall be coming with the first light,
> when the first songster of the day leaves the roost
> and stretches out his well-plumed neck to crow.
>
> Theocritus, *Idylls* XVIII 55–57

> The first light has already passed, Chrysilla,
> and the early cockerel has long been the herald
> to bring forth the grudging dawn of day.
> Away with you, most spiteful of birds, who forces me

from home to endure the endless chatter of students.
Are you getting past it, Tithonus?[1] If not, why
have you driven Aurora so early from your bed?

Antipater of Thessalonica, *Greek Anthology* v 3

Damn cockerel! Why have you snatched my treasured sleep?
The sweet image of Pyrrha has flown from my bed and gone.
Is this your return for all my care, you ill-fated fowl,
in making you king of the flock of egg-layers in my palace?
I swear by the altar and sceptre of Sarapis,[2]
that no longer shall you crow by night,
but you will bloody the altar I swore by.

Argentarius, *Greek Anthology* IX 286

While Pliny makes the same points more prosaically:

Nearly equal in their sense of self-importance are our nightwatchmen, whom
nature has designed to wake up mortals and interrupt our sleep. They understand
astronomy, and they mark every three-hour interval in the daytime with their
crowing, go to bed with the sun, and at the fourth watch of the night summon us
back to our business and work, not allowing the sunrise to catch us unawares;
they herald the coming day with their songs and beat their wings against their
sides to herald the songs themselves. They rule over their own race and exercise
their sovereign power in whatever house they live.

Pliny, *Natural History* x 46–47

As for unwelcome bird alarms at the other end of the day, one example
may suffice. This is from Aristophanes' play *Lysistrata*, in which the women are
staging a sex strike. They have abandoned their husbands to occupy the
Acropolis, but are still getting interrupted nights:

I'm a wreck through lack of sleep here, what with these owls
calling all the time.[3]

Aristophanes, *Lysistrata* 760–61

---

[1] Tithonus (the consort of Aurora) had the misfortune to be granted immortality but not eternal youth, so was failing in his conjugal duties.

[2] A Graeco-Egyptian god who had cults in the Mediterranean region.

[3] 'Calling' not 'hooting' (the usual translation) because this would probably have been the little owl *Athene noctua*, which had special associations with Athens and the Acropolis (see p. 259 **5.3**) and has a range of penetrating alarm calls, quite unlike the hooting of the tawny owl *Strix aluco*. Another possibility is scop's owl *Otus scops*, which can maintain its repetitive 'BBC time-signal' call right through the night.

1.11 Cockerel mosaic. Detail from a Roman mosaic pavement of the second century AD at Acholla, Tunisia. Probably a *xenia* (hospitality) motif, with which wealthy hosts adorned their floors to welcome guests with the promise of good fare.

A quite different measure of time is that of the span of a human life. And here the most favoured species for comparison in the folklore was the long-lived crow or raven, though there was some disagreement just what the ratio of bird to human longevity was. Hesiod pitches it at nine times for the crow (and an absurd 108 times for the raven):

> The noisy crow lives out nine generations of old men;
> but a stag's life is four times a crow's,
> while a raven sees three stags grow old,
> and the phoenix outlives nine ravens;
> while we outlive ten phoenixes
> —we, the nymphs with beautiful tresses,
> the daughters of Zeus Almighty.
>   Hesiod, *Precepts of Chiron* 3

Aristophanes cuts that back to five for the crow:[1]

> CHORUS OF BIRDS So, will men still reach old age—that's surely in the gift of the
>   gods?
> Or must they die young, then?
> PEISETAERUS   Goodness, no. You birds will add three hundred
>   or more years to them.
> CHORUS   But from where?
> PEISETAERUS   Where from? Why, from yourselves!
> Don't you know that the noisy crow lives out five generations of men?
> EUELPIDES Blast it. We'd clearly do better to be ruled by birds than by Zeus then.
>   Aristophanes, *Birds* 606–10

The Roman satirist Martial, on the other hand, uses the longevity of crows merely to embellish an insult to a woman:

> She was the daughter of Pyrrha, the stepmother of Nestor,
> she was grey-headed when Niobe saw her as a girl,
> she's the woman the aged Laertes called his grandmother,
> Priam knew as his nurse and Thyestes as his mother-in-law.
> Now Plutia,[2] older than any crow, is at last laid in this tomb,
> Still itching for sex, along with bald old Melanthion.
>   Martial, *Epigrams* x 67

*   *   *

Time was the fourth dimension in which the physical world was perceived and it made good sense to adopt ways of measuring it drawn directly from lived and observed experience. The cyclical changes of the days, months, and years provided the obvious framework, and all these were marked by corresponding changes in the natural world in the cycles of waking and sleeping, growth and decay, and the migratory movements of birds and other animals. We share with many animals and plants circadian[3] rhythms attuned to the alternation of day and night in their twenty-four hour cycles, and so—it is reasonable to suppose—we may also share with them some deeply embedded sensitivities to the

---

[1] This is still a grossly exaggerated longevity. A crow's normal life span is probably around ten years, while a likely maximum for a raven is around thirty years, though there have been claims of fifty years in exceptional cases.*

[2] These comparisons of Plutia with figures of legend are just meant to imply unimaginable antiquity.

[3] From the Latin *circa diem*, 'around a day'.

seasonal cycles, which explains our physical and emotional responses to these too. Is this why we welcome each spring with a renewed sense of expectation and recognition?

Time is the abstract measure of such changes but is itself imperceptible, of course, and this led to various theoretical puzzles in the ancient world. Most philosophers who pondered the nature of time connected it with the idea of change, since without change, they argued, we would have no concept of present, past, or future and no reason to measure the passing of time or any means of doing so. The only timeless world would be one in which there was no sensory experience, no movement, and no change. These were among the defining characteristics of Plato's perfect world of unchanging and everlasting Forms, of which the present world was supposed to be just an imperfect image; and similar 'ideal' worlds are posited by some post-classical religions, though it is common for their adherents nonetheless to imagine themselves enjoying at least some of their present capacities and advantages in them.

But back to the here and now, there is another important dimension of the sensory world as we experience it and that is the dimension of sound, which is the topic of the next chapter.

4

Soundscapes

The first work of science fiction in Western literature is Lucian's *True History*, a fantasy about space travel. It is a parody of the improbable stories and travellers' tales in works like Homer's *Odyssey*, Ctesias' *Indica*, and Herodotus' *History*, all of which Lucian explicitly criticizes for blurring facts with fictions. In his own novel (which he cheerfully says is also a pack of lies) he describes a trip to the moon, where he encounters many weird and wonderful things. For a start, the people up there seem to have a quite different sensory apparatus from ours. They sniff up the fumes from their food instead of eating it; they sweat milk; they have removable eyes; and their ears are the leaves of plane trees (except for the 'acorn-men', who have wooden ones). They also have some impressive surveillance equipment in their royal palace:

> A huge mirror is positioned over a shallow well. Anyone who descends into the well can overhear everything that is being said by the people back on earth. And if he looks into the mirror he can see every city and all the different peoples, just as if he were standing next to them.
> Lucian, *A True History* 1 26

Like all good science fiction writers, Lucian seems here to be inviting people to reflect on their own condition by comparing it with something radically different. But things move on. Google Earth can now match Lucian's mirror in representing our cityscapes and streetscapes, and various intelligence agencies are doing their best to capture all the conversations in them.

In most modern cultures sight is regarded as the primary sense, followed by hearing and the others in some sort of descending sequence. Our whole language reflects this assumption. 'I see,' we say, meaning 'I understand,' and we have expressions like 'see for yourself', 'watch what you're saying', and 'seeing is believing'. There are good biological and practical reasons for this, of course. As a species we rely hugely on sight to interpret the world, navigate round it, and engage with it. All this applied as much to the ancients as to us, and their languages reflect it, too. The Greek word *oida*, 'I know', means literally 'I have seen', while the Latin word *video* has much the same range as the English 'I see'. Similarly, the Greek words from which we derive 'theatre' and 'theory' are in turn derived from their word for 'seeing'.

But there are important differences too. Ours is a largely literate culture and we rely very heavily on our ability to read, write, record, document, print, and more recently to film and to digitize. Vision is the faculty through which we acquire and transmit much of our knowledge. The Greek and Roman cultures, by contrast, were largely oral ones, where the spoken word was the primary means of communication.* Perhaps less than 10 per cent of the population was functionally literate and most of the business of politics, law, and education was conducted out loud. Rhetoric was therefore one of the most prized professional skills. Remember, too, the importance of theatre as a principal cultural medium and the fact that a key element in theatre and other festivals was the accompanying choral music. That music is wholly lost to us, bar a few fragments of scores, so we are even more inclined now to think of the great classical plays as literary texts rather than the audio-visual dramatic performances they really were. We know that Homer was actually *composed* orally and that all poetry was regularly recited, often with musical accompaniments. Lyric poetry, for example, is literally 'poetry for the lyre'. Byron had this right:

> The isles of Greece, the isles of Greece
> Where burning Sappho loved and *sung*.
> Byron, *Don Juan* (1820), Canto III

Prose works too would often be read out loud, and historians like Herodotus gave public readings of their compositions. Silent reading on one's own is generally thought to have been a much later development.*

An oral culture of this kind is likely also to be an aural one, which has greater sensitivity not only to human speech but to the medium of sound more generally as a way of engaging with the world we live in—the way we attend to it, perceive it, and think of it. Add to this the technological fact that the ancients had none of our optical aids like spectacles, binoculars, or telescopes, and one can begin to imagine some interesting differences between our world and theirs. There is a lot we don't know. We can read ancient texts but we aren't really sure what they would have sounded like read out loud, as they usually were.* The tones and stresses in the pronunciation of ancient languages might have made them sound as foreign to us as Chinese does now to Western ears. The music is lost, too, and it has been remarked that we might be less inclined to think of the ancient Greeks as the fathers of Western rationalism if we could actually hear the music they so much admired.*

There are certainly plenty of references in classical literature to the importance of the soundscape. Ovid gives a wonderful description of how news, rumour, and misinformation were spread in the days before social media performed this function. This passage comes from his *Metamorphoses*, a retelling of the stories from myth and legend:

There is a place in the centre of the world between land,
sea and sky, where the three realms of the universe meet.
From here everything can be observed, however far away,
and every word reaches its listening ears. Here Rumour
dwells in the home she has chosen on a high mountain-top.
She has given her house countless ways in and a thousand
apertures, with no doors to block the entrances. It lies open
day and night. The whole structure is of echoing brass
and is full of noises, repeating and returning what it hears.
There is no quietness within, no silence in any part,
yet no loud clamour either, just murmured whispers
like those of the waves of the sea heard from afar
or the sound of the last rumbles of thunder
when Jupiter has crashed the dark clouds together.
Crowds fill the halls, shadowy presences that come and go,
and everywhere wander a thousand rumours,
false mixed with true, and confused words flit around.
Some of them fill idle ears with their talk, while others
go and tell elsewhere what they have heard, while the story
grows in size and each new teller adds to the report.
Here live Credulity, here too are Rash Error,
unfounded Elation and anxious Fears,
here sudden Discord and Whispers from sources unknown.

Rumour herself monitors all that is done in heaven, on land
and sea, and searches the world for news.

Ovid, *Metamorphoses* XII 39–63

In personal relationships, too, sounds can matter. Sappho's famous love poem
makes as much reference to the voice as to the looks of the girl she desires, and
even her own speech and hearing are affected:

He must be in very heaven
that man who sits close by you
and listens to your sweet voice
and your lovely laughter—truly, it
makes my heart leap in my breast,
for if I look at you just a moment
speech fails me, my tongue is paralysed,
and at once a light fire runs under my skin,
my eyes are blinded, my ears are drumming,
the sweat runs off me, I shake all over,
I am paler than grass, and I feel
not far off dying…

Sappho, fr. 31

Another envious lover ranks sound well above sight:

Melite, you have the eyes of Hera, Athene's hands,
the breasts of Aphrodite and the feet of Thetis.
Blessed is the man who looks on you,
thrice-blessed the one who hears you speak,
a demi-god who makes love to you,
and an immortal who marries you.

Rufinus, *Greek Anthology* v 94

Of less romantic interest are the frequent references in literature to the ambient
noise in the city.* Seneca describes the din of the street, which he has to block
out while studying:

…the carriages running past, the builder who lodges here, the local metal-grinder,
the fellow performing with pipes and flutes by the fountain jets, who is not singing but shouting.

Seneca, *Letters* 56.4

Worse still, he has the misfortune to live over a bathhouse and says the cacophony of noise from assorted clients in various conditions of pleasure or distress 'makes him hate his own ears'.

By contrast, the whole natural world was experienced as a source of sounds that were more communicative than distracting. Indeed, the priests and priestesses of the famous oracle at Dodona in north-west Greece were supposed to interpret its meanings from the rustlings of oak leaves in the surrounding groves. And the poet Ausonius (fourth century AD) is complaining in this 'verse letter' to a tardy correspondent that his silence has been positively unnatural:

> Even the rocks respond to one and speech is returned
> from echoing caves, as from reverberating woods;
> sea-cliffs cry out, streams voice their murmurs,
> and the hedgerows where bees feed whisper to us.
> Reedy banks make their own tuneful music,
> and the pine has tremulous words with its winds.
> When the light eastern breeze leans into shrill leaves
> wild strains resound through woodland groves.
> Nature has made nothing mute. Neither birds of the air
> nor mammals are silent, and even the serpent hisses,
> while shoals in the deep sigh in a faint semblance of voice.
>
> Ausonius, *Letters* XXIX 9–19

In the countryside itself the sounds tend to be soothing. The Sicilian Greek pastoral poet Theocritus composed a series of *Idylls* celebrating rural life and landscapes, and it is striking how often he uses sounds, both natural and man-made, to evoke the mood. The collection begins:

> Sweet is the music from the whispering[1] pine
> over there beside the springs, master goatherd,
> and sweet the music from your piping…
>
> Theocritus, *Idylls* 1 1–3

And here he is describing the sounds of high summer:

> Over our heads many an aspen and elm stirred
> and rustled, while nearby the sacred water
> of the nymphs murmured, welling from their cave.

[1] *Psithurisma*, a beautifully onomatopoeic word.

In the shady foliage of the trees the dusky
cicadas were busy chirping, and some songster murmured[1]
his laments, high up in the thorny thickets.
Lark and finch were singing, the turtle dove crooned,
and bees hummed and hovered, flitting about the springs.

   Theocritus, *Idylls* VII 135–42

1.12 Pastoral scene on a silver dish, probably from late first century BC. A male figure, possibly representing the poet Theocritus (third century BC) in the guise of a goatherd, sits with his dog. Another possible allusion is to Virgil's *Eclogues* (42–39 BC), a series of bucolic poems that had Theocritus' *Idylls* as its literary model.

---

[1] No one really knows what this 'songster' (*ololugon*, literally 'moaner') is. In some other references the word clearly means a frog, but the context here suggests a bird. The nightingale might be the likeliest candidate but for the season (harvest-time, when nightingales would have stopped singing), so I have translated indeterminately, as may indeed have been intended.*

Natural sounds predominate, too, in the wilder landscapes inhabited by the shepherd–god Pan, one of whose epithets is *philokrotos*, 'lover of rhythmic noise' (beat music). Here the song of one bird in particular stands out:

> Then at evening, returning from the chase, his sounds
> ring out, as he plays sweet music on his reed pipes.
> No bird can surpass him in song, not even the one
> who when spring is in full-blossomed flower
> pours forth her honey-toned lament amid the leaves.
> Then the clear-voiced mountain nymphs join him,
> dancing with nimble feet as they sing their songs
> by the spring of dark water, while Echo spreads
> the sounds from her mountain-top.
> *Homeric Hymn* (to Pan) XIX 14–21

That bird was the nightingale. With the possible exception of the eagle, the nightingale must be more often invoked in ancient literature than any other bird. And the reference is almost always to its voice. The nightingale has provided the perfect image—in this case a sound image—for poets from Homer to Keats through which to evoke particular places and moods. The places are wild, or at least thickly wooded, and the mood is generally one of lament. The fascination with the nightingale's song depends partly on its extraordinary melodic qualities, but partly also on the sense of mystery surrounding the bird. The nightingale famously sings by night as well as by day; and in the hours of darkness, when it is usually the only bird singing, the power, purity, and intensity of the song are accentuated by its isolation. The bird is of course invisible at night, but it is also very hard to see by day since it favours dense woodland habitats and tends to conceal itself in deep cover. Moreover, it is a summer migrant and sings for only a brief season, beginning when it arrives (usually in mid-April in England) and ceasing altogether in June.

All this has made the nightingale an iconic bird. Everyone knows about the nightingale, but relatively few people nowadays have ever heard one and even fewer have actually seen one. Little wonder then that the bird not only provides us with ready literary images but is also surrounded by a huge symbolic web of myth and legend.* I shall return to the mythology later but here I want to concentrate on the voice.

In Homer, our earliest Western author, the nightingale is already established as a familiar songster. Penelope is describing her grief to the stranger (who is in fact her returning, but so far unrecognized, husband, Odysseus):

> But when night falls and sleep comes to everyone,
> I lie on my bed, racked by sharp anxieties that cluster
> thickly around my throbbing heart in my mourning.
> Just as when the daughter of Pandareos,[1] the greenwood
> nightingale, sings her lovely song at the start of spring,
> perched among the dense foliage of the trees, and keeps
> pouring out the varied notes of her many-toned voice,
> lamenting her child...
>
>   Homer, *Odyssey* XIX 515–22

In this passage Sophocles is describing Colonus, a village outside Athens,[2] to which Oedipus, now an old man, is returning to seek his final sanctuary:

> White Colonus...
> favoured haunt of the clear-voiced nightingale
> who for ever warbles in the green glades,
> keeping to the wine-dark ivy
> and the untrodden grove of the god,
> thick with leaves and fruit,
> untouched by sun or the winds of any storm.
>
>   Sophocles, *Oedipus at Colonus* 670–76

And Oedipus, we should remember, is by now a blind man, for whom the sounds of this place of refuge might be all the more important.

In Aristophanes' play *The Birds*, Tereus, the hoopoe, is asked to go into the thicket and awaken his consort, the nightingale:[3]

> Come, awake, my mate, my partner in melody,
> loosen the strains of the wondrous songs
> from your divine mouth with which you lament
> Itys, your child and mine, whom we grieve so tearfully,
> your voice quavering with the liquid notes from
> your vibrant throat.
>
>   Aristophanes, *Birds* 209–14

---

[1] In this myth, Aëdon was the daughter of Pandareos and was transformed into a nightingale that endlessly lamented the son (Itylus) she had killed. There is also a quite separate Greek myth about the nightingale, involving Tereus, Procne, and Philomela (see p. 279).

[2] Now a very noisy, built-up suburb...not frequented by nightingales.

[3] There are some possible double entendres here, since 'waking the nightingale' was coarse slang for arousing female sexual passion, and in that context 'the thicket' is ambiguous, too.

The same themes and epithets recur in the many poetic references to nightingales in both Greek and Latin poetry,* and these raise some interesting questions of perception, and perhaps of identification too.

In the first place, why should the nightingale's song so often be associated with lament? One explanation given is that this was a consequence of the myth about Aëdon (also the Greek word for a 'nightingale') grieving for her murdered son, Itys (or Itylus, see p. 50 n.1). But that seems the wrong way round. You would expect a myth to express an existing belief or perception, by way of explaining them, not to *cause* them.

Perhaps we should try a different tack. It was a common fallacy, as illustrated in the passages quoted from Homer and Aristophanes above, that singing nightingales were female. Is that relevant? Lament for the dead was a highly formalized convention in the ancient world, involving women and women's voices in particular.* Perhaps the high-pitched wavering trills that were part of the ritual act of female ululation recalled the 'sobbing' notes in the nightingale's standard repertoire. In the later Western Romantic tradition, by contrast, the nightingale's song is more often associated with emotions of exhilaration, joy, and the rebirth of spring:*

> …thou, light-winged Dryad of the trees
> in some melodious plot
> of beechen green, and shadows numberless,
> singest of summer in full-throated ease.
>
> Keats, 'Ode to a Nightingale'

> …and her renown
> hath made me marvel that so famed a bird
> should have no better dress than russet brown.
> Her wings would tremble in her ecstacy
> and feathers stand on end as 'twere with joy
> and mouth wide open to release her heart
> of its out-sobbing songs – the happiest part
> of summer's fame she shared…
>
> John Clare, 'The Nightingale's Nest'

Coleridge calls the bird 'the merry nightingale' and explains its literary reputation as a mere projection on the part of unhappy listeners who:

> First named these notes a melancholy strain
> And many a poet echoes the conceit…

Whereas, he asserts:

> ...we have learnt
> a different lore: we may not thus profane
> nature's sweet voices, always full of love
> and joyance! 'Tis the merry nightingale
> that crowds, and hurries, and precipitates
> with thick, fast warble his delicious notes,
> as if he were fearful that an April night
> would be too short for him to utter forth
> his love-chant, and disburthen his full soul
> of all its music!
>
>   Samuel Taylor Coleridge, 'The Nightingale· a Conversation Poem'

Anthropomorphism, of course, can apply in both directions. Nightingales are neither mournful nor merry by constitution.

Anyway, are we even sure these are all nightingales that the classical authors were describing? The passage in which Sophocles evokes the charms of Colonus through its singing nightingales (above p. 50) is worth a closer look. There are at least a dozen warblers to be found in Greece in summer, all of them vocal. Several of them might have been singing in the Colonus groves in early summer, and three in particular are possible confusion species. The Orphean warbler is a wonderful songster, as its name suggests, and the olivaceous and olive tree warblers are both also quite tuneful to our ears. All three can sing from deep cover and so remain inconspicuous and hard to identify by sight alone. Moreover, the Greek word I translated as 'warbles' (*minuretai*) is an unusual one, which in its other occurrences suggests a continuous low murmuring, more like the scratchy burbling of a song or sub-song from one of these other species rather than the full organ notes of a nightingale with all the stops out. Perhaps Sophocles is describing one of these other songs exactly as he heard it? Or maybe 'nightingale' here stands generically for all these vocalists and just means 'warbling bird'? Nightingales are, in fact, more closely related to thrushes than they are to the warbler family, but no doubt then, as now, people thought of them as 'warblers' because of their songs.[1] And as we know from our own times, 'nightingale' is a sort of cultural construct, which everyone identifies with but only few could actually identify.*

---

[1] 'Ten thousand warblers cheer the day, and one / The live long night',
    William Cowper, 'The Task' (1785).

The nightingale wasn't the only bird whose singing may have been appropriated by the poets for their own purposes. The kingfisher is also associated with laments, and Euripides' chorus of captive Greek women in Tauris (Crimea) makes just that connection:

> Halcyon, the bird who
> along the rugged sea-breakers
> sings your song of sorrow,
> understood by those who know
> you for ever lament your mate.
> I match my lament to yours,
> a bird without wings.
>
>   Euripides, *Iphigenia in Tauris* 1089–95

It's true that the kingfisher does have a song of sorts—a jumble of high-pitched whistles, which could be thought of as a kind of keening. But the song is very rarely heard, and it seems unlikely that even the bird's much commoner shrill flight calls could explain the many literary references.* However that may be, it is interesting that such a visually striking bird should be mythologized mainly for its dissonant voice, and categorized along with the melodious nightingale as the voice of mourning.

Even more ornithological liberties are taken with the swan's voice. There was an early belief, which hardened into orthodoxy and later acquired proverbial status, that swans sang, particularly just before their death.* In fact, mute swans, the species of swan most likely to be encountered (though still uncommon) in Mediterranean wetlands, are indeed largely mute, apart from various threatening hisses and tuneless gurgles and rumblings. Various earnest attempts have been made to rationalize the myth by suggesting that it might have been inspired by the bugling, ocarina calls of another species, the whooper swan, which is certainly a highly vocal bird and was probably then, as now, an occasional winter visitor to Thrace and the Evros Delta. It was even suggested by the nineteenth-century German zoologist Peter Pallas that the convoluted trachea of the whooper could produce a slow, wailing, flute-like sound as the air expired from its collapsing lungs.* It seems doubtful whether the fortuitous experience of a single dying whooper could have started such a persistent legend, but if one has to relate this to some acoustic effect then perhaps the rhythmical whistling note of the mute swan's wing-beats in flight is a stronger candidate than any vocal sound. Indeed, there is possible support for that hypothesis from two ancient sources:*

Phoebus Apollo, even the swan sings in praise of you,
with the clear sound of its beating wings, as he alights
on the bank of the eddying river Peneus.

> *Homeric Hymn* (to Apollo) xxx 1–2

With such strains did the swans—
tio-tio-tio-tio-tynx –
beating their wings in harmonious chorus hail Apollo
tio-tio-tio-tio-tynx

> Aristophanes, *Birds* 769–73

1.13 Apollo and the swan. Detail from a painted mixing-bowl from Apulia, Italy, 340–330 BC. Apollo is portrayed with various of his usual symbols: the sun, a laurel branch, a leopard, and in particular the swan, which was thought of as his special minstrel or messenger. The swan's bill in this image looks somewhat more like the smooth bill of a whooper swan (*Cygnus cygnus*) than the knobbly bill of a mute swan (*Cygnus olor*), but that may be to over-interpret the rendering.

But these also point beyond literal explanations to the mythical connection of the swan with Apollo, the god of prophecy and music, which would suggest a deeper interpretation.

In any case, there were sceptical objections voiced about 'swan-songs' even in the ancient world, briskly expressed, for example, by Pliny:

> There is this story about the doleful songs of swans at their death, a false one, as I judge from various tests of experience.
>
> Pliny, *Natural History* x 63

Who knows what 'tests' he had in mind? A far more disarming and ironic put-down is given by Socrates in Plato's account of his last conversations in prison before his execution. He explains to his friends why he does not regard death as a misfortune to be feared, and cheerfully debunks all these references to the 'birds of sorrow' as emotional transference. The 'swan-song' becomes a metaphorical celebration of the life to come:

> You seem to think that I am less of a prophet than the swans which, when they feel that they are to die, sing more and better than they ever have before, happy in the knowledge that they are departing this life to join the god they serve. But humankind, because of their own fear of death, misrepresent the swans and claim that they sing their last in sorrow, bewailing their own death. They ignore the fact that no bird sings when it is cold or hungry or has some other cause for distress—not even the nightingale, the swallow, or the hoopoe, which are said to sing in lamentation. I don't think these birds sing from distress, any more than the swans do, but I believe that because the latter are Apollo's birds they are prophets with foreknowledge of the advantages of the other world so they sing and rejoice on that day more than any other. I regard myself as a fellow servant with the swans, dedicated to the same god, and have received from our master a power of prophecy equal to theirs. I therefore leave this life no more despondent than they do.
>
> Plato, *Phaedo* 84e–85b

Socrates also mentions the swallow here as another 'lamenting bird'. Here too the perceptions seem different from ours. We tend to think of the swallow's song as a sweet, pleasing chatter, but that wasn't necessarily the way the ancients heard it. In Homer it is compared to the 'twanging of a bow-string' (*Odyssey* XXI 411). In drama it becomes a metaphor for a tuneless babble. Aeschylus talks of Cassandra's 'outlandish barbarous speech like a swallow's' (*Agamemnon* 1050–51); while

Aristophanes, in the worst ethnic slur he can think of, compares a hated Athenian demagogue with a foreign accent to 'the Thracian swallow, shrieking horribly, who sings from his barbarous[1] perch' (*Frogs* 678–82). And Theophrastus in his book on different human character types, says that the 'garrulous man' is 'a greater chatterer even than the swallows' (*Characters* VII 7). Finally, in a witty little poem in the *Greek Anthology* the swallow's voice is even likened to that of an insect:

> Honey-fed maiden of Attica, a chirruper seizing a chirruping
> cicada, you're taking him as food for your wingless chicks,
> chirruper preying on chirruper, winged on winged,
> host on guest, one summer visitor on another.
> Won't you drop him quickly? It isn't right or just
> that singers should die in the mouths of singers.
>   Euenus, *Greek Anthology* IX 122

Another comparison that sounds odd to our ears is the occasional rendering of the cock's crow as 'cuckoo'.* But is that description, analogy, or metaphor? It's hard to be sure.

To end this series of species, we should consider briefly two birds whose songs are greatly valued now but receive very little attention in classical literature. Theocritus mentioned the lark's song in the passage quoted above from *Idyll* VII (p. 48), but this is a rare positive reference. Indeed, its reputation seems to have been decidedly negative. The poet Dioscorides quipped in an epigram that 'among musical illiterates even a lark sings more tunefully than a swan' (*Greek Anthology* XI 195). Perhaps that is because the commonest local lark species in the region would have been the crested and short-toed larks, which have much less attractive songs than the skylark.* The blackbird too is mentioned only very rarely as a songster, though it is another modern favourite.* Gaps and absences in the record like these can be harder to spot but may be just as telling as explicit cases of apparent contrasts between one culture and another.

It is difficult to know what to make of all these ancient representations and misrepresentations of the voices of species like the nightingale, swan, kingfisher, and swallow, all of them iconic birds in Western culture. The connection with lamentation seems significant. Indeed, all these species are mentioned together in that context in these (highly rhetorical) passages from the pastoral poet Moschus (second century BC):

---

[1] The word *barbaros* in these two references refers to foreigners or 'outsiders'—that is, people who couldn't speak Greek properly.

> Wail your dirges, you swans, by the waters of Strymon
> and let flow such songs of sorrow with grieving voices
> as in old age you may sing from your throats.
>
> Moschus, 'Lament for Bion' III 14–16

But nothing, he said, could compare with the song of mourning for the poet:

> Never so lamented the Sirens by the shore,
> never so sadly sang the nightingale in the crags
> or so wailed the swallow amid the long hills,
> nor the cries of Keÿx for the woes of Halcyon,
> nor the song of Kerulos over the dark waves.[1]
>
> Moschus, 'Lament for Bion' III 37–42

It may also be relevant that these birds are all personified in mythology, often as females, with 'explanations' given for their sad fates and subsequent grieving. Would that support a feminist interpretation of their symbolic role as victims? But there is no single, clear, and certain interpretation. The more evident common factor is that it should be their *voices* that attracted this attention.

*   *   *

This emphasis on sound is further illustrated in ancient attempts to explain the origins of bird names. The Roman scholar Varro (116–27 BC) offered some speculative etymologies of this kind. He starts with the whole class of *oscines* (now the scientific name for a sub-order of Passerines), which he derives from *os* ('mouth') and *cano* ('sing'); and he goes on to suggest that the following are named after their characteristic calls: *upupa* ('hoopoe'), *cuculus* ('cuckoo'), *corvus* ('raven'), *hirundo* ('swallow'), *ulula* ('barn owl'), and *bubo* ('eagle owl'). These all seem convincing, except for the swallow; but he then rather spoils it by tacking on the names of *pavo* ('peacock'), *anser* ('goose'), *gallina* ('hen'), and *columba* ('dove'), all of which have quite different origins; and he also offers the ingenious but unlikely suggestion that *luscinia* ('nightingale') is derived from *luctuose canere* ('sorrow-singer'). The much later encyclopedist Isidore of Seville (seventh century AD), whose work retained authoritative status for a further thousand years, added the examples of *ciconia* ('stork'), *coturnix* ('quail'), *cygnus* ('swan'), *graculus* ('jackdaw'), *grus* ('crane'), and *milvus* ('kite'). Several of these too are unconvincing,

---

[1] These capitalized mythological figures are obscure. Keÿx elsewhere seems to be a tern, but they are all alternative kingfisher names too.* See also p. 280 for the Latinized form 'Ceyx'.

but it is sometimes as interesting to see what people believe to be the case in folk
etymologies of this kind as it is to trace the 'true' derivations.*

In the same spirit, both Varro and Suetonius catalogued a number of specialized Latin verbs representing different animal calls, some of which are clearly
onomatopoeic. And these were probably the source for the nerdy linguistic tests
that the Roman emperor Geta (AD 189–211) used to set for the grammarians of
his day, as reported in the *Historia Augusta* (a collection of imperial biographies).
Here is a selection from their composite lists:*

lambs *balant*	pigs *grunniunt*
camels *blatterant*	horses *hinniunt*
frogs *coaxant*	mice *mintriunt*
storks *crotolant* (the bill-rattling	pigeons *minurriunt*
display)	bulls *mugiunt*
owls *cuccubiunt*	peacocks *paupulant*
swans *drensant*	sparrowhawks *plipiant*
geese *gingriunt*	lions *rugiunt*
hens *glocidant*	ducks *tetrissitant*

There are also lots of attempts to represent some of the most familiar bird
calls in crude transliterations. Where we have 'cuckoo', 'tu-wit-tu-woo', and 'cock-
a-doodle-do', the ancients had 'kokku', 'tu-tu', and 'co-co-co-co'.* But by far the
best of these attempts at mimicry is the splendid invocation of the birds in
Aristophanes' play by Tereus, the hoopoe. He tells us that he was the one who
taught the birds to speak and will act as their intermediary (*Birds* 199–200). He
first mimics himself with an extended 'epopopopopopopopopoi'; then adds an
impression of the nightingale he has just coaxed out of the thicket 'iō, iō, itō, itō,
itō, itō, itō'; and he goes on to mimic a series of other, not always identifiable,
birds in what must have been, on stage, a virtuoso performance. In the vocal
extravaganza that follows we hear this medley as the hoopoe summons birds
from their different named habitats in fields, gardens, hills, wetlands, and the
sea: 'tio tio tio tio tio tio tio tio trioto trioto totbrix'; 'attagen attagen'; 'torotoro-
torotorotix'; 'kikkabu'; and 'torotortorolililix' (*Birds* 227–62). The only ones here
that can be plausibly identified are 'attagen' (black francolin) and 'kikkabu' (little
owl), both on the basis of more transparent uses elsewhere. As for the others,
anyone can play this game, and eager commentators have suggested all of the
following as candidates: partridge, house sparrow, corn bunting, white wagtail,
starling, wryneck, woodcock, godwit, flamingo, Sardinian warbler, Orphean
warbler, lesser whitethroat, nightjar, house martin, robin, mistle thrush, great

tit, blackbird, woodlark, and black-headed bunting.* Really? Isn't that trying a
bit too hard? Aren't some of these vocal effects more likely to have been conceived as generic bird sounds, created at least partly to suit the demands of
metre and the accompanying music? The connections made between bird song
and music are worth pursuing further.

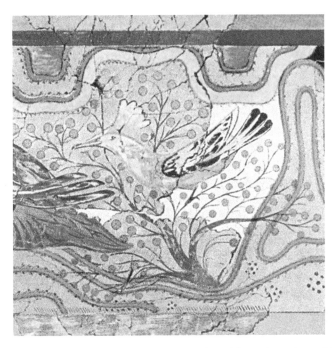

1.14 Hoopoe. Detail from the famous 'Partridge fresco' from the Palace of Minos at
Knossos, c.1500–1100 BC. The Greek name for the hoopoe was the onomatopoeic *epops*,
which recurs in its current scientific name *Upupa epops*.

Aristotle makes an interesting comment about song learning:

> Among small birds some have songs that are different from their parents, if they
> have been reared away from the nest and have heard other birds singing. A night-
> ingale has before now been observed teaching her young how to sing, which sug-
> gests that language is not natural in the way that voice is. Humans all have the
> same voice but not the same language.[1]
>
> Aristotle, *History of Animals* 536b14–20

---

[1] The word used here for 'language' is *dialektos*—that is, the kind of language that varies by country
and region. This striking thought anticipates some modern ornithological research on bird songs.*

And the encyclopedist Pliny elaborates the analogy between nightingale song and music:

> Nightingales are the most remarkable birds. They sing continuously for fifteen days and nights on end when the buds are bursting into leaf. The voice is so loud in relation to their small size and the supply of breath so continuous; then there is such a consummate knowledge of music in the individual bird—it modulates the sound, at one moment drawing out one sustained note in a continuous breath, at another adjusting the breathing to vary it, now punctuating it with pauses, now prolonging it to link phrases, now extending it in an encore; or suddenly it lowers the tone, sometimes just murmuring to itself, or the note is at will made full, bass, treble, throbbing, extended, tremulous—soprano, mezzo, or baritone. In short, that tiny throat contains everything that human art has devised in the elaborate mechanism of the flute.
>
> Pliny, *Natural History* x 81–82

This musical ability made nightingales popular cage-birds, of course, and Pliny goes on to discuss the price of the best songsters as well as various artificial means of imitating nightingale song. He describes people who can mimic a nightingale song, either mechanically by blowing into a specially fashioned reed or vocally by some form of tongue control, all of which irresistibly recalls the celebrated case of the cellist Beatrice Harrison duetting with nightingales for the BBC in their first ever outside broadcast on 19 May 1924 (with a trained mimic in the bushes as a back-up, I suspect).*

Various writers had linked the origins of human music with the appreciation of bird song. 'I know the tunes of all the birds,' said the poet Alcman, and gives the (perhaps surprising) example of the partridge:

> These words and this melody,
> Alcman invented and articulated,
> by transcribing the voice of partridges.
> Alcman thus makes it clear that he learned to sing from the partridges. And that is why Chamaeleon of Pontus said that the invention of music was conceived by the ancients from the sounds of birds singing in the wild.
>
> Athenaeus, The Intellectuals' Dinner Party 390a

And the Roman didactic poet Lucretius, in a passage explaining the evolution of human culture, is quite specific:

> Men learned to imitate by mouth the liquid notes
> of birds long before they could join together
> singing tuneful songs to delight the ear.
>
> Lucretius, *De rerum natura* v 1379–81

1.15 Alcman and partridges. Detail from a large floor mosaic celebrating literature and the arts, from Jerash in Jordan, late second to third century AD. The poet Alcman is pictured with partridges, here the Near Eastern species the chukar (*Alectoris chukar*), whose ancient Greek name (*kakkabis*), like its English one, is onomatopoeic from its grating calls, which are scarcely musical. Indeed, the generic Greek word for partridge was *perdix*, which is thought to be a rare case of anal not oral onomatopoeia, derived from the verb *perdomai* ('to break wind'), a sound that supposedly recalled the drumming wing-beats of a covey of flushed partridges.

The thought that birds were the source of human music is a very large claim. It has its counterpart in more modern suggestions, by Darwin and his successors, that vocalizations by birds and other animals had a formative effect on the development of human language:

> The sounds uttered by birds offer in several respects the nearest analogy to language, for all the members of the same species utter the same instinctive cries expressive of their emotions…I cannot doubt that language owes its origin to the imitation and modification of various natural sounds, the voices of other animals, and man's own instinctive cries, aided by signs and gestures.
>
> Charles Darwin, *The Descent of Man* (1871), ch. 3*

But the claim was an even stronger one in the ancient world, given the central importance of music in classical (particularly Greek) culture. Think of all our words in this field with Greek origins: music, melody, harmony, symphony, polyphony, antiphony, rhapsody, lyric, orchestra, organ, chorus, hymn, paean, chord, tone, rhythm, chromatic, syncopation, and others. Music permeated ancient social and cultural life at every level: both in public events such as festivals, music competitions, funerals, weddings, and harvest celebrations; and in the daily round of domestic life as work-songs, folk-songs, and recitations at dinner parties and private entertainments. Music also formed a major part of education. Indeed, the Greek word *mousike* had a much wider reference than its English counterpart—it covered all those activities inspired by the Muses and so came to stand for the creative arts more generally. 'Let me not live a life without music,' sang the chorus in a Euripides play, and there were many similar

1.16 Musical performance. A Muse plays a harp, while behind her another one fits a new reed to her pipe, and the poet Musaeus, standing before her, holds an eight-stringed tortoiseshell lyre; a *kithara* (from which we ultimately get the word 'guitar') hangs on the wall. Attic red-figure vase, c.440 BC.

references in tragedy to lives blighted by war as being 'music-less', 'chorus-less' and 'lyre-less'.* It was this belief in the crucial importance of *mousike* to human flourishing and the transmission of shared values and traditions that explains its moral status as a supposed determinant of character and behaviour. And this led Plato (rather frighteningly) and Aristotle (more pragmatically) to recommend educating people in the kinds of music most likely to promote politically desirable forms of emotional development and civic behaviour.* Music mattered more then, as the whole dimension of sound may have done.

I am not arguing, of course, that the ancients had different physical capacities from us for perceiving sound, as Lucian's spies in the well did. But I think the quotations in this chapter do suggest some significant cultural differences in how they might have perceived the natural soundscape, including the birds, which are among its most vocal and musical inhabitants. There would certainly have been a greater *density* of sound from the natural world then, because there was so much greater an abundance of wildlife. There would also have been a very different *balance* in the sounds, since there were far fewer competing mechanical noises. Their world would have sounded very different from ours.

PART 2

Birds as a
Resource

And God blessed them, and God said unto them, 'Be fruitful, and multiply, and replenish the earth, and subdue it: and have dominion over the fish of the sea, and over the fowl of the air, and over every living thing that moveth upon the earth'.

Genesis 1:28 (*c*.sixth century BC)

So we can clearly infer that plants exist for the sake of animals as they develop, and animals for the good of humankind—the domestic species for his use and sustenance, and most if not all the wild ones for his sustenance and for various kinds of practical help as a source of clothing and other items. If nature therefore makes nothing without purpose or in vain, it follows that nature has made all these other species for the sake of humans.

Aristotle, *Politics* 1256b15–23

The brute creation are his property,
Subservient to his will, and for him made.
As hurtful these he kills, as useful those
Preserves; their sole and arbitrary king.

William Somervile, *The Chase* (1735), Bk IV, lines 8–9

2.1 Peacock palace. The peacock is the national bird of India (hence the full proper name Indian peafowl *Pavo cristatus*), celebrated here in the Mor Chowk ('Peacock Courtyard') at the City Palace, Udaipur, Rajasthan Province. The peacocks are modelled in high relief and set in a mosaic of coloured glass in alcoves in the courtyard. Peacocks had reached Greece, probably via Persia, by at least the fifth century BC and came to be valued in several different roles: as exotic curiosity in captive collections, as culinary luxury, as commercial resource, and as symbolic icon in art, ritual, and myth.

Introduction

Part 1 illustrated how birds were perceived as a very conspicuous and significant part of the natural world they shared with human beings. But they were
also thought of as one of its resources, to be exploited as need be for human
purposes, and this is the theme of part 2. In particular, birds represented a
source of food, in a world where for most of the population the food supply was
always precarious and the spectre of scarcity or real famine was never very far
away.* Hunting provided one source of meat and protein, the farming of domesticated livestock another. There is a chapter on each of these topics and they
provide the raw material, so to speak, for the central chapter on cooking and
eating, which explores the tastes, processes, and rituals behind the consumption
of birds as food.

These were, of course, all forms of exploitation, and there was no sentimentality about them. People were not only 'close to nature' in the sense explored in
part 1, but most of them would have had a direct and personal experience of the
meat supply chain which, like life in Thomas Hobbes's envisaged state of nature,
was no doubt nasty, brutish, and short. They would have seen animals and birds
being trapped, killed, dismembered, and prepared either for the pot or for
sacrifice,[1] and seen these things at very close quarters and as an everyday event.
This is a quite different situation from that of the modern Western consumer
buying pre-packed and ready-to-cook meats, whose original embodiments are
by then unrecognizable and whose experiences in the transformation are not
seen (or heard). One can argue that our more distant and sanitized connections
with the sources of our meat are less honest and less humane.*

At any rate, there were few moral or aesthetic scruples about the slaughter of
edible creatures in the ancient world, except on the margins of mainstream

---

[1] On animal and bird sacrifice, see chapter 18.

culture. A few minor religious sects like the Orphics and Pythagoreans did believe in some sort of 'community of souls' between animals and humans, and in later Stoic and Christian writings there are some interesting speculations about 'animal rights', which we shall look at in chapter 10. But the general view would have been that expressed in the epigraphs to part 2 above: animals were there for humans to use in whatever ways they wished and had the practical means to accomplish.

This would also, of course, have been the prevailing view in Western Europe up to the Enlightenment. Keith Thomas in his survey of changing attitudes to the natural world in England from 1500 to 1800 documents case after case of this and takes as an epigraph to his chapter 'Human ascendancy' the following quotation:

> Ask any one of the undistinguished mass of people, for what purpose every thing exists? The general answer is, that everything was created for our practical use and accommodation!...In short, the whole magnificent scene of things is daily and confidently asserted to be ultimately intended for the peculiar convenience of mankind. Thus do the bulk of the human species vauntingly elevate themselves above the innumerable existences that surround them.
>
> G. H. Toulmin *The Antiquity and Duration of the World* (1780)

Moreover, Christian theologians gave their cheerful support to such ideas. Genesis had, after all, already made clear what man's rights in the matter were:

> And the fear of you and the dread of you shall be upon every beast of the earth, and upon every fowl of the air, upon all that moveth upon the earth, and upon all the fishes in the sea; into your hand are they delivered. Every moving thing that liveth shall be meat for you; even as the green herb have I given you all things.
>
> Genesis 9.2–3

Ingenious doctrinal explanations were found to justify every form of human exploitation of the animal world, to the point where the Cambridge theologian Henry More could say in 1653 that cattle and sheep had only been given life by the Creator in the first place so as to keep their meat fresh 'until we shall have need of it'.*

The ordinary person in the ancient world would not have felt the need for these theoretical contortions to justify their traditional habits. Conditions were hard anyway and were made even more insecure by the vagaries of weather and warfare. Communities were very dependent on the annual harvest since there were no central food supplies to draw on, and both imports and exports of foodstuffs were always subject to favourable sea conditions and trading relationships. Self-sufficiency was therefore a necessary ideal, for families and cities alike, and birds represented one resource that satisfied all the requirements of taste, diet, availability, and economy.*

5

Hunting and Fowling

Hunting served a number of different practical and social functions in the ancient world. Firstly, there was the primitive need to defend oneself and one's community against dangerous beasts in a wild environment where humankind was far from always dominant: hence the heroic exploits memorialized in early myth and epic—Heracles slaying the Nemean lion, the Calydonian boarhunt, and Odysseus killing the great boar of Parnassus.* The hunting of animals like the boar and stag was also seen as a test of manhood, and good training in the arts of war, especially for the social and military elite who could support the expense of horses and hounds, and the slaves to look after them. The hare was a particularly favoured quarry, also hunted with hounds but in this case with the hunters mainly on foot, in the manner of modern-day beagling.

Another specific purpose of hunting, which has no direct analogy in our culture, was for competitive gift exchange in homosexual courtship. Various Attic vases from the sixth century BC onwards show how older men would bring back the day's catch and eagerly 'say it with foxes' (or hares) to charm their young boyfriends.* These lovers' gifts could also be of birds, as Aristophanes describes when he has the leader of the chorus explain how birds can act as the agents of Eros, assisting in difficult seductions:

> Many pretty boys still of the right age keep holding out,
> but thanks to our power their lovers do get between their thighs,
> with gifts of quail, gallinule, goose, or Persian cockerel.[1]
>
> Aristophanes, *Birds* 705–07

---

[1] The purple gallinule (swamp-hen) is the surprise here—a sort of gigantic moorhen, now extinct in Greece but present in suitable marshes in the classical period and sometimes kept as a pet (see **8.3**, pp. 138–39).* On the cockerel as the 'Persian bird', see p. 36.

2.2 Lover's gift. A man presenting a boy with a cockerel and reaching forward suggestively. Attic red-figure cup, c.470 BC.

We shall return to the metaphor of erotic pursuit at the end of this chapter.

There were, of course, many variations in practices both across different states and over time. It is always risky to make confident judgements to the effect that 'the Greeks (or Romans) believed...', when classical civilization spanned a thousand years and included even more semi-independent polities. In Sparta, for example, hunting animals was seen very much as a form of military training, supported by the state, and not at all as a sport for the leisured; it also extended there into the more sinister forms of 'man-hunting', where escaping helots (the serf class) were systematically hunted down and either recaptured or culled.* But one can say that over much of Greece in the classical period hunting large animals was mainly an upper-class sport, and prowess in the trinity of hunting, athletics, and warfare helped to define a particular male and social ethos. Later on, organized aristocratic hunting parties on a large scale became a favoured pursuit for wealthy Macedonian kings and Roman noblemen. And they in turn sponsored the debased sporting spectacles of the Circus for consumption lower down the social ladder—for example, the *venationes*, which were staged fights between exotic animals (including crocodile, hippopotamus, elephant, and lion) and the human *bestiarii* ('hunters').

The hunting and trapping of birds, by contrast, was generally much more a countryman's pursuit and one motivated far more directly by the needs of the family pot and the local market. The quarry ranged from large game like bustard, partridge, and crane through wildfowl, waders, and pigeons, to all manner of smaller birds like thrushes, nightingales, warblers, larks, buntings, sparrows, finches, and even cuckoos*—anything, in short, judged edible or saleable. This was hunting for a practical purpose not for sport alone.

Plato has his lawgivers roundly dismiss all forms of hunting, except the manly activity of hunting with horses and dogs, as 'lazy pursuits', and says that birding in particular is a 'crafty kind of craving' and 'not at all the thing for a free man' (*Laws* VII 823b–824a). And Oppian, the presumed author of the verse treatise *On Hunting*, makes it clear that of the three kinds of hunting—angling, fowling, and hunting wild animals—the first two have none of the danger, and therefore neither the prestige nor social cachet, of the last:

> God has granted mankind three kinds of hunting
> – in the realms of the air, earth, and the lovely sea;
> but these sports are quite unequal, for how could
> drawing a gasping fish from the ocean depths
> or plucking birds from the air above compare
> with fighting deadly beasts on the hillsides?
> Not to say that for the angler, let alone the fowler,
> their hunting is without toil; but their toil comes only
> with pleasure not gore and they are not bloodied.
> The angler sits himself on the rocks beside the sea
> with his curving rods and deadly hooks
> and catches in comfort the shimmering fish.
> Pure pleasure, when he hooks it with his barbs of bronze
> and pulls through the air the gasping dancer of the sea,
> as it leaps up high above the waters of the deep.
> The fowler too has pleasant work, for he carries
> to his hunt neither sword, nor knife nor brazen spear;
> his only companion into the woods is the hawk,[1]

---

[1] One should not assume this is a reference to traditional falconry, however (see chapter 9).

together with his long strings and sticky yellow lime[1]
and the reeds that push their way through the air.

Oppian, *On Hunting* 1 47–65

He then drives the point home with a series of unflattering comparisons:

Hunters kill wolves, fishermen catch tunny; trappers
take sheep, the fowlers with the reed take doves;
the hunter with hounds catches bears, the angler bream;
the mounted hunter takes tiger, the fisherman spears mullet;
trackers hunt boar, and bird-limers…nightingales.

Oppian, *On Hunting* 1 72–76

2.3 Hunting and fishing scene. Fresco from an Etruscan burial tomb in Tarquinia, Italy (530–520 BC), which is remarkable for its evocation of colour and movement in the representation of the boys, and of the dolphins and birds (gulls and wildfowl?) they are hunting. The elaborately decorated tomb would have been constructed for an aristocratic family, and its vivid imagery was perhaps a celebration of the active, privileged life they hoped to take with them to the underworld.

---

[1] Bird-lime, made from mistletoe berries, was a sticky substance daubed on places where birds might perch so that they would get stuck fast there. Pliny gives the recipe in his *Natural History* XVI 94. More recent concoctions have also incorporated holly bark, linseed oil, treacle, and fig sap.*

In another long didactic poem, *On Fishing*, to which *On Hunting* seems to have been a later companion volume, Oppian suggests that fowling was also easier than angling:

> Those who make the preparations to kill birds
> have an easy time of it and a conspicuous prey to hunt:
> some birds they take by surprise, asleep in their nests,
> others are caught on limed reed-stems;
> and others entangle themselves in outstretched nets,
> seeking the roost but finding an unhappy place of rest.
>> Oppian, *On Fishing* I 29–34

But fowling did have its technical skills and equipment, too. Bird-catchers were often specialists, who had at their disposal an alarming array of traps, nets, snares, lures, and decoys and considerable expertise in deploying them all. There is a charming epigram in the *Greek Anthology* in which an old bird-catcher dedicates his kit to Pan:

> These old tatters of my hunting-net, and triple-twisted
> foot-snare and stretched meshes,
> broken cages and nooses to tighten round the neck,
> pointed stakes sharpened by fire,
> the sticky secretions of the oak and the rod
> slimy with mistletoe that entraps birds,
> the triple-spun draw-string of the fraying old spring-net
> and the snare for the bugling crane—all these,*
> Craugis the huntsman, son of Neolaidas,
> an Arcadian from Orchomenos,
> dedicated in your honour, Pan, God of High Places.[1]
>> Antipater of Thessalonica, *Greek Anthology* VI 109

There are many other references indicating that hunting and fowling were popular everyday activities, both as sport and as contributions to the domestic economy. Sophocles in his famous 'Ode to Mankind' even names hunting as one of the defining human capacities:

> Many wonders there are, but nothing more wondrous than man.
> He travels the grey ocean in the stormy south wind,
> and makes his way through the surging surf.

---

[1] Like most Greek gods, Pan had a whole series of roles and attributes. He was, among other things, the local god of Arcadia and the god of goats, shepherds, mountains, and the hunters of small game (Artemis had the portfolio for big game).

Even Earth, the greatest of gods, everlasting and untiring,
he wears away as he turns the soil
with his team of horses and his ploughs
that pass up and down, year after year.

With his woven nets he snares the race of light-witted birds,
the tribes of savage beasts, and the creatures of the seas,
ingenious as he is. And with his cunning arts
he masters the animals that roam the wild and the hills,
and he tames the shaggy-maned horse with yoke and bit
and the tireless mountain bull.

    Sophocles, *Antigone* 333–52

The pleasures of hunting are often celebrated too:

How pleasant to lie—now under the ancient holm-oak,
now on the well-rooted grass.
Meanwhile streams glide between high banks
and birds sing plaintive songs in the woods;
rivulets gurgle in pure flowing streams,
and so invite soft slumbers.
But when the heavens thunder in winter's turn,
bringing rains and snow,
one either drives fierce boars with a pack of hounds
hither and thither into the waiting toils,
or on a smooth pole stretches out wide-meshed nets—
a trap for greedy thrushes,
and captures in a snare the timid hare and migrant crane—
sweet prizes both.
Amid such delights, who does not forget
the unhappy cares love brings.

    Horace, *Epodes* 11 23–38

But this is the time to pick the acorns from the oak,
the laurel berries, the olive, and the blood-red myrtle;
time also to set snares for the cranes and nets for the stag,
to chase the long-eared hares and to bring down the does
by whirling the hempen thong of a Balearic sling,
when the snow lies deep and the rivers flow with ice.

    Virgil, *Georgics* 1 305–10

Oppian declares more generally that it is through hunting that man demonstrates his almost god-like domination of nature:

Lord of the Earth, next listen to me and take note
that nothing is beyond the means of man[1] to achieve,
either on Mother Earth or across the vast expanse of the sea;
to be sure, someone created humankind as a race comparable
to the blessed gods, though endowed with less strength—
whether it was the many-talented Prometheus, son of Iapetus,
who made the race of man in the image of the blessed gods,
mixing earth with water and anointing his heart
with divine unction, or are we descended from blood
that flowed from the Titans; for there is nothing finer than man,
apart from the gods, and only to these immortals shall we yield.

2.4 'Bird-catcher' cup. Ionian black-figure cup from eastern Greece, *c*.550 BC, featuring
a bearded man between two trees (or vines). In the foliage are two birds, a nest with four
nestlings, and a partially concealed snake and grasshopper. The man is usually identified
as a bird-catcher, but he could be the god Dionysus, given the latter's connections with
wine and wild animals.

---

[1] 'Man' translates the rare poetic term *merops*, derived perhaps from *meiromai* ('dividing') + *ops* ('the
voice'), i.e. 'articulate'. Curiously, *merops* is also the ancient Greek term for the 'bee-eater' and the current
scientific name for that genus.

How many wild beasts, roaming the mountains in fearless might,
does mortal man extinguish despite their overweening pride,
how many tribes of birds that wheel through the clouds and skies
does he capture, despite his own earth-bound form!
  Oppian, *On Fishing* v 1–14

From the birds' point of view, this all feels rather different, of course. The chorus of birds in Aristophanes' play, who are being asked favours by their human supplicants, have several complaints to make along these lines. First, they complain that they have been betrayed by one of their own number, Tereus the hoopoe, who had welcomed the human intruders into their territory:

Help, help!
We're betrayed and defiled.
This was our friend, who ate alongside us
in the fields that feed us all.
He's broken our ancient laws,
he's broken the birds' sacred oaths.
He's led us into a trap
and cast me out among
a foul, defiling race, that
since its first creation
has been brought up to be
my enemy.
  Aristophanes, *Birds* 327–35

Then they are reminded how they are abused:

Now you are treated like slaves, foreigners, and fools.
These days they attack you
as if you were lunatics: why, even in temples
every bird-hunter is after you,
setting up nooses, snares, sticky twigs,
traps, nets, toils, and decoys.
Then when they've caught you they sell you whole;
the customers feel up your flesh,
and if they go ahead they don't just
roast you and serve you up,
but they coat you with grated cheese,
add seasoning, oil, and vinegar,
prepare a further sweet and greasy dressing
and pour it over you hot,

when you are hot already,
like barbecued carrion.

    Aristophanes, *Birds* 523–37

And finally, the birds turn the tables and issue a warning:

So we want to make our own proclamation here and now.
Anyone who kills Philocrates, the sparrow man,
will get one talent, or four if you take him alive,
since he's the man who sells finches on a string for seven an obol;[1]
furthermore, he abuses thrushes by puffing them up for display,
and crams the noses of blackbirds with their own feathers;
and when he's caught pigeons he keeps them captive
and forces them to act as decoys while tethered in a net.
This, then, is our announcement. And if anyone here keeps
caged birds in his house, we order you to release them.
If you disobey, you will be arrested by the birds
and it will be your turn to be tied up and serve us as decoys.

    Aristophanes, *Birds* 1076–87

This anthropomorphic role-reversal had its comic force only because of its absurdity. There was no squeamishness about such things in the ancient world. Indeed, what must be the earliest reference to fowling in European literature occurs in a particularly macabre context. Odysseus' son, Telemachus, is taking revenge on the women who serviced the suitors in his father's palace during Odysseus' long absence on his travels back from Troy:

'I will inflict foul and dishonourable deaths
on these women who poured abuse both on me
and my mother and slept with her wooers.'
So he spoke and fastening the cable of a dark-prowed ship
to a great pillar he threw the end over the round-house,
tightening it so their feet would be high off the ground.
And just as when long-winged thrushes or doves
are caught up in a snare that has been set in a thicket—
seeking their roosts but finding their repose in disaster;
so, these women were lined up and around their necks
nooses were laid to ensure them horrendous deaths.
Their feet twitched a little while, but not for very long.

    Homer, *Odyssey* XXII 462–73

---

[1] The obol is the smallest unit of currency in Greece and there were 6 obols to the drachma.

Thrushes of various kinds were an especially common quarry and appeared regularly on menus, but in one poetic conceit a fine distinction is made between a thrush and a blackbird, on the grounds that the latter is the better singer:

> Of two snares, the one caught a fat thrush
> in its horse-hair noose, the other a blackbird.
> Now, the one did not release the plump thrush
> from the twisted fibres round its neck
> to see again the light of day,
> but the other did set free its holy prey.
> So, there is mercy for songsters,
> my friend, even among deaf snares.
>
>   Antipater of Sidon, *Greek Anthology* IX 76*

2.5 Limed thrush. A song thrush (*Turdus philomelos*) caught fast on a limed stick. Illegal liming is still widely used in some Mediterranean countries to trap migrant birds like thrushes and warblers as delicacies for the table; *ambelopoulia* is still a traditional (but now illegal) dish in Cyprus.

What we would think of as 'game birds' were also much sought by trappers. The Latin author Nemesianus seems to be describing a black grouse, or possibly a capercaillie, in this fragment from his lost poem on bird-catching:

… and the *tetrax*, which at Rome they have started to call the *tarax*.
This is by far the most stupid of birds, for this reason:
though it has perched there watching the snares laid for it,
it still runs headlong into disaster, mindless of its own safety.
Your job, when you find the meshes of the net drawn tight,
is to hurry up and carry off your prey with its beating wings,
since it will be quick to shake off the treacherous entanglements
around its neck and with a raucous call deride the designs
of its master and gladly enjoy its peace again in freedom.
It builds its nest near Peltinum at the foot of the Apennines,
where the sun casts its rays over the outspread fields.
Its neck is like the colour of ashes, and its dappled
back is marked with dusky flecks like a partridge.
The guardian of the Capitol is no larger in size,
nor are the birds whose flight taught you, Palamedes, letters.[1]
Often have I seen a slave staggering under the unmanageable
weight of a huge charger, when he carries in a meal of these birds
which a consul or new praetor has laid on for a circus celebration.

Nemesianus, *On Bird-Catching* fr. 1

Quail were far commoner and a cheap and tasty addition to the pot. They were easiest to catch when arriving exhausted after their migrations over the Mediterranean. Sometimes they needed staging posts, which is reputedly why Delos in the Aegean was called Ortygia ('Quail Island'), but often they would arrive on the mainland en masse and flop down in the nearest cover. The historian Diodorus Siculus (Diodorus 'the Sicilian') describes how an impoverished community in a desert region on the coast between Syria and Egypt took advantage of such incursions:

Nevertheless, although these people had been expelled and forced to occupy a desert region that lacked almost everything of practical use, they contrived a form of life that was adapted to the dearth surrounding them, since nature forced them to devise every possible means of alleviating their destitution. For example, they cut down reeds from the neighbouring marshes and split these to make long nets. They then set these up on the beach for a distance of many stades[2] and used them to hunt quail. For these arrive in large coveys from the sea and they caught sufficient numbers of them in their traps to provide themselves with food.

Diodorus, *Bibliotheca historica* 1 60

[1] The 'guardians of the Capitol' were the geese who gave the alarm against invaders (see pp. 178–79). Palamedes is credited with inventing some of the Greek letters (for example, Λ and Δ) in imitation of cranes in flight (see pp. 293 and 411).
[2] There were about 8 stades to the mile.

2.6 Quail hunt. Fresco from the tomb of Nebamun in Thebes, Egypt, *c.*1350 BC, showing men catching quails with a net.

This particular example would have occurred on the quails' returning migration south, when there would be the further advantage for the local people that the birds would have fattened themselves up to supply them with the energy and stamina for these very long journeys. The huge numbers in these migrant flocks are attested in several sources. Even after due allowance is made for exaggerations, misunderstandings, and tall stories, these still suggest an abundance quite unknown in the modern world, after centuries of systematic hunting and habitat destruction have finally taken their toll.* Aristotle and Pliny are here discussing migrations more generally, but were particularly struck by the seasonal movements of quail:

> When there is a fall of quail, if the weather is fine or the wind is from the north, they pair off and stay put, but if the wind is from the south they have difficulties since they are not strong fliers and that wind is humid and heavy. The hunters, therefore, try for them during these southerly winds. In good weather they avoid flying because of their body-weight; they are bulky birds, which is why they cry out in flight—because they are suffering. Now, when they make landfall after migrating they do not have leaders; but when they are setting off from here they

are accompanied by the wryneck, the quail-mother, the eared owl, and the rail,[1] which actually calls out to them at night, so that when the hunters hear that call they know that the quail are leaving.

Aristotle, *History of Animals* 597b9–20

In considering this migration of birds of passage over seas and land we should now turn to smaller birds that have a similar nature. For however much the size and bodily strength of the species mentioned above [cranes, storks, geese, and swans] may seem to encourage them to migrate, the quail always arrive before the cranes in fact, though the quail is a small bird and when it arrives it prefers to stay on the ground rather than fly aloft. But they too migrate here by flight in the same way, though not without causing danger to sailors when the birds are approaching land. For they often land on the sails—always at night—and so sink the ships.

Pliny, *Natural History* x 64–66

There is even a biblical precedent in the Old Testament for this phenomenon of massed quail migrations. Moses and the Israelites in the wilderness are blessed with a fall of quail to provide a meat dish to go with the manna from heaven:

And there went forth a wind from the Lord, and brought quails from the sea, and let them fall by the camp, as it were a day's journey on this side and as it were a day's journey on the other side, round about the camp, and as it were two cubits high upon the face of the earth. And the people stood up all that day, and all that night, and all the next day, and they gathered the quails: he that gathered least gathered ten homers:[2] and they spread them all abroad for themselves around the camp.

Numbers 11.31–32

Quail and partridges were also caught on a smaller scale with other techniques, including decoys, mirrors, and scarecrows:

---

[1] These identifications are somewhat speculative. The *glottis* ('tongue-bird') sounds very like the wryneck, which does have a long tongue and which migrates at the same time as quail. The *ortygometra* ('quail-mother') seems from other descriptions to be the corncrake (still called the *ortygometra* in modern Greek), which might also associate with migrating quail. The *otos* ('eared owl') could be any one of three smaller owls with ear-tufts (long-eared, short-eared, and scops); these were probably confused but it is more likely to have been the last in this context. And the *kychramos* might be either the water rail or the little crake, both of which migrate and call by night.

[2] Two cubits' height would be about 100 cm or just over 3 feet; and a 'homer' was about 365 litres or 80 gallons. The indefatigable compiler of hunting statistics, Hugh Gladstone, 'established by experiment that about 32 quail will go into a one gallon measure' and calculated that on this basis Moses and his party might have harvested over 9 million birds.* The bonanza ends badly for the Israelites, though (Numbers 11:33–34).

The leader of the wild birds rushes forward to challenge the decoy partridge to fight. Then after he has been caught in the nets another one comes forward to make a similar challenge. That is how they behave if the decoy is a male, but if the decoy is a female and is calling and the leader challenges her, then the others mob him and strike him, driving him away from the female because he is making advances to her and not to them…. Often too a female sitting on eggs stands up when she sees the male paying attention to the female decoy and makes a challenge of her own, crouching submissively in order to mate with him and draw him away from the other female. Partridges and quails become so sexually excited at the prospect of mating that they throw themselves on the hunters and often settle on their heads.

    Aristotle, *History of Animals* 614a10–30

When quails are in their mating season, if one sets up a mirror in their path and then positions a noose in front of the mirror, they will run towards the reflection in the mirror and be caught in the noose.

    Athenaeus, *The Intellectuals' Dinner Party* 393a

Quail are hunted with nets by night, with the older birds calling out; the others run towards the calls and fall into the long hunting nets. By day, one way of catching them is as follows. Someone spreads out a mesh-net on the ground; he then stretches a cloak over his head and holding it up screened with reeds on each side he moves it around, advancing step by step. The birds are alarmed by this, and fleeing towards the shadow of the garment being waved about this way and that, they fall into the meshes of the nets.

    Dionysius, *On Birds* III 9

There are further unconventional techniques mentioned for catching other species:

Jackdaws are a similar case, because of their instinctive fascination with themselves. They excel all other species in their cunning, but nonetheless when a bowl full of oil is set before them, there are those that stand on the rim, look down at their reflections and plunge in headlong. Their wings become saturated in oil and clogged up—and that's why they are caught.

    Athenaeus, *The Intellectuals' Dinner Party* 393b

The eared bird is like one of the owls and has tufts by its ears. Some call it the 'night raven'.[1] It is a trickster and a mimic, and can be caught by one hunter dancing

---

[1] See p. 83 n.1 for the 'eared owls'. Another possibility is the night heron (scientific name *Nictocorax nictocorax*, and current vernacular name in modern Greek *nyktokorakas*), which has a sort of 'dance' and a hoarse call somewhat like a raven.

to get it to dance in response and another going round behind it and taking it, as one does an owl.

Aristotle, *History of Animals* 587b

The storm petrel[1] is caught by the use of foam. These birds peck at foam, so they hunt them by spraying it at them. The flesh has a good taste generally, but the rump is the one part that smells of mud. They grow fat.

Aristotle, *History of Animals* 620a

Neither the great crested grebes nor the diving birds[2] nor the little grebes can escape the hunters, even if they stay all day on the water, since the men trap them by means of a trick. When the surface of the water is calm and still, they set off in a skiff without oars and sail gradually towards them so that the birds are not scared off by the sound of rowing. One of the men stands on the stern with a net, while another is on the prow easing the boat gradually forwards with the rudder and holding a lantern to attract the birds' attention. They approach the boat, thinking they are seeing not a light but a star. When they get near, the hunter hides the lamp down in the boat so that the birds don't realize the deception. He then unfurls his net, makes a long cast over them, and hauls in a good catch.

Dionysius, *On Birds* III 25

A skilled archer might also bring down birds with a well-aimed arrow. The wounded hero Philoctetes, abandoned for dead on an island, has only his bow to help him:

So time passed for me, day after day,
and all alone in this cramped cave
I had to care for myself. This bow supplied
my stomach's needs, downing doves on the wing.
And whenever my string-sped arrow struck home
I crawled along in pain towards it,
dragging my lamed foot behind.

Sophocles, *Philoctetes* 285–92

And the Latin poet Propertius confesses in a love letter to his girlfriend that though he wasn't man enough to go after big game he could shoot down a bird:

---

[1] Storm petrel seems a reasonable conjecture for *kemphos* (see p. 23 n.2). Because the bird was (supposedly) so easily captured by these means, *kemphos* came to become slang for 'simpleton'.

[2] *Dutinos* just means 'plunger' and could well refer to a small diving duck. There is some contextual support for the two grebe identifications (*thrax* and *kolumbos*).

Yet I wouldn't dare take on the mighty lion
or dash to confront the wild boar of the fields.
I feel brave enough if I catch the timid hare
or shoot down a bird with my bow and arrow.

Propertius, *Elegies* II 19.21–4

The largest quarry we hear about is the ostrich, which did seem to count as big game. Indeed, Aristotle was unsure whether to classify the ostrich as a bird or a terrestrial animal. As far as hunting went, this was a quarry for Eastern princes and their guests on safari, who hunted it on horseback as they would large animals. Ostriches would also occasionally be taken by horsemen from armies on the move, who would have welcomed such a substantial supply of meat in the desert regions of north Africa and Asia Minor. For the common man, however, the ostrich was just an exotic foreign curiosity that he would have heard about indirectly from travellers to those parts. Here is a selection of anecdotes about hunting them:[1]

2.7 Hunting scene. Detail from a Roman mosaic pavement from Utica, Tunisia, AD 220–225. Men in boats are hunting various kinds of exotic game with nets, including boar and ostrich (though marshlands would not be a natural habitat for the latter).

Indeed, I have seen with my own eyes the great marvel
of another double ancestry, the 'camel with sparrow'.[2]

---

[1] See also the discussion of 'travellers tales', pp. 197–99, and on Aristotle's taxonomy pp. 231–32.

[2] The Greek word *strouthos* could mean either 'ostrich' or 'sparrow' (maybe a sort of linguistic joke), and this odd combination, 'camel-sparrow', survives in the ostrich's modern scientific name *Struthio camelus*. In Latin its name was *struthio*, but the bird was also sometimes known as the *passer marinus* ('sea sparrow') because it was brought to the Roman circuses from lands overseas.

Although that is numbered with the light birds of the air
and is itself winged, I shall celebrate it in my verses,
since the varied range of our hunting does include it.
For the lime, so deadly to birds, is powerless in this case,
as are the reed stems pointing upwards in the air;
instead you need horses and swift hounds and unseen bonds.

Oppian, *On Hunting* III 482–89

… the mighty Libyan bird, when pressed by the cries
of the hunters, runs across the hot sands and flies along
in a cloud of dust, its wings angled to catch the wind;
but when it hears the sound of footsteps close behind
it forgets its flight and stands, eyes closed and head averted,
believing, ridiculous bird, that it is hidden from those
it cannot see itself.

Claudian, *Against Eutropius* II 310–16

The ostrich is caught by using horses. It runs in a circle round the edge of a wide circuit, but the horsemen can intercept it by describing an inner circle, and by thus travelling a shorter distance they can eventually hunt it down when it becomes exhausted with running.

There is also another way to catch it…When the ostrich is thus preoccupied [at the nest], the person who has been observing her—not any old fool but someone experienced in this kind of hunting—sets some sharp spears upright in the ground round the nest, points uppermost with the metal shining; then he withdraws and lies in wait for the outcome. The ostrich in due course returns from where she has been feeding, drawn by a powerful love of her chicks and longing to be with them again. First, she casts her eyes round, looking nervously this way and that in case someone should be watching her. Then, overcome by the stimulus of her intense desire, she spreads her wings like a sail, dashes in at a run, and meets a pitiful death, entangled and impaled on the spears. Thereupon the hunter moves in and seizes the young birds along with their mother.

Aelian, *On Animals* XIV 7

Ostriches were variously known as 'Libyan' or 'Arabian' birds. There were in fact two different subspecies in the ancient world. The African (Saharan) ostrich (*Struthio camelus camelus*) is now very rare in the region, while the Arabian one (*Struthio camelus syriacus*) became extinct some time in the mid-twentieth century. Both these declines were the result of intensive hunting over the last 150 years, as the use of vehicles and guns made it progressively easier to pursue and kill the birds.

The ostrich represents an exception in all sorts of ways. Another kind of
exception comes from one of the few classes of birds that were *not* hunted. This
is from the Roman playwright Terence:

> ...no one tries to net birds like a hawk or a kite,
> birds that do us harm; they set them for those that don't,
> because there's some return on the latter
> while the others are just a waste of time.
> Terence, *Phormio* 331–32

The ancients trapped and ate all manner of birds, so why did they draw the line
at birds of prey? And why for that matter do we? Is it on grounds of taste or
because they are judged unhealthy and taboo as carrion eaters? How might
birds of prey 'do us harm' ('male faciunt')? One suddenly realizes how little we
know about what's going on here. Anthropologists can help to some extent. In
her classic monograph *Purity and Danger*, Mary Douglas examines the case of
the biblical 'abominations' in Leviticus and Deuteronomy. It is striking that
birds of prey and other eaters of meat, fish, and carrion like the raven, owl, stork,
heron, cormorant, and pelican figure prominently in the lists of dietary prohibitions
there, though the position is confused by the uncertainty of several of the
standard biblical translations of the species involved, as well as by the presence in the list of a few other outriders (hoopoe, nightjar, and cuckoo).
Douglas argues that such species may have been regarded as 'anomalous' and
therefore to be avoided:

> But in general the underlying principle of cleanness in animals is that they shall
> confirm fully to their class. Those species are unclean which are imperfect mem-
> bers of their class, or whose class confounds the general scheme of things.*

As we shall see in later chapters, several of these species were also regarded as in
some sense sacred, symbolic, or (literally) ominous, and that may also be relevant to their exclusion from the attentions of the hunters. As far as the majority
of other species is concerned, the hunting tradition has persisted strongly to this
day in the Mediterranean countries and the old technology is still very much in
use alongside the new. What has changed is the range and number of birds
killed and the effects on the populations of species already threatened by habitat
loss and changing agricultural practices. In the ancient world the hunting was in
most cases 'sustainable' because it was relatively inefficient and was more directly
determined by the needs of the table. What was actually *on* the table is the sub-

ject of the next chapter, but we end this one with two extracts exploiting the metaphorical connection between the hunting of birds and the pursuit of a loved one.

The first is an epigram attributed to the Hellenistic poet Rhianus, in which the poet envies the bird captured and held by the hunter:

> Dexionicus with mistletoe-lime from the green plane tree
> went hunting and trapped a blackbird by the wings,
> and the holy bird cried out in grief and despair.
> And I declare to you, Gods and Graces of blooming love,
> were I a thrush or blackbird in the hands of that man,
> I too would cry out and shed a tear, but a sweet one.
>
> Rhianus, *Greek Anthology* XII 142

The second comes from the romantic novel by Longus, *Daphnis and Chloe*. Under the excuse of doing some winter birding, Daphnis sneaks into the garden of the cottage where Chloe is cloistered with her parents, hoping to get at least a glimpse of her:

> Huge numbers of birds used to gather round this shrubbery in winter, through the lack of food elsewhere—lots of blackbirds, thrushes, pigeons, and starlings along with all the other birds that feed on ivy berries. So Daphnis set off there one day under the pretence of birding. He had filled his bag with honey-cakes, but to keep up the pretence had with him also his bird-lime and nets. The place was not more than a mile or so away, but the fresh snow presented him with quite a challenge. However, love will always find a way, even through fire, water, and Scythian snows. He therefore toiled on to the cottage, and after shaking the snow from his thighs he set his traps and smeared lime on his sticks. Then he sat down to await the birds … and Chloe.
>
> The birds came in their crowds, quite enough to keep him fully occupied gathering them in, killing them, and plucking them. But no one stirred from the cottage, not a man, woman, or domestic chicken; they all stayed inside in the warm. So Daphnis was at a complete loss what to do, since his luck with the birds was less than auspicious.
>
> Longus, *Daphnis and Chloe* III 5–6

And here we have not only two kinds of pursuit, but two kinds of birds as well. There is a verbal play on the two senses of the Greek word *ornis* in the final line—a bird and an omen—and this double sense is a theme running through the present book, which helps to explain why birds mattered so much in ancient culture and how they were, literally 'significant'.

6

Cooking and Eating

The historian H. D. Kitto memorably remarked that the average Greek diet consisted of two courses, the first a kind of porridge and the second a kind of porridge. What is true about this dubious statement is that most ancient diets were very different from modern ones and far less varied. The 'Mediterranean diet' then would have been based around the classic triad of wheat, olive oil, and wine. The staple food would have been largely vegetarian: cereals like wheat and barley for bread (and indeed porridge) to provide the calorie intake, supplemented with vegetables, fruit, cheese, olive oil, and various spices. Fish would have been eaten when available, but meat was more of a luxury, at least for the ordinary citizen. The best animal meat was reserved for sacrifices to the gods and for special feasts and festivals, though the family pot might be improved with more regular additions of cooked meats from hunted and farmed animals, including birds. Things were different for the upper classes, especially in Roman times when the expansion of trade, empire, and foreign contacts brought new foods, cooks, and menus to aristocratic tables and led to predictable excesses and bizarre recipes.*

In this chapter, like the last, we must remember that practices will have varied considerably across times and places, and not only according to social class. Sparta again represents an extreme example, where a 'Spartan diet' was both spare and challenging. It typically included the notorious black broth, reputedly made from boiled pork seasoned with salt, vinegar, and blood, which was designed to give Sparta's fighting men their strength and endurance and give them an advantage over their more self-indulgent enemies. Indeed, one sybaritic visitor was reputed to have exclaimed after being entertained at the soldiers' mess, 'Now I understand why Spartans do not fear death.'* There were also sects like the Orphics and Pythagoreans who practised a form of vegetarianism based on religious beliefs about the transmigration of souls between animals and humans. So, large cultural generalizations are likely to be unreliable and the extracts that follow must be read more as a selection of examples than demonstrations of any single overarching thesis.

The sources are limited and unbalanced in another way, too. Most of the references in literature to birds as food items are incidental and unsystematic. They tend to crop up as contextual detail in the plays of comic dramatists like Aristophanes in the Greek world and Plautus and Terence in the Roman, from which one can infer something about the usual diets of the ordinary people portrayed. The more explicit comments about menus occur in the writings of Roman satirists like Horace, Juvenal, and Martial, who are deliberately mocking the fancy gourmet meals and excesses that were a part of early imperial society in Rome. The late Greek writer Athenaeus is another good source, but he is reporting an imagined high-table conversation between a group of intellectuals, who are demonstrating their erudition by quoting other authorities on various cultural curiosities. We therefore learn more from these authors about the exceptional and exotic than we do about the ordinary and familiar, and the selections that follow reflect that imbalance. There are also important medical writings dealing with questions of diet that discuss the properties of different species of birds, but I reserve these for chapter 12 on medicine.

Descriptions of local markets can sometimes give us a good idea of which birds were in fact available as food for the average household.* Aristophanes describes one such in what is the oldest surviving ancient comedy, the *Acharnians*, produced in 425 BC, a few years after the start of the great war between Athens and Sparta. The war was having a devastating effect on Athenian agriculture since the Spartans were invading Attica each spring to slash and burn all the crops, so Aristophanes has the hero of the play, the decent but despairing farmer Dikaiopolis, negotiate his own personal peace with Sparta and her allies and open a private market. A rustic Boeotian appears from central Greece to do some trading:

> BOEOTIAN Buy anything you like from what I've brought,
> any of these birds or beasts you fancy.
> DIKAIOPOLIS Hi there, Boeotian bap-eater. What have you got?
> BOEOTIAN Absolutely all the good things Boeotia offers:
> marjoram, pennyroyal, rush-matting, plantain for wicks;

and ducks, jackdaws, francolins,[1] coots, plovers, and grebes.
DIKAIOPOLIS That's a real fall of birds you've blown
into my market-place with this fowl weather from the north.
    Aristophanes, *Acharnians* 872–80

That is quite an interesting list, if it is to be taken literally rather than as a jibe at
the outlandish habits of the country bumpkins of Boeotia. The water birds
mentioned here would probably have come from Lake Copaïs in central
Boeotia, now drained but then a large freshwater lake with extensive marshes.
A few lines later the Boeotian trader mentions it as a source of otters and eels
too. Jackdaws may seem more surprising as a menu item, though of course 'rook
pie' has been a traditional and popular rustic dish in England for centuries, and
still appears on the table in some nostalgic feasts.*

In another play by Aristophanes, *Assembly Women*, we hear about the variety
of ingredients that might crop up in a more elaborate meal. The women of
Athens in this play have succeeded in seizing power (political and sexual) from
the men and are now celebrating with a public banquet. The dishes are all run
together here as one gigantic compound word,[2] conveying perhaps both breath-
less excitement and the medley of ingredients in the stew. There is also some
comic bathos in the final menu item:

Look lively, lanky legs,
and see what we're serving:
a dishy-fish-slicy-sharky-dogfishy-
bits-and-pieces-of-bass-fishy-in-strong-pickley-
silphium-seasoned-honey-soaked-
thrush-upon-blackbirdy-dovey-pigeony-
chickeny-roast-cooty-wagtaily-
rockdovey-hare-dipped-in-winey-
tastily-winged-thingummy.
So now you've heard that
get yourself a plate quickly,
and kick up the dust. But take
for your afters…some porridge.
    Aristophanes, *Assembly Women* 1167–78

---

[1] Black francolins (*Francolinus francolinus*) are related to the partridge and were once common in the
Mediterranean but were hunted out by the nineteenth century. The bird is still native to Cyprus and
parts of southern Turkey, and some reintroductions have been recently attempted in Italy.
[2] The longest recorded word in Greek literature (or perhaps any literature) at 170 letters and seventy-
nine syllables in the original, though the text is uncertain in places and some of the identifications of
ingredients are speculative.

But the species that probably crops up most in these descriptions of birds for the table is the thrush.[1] Elsewhere in the *Acharnians* Aristophanes talks about 'providing some thrushes for a feast for a drachma' (960–61), 'impaling thrushes on spits' (1007) and 'roasting them' (1011), and 'bringing thrushes for a feast' (1104, 1108), which are 'tastier than locusts' (1116); and there are a lot of other casual references to thrushes as delicacies elsewhere, especially in comedy.* Athenaeus is the source for a potpourri of further information about thrushes.* He quotes fragments from a host of otherwise largely unknown authors—that is, unknown now but not necessarily minor ones in their own day (the history of text survivals has not always been fair in this respect):

Roast thrushes with pastry cakes flew down your throats.
  Teleclides, *Amphictyon*

Roast thrushes ready for stewing,
flitted round their mouths, just asking to be swallowed.
  Pherecrates, *Miners*

A. What should I buy for the pot, then?
B. Nothing too pricey. Keep it simple. Just some hares,
if you come across any, and as many ducks as you like,
thrushes and blackbirds, and plenty of small birds.
A. Fine.
  Nicostratus (or Philetaerus), *Antylla*

At the feast of Amphidromia it's usual
to roast a slice of Chersonesian cheese,
and stew some cabbage shining with oil,
and bake the breasts of plump lambs,
and pluck pigeons and thrushes with some finches ...
  Ephippus, *Geryon*

And, finally, from Plato (the comic poet not the philosopher), an extract with a host of sexual innuendoes:

If you want to get to see Phaon
you'll have to make some advance payments.
First, a sacrifice to me as the Tender of Youths:

---

[1] More exactly, the thrush family: mistle thrushes and blackbirds would have been residents, but song thrushes, redwings, and fieldfares were common migrants and were both trapped (see p. 80) and even reared (see pp. 122–23) for the pot.

an uncastrated cake, a pregnant scone of the finest meal,
sixteen perfect thrushes mingled with honey-sauce,
and twelve hare cutlets shaped like crescents.
    Plato, *Phaon*

Athenaeus also refers to a short epic poem attributed to Homer, entitled 'For
Thrushes', so called 'because when Homer sang it to the children they would
give him thrushes as a gift'. Thrushes remained a popular dish throughout the
whole classical period. We even find them listed as a relative luxury in Diocletian's
Edict of AD 301, in which he tried to control the galloping inflation of the day by
announcing rigid price controls on a 'basket' of over 1,000 common items of
purchase, including various foodstuffs. The maximum price for thrushes was

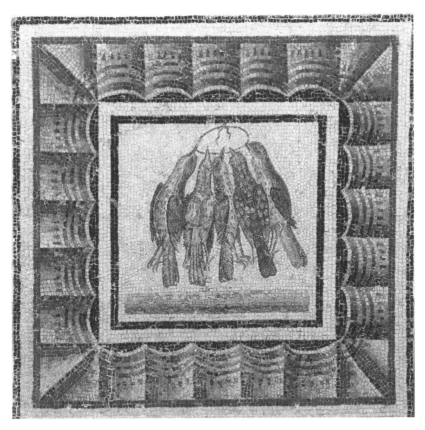

2.8 A hoop of thrushes for the table. Mosaic from the Roman settlement at Thysdrus
(a Roman/Berber town near present-day El Djem, Tunisia). See also **2.5**.

fixed at 60d. (denarii) for ten, compared with 20d. for ten starlings and 16d. for ten sparrows.[1]

Thrushes were clearly regarded as choice and readily available fare, both for ordinary people and the gourmet, though the latter might find the more ingenious ways of incorporating them into menus. In Petronius' *Satyricon* we have a vivid picture of the 'Feast of Trimalchio', a particularly gluttonous occasion, in the course of which a huge roasted boar is presented for the table:

> Carpus the Carver, who had cut up the fowls, did not come forward to divide the boar. Instead, some bearded giant with bands wrapped round his legs and sporting a brocaded hunting jacket, drew out his hunting-knife and plunged it violently into the boar's flanks. Upon the incision thrushes flew out from inside the boar. Bird-catchers were on hand with their limed twigs and as the birds fluttered round the dining room they caught them in no time at all. Trimalchio then ordered each guest to be given his own share of the meal.
>
> Petronius, *Satyricon* 40

In a later passage in the same work we hear of more excesses, literary as well as culinary. Trimalchio is here reportedly quoting the poet Publilius Syrus:

> The ramparts of Rome collapse in the gaping jaws of greed.
> For your palate the caged peacock is reared,
> clothed in his plumage of Babylonian gold;
> for you, the guinea fowl and the capon too.
> Even the stork, our beloved guest from afar,
> a model of piety, with its slender legs and noisy rattle,
> a bird exiled by winter but harbinger of warmer days,
> now nests in your saucepot of decadence.
>
> Petronius, *Satyricon* 55

Elsewhere we learn of other legendary Roman extravagances, notably the 'Lucullan feasts' of the Roman general of that name (see pp. 122–23), and more especially those of the outrageous Heliogabalus, who was emperor from AD 218 to 222. Edward Gibbon said of him, 'To confound the order of the season and climate, to sport with the passions and prejudices of his subjects, and to subvert every law of nature and decency, were in the number of his most delicious amusements.'* These 'amusements', as recorded in the *Historia Augusta*, included a dish of nightingales' tongues and a party trick of suffocating his guests with flower petals:

[1] The denarius was a small silver coin and the commonest unit of Roman currency. It was remembered in the UK up to 1971, along with two larger Roman denominations, as the *d.* in Ls.d. (*Librum, solidus, denarius*).

He had couches made of solid silver for use in his dining-rooms and bedchambers. In imitation of Apicius he often used to dine on camel-heels and the cocks-combs cut from living birds, and the tongues of peacocks and nightingales, because he was told that anyone who ate them was safe from the plague. Moreover, he served his palace officials with huge platters filled with the entrails of mullet, flamingo brains, partridge eggs, thrush brains, and the heads of parrots, pheasants, and peacocks ...

He fed his dogs on goose livers...He sent grapes from Apamea to the stables for his horses, and he fed his lions and other wild animals on parrots and pheasants. And for ten days running, with thirty portions a day, he served sows' udders with their wombs, and also peas with gold, lentils with onyx, beans with amber, and rice with pearls; he also sprinkled pearls in place of pepper on fish and truffles. In a dining-room with a reversible ceiling he once engulfed his guests with a cascade of violets and other flowers, so that some of them died, unable to breathe or to crawl up to the surface.

Historia Augusta, 'Elagabalus' xx 4–xxi 5

But the species we hear about as more regular dinner fare include pigeons, turtle doves, game birds (especially quail and partridge), larks, finches, sparrows, wild duck, warblers, perhaps more surprisingly coot, and even jays, though the last was evidently not to everyone's taste:

The so-called *chennia* (which is a small quail) are referred to by Cleomenes in his 'Letter to Alexander', who talks about 'ten thousand smoked coots, five thousand thrushes,[1] and ten thousand quail'. And Hipparchus in the 'Egyptian Iliad' remarks:

The life the Egyptians lead does not appeal,
for ever plucking quail and slimy little jays.

Athenaeus, *The Intellectuals' Dinner Party* 393c

This mention of jays illustrates some of the problems of translating ancient bird names. 'Jay' translates the Greek word *kitta* here (elsewhere *kissa*), and it is clear from descriptions of the *kitta* in Aristotle and other sources that this was undoubtedly a jay (indeed *kissa* is still the modern Greek word for that bird). Athenaeus was writing his account of this dinner-party conversation in Greek in about AD 200, while the Hipparchus quoted here was probably a Hellenistic poet of a few centuries earlier. There were certainly jays in Greece in this period, but there are most unlikely to have been any in Egypt, the setting for Hipparchus' poem (and where Athenaeus himself came from). There are none there now, at

---

[1] I translate *tulas* as the generic 'thrush' here, though that is usually *kichle* and the more specific redwing *Turdus iliacus* is a possibility.

any rate. Could Hipparchus have had some other species in mind—for example, a bulbul (common in north Africa), or was this just an ignorant mistake? Some translators, however, take a quite different tack and choose to translate *kitta* as 'magpie', presumably on the grounds that its Latin equivalent, *pica*, later came to denote 'magpie' as well as 'jay' when magpies expanded their range into the Mediterranean. Pliny, writing in the first century AD, has a helpful note on this, in the course of discussing how local some distributions of birds are:

> The kinds of *pica* that are distinguished by their long tails and are called the 'chequered pie' were previously rare, but have now begun to be seen between the Appenines and Rome.
>
> Pliny, *Natural History* x 78

There seems to have been no ancient Greek word for 'magpie', and the assumption must be that the species was rare or absent in the region earlier, since one would otherwise have expected such a conspicuous bird to have been separately named.

This little digression illustrates a triple problem translators face: firstly, the ancients did not always make the same taxonomic distinctions that we do; secondly, the distinctions they did make, like ours, may change over time; and thirdly, the distribution of species changes over time too and in ways we cannot always now reconstruct.[1] The modern Greek word for 'magpie', by the way, is the recognizably onomatopoeic *karakaxa* and its scientific name is now firmly *Pica pica*.

Whichever of these species was intended in this epigram from the Latin satirist Martial, writing in the first century AD, it is clear that *pica* was not the epicure's choice:

> Since I've lost my meal ticket[2] as a paid client,
> why don't you and I get the same menus?
> You have oysters fattened in the Lucrine lake,
> while I have to cut my lips sucking a mussel.
> You get the fancy mushrooms, I have fungi fit for pigs.
> You are served turbot, I get the little bream.
> You gorge on fine fat-arsed turtle dove,
> I'm given a *pica* that died in its cage. Why, Ponticus,
> do we dine separately when we are dining together?
> The dole's over. So be it. Let's eat the same meal.
>
> Martial, *Epigrams* III 60

---

[1] See also the discussion of translation issues in the appendix, pp. 363–67.

[2] The *sportula* was a sort of food dole given by rich patrons, either in the form of a cash subsidy or, as here, a meal, which might be an inferior one.

2.9 Jay. Detail from the garden fresco in the House of the Gold Bracelet at Pompeii, AD 30–50, depicting a jay (*Garrulus glandarius*) among oleanders and strawberry trees. The plumage details suggest that the fresco painter cared about representational accuracy and was not just creating fanciful ornamental images.

Martial's satires on Roman mores are a wonderful source for the tastes of both low and high society. We hear about 'a pigeon dripping in its gravy' (II 37), 'a hoop heavy with fat thrushes' (III 47), 'lapdogs chewing goose livers' and 'turtle-dove rumps presented to boy-lovers' (III 82). Then in Book XIII he reels off a whole series of short riddles and scurrilous jibes about menu items involving birds:

> *A bunch of thrushes*
> You may prefer garlands woven with roses or rich nard,[1]
> but I like one made of thrushes.
>   Martial, *Epigrams* XIII 51

---

[1] The spikenard, an Eastern plant with an aromatic oil and root.

Ducks
Serve the duck whole by all means,
but only the breast and neck are tasty;
send the rest back to the cook.

    XIII 52

Turtle doves
When I get a fat turtle dove,
it's goodbye lettuce;
and you can keep your snails.
I won't waste my appetite.

    XIII 53

Goose liver
See how the liver grows even larger than the large goose.
You'll say in amazement, 'Where on earth did that grow?'

    XIII 58

Fatted hens
The compliant hen is fed on sweet meal
and in darkness. How ingenious the palate is.

    XIII 62

Capons
Lest the cockerel loses weight from too much sex,
he has lost his testicles. Now he's a real *gallus*.[1]

    XIII 63

Partridges
This bird is very rarely served at Ausonian tables:
it's a game you often like to play in the pool.[2]

    XIII 65

Ringdoves
Ringdoves obstruct and dull your loins:
so, if you're thinking of sex,
don't eat this bird.

    XIII 67

---

[1] Untranslatable pun on *gallus*, which is both a cockerel and a Galatian priest of Cybele (hence a eunuch).
[2] Another pun: *perdix* in Greek is a partridge and the verb *perdomai* means farting (see **1.15** p. 61).

Peacocks
If you admire him when he spreads his jewelled wings,
how can you hand him over to the cruel cook, you brute?
    XIII 70

Flamingoes
My name comes from my scarlet wings,[1]
but my tongue is a treat for gourmets.
What if my tongue could tell tales?
    XIII 71

Woodcock
Am I woodcock or partridge?
Who cares, if the taste's the same?
Partridge is dearer, that's why it tastes better.
    XIII 76

Pliny lists a number of rare birds that he says are now imported for the Roman table and gives some incidental (but sometimes doubtful) information about the changing distributions of some of the species he identifies:

Apicius, that most insatiable gorger of all gluttons, took the view that the tongue of the flamingo was the most exquisite taste of all. The francolin is a very famous Ionian bird. It is normally very vocal but when captured it falls silent. It used to be counted as one of our rare birds, but it is now found also in Gaul and Spain. It has even been caught in the region of the Alps, where there are also cormorants, birds that are a speciality of the Balearic Isles, just as the alpine chough (which is black with a yellow beak) and the very tasty grouse are of the Alps. This grouse gets its name from its tufted 'hare's foot', though the rest of it is all white, and it is the size of a pigeon.[2] Outside that terrain it is difficult to keep it fed, as it doesn't become domesticated and quickly loses its flesh. There is also another kind of grouse that differs from quail only in size; it is yellow in colour and very acceptable for the table. Egnatius Calvinus, governor of the Alpine Region, has reported that the ibis, which is an Egyptian speciality, has been seen by him there as well.

---

[1] *Phoenicopterus* is literally 'scarlet-wing', and the current scientific name of the greater flamingo is *Phoenicopterus roseus*.

[2] Evidently a ptarmigan (*Lagopus lagopus*). The generic name for 'grouse' is *lagopus*, literally 'hare's foot'. The 'yellow' grouse that follows might possibly be a sandgrouse (*Pterocles sp.*), as might the 'new birds' mentioned next, since the sandgrouse is a characteristically 'irruptive' species, with sudden population changes and movements.

There also arrived in Italy at the time of the Civil War battles around Bedriacum
north of the Po the 'new birds', as they are still called, which look like thrushes and
are a little smaller than pigeons in size, and these have a very agreeable taste. The
Balearic Isles provide us with the even more splendid gallinule. From there too
the raptor called the buzzard is very well regarded for the table, as is the demoiselle
crane (*vipio*), which is their name for the smaller crane.

Pliny, *Natural History* x 133–35

2.10 Trussed flamingo. Detail from a Roman mosaic of the late second century AD at
Thysdrus (a Roman/Berber town near present-day El-Djem, Tunisia). Flamingoes
(*Phoenicopterus roseus*) were familiar (and unmistakable) birds of wetlands in the
Mediterranean and the Nile Delta and became a luxury item for the table (see p. 107
for a menu).

Other exotic birds for the table, mentioned by Athenaeus (65e), include parakeets and small falcons (perhaps lesser kestrels). But one can never be sure in

such cases what is being said purely for dramatic effect and what is to be taken literally. The peacock, flamingo, stork, and crane, however, certainly did feature regularly on upper-class menus, and these extravagances also produced a predictable reaction from contemporary satirists:

> You should whet your appetite with exercise.
> The man who is fat and pale from over-indulgence
> will find no remedy in oysters or trout or foreign grouse.
> But if a peacock is set before you, I know I can't stop your
> urge to tickle your palate with that rather than a pullet.
> You're seduced by vanities—a rare bird that costs gold
> and makes such a show with its outspread tail.
> As if that mattered! Do you feed on the feathers
> you so admire? Is it such a fine fowl when cooked?
> Come on! Although the meat's no better, you prefer
> one to the other, duped by its better appearance!
>
> Horace, *Satires* II 2.23–30

Horace goes on to give other examples of the passing fashions in taste, and concludes that people are, literally, gullible:

> So, should someone now proclaim roasted gulls to be delicacies,
> the youth of Rome would be quick to embrace this new depravity.
>
> Horace, *Satires* II 2.51–52

In a later satire he describes a particularly ostentatious dinner party where the guests eventually vote with their stomachs and their feet:

> Then the servants follow in, bearing on a huge platter
> a crane's dismembered limbs , showered with salt and meal,
> and the liver of a white goose, fattened with rich figs,
> and the severed limbs of hares—so much tastier, they said,
> than if eaten with their loins. Then we saw blackbirds served
> with their breasts burned off and pigeons without rumps—
> real dainties, if our host hadn't insisted on lecturing us about
> all their facts and features. So we took our revenge on him,
> running off without tasting a thing, as if Canidia[1] had poisoned it
> with a blast of her breath, deadlier than African serpents.
>
> Horace, *Satires* II 8.85–95

---

[1] A famous witch, see Horace, *Satires* I 8.24.

Horace tends to be ironic; but Juvenal is more often angry, in this case at the selfish greed of a rich patron:

> But who can bear such stingy extravagance?
> What a monstrous gullet that serves up for itself
> whole boars, an animal created to be shared at parties!
> The punishment is instant, however, when you disrobe,
> bloated, and carry an undigested peacock to the baths.
> Result: sudden death before you've even made a will;
> the un-sad news goes quickly round the dinner circuit,
> and the funeral is applauded by your furious friends.
>
> Juvenal, *Satires* 1 139–45

The snobbery in such cases can be as bad for you as the food. Horace imagines the pleasures of a more self-sufficient country life, where a modest wife makes house and home ready for her husband, who has been working the land:

> She piles the sacred hearth with seasoned wood
> to greet her weary husband on his return;
> gathering the flock in the wicker pen,
> she drains their swollen udders;
> and drawing the year's sweet wine from the jar,
> she prepares a meal unbought.
> No Lucrine shellfish could delight me more,
> nor any turbot nor exotic wrasse,
> should the thunderous eastern waves
> of winter drive them to our shores.
> No fowl of Africa[1] nor any Ionian francolin[2]
> would descend to my belly more pleasantly
> than olives picked from the laden branches
> of our own trees, or the leaves of the meadow sorrel,
> or mallows, so healthy for bodily ailments,
> or a lamb sacrificed at the feast of Terminus,
> or a kid rescued from the wolf.
>
> Horace, *Epodes* 11 43–60

For his part, the poet, Statius, is just grateful for a simple meal and good conversation:

---

[1] A helmeted guinea-fowl (*Numida meleagris*).

[2] This could be any game bird, but the epithet 'Ionian' (from Asia Minor) suggests a black francolin (*Francolinus francolinus*).

That dinner slipped deep into my soul,
and stayed unconsumed. For it was no mockery of the belly
we devoured, fine dishes sought from distant climes;
no wines to match in age our traditional Annals.[1]
Unhappy people, who need to distinguish
the bird of Phasis from the crane wintering in Rhodope,[2]
or who must know which goose yields the better innards,
and why a Tuscan boar is nobler than an Umbrian one,
and on what seaweed slippery shellfish rest most easily!
For us, true love and talk sought from the heart of Helicon[3]
and pleasant banter consume a winter's night
and banish gentle sleep from our eyes.

Statius, *Silvae* IV 6.4–14

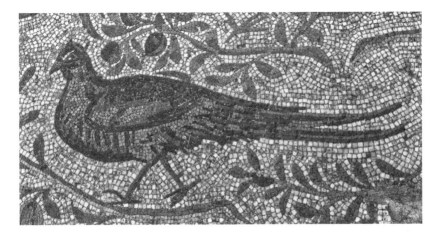

2.II Pheasant. Detail from a mosaic in the Villa of the Aviary at Carthage, early third century AD. The pheasant was introduced into Athens in the 420s BC, and spread from there throughout Greece and Rome. It was sometimes known as 'the bird of Phasis' (as in Statius' poem quoted here). Phasis was a river at Colchis on the Black Sea (now part of Georgia) where pheasants were abundant in the wild, and the bird's scientific name is now *Phasianus colchicus*.

The demand for ever more elaborate feasts required some experts in the kitchen, of course. Domestic slaves did most of the cooking in ancient Rome in

---

[1] *Fasti*, the Roman almanac, setting out the days of the year, festivals, and official events.
[2] Rhodope was a mountainous region in north-east Greece. For Phasis, see **2.II**, caption.
[3] Helicon was the traditional home of the Muses, so this suggests a more elevated kind of conversation than the snobberies of small distinctions between luxury dishes.

all but the very poorest families, and there would have been competition among employers for the best of these, who might thereby attain some special status in the household. But in the upper-class establishments that put on the sort of banquets that are being satirized above, there were serious connoisseurs and gourmets involved too, either as professional chefs for hire or as the hosts doing the hiring. One such was the notorious Roman glutton Apicius, already mentioned, who lived in the first century AD, a contemporary of the emperors Augustus and Tiberius, for whom he may have acted as culinary consultant.

We have already heard from Pliny of Apicius' predilection for flamingo tongues. Athenaeus tells the story that Apicius also spent much of his time gorging on seafood at his home town of Minturnae in Campania, which was famed for its large and succulent shrimps. Hearing of even larger ones reported from Libya, however, he at once set out on the long and arduous journey there over stormy seas; but as he approached the Libyan coast he sampled some shrimps the local fishermen had eagerly sailed out to offer him, and judging them no superior to those at home, he turned round without even landing and sailed back to Campania.

A recipe book in the name of Apicius (but probably not produced in this form until much later) illustrates the sophistication of the cuisine available during the Roman Empire and the extensive use of spices and sauces to titillate the palette. A whole section is devoted to the preparation of dishes involving birds, from which these are extracts involving the more exotic species:

Sauces for boiled ostrich
Ingredients: pepper, mint, roasted cumin, celery seed, dates or Jericho dates, honey, vinegar, cooking-wine, fish-sauce, and a little oil.[1] Put in a saucepan and bring to the boil. Thicken with cornflour, and then pour over the pieces of ostrich in the serving-dish. Sprinkle some pepper on top. Alternatively, if you want to cook the ostrich in the sauce, add spelt-grits.
     Apicius, *Recipes* VI 1.1

Sauce for crane, duck, or chicken
Ingredients: pepper, onion, lovage, cumin, celery seed, plums or damsons, must, vinegar, fish sauce, reduction of must, and oil. Cook all this. When you cook

---

[1] A number of the translations of the ingredients listed are somewhat speculative. 'Cooking-wine' translates *passum*; while *liquamen* is some kind of 'fish sauce' that seems to feature in every recipe.

crane, make sure the head does not touch the water but stands clear of it. When cooked, wrap the crane in a hot cloth and pull off its head together with its sinews, leaving the flesh and bones behind, since you cannot eat it with the sinews left in.

VI 2.2

Sauce for flamingo
Pluck, wash, and truss the flamingo and put it in a saucepan. Add water, salt, dill, and a little vinegar. Halfway through the cooking, add a bundle of leek and coriander and cook it with the bird. Just before it is fully cooked, put in reduction of must to give it colour. Put the following ingredients in a mortar: pepper, cumin, coriander, root of silphium, mint, and rue; and then pound them. Wet with vinegar, add some reduced sweet wine, and pour some of the sauce over it. Pour the rest of the sauce back into the same pan and thicken with cornflower. Then pour the sauce over the bird and serve.
The same recipe serves for parrot.

VI 2.21

Other inventive recipes are given for 'crane with turnip', 'boiled partridge, francolin, and turtle dove', and 'sauce for any well-hung bird'. There are finally recipes for fifteen different ways of preparing chicken, including such specialities as chicken à la Parthian, Numidian, Vardanian, and Frontonian, presumably named after regional varieties and famous chefs. Several of Apicius' instructions are quite elaborate, but distinctly short on quantities and timings, so probably come into the category of 'Don't try this at home.'

Farming

In a famous passage the Greek historian Thucydides reflects on a distortion in our perceptions of the great cities of the past. If we judge them just from their material remains, he says, we risk seriously misjudging their former importance. Consider the two great powers of his own day, Athens and Sparta:

> Just suppose the population of Sparta was wiped out and all that was left of the city were its shrines and the foundations of its buildings. I think that years later future generations would find it hard to believe that its power matched up to its reputation. Yet in fact the Spartans occupy two-fifths of the Peloponnese and are leaders of all its peoples as well as of many allies beyond. Nevertheless, because they are not united in one city and have no lavish shrines or public buildings but live instead in village settlements in the traditional Greek manner, they would be underestimated. On the other hand, if the Athenians were to suffer the same fate they would be thought twice as powerful as they actually are, just on the evidence of the remains you can see. One should therefore keep an open mind and not judge cities by their appearances rather than by their actual power …
>
> Thucydides, *The War of the Peloponnesians and the Athenians* I 10.2−3

But this passage also points to another distortion, and in some ways a more profound one—that is, in our perceptions of the importance of cities in general. For much of the classical period Greece and Italy were predominantly agrarian societies, and most people, whether they lived in towns or in the surrounding countryside, were peasants who made their livelihoods in agriculture. The cities were very small by modern standards[1] and were for a long time largely dependent on the produce of the fields. By the time of the later Roman Empire the patterns of employment had changed somewhat, but the products of domestic agriculture were still crucial for the maintenance of the huge empire overseas. Another social critic, Libanius, could still makes this observation as late as the fourth century AD:

> One might say that cities are founded upon the fields and that these are their firm footings. From the fields come their wheat, barley, grapes, wine, and oil—the sustenance for men and for other living creatures too. If there were no oxen, ploughs, seeds, plants, or herds of grazing cattle, then there would never have been any cities. And once cities were created their fortunes have been dependent on the countryside, and both their successes and failures arise from that source.
>
> Libanius, *Orations* 50 ('On the peasantry') 34

The relative invisibility of the countryside in the ancient world reflects the preoccupations of our sources, which focus overwhelmingly on the achievements and activities of the cities. A modern historian, Robin Osborne, calls this the 'paradox of the Greek city':

> In literature and art the countryside of the Greek city is never described and rarely discussed. In reality the whole population was intimately involved in the life and production of the countryside and the town never began to be independent of the countryside around it. The Greek city was not a town and its territory, as it has sometimes been described; it was a variously peopled landscape.*

Modern scholarship has largely reflected this bias, and has even exaggerated it since, as Thucydides predicted, subsequent generations have focused their attention on the magnificent cultural heritage of the ancient world—the architecture, art, and sculpture that we can still see and the extraordinary flowering of literature and philosophy that we can read. The voice of the countryside is rarely heard, and then only incidentally. We have to piece together a picture of this 'variously peopled landscape' from a range of archaeological remains and literary sources, each of which may illustrate just one facet of it.*

[1] The modern metropolitan population of Athens is about 3.7 million. Ancient figures are hard to reconstruct from official records, but Athens at the height of its power in 431 BC probably had a population of some 30,000 male citizens, so perhaps a total citizen body (excluding slaves) of about 120,000.

The farming of the landscape and the exploitation of its natural resources was, of course, one major influence on its changing profile and on the diversity of wildlife it supported at different times. We have seen this already from the work of writers like Hesiod, Aratus, and Theophrastus in the chapters on the seasons and the weather. In contrast to the present day, however, farming will actually have favoured biodiversity in some ways. Small-scale, low-intensity agriculture, which was all that the terrain and the technology permitted, will have increased the diversity of habitats and food sources for birds and thereby the diversity and abundance of the birds themselves.

On the whole, however, birds play little part in descriptions of farming the land, beyond references to them as portents of weather, markers of seasonal changes, and occasional pests on the crops.* The present chapter deals more especially with the topic of farming the birds themselves, in particular domesticated birds like geese, ducks, chickens, and pigeons, though more exotic species were also introduced into some farmyards and aviaries later.

*   *   *

For a good part of our period we have to rely on stray literary references to rearing fowl as part of managing smallholdings in a mixed domestic economy. Geese, for example, already feature in Homer's heroic age. Odysseus' wife, Penelope, has been faithfully awaiting his return for twenty years, while her importunate suitors are literally eating her out of house and home. However, a stranger has arrived (Odysseus, as yet unrecognized), and she tells him a dream she has had about her flock of geese:

> Twenty geese I have at my house. They come from the pond
> to eat the grain, and it warms my heart to watch them.
> But down from the mountain came this huge, hook-beaked eagle,
> who broke all their necks and killed them; and their bodies lay
> strewn around the halls, while he soared off into the bright sky.
> I wept and wailed, even though it was only a dream,
> and the fair-haired Achaean women gathered around me
> as I cried bitter tears because the eagle had killed my geese.
> Then back he came again, and sitting on a projecting beam
> the eagle checked my tears, speaking in a human voice:
> 'Take heart, daughter of far-famed Icarius,
> that was no dream, but a reality that will come to pass.
> The geese were your suitors and I, who before was the eagle,

have now come back again as your husband,
who will unleash a gruesome fate on them all.'
So he spoke and sweet sleep released me from my dream.
I then looked around and saw the geese still in the yard,
feeding just as before on the grain by the trough.

   Homer, *Odyssey* XIX 536–53

2.12 Woman with goose. A woman is shown playing ball while her pet goose watches her. There were often strong relationships between pets and their owners (see chapter 8). Red-figure amphora, 470–460 BC.

Later on, in the fifth century BC, authors like Sophocles and Plato also refer to domestic geese, and Plato even mentions the existence of 'goose-farms and crane farms' in Thessaly;* but there is little systematic discussion until agriculture itself became more organized in the Roman era with the growth of large estates and an industrial scale of production. We then get long practical handbooks from the three great writers on Roman agriculture—Cato, Varro, and Columella—supplemented in a more amateur way by the indefatigable encyclopedist Pliny.

The detailed descriptions in these technical treatises are sometimes given a richer human context in more literary works by Cicero, Horace, Martial, and in particular Virgil, whose *Georgics* are a celebration of the traditional rural virtues and of a life lived in conformity with nature. This chapter draws on all these authors and ends with some further reflections on the relationship between town and country to bring us full circle.

Varro and Columella commence their accounts with very useful bibliographies of previous writers on the subject, both Greek and Roman.* They list some fifty Greek predecessors, most of whose works are now lost, except for Hesiod's *Works and Days* and Xenophon's *Oeconomicus* (neither of which deals with farmyard birds). I therefore quote mainly from the three major Latin agricultural authors, who themselves represent a progression both in the professionalism and the detail of their accounts.

Columella says of Cato (234–149 BC) that 'he was the first to give Agriculture a Latin voice' (1 1.12). Cato's book is rather scrappy, in fact, and he has relatively little to say about poultry farming in general; but he does give some brisk advice about cramming birds for the table:

> To fatten hens or geese. Coop up young hens which are just starting to lay. Make balls of moistened flour or barley-meal, soak them in water and push them into their mouths. Increase the amount gradually day by day, judging what is sufficient from their appetite. Cram them twice a day and at midday give them something to drink, but then don't place any water before them for an hour. Feed a goose the same way, except that you let it drink first and then give it food and drink twice a day.

The regime for pigeons requires more intimate attention:

> To fatten young pigeons. When you have got hold of the bird, first feed it boiled and toasted beans, blowing them from your mouth into theirs, and do the same with water. Repeat this for seven days. Next clean some crushed beans and spelt. Let a third of the beans come to the boil and then add in the spelt, keeping it clean, and boil thoroughly. When you have emptied this from the pot, grease your hands with oil and knead it fully, a little in the first instance then more, oiling and kneading until you can make little balls of it. Then after soaking it, feed it to them in manageable quantities.
> Cato, *On Agriculture* 89–90

Varro and Columella give similar instructions for fattening fowl, with a few variations in the recipes and the timing of operations, but they reach this point by a rather different route. Varro starts with an impressive-sounding analysis. He first distinguishes three kinds of farming: agriculture, animal husbandry in the fields (sheep, goats and cattle), and husbandry around the farmstead (smaller domesticated creatures). He then subdivides the last class into fishponds (*piscinae*), hare-warrens (*leporaria*), and aviaries (*aviaria*); and aviaries in turn subdivide into those that need only land (for peafowl, turtle doves, and thrushes) and those that also need water (for geese and ducks). This process of subdivision continues remorselessly, but gets hopelessly over-complicated as other principles of analysis are superimposed, according to one of which chickens end up in an odd class together with dormice, snails, and bees, because each of these is introduced into the estate rather than being initially acquired by hunting. More importantly, however, Varro also recognizes an underlying historical and social dimension, marking the development from ancient habits of frugality to a later taste for luxury:

> For example, in the first stage our ancestors just had two aviaries, one an enclosed pen on the ground in which the hens fed—from which the returns were eggs and chicks—and the other above ground, either in lofts or on the roof of the villa where the pigeons lived. But now these aviaries have changed their name and have become 'bird-houses', constructed to gratify the sophisticated palates of their owners and containing more buildings in which to house thrushes and peahens than whole villas used to have in the old days.
>
>   Varro, *On Agriculture* III 3.6–7

When he has finally worked through these taxonomic obsessions, Varro turns out to be far more interested in the production of these table-birds for the gourmet than he is in the ordinary barnyard fowl that were a staple of the domestic rural economy. He devotes most of his attention to the construction of these luxury 'bird-houses' (*ornithones*), the rearing of the various market specialities in them, and the large profits an astute capitalist can make from this business.

Columella by contrast is far more practical in the organization of his material. He defers discussion of outlying enclosures like aviaries, apiaries, and *vivaria* (enclosures for wild animals), and begins instead with the primary activity of rearing domestic poultry:

> First, then, I deal with what can be reared within the precincts of the farm. As regards the other birds and animals, it may perhaps be questioned whether country people should keep them at all, but keeping hens is quite a standard part of

farming practice. Hens fall into three classes: farmyard, rustic, and African.[1] The farmyard fowl is the kind commonly seen on almost every farm…and of these three classes the female farmyard fowls are the ones properly called 'hens', the males being 'cocks' and the half-males 'capons', which are called this because they have been castrated to remove their sexual appetite.

Columella, *On Agriculture* VIII 2.1–3

2.13 Farmyard scene. A country residence at Tabarka, near Tunis, with a walled courtyard and massive corner towers. The livestock includes pheasants, geese, and ducks. Mosaic lunette of the late fourth century AD.

Columella then distinguishes the best breeds of the farmyard hen. He pays tribute to the science of rearing poultry developed in Greece (particularly in the island of Delos), though he warns against various Greek and Persian strains of chickens that were bred for their appearance and fighting spirit but were not such good layers:

We, however, much prefer our native breed. We do not share the Greek concern with preparing the fiercest birds they could find for competition and fighting. Our objective is to establish a source of revenue for a hard-working master of a

---

[1] The 'African' birds are guinea-fowl, while the 'rustic' ones may be either feral birds of some kind or genuinely wild species like partridges or hazel-hens.

household, not for a trainer of aggressive birds, whose whole income, wagered on
a gamble, is usually snatched from him by a victorious fighting-cock.

VIII 2.4–6

He then gets down to the detail, which occupies nine whole chapters. Two hundred birds is about the limit one poultry-keeper can manage, he says, assisted by
'an old woman or boy' to keep an eye on strays. Birds of red or dark plumage
with black wings are to be preferred to white ones, which tend to be delicate and
not very long-lived or prolific; moreover, 'being very conspicuous through their
striking whiteness they are more often predated by hawks and eagles'. Temperament
and character are important too:

> These male birds, although they are not being prepared for fighting or to win
> competitions, are nevertheless to be prized for their breeding if they are proud,
> lively, watchful, ready to crow frequently, and not easily frightened; for they need
> to fight back on occasion and kill a snake that rears up in threat or some other
> dangerous animal.
>
> VIII 2.11

And that leads to an interesting comment about cross-breeding, which was of
course identified by Darwin some 2,000 years later as an important clue to
understanding the processes of evolution.* The Rhodian and Median strains,
Columella says, are rather lazy about sitting on their eggs and hatching them, so
their eggs are best removed and given to the 'ordinary hens' to brood and bring
up the chicks. The Tanagran and Chalcidian, on the other hand, are a better
compromise between the size of the foreign strains and the disposition of the
native birds:

> But of all these kinds the best are the cross-bred chickens, which our native hens
> have produced after conceiving them by foreign males; for they exhibit the same
> physical appearance as their fathers, together with the sexual appetite and fertility
> of the native birds.
>
> VIII 2.13

He then moves on to exact instructions for the siting, dimensions, and internal
architecture of the hen-houses, right down to details like ensuring that the
perches are cut square and not rounded, in order to give the birds a securer grip
and avoid fouling themselves by slipping into the dung on the loft floor. In fact,

a great deal of attention is given to health and safety issues in the coop, with ingenious provisions for guarding against vermin and fleas and keeping the drinking-water clean, while at the same time ensuring a balanced diet and a supply of dust and ashes for the birds with which to clean their feathers. But this is, in the end, a form of intensive farming, as becomes clear when Columella gets to the question Cato introduced of fattening selected hens for market:

> The place required for this purpose should be very warm but have little light. The birds should be shut up separately in quite narrow, hanging cages or wicker baskets and confined in so small a space that they cannot turn round. They should, however, have openings on either side, one through which they can put their head and the other through which they can put their tail and rear-end, so that they can both take their food and expel it when digested, without becoming fouled with excrement.
>
> VIII 7.1–2

Varro has a similar description of this grim process and concludes with a striking phrase: 'they are shut up in a warm, cramped, and darkened place, because movement on their part and light release them from the slavery of fat' (III 9.19). This may, of course, still be relatively humane treatment compared to some of the conditions we hear of in modern factory farming.*

Both Varro and Columella deal more briefly with geese, partly, as they say, because they involve less work for the farmer. We have already seen that geese had been kept on small estates as early as Homeric times. Domestic stock of this kind would presumably have descended from wild greylags, which still breed in northern Greece but which would have been much more widespread then. For commercial farming, however, white birds were to be preferred to the wild or 'mottled' ones. Varro refers to large flocks belonging to Roman noblemen in the first century BC and he uses the Greek name for a goose farm, *chenoboscion*, which suggests that these were common in the Greek world before then, too.

Columella explains why geese were a favourite choice with farmers:

> I now come to the kind of birds the Greeks call 'amphibious' because they like fodder not only from the land but also from water, and their natural environment is as much standing water as earth. In this category the goose is particularly popular with farmers because it doesn't require much attention. It also keeps sharper watch than a dog, since by its honking calls it betrays the presence of anyone lurking around, just as the geese did, so tradition has it, when the Capitol was under

2.14 'The geese of Meidum'. A famous wall-painting from a tomb at Meidum in Lower Egypt, of the Fourth Dynasty (2575–2464 BC). It depicts, with considerable accuracy, three species of geese that would have visited the Nile wetlands in winter: bean geese (*Anser fabalis*) at either end, two white-fronted geese (*Anser albifrons*) facing left, and two red-breasted geese (*Branta ruficollis*) facing right. The first and third of these would have been much rarer than the second, but all three might have featured in ornamental collections.

siege and they were the ones to give a noisy warning of the approaching Gauls, while the dogs remained silent.... So, we are in favour of keeping geese, not because they yield great profits but because they take so little work.

Columella, *On Agriculture* VIII 13.1–3

He then sets out, again in detail, everything the farmer needs to know about the diet of geese and the construction of their goose-pens, the breeding and rearing of the goslings, and the protective measures required against predators like snakes, cats, and weasels.

Pliny tells various stories about cases of affection between geese and people, but then unsentimentally lists some more practical uses geese have too:

But our fellow countrymen are wise enough to know geese through the excellence of their livers. With a regime of stuffing, the liver can be made to grow very large, and once it has been removed it can be enlarged even further by soaking it in a mixture of milk sweetened with honey. It is an open question whether the consul Scipio Metellus or his contemporary Marcus Seius was the first to invent this great boon for humankind. But it is agreed that Messalinus Cotta, son of the orator Messala, was the man who invented the recipe for grilling and pickling the soles of their feet together with cockerels' combs.

Pliny, *Natural History* X 52

Goose feathers represent another product:

There is a second income to be had, from the feathers of white geese. In some places they are plucked twice a year and they grow a replacement coat of feathers. The feathers closest to the body are the softer ones, and those from Germany are held in particular regard. The geese there are white but smaller; they are called *gantae* and their feathers are priced at five pence per pound. As a result, the officers in charge of auxiliary troops are often charged with sending whole cohorts away from sentry duty at an outpost on a goose-hunt; and the demand for luxury has advanced to such a point that even the men insist on having goose-feather bedding under their necks.

Pliny, *Natural History* X 53–54

Pliny also tells an interesting story about driving geese large distances overland, which recalls the accounts in Daniel Defoe of geese being marched in droves of up to 2,000 from Norfolk to the London market.* The geese in Pliny's account, however, must have been travelling some 1,000 miles (from modern-day Normandy to Rome), and crossing the Alps too in the course of their forced march:

> A remarkable fact about this bird, however, is their journey on foot all the way from Morini in Gaul to Rome: when they get tired they are promoted to the front rank, and the rest of the flock then instinctively propel them forwards from the rear.
>
> Pliny, *Natural History* x 53

Julius Caesar makes the unlikely suggestion in his generally very factual war memoirs that in Britain geese were regarded more as pets than produce. He said that the Britons 'thought it wrong to partake of hare, cockerel, or geese, but they keep these instead for reasons of affection and pleasure' (*Gallic War* v 12).

Chicken and geese will reappear in later chapters, but we now survey the rest of the farmyard.

Ducks are another of the 'amphibious birds'. Varro describes how he made a special platform over a pond in his aviary so that, while they were dining *al fresco*, his guests could watch the ducks swimming around. He also gives a detailed account of the construction and operations of a more serious 'duck-farm' (*nessotrophion*, another Greek term), in which the birds could be reared commercially. Particular attention is paid to protecting them from predators:

> All the walls are smoothed with plaster, so that no polecat or other beast can get in to harm them; and the entire enclosure is covered with a wide-meshed net to stop eagles from flying in and the ducks from flying out.
>
> Varro, *On Agriculture* III 11

The kinds of ducks farmed seem to be mainly mallard (*anates*), but we also hear of *querquedulae* (which could be either teal or garganey) and some unidentifiable *boscides* (Columella VIII 15.1) and *phalarides*, which were said to have originated in Seleucia and Asia (Pliny x 67).

Pigeons and doves were commonly kept in dovecotes, which attracted feral and wild birds as well as the (mainly white) domesticated ones. Many of these were kept for pleasure, but the serious breeding and fattening of birds for the table was done in specially constructed pigeon-houses (*peristerotrophia*), which could hold up to 5,000 birds. These were looked after by a professional pigeon-keeper (*pastor columbarum*), one of whose main duties was to keep the place clean and clear out all the droppings, which could then be recycled as premium

2.15 Nilescape. Mosaic from the House of the Faun, Pompeii, second century BC, featuring waterfowl, a frog, and a kingfisher among lotus plants. The birds are poorly depicted but seem to include: two mallards (front), two Egyptian geese (back left), and possibly—judging from the bills—two purple gallinules (back right).

fertilizer (Varro III 7.5). And Varro now gives his account of the techniques for fattening up young birds, the 'squabs'. If Cato was brisk on this topic (see p. 113), Varro is more straightforwardly brutal:

> Those who professionally fatten up squabs to increase their market value enclose them in cages as soon as they are covered in down. Then they stuff them with masticated white bread, twice a day in winter and three times in summer (morning, noon, and evening in summer, while in winter they omit the middle feeding). When they start to grow feathers they leave them in the nest with their legs broken, and put them in with their mothers so that they can enjoy an even richer diet, since the mother birds feed themselves and their squabs all day long. Birds reared in this way become fatter, faster than others, and their parents become white.
>
> Varro, *On Agriculture* III 7.10

Turtle doves had to be treated differently:

> It is pointless to rear turtle doves, since this species neither lays eggs nor hatches its young in an aviary. A flight of doves is ready for cramming in the condition in which they are caught, and they can therefore be fattened with less trouble than other kinds of bird—though not in all seasons, since in winter, despite the work devoted to them, they grow only with difficulty; moreover, their price comes

down because of the abundance of thrushes on the market then. During the summer, by contrast, they grow fat of their own accord if they have easy access to food.

Columella, *On Agriculture* VIII 9

They were also housed differently, on simple mat platforms, on which they had
a constant supply of millet to fatten them, with nets spread around to prevent
them flying about and so losing precious bulk.

Thrushes, however, were the prime crop, which according to Varro 'made the
term "bird-house" synonymous with gain' (III 4.1). For example, his aunt's Sabine
farm, where the birds were 'common in the area,'[1] had some 5,000 thrushes in its
aviary, and these were sold for three denarii apiece. These were birds trapped
and then fattened in a specially constructed domed building (*testitudo*) or a
peristyle roofed with tiles or netting. Other species kept in this area might
include high-value birds like quail and ortolans (*miliaria*).[2] Thrushes were kept
for pleasure as well as for market, and the epicure Lucullus tried to construct an
aviary that combined these two purposes:

> Under one roof he had both a bird-house and a dining-room, where one could
> dine in great comfort and watch some of the birds lying cooked on the dish and
> others fluttering around the windows of their cage. But this was an unsatisfactory
> experiment. For the birds flying behind the windows did not afford as much
> pleasure to the eyes as the offence the nasty smell caused to the nostrils.
>
> Varro, *On Agriculture* III 4

Lucullus did, however, succeed in keeping a year-round supply of thrushes for
the table, as indicated by the following anecdote about the general Pompey, who
had a reputation for plain living:

> Once when Pompey was ill and was off his food, his doctor prescribed that he have
> a thrush to eat. But when his staff failed to find any on sale despite their searching—
> since it was out of season for them—someone suggested that they could get some
> at Lucullus' place where they were kept all the year round. 'What!' said Pompey,

---

[1] These thrushes (*turdi*) are usually translated as 'fieldfares', though wild ones could have been common only in winter, when there would have been a big influx of all the thrush species migrating south,
including redwings and blackbirds. Mistle and song thrushes were resident as well as migratory, but only
thinly distributed.

[2] *Miliaria* is usually translated 'ortolans' since that species of bunting did become a celebrated gourmet
dish. It may just have meant 'bunting', though; at any rate *miliaria* later become the generic scientific name
of the corn bunting *Miliaria calandra*.

'Must a Pompey have died, if a Lucullus wasn't living a life of such luxury?'
Whereupon he dismissed his doctor and took something easier to get hold of.

   Plutarch, *Life of Pompey* II 3

Last in this muster of farmed species is the peacock. This charismatic bird is
treated in several chapters of this book, since it was important to the ancients in
a number of different ways—as exotic curiosity, symbolic icon in art, ritual, and
myth, culinary luxury, and commercial property. Peacocks were known to have
originated in India, and probably reached ancient Greece via Persia, as did the
domestic cock, hence the nickname 'Persian bird' for both species. Peacocks
were certainly present in Athens by the fifth century BC, when they were on display in private collections, and they were being farmed in Italy from at least the
second century BC. Pliny tells us that they were first introduced into Rome for
the table by the orator Hortensius (114–49 BC), a friend and fellow gourmet of
Lucullus, and he describes the large profits being made by the middle of the first
century BC.* But from the start there was a certain ambivalence about whether
peacocks should be kept as a hobby or a business proposition:

> Keeping peacocks is more a matter for the city-dwelling householder than for the
> hard-nosed countryman. Yet, it isn't an irrelevant activity for the farmer who is
> out to acquire from any source he can some pleasures with which to beguile the
> loneliness of country life. Indeed, the charm of the birds delights visitors as much
> as it does their owners.
>
>   Columella, *On Agriculture* VIII 11.1

Columella recommends keeping them on small wooded islands, where they will
be safe from predators and can largely look after themselves; but if they are to
be farmed more intensively they will need a special peacock-house (*stabula pav-
onum*) and a resident keeper to supervise the laying and rearing and occasionally
to intervene in cases of male competition:

> The male birds are then each driven into their own enclosures with their hens to
> prevent them from quarrelling, and the food is distributed equally among the whole
> flock. For even in this species there are aggressive males who deny both food and sex
> to those males weaker than themselves, unless they are kept apart this way. It is gen-
> erally in sunny places that the desire for intercourse seizes hold of the male birds,
> when the wind begins to blow from the west, that is from mid-February until March.
> The sign of sexual excitement is when the male covers itself with its bejewelled tail-
> feathers, as if admiring itself, and 'makes a wheel', as the saying goes.
>
>   Columella, *On Agriculture* VIII 11. 7–8

Varro adds the commercial point:

> As for peacocks, it is within the memory of our own times that they began to be
> kept and sold for a high price. For example, Marcus Aufidius Lurco is said to
> make 60,000 sesterces from them a year. If you have an eye to the profit you need
> to have fewer males than females; but the reverse if you are more concerned with
> the pleasure, since the male is the more beautiful of the two.
>
> Varro, *On Agriculture* III 6.1

* * *

And this takes us back to the relationship, and sometimes the tensions,
between town and country life. Columella had made the point that keeping
peacocks might be more a hobby for the city-dweller, playing with the idea of
a country estate decorated with exotic species of birds, than a serious proposition for a real farmer who actually lived and worked in the countryside. The
pull of the countryside had already become something of a literary theme,
whose origins one can perhaps trace right back to such passages in Homer as
the idealized farm scenes worked into the decorated shield of Achilles (*Iliad*
541–72) and the sequestered orchards of Alcinous (*Odyssey* 112–32). Indeed
Thucydides, whose remarks on cities introduced this chapter, goes on to
describe later how hard the Athenian people found it to accept their forced
evacuations from the countryside to the city in wartime, because the countryside *was* their city (II 14, 16–17). Greek religion and its cults and festivals were
often rooted in the countryside rather than in the cities and these attachments
went very deep.*

So it is unsurprising that urban perceptions of the countryside, whether
driven by nostalgia, snobbery, or ignorance, should change as cities became
steadily larger and a higher proportion of the population lived in them.[1] There
will surely have been a difference in viewpoint too between small farmers serving a local area and the landowners of large *latifundia* serving a much larger and
more distant market. At any rate, the relationship between town and country
became a regular trope in Latin prose and poetry, particularly in the work of
Cicero, Horace, Virgil, and Martial.*

---

[1] The modest population figures for Athens in the fifth century BC are quoted on p. 110 n.1. The total
population of Rome by the first century AD was more like 1 million, and possibly a good deal more.

Martial here compares a friend's rough but productive 'organic' farm with a 'civilized' and rather sterile, villa:

> Bassus, the Baian villa of our friend Faustinus,
> does not keep whole acres of wasted space,
> laid out in useless myrtle plantings,
> barren planes, and clipped hedges of box.
> He delights in a true, unkempt countryside.
> Here, grain is tightly crammed into every corner
> and many a wine-jar is fragrant with autumns past.
> Here, with November gone and winter threatening,
> the uncouth pruner brings home the late grapes.
> Bulls in the deep valley bellow fiercely,
> and the young hornless steer itches for the fray.
> The mucky yard is thronged with roaming fowl—
> the honking goose and the spangled peacocks,
> the flamingo, named after its flaming plumes,
> the painted partridge, the speckled guinea-fowl,
> and the pheasant of the heathen Colchians;[1]
> proud cockerels tread their Rhodian wives
> and the dovecotes are loud with the clatter of wings—
> here croons the pigeon, there the waxy turtle dove.

The rest of the farmyard teems with activity too, and employees, friends, and neighbours all collaborate cheerfully:

> The day's work done, the neighbour gladly comes to dine
> and the ample fare is not hoarded for the morrow.
> All join in the feast, and the well-fed attendant
> has no cause to envy the tippling guest.
> By contrast, you in the suburbs starve in genteel fashion:
> from your belvedere you survey only laurels,
> secure since your Priapus[2] need fear no pilferer;
> you feed your vine-dresser on corn from the city
> and you lazily import for your painted villa
> cabbage, eggs, chickens, apples, cheese, and new wine.
> Should you call this a country farm or a second town house?

Martial, *Epigrams* III 58

---

[1] See p. 105 **2.11** for the Colchis connection. We hear less about pheasants in the literature than one might expect, relative to the other imported species like guinea-fowl, peacock, and cockerel, though there is archaeological evidence that they were reared and eaten in Roman Britain at least.*

[2] The god of procreation, and hence protector of gardens and vineyards.

Martial is jeering about urban pretensions, but Horace makes the more philo-sophical point that the good life can best be realized in the country:

> If our duty is 'to live in harmony with nature'
> and we must first choose a place to site our home,
> then where could be better than this countryside bliss?
> Are winters milder elsewhere, or breezes more welcome,
> tempering the fury of the Dog Star or the onset of the Lion,
> when maddened by the piercing shafts of the sun?[1]
> Where does envious care less disturb our slumbers?
> Does grass look or smell worse than your Libyan mosaics?
> Is the water bursting its lead pipes in city streets any purer
> than that which bustles and chatters downhill in the brook?
> Come on! Amid your coloured columns you are nursing trees,
> and you're glad your mansion has that distant view of fields.
> You can drive nature out with a pitchfork but she'll soon be back,
> and will slyly break through your fond follies in triumph.
>
> Horace, *Epistles* 1 10.12–25

This recognition that nature and culture are inextricably connected leads us nicely to the next part, in which we shall be looking at birds in everyday life, not so much as a resource to be exploited but as creatures sharing human domestic spaces as commensals and familiars.

---

[1] The Dog Star is Sirius (from Greek, 'the scorcher'), which rises on 20 July, heralding the 'dog days' of intense heat. The sun enters the constellation of Leo on 23 July.

PART 3

Living with Birds

Then there are the wild beast fights, two a day for five days. A magnificent spectacle, of course—who could deny it. But what possible pleasure is there for a man of sensibility, when either a puny human being is being savaged by a more powerful beast or some splendid animal is run through with a hunting-spear? And even if this is quite a sight, it's one you've often seen before, and as a spectator I saw nothing new in it. The last day involved the elephants and on that occasion the mob of people was greatly impressed but showed no pleasure in it. Indeed, the subsequent emotions were a kind of compassion and a feeling that the huge creatures shared some sort of fellowship with the human race.

Cicero, *Letters to Friends* VII 1.3

Having proved mens and brutes bodies on one type: almost superfluous to consider minds.

Charles Darwin, *Notebooks on Transmutation of Species* (1838–39) IV 47

3.1 House of Livia. A house built near Rome in the period 30–20 BC by the Emperor Augustus for his wife, Livia. There are sumptuous frescoes in the *triclinium* (dining-room), portraying a wide range of colourful birds, flowers, fruits, and bushes in a restful garden setting. The site was known as the Villa ad Gallinas Albas ('House of the White Chickens') because at her betrothal Livia was supposed to have been visited by a white hen holding a laurel branch. This was taken to be a good omen, presaging good fortune and evergreen life, and symbolizing the peace and prosperity of the Augustan reign.

Introduction

Part 2 explored some of the more destructive forms of avian exploitation in the ancient world, in which birds were hunted and farmed for human consumption with little thought—and certainly no sentimentality—about what other value they might have for people. 'Value' is a capacious notion, of course, which can include ideas both of intrinsic worth and of utility. Those who today emphasize the importance of the natural world tend to employ one of two different kinds of argument: either they urge that nature matters to us 'for its own sake' or they point to the quantifiable benefits or 'services' it provides us with.* That general distinction recurs, of course, in analogous political disputes about the value of education, culture, or science, though in all these cases too the underlying assumptions are often murky and inexplicit. We shall consider later whether the ancients can be said to have valued the natural world, and by implication birds, for their own sake, and if so in what sense. This is by no means straightforward, since the issues presented themselves in very different ways in these early cultures. The evidence has to be teased out from a range of literary sources, of which only a few philosophical and zoological writings seem to bear directly on such questions, usually in the course of considering what biological and cognitive capacities humans and animals might share and what the implications of these similarities might be.

First, though, we shall look rather at the other practical and social benefits birds were thought to confer, beyond that of being just a source of food. This is the more collaborative end of the scale of utility, where birds are valued for their specific uses and roles but are not necessarily harmed in the process. And some of these examples will in turn be seen to bear on, and perhaps to some degree undermine, the idea of a sharp dichotomy between the intrinsic and the utilitarian arguments for the value of the natural world.

Biologists distinguish between various forms of relationship different organisms can have with each other. *Symbiosis*, which comes from the Greek words for 'living together', means just that: an intimate relationship where two species share the same living spaces, like the cattle egret and the livestock it accompanies. Here the relationship is mutually beneficial since the egrets feed not only on insects the cattle have disturbed but also on the ticks they may be hosting on their bodies. *Commensalism*, from Latin for 'sharing the same table', is usually defined as a narrower notion where only one partner benefits directly from the relationship, though without harming the other, like the swallow nesting under the eaves of your house. In *parasitism*, by contrast (from Greek meaning 'feeding beside', thus 'eating from someone *else's* table'), one partner benefits but the other is actually harmed, as in the case of the cuckoo, whose young displace those of its unfortunate host. The overall balance of advantages can get quite complicated, however, where the parasite harms its host species but may benefit other species, like the ticks that plague the cattle but are food for the egrets, or the mistletoe that weighs down a tree but may provide good nesting sites and nutritious food for birds.

The connections between birds and people in the ancient world exhibit examples of all these complicated interrelationships and others besides. More informally, there is a spectrum that leads from crude exploitation at one end of the scale through to more benign forms of use, cooperation, partnership, or even affection at the other. In chapter 8 we shall see birds sharing domestic spaces as commensals and being treated as exhibits, pets, mimics, or familiars with whom one can forge relationships of a kind. Chapter 9 then deals with the part birds played in sport and public entertainments, while chapter 10 goes on to consider other public arenas, in which birds performed such socially useful roles as scavengers, sentinels, and messengers.

8

Captivity and Domestication

Sometimes an incidental reference in ancient literature reveals something quite unexpected. We have this fragment of a speech by the fifth-century orator Antiphon, which seems to be referring to a private peacock zoo in Athens:

> On the first of the month anyone who wished to see the peacocks was admitted, but anyone who came to see them on any other day was disappointed. And this has been the practice not just for the last day or so but has been going on for over thirty years.
>
> Antiphon fr. B12 (Athenaeus 397c–d)

A zoo? When were they invented? And why peacocks?

The idea of a zoo, where the public can see wild creatures at close quarters, is in fact a very ancient one. Archaeologists have excavated the remains of what may be the world's earliest zoo, dated to about 3500 BC, at Hierakonpolis ('City of hawks') in ancient Egypt, where they found the bones of elephant, hippo, baboons, and wildcat, whose locations and stomach contents suggested that they had been fed by human 'keepers'.* Later pharaohs like Akhenaten (1379–1361 BC) certainly maintained zoos, as did various Assyrian rulers like Ashur-bel-kala (1074–1056 BC), and the biblical figures of Solomon of Israel (tenth century BC) and Nebuchadnezzar of Babylon (sixth century BC).

3.2 Garden of a private estate. An enclosed ornamental pool, with fish, lotus, and wild-fowl (including Egyptian geese, *Alopochen aegyptiaca*), surrounded by date-palms and fruit trees. Detail from a wall-painting from the Tomb of Nebamun, Thebes, Egypt, *c.*1350 BC.

Other Eastern potentates continued this tradition with their hunting parks and 'paradise gardens,'[1] but the most famous royal collection we hear about in the Graeco-Roman period is that of Ptolemy II ('Philadelphus') at Alexandria in Egypt in the third century BC. His great passion was collecting elephants, but he was also keen to display other exotica. Athenaeus describes at length an extraordinary carnival procession that Ptolemy mounted, which included spectacular floats celebrating the god Dionysus, drawn by teams of elephants, camels, oryxes, antelopes, ostriches, and human slaves. It included one huge exhibition piece mounted on a cart pulled by 500 men:

[1] A Persian speciality, the word 'paradise' being derived via Greek from the Old Persian *pairi-daeza*, 'walled around' (see Xenophon, *Anabasis* I 2.7).

On top of this was constructed a deep cave, thickly covered with ivy and yew. From it there flew out along the whole course of the procession doves, wood pigeons, and turtle doves, with ribbons tied to their feet to make it easy for the spectators to catch them.

Later on in the procession came floats depicting foreign conquests in India and Ethiopia and hunting scenes:

Next came 150 men carrying trees, on which were draped wild animals of every sort and birds. Then there were carried by in cages parrots, peacocks, guinea-fowl, pheasants, and other Ethiopian birds,[1] all in vast numbers.

Athenaeus, *The Intellectuals' Dinner Party* 200b, 201c

Ptolemy's collection was the predecessor of those maintained by Roman emperors for the more specific purpose of the gruesome public entertainments in the Circus, which I deal with in chapter 9 on sport. These earlier rulers seem to have established their private collections mainly to demonstrate their wealth and power and to impress both their subjects and their enemies. But what were the motives and reactions of the spectators, and how have these changed over time? There may be clues in the later history of zoos and their etymologies.

These ancient royal collections were really menageries, not zoos in the modern sense, since there was no scientific or educational purpose behind them. They gratified a sense of curiosity and offered a form of personal contact with the foreign and the exotic; and they also reassuringly emphasized the degree of human ascendancy over these fierce and dangerous wild creatures, which had been reduced by captivity to mere playthings. There were many animal collections of this kind in Europe in medieval times, one of the most famous being that in the Tower of London, established by King John in 1204. It was opened to the public in the sixteenth century, mainly so that they could look at the lions and other big cats, which were the principal exhibits. But there were also a few birds in the collection, including a 'bald eagle with a white head and neck' (more likely a white-tailed eagle at this date), two 'Swedish owls' [great grey owls], of a great Bigness, called Hopkins', and some golden eagles, which the ornithologists John Ray and Francis Willughby report seeing in the late 1660s when they visited what they called 'the Royal Theriotrophium'. By the eighteenth century visitors were being charged three half-pence admission, or 'the supply of a cat or a dog to be fed to the lions.'*

[1] Perhaps ibises and egrets, which would have been showy and exotic, but there are many possibilities.

The French word *ménagerie* originally referred simply to the management of household stock in a *ménage*; it gained its broader sense in seventeenth-century France when Louis XIV was establishing his prestigious royal menageries—at Vincennes, which was used mainly to stage gory fights in an amphitheatre between large beasts like tigers and elephants, and at his show-piece, the Palace of Versailles, which catered for gentler pleasures in a parkland or garden setting. The word *ménagerie* was defined in the French *Encyclopédie méthodique* of 1782 as an 'establishment of luxury and curiosity'.* These aristocratic menageries later evolved into more popular forms of entertainment, particularly when they gave rise to travelling shows and circuses from the eighteenth century onwards.

Modern zoos were an invention arising from the nineteenth-century fascination with natural history and its classification, and from the growing access to foreign places where previously unknown specimens could be collected. One of the first and most important to be established was the London Zoo, or to give it the full name it had when it was founded by Sir Stamford Raffles in 1826, the Gardens and Menagerie of the Zoological Society of London, whose original declared purpose, as the Greek-derived 'Zoological' suggests, was 'the study of animal life'. The original prospectus of 1825 deliberately made the contrast with the ancient world:

> Rome, at the period of her greatest splendour, brought savage monsters from every quarter of the world then known, to be shown in her amphitheatres, to destroy or be destroyed as spectacles of wonder to her citizens. It would well become Britain to offer another, and a very different series of exhibitions to the population of her metropolis; namely animals brought from every part of the globe to be applied either to some useful purpose, or as the object of scientific research, not of vulgar admiration.*

The Regent's Park Gardens were not in fact opened to the public until 1847; the popular name quickly became just the 'London Zoo' and it has ever since been a huge tourist attraction.

In the late twentieth century some zoos sought to distance themselves from the nineteenth-century concept of zoos as collections and re-described themselves as 'conservation parks' or 'bioparks' to reflect a larger and more responsible attitude to the whole natural environment. Indeed, in 1993 the New York Zoological Society changed its name to the Wildlife Conservation Society and rebranded all the zoos under its jurisdiction as 'wildlife conservation parks'.

Similarly, the current official mission of the London Zoo, now called the ZSL (Zoological Society of London), is 'to promote and achieve the worldwide conservation of animals and their habitats'.

*   *   *

These examples serve to illustrate some of the social and political functions such establishments have served and the ways in which they responded to changing public attitudes to wildlife. As so often, however, the evidence from the classical world is far more sketchy and discontinuous. The earliest wildlife collection we hear about in ancient Greece was the private peacock exhibition I cited at the start of this chapter (and no such word as 'zoo' is used at this point). This collection was said to be owned by one Demus, son of Pyrilampes, in the late fifth century BC and was visited, Athenaeus tells us, by 'many from Sparta and Thessaly who came to see the peacocks and tried to obtain some of their eggs' (397c–d). The reference occurs in a legal speech by the orator Antiphon, entitled 'On the prosecution of Erasistratus in the matter of the peacocks', in which he appears to be accusing the defendant of stealing either the birds or their eggs.

Aelian comments on the same establishment, which evidently traded very successfully on the allure of the peacock's beauty:*

> The bird is well aware of the reactions it prompts, and just as a pretty boy or lovely woman displays their best physical features, so the peacock flaunts its feathers in an orderly succession. Indeed, it looks like a flowery meadow or a painting worked with many hues of colour, which an artist must sweat over to convey its special natural qualities. And it reveals its willingness to exhibit itself by allowing bystanders to take their fill of gazing at the spectacle as it turns this way and that; and it makes every effort to show off the full range of its plumage features, with an arrogant display that surpasses even the finery of the Medes and the embroidery of the Persians.
>
> The peacock is said to have been introduced into Greece from foreign parts. For a long time it was a rare sight and used to be shown to lovers of beauty for a charge. At Athens they let men and women in to examine the birds on the first of the month and turned a profit from the spectacle. They used to value the cock and hen at 10,000 drachmas,[1] according to Antiphon in his speech against Erasistratus.

Aelian, *On Animals* v 21

---

[1] Impossible to convert into today's values but, as a yardstick, 1 drachma per day was the standard naval pay in a Greek fleet at this period (Thucydides VIII 29.1–2), so peacocks were seriously expensive.

3.3 Peacocks. Detail from a mosaic in the early Christian basilica at Aquilea, *c.*400 AD. Aquilea was a large city in Roman times, situated at the head of the Adriatic in north-eastern Italy.

We know there were aviaries, too, by at least the fifth century BC. They were kept by pigeon-fanciers and others, and here there is a word, *peristereon*, a 'pigeonry'. In one of his philosophical dialogues between Socrates and an acquiescent respondent, Plato uses the analogy of pigeons in an aviary to explore a subtle distinction between possessing certain kinds of knowledge and having access to them. He likens the birds to elusive items of memory, which suggests that aviaries were commonplace:

> SOCRATES. ... So let us imagine in each soul an aviary filled with all kinds of birds, some in flocks keeping themselves apart from the others, others in small groups, and some on their own flying here and there among them all.
>
> Plato, *Theaetetus* 197c–d

Little aviaries of the kind referred to here were presumably just an extension of the practice of having one or more caged birds in the home. As we saw in chapter 7 on farming, by the first century BC in the Roman period the concept of an aviary had expanded to include large-scale commercial aviaries, which were managed to produce birds mainly for consumption but also in some cases for the private pleasure of their owners (see pp. 114–24). Varro describes his own very elaborate aviary, which was set on the banks of a private stream and displayed two collections: one of water fowl in a specially designed enclosure complete with duck-sheds, fish-basins, a waterwheel and a water clock; and one of songbirds 'in what is effectively a miniature bird theatre, with graduated seating, brackets being fastened to all the columns at frequent intervals to serve as perches' (*On Agriculture* III 5.13–14).

Roman emperors might maintain similar establishments for their pleasure, like the extensive aviaries of the emperor Severus Alexander (r. AD 222–35):

> He did have one particular kind of amusement in the palace, in which he took a special delight and from which he gained some relief from the cares of public life. These were the aviaries he had set up for peacocks, pheasants, cockerels, ducks, and partridges. He derived enormous pleasure from all these, but most of all from his doves, of which he was said to have possessed some 20,000. To stop the food for these becoming a drain on his annual resources he had slaves raising revenue to maintain the doves from the produce of the eggs, squabs, and chicks.
>
> *Historia Augusta*, 'Severus Alexander' XLI 6–7

We shall focus here, however, on the ordinary domestic household, in which birds often came to be treated as family pets. Quite a wide range of species seem to have been kept and for a number of different reasons.

The crow family generally was a popular choice. A jackdaw and a crow are the species chosen to acts as guides to the two Athenians at the start of Aristophanes' play *The Birds* when they set out on their quest to infiltrate the kingdom of the birds; and we are told that they were acquired at the bird market for 1 and 3 obols respectively, so they must have been quite common pets as well as familiar wild birds. Jackdaws made clever performers for pretentious householders to show off. Theophrastus, in his deadly accurate sketches of different character types, gives this example of the behaviour of the 'man of petty pride':

> He has the trick of keeping a pet jackdaw in the house, buying it a little ladder and fashioning a tiny shield for it to hold as it hops up and down the ladder.
>
> Theophrastus, *Characters* 21.5

Jackdaws were also natural candidates for leading roles in several of Aesop's moral fables.* We are reminded in this one that they were sometimes unwilling captives:

> A man caught a jackdaw and tied a piece of string round its foot to give it to his child as a present. But the bird could not bear to live its life in human company, so taking advantage of a momentary opportunity it made its escape back to its own nest. However, its bonds became caught up in the branches and it was unable to fly away. As it was dying there, the jackdaw said to itself, 'What a wretched fool, I am. Since I couldn't bear to be a slave in human society I made the mistake of losing my life altogether.
>
> Aesop, *Fables* 131 (Perry)

Magpies became a familiar species in the region only quite late on (see p. 98), so it was probably an exotic touch to have a magpie as part of the striking tableau that greeted guests arriving for Trimalchio's over-the-top dinner party in Petronius' 'Feast of Trimalchio':

> Right at the entrance there stood a porter in a leek-green uniform with a cherry-coloured belt, shelling peas into a silver dish. Over the doorway hung a golden cage, in which a pied magpie greeted visitors. But while I was taking all this in and gawping, I nearly fell backwards and broke my legs. For there on the left as you went in, not far from the porter's lodge, was a huge dog on a chain; it was painted on the wall and written in capital letters above it were the words, BEWARE OF THE DOG.
>
> Petronius, *Satyricon* 28–29

Purple gallinules (the 'purple birds') must have looked like even more exotic accessories in wealthy establishments, though in this case they were probably much commoner in the region then than they are today. Their strange appearance and reclusive habits in the wild perhaps contributed to the credulous anecdotes they tended to attract.

> The purple gallinule is the most splendid of all creatures and the most aptly named. It likes to dust itself, and it bathes in the way pigeons do, but it doesn't commit itself to the dust-bath or the washing until it has walked a certain number of steps to reassure itself. It cannot bear to feed with people watching and for that reason it is retiring and eats from within cover. It is subject to violent jealousies and keeps a close eye on the married females; and if it catches the mistress of the household in adultery it strangles itself. It doesn't fly high. Yet people do take great pleasure in having them and they look after them with much care and

attention. As a rule they seem either to be kept in fancy and seriously rich households or to be let into temple grounds, where they wander about and range freely
with the status of sacred birds within the precincts.

Aelian, *On Animals* III 42

3.4 Purple gallinule. A dramatic, if faded, image from the garden fresco in the House of
the Gold Bracelet at Pompeii, AD 30–50. This exotic bird was sometimes a lover's gift as
well as a household pet (see p. 71). It must have owed much of its attraction to its striking purple colour, which was associated with high status and power, particularly in
Roman culture. Its Greek name *porphurion* ('purple bird') survives in the modern scientific name of *Porphyrio porphyrio*. The common generic name has recently been changed
from 'gallinule' to 'swamp-hen'.

The most famous pet bird in ancient literature, however, concerned a far
more ordinary species: the 'sparrow'. The Roman poet Catullus addressed a
series of poems to the love of his life, Lesbia, tracing the course of their affair
through the first innocent longings to disillusionment and the final bitter rejection. The first two poems in the cycle concern Lesbia's pet bird, described as a
passer, which is conventionally translated as 'sparrow' and is indeed now the
generic scientific name for our urban house sparrow, *Passer domesticus*. But was
it in fact a sparrow? The only internal clues are that it nestles intimately in her
lap, nips her occasionally, and calls in a way Catullus describes with the rare verb
pipiabat ('cheep', 'chirp', 'chirrup', 'peep', or 'pipe'?). Alternative identifications suggested include a bullfinch (which make devoted pets and do 'pipe'), other finches

(goldfinch or chaffinch, both common cage-birds), a blue rock thrush (still called *passero* in modern Italian, but a much larger bird with a fluting song), or some other kind of sparrow (tree, Italian, or Spanish, all of which 'chirp'). Or could the sparrow have been a purely literary invention, an erotic symbol of some kind? * 'Sparrows' do have this slang sense in many languages, and Catullus' readers might even have remembered the famous Sappho poem invoking Aphrodite, whose chariot was drawn through the skies by 'fine, fleet sparrows.'*

3.5 Girl with two pet doves. Marble relief from the island of Paros in the Aegean, *c.*450–440 BC. The sculpture is on a *stele* (upright stone pillar), a grave marker for the little girl who is shown in a tender moment with her pets. Paros was famed for its translucent white marble, which could be worked in the sort of exquisite detail illustrated here.

All we know about the word *pipiabat*, apart from the onomatopoeia, is that in one of its other two attested uses it refers to young unhatched chickens calling from within the egg (Columella VIII 5.14) and in the other to human children (Tertullian, *Monogamia* 16). Scholarship alone won't resolve this identity problem, so decide for yourself after reading the poems. I go for a generic solution, since I suspect that *passer* was used in the vernacular for any small bird, as it has often been in later history. Think, for example, of the famous passage in St Matthew's Gospel, 'Are not two sparrows sold for a farthing?' and the wonderful image in Bede, comparing the life of humankind with 'the swift flight of a lone sparrow through the banqueting hall'. In scientific terminology too 'passerine' stands for the whole class of perching songbirds, more than half the world's species of birds.*

A minor mystery, which really *is* a scholarly question, is whether Catullus' two poems were in fact originally one, joined together by some verses now lost in the precarious manuscript tradition. I follow the current consensus and present them separately here. The first of the pair (which is one long sentence in the Latin) does perhaps carry some erotic charge in envying the physical intimacy the bird has with his mistress:

> Little bird, my sweetheart's pet,
> whom she likes to play with, hold to her bosom,
> and offer her fingertips to be pecked,
> provoking your sharp nips,
> whenever it takes my lovely darling's fancy
> to play some favourite game with you,
> so that when her fiercer longings subside,
> she may find some relief from her pain;
> would that I too could play with you thus
> and allay the sad cares of my own heart,
> as welcome a gift to me, as they say
> the golden apple was to that swift girl,[1]
> whose girdle it loosened, too long tied.
>
> Catullus, *Poems* 2

The second poem is the better-known one, however:

> Mourn, all you gods of love and desire
> and all people deeply touched by love!
> My sweetheart's little bird is dead,
> that little bird, my sweetheart's pet,
> which she loved more than her own eyes.
> He was her honey, who knew her
> as well as a girl knows her own mother.
> Nor would he stir from her lap,
> but hopping about here and there
> would ever chirp for his mistress alone.
> Now he travels the darkened path

---

[1] Atalanta, who promised that she would give herself to any suitor who could outrun her, while those who failed would be killed. Hippomenes won this risky footrace by casting in her path golden apples that she paused to gather, perhaps willing the consequences.

to that place whence none may return.
A curse on you, cursed shades of Orcus,[1]
who devour all pretty things.
What a pretty bird you've robbed me of.
What a shame, poor little bird,
that because of you, my sweetheart's eyes
are red and swollen with crying.

    Catullus, *Poems* 3

*   *   *

There are many other references in classical literature to birds given as presents, whether to become family pets or for sport or for the table.* But the most usual reason for keeping birds seems to have been because of their voices. Nightingales were greatly prized singers, of course. Pliny gives an excellent description of nightingale song (see p. 60) and goes on to tell us that the best songsters were consequently very expensive:

> They therefore command the same prices as those paid for slaves, indeed higher prices than used to be paid for armour-bearers in days past. I know of one bird, which was given as a present to Agrippina, wife of the emperor Claudius, that went for 600,000 sesterces,[2] though it was admittedly a white one, which is almost unprecedented. Cases have often been recorded of nightingales that have started to sing when ordered and have duetted with a musical instrument.
>
>   Pliny, *Natural History* x 83–84

Aelian thinks the bird actually sings better in company:

> I gather from Charmis the Massilian that the nightingale is a bird fond of music, and indeed of fame. At any rate, when it is singing to itself in deserted places the bird sings a simple, spontaneous melody. But when it is in captivity and has an audience, then it starts to sing more varied notes and trill tunes of melting beauty.
>
>   Aelian, *On Animals* v 38

---

[1] A god of the underworld, hence the underworld itself.

[2] A huge sum, though a sestercius was a very small denomination, a quarter of a denarius (see p. 96 n.1), and this was, after all, a gift from an emperor. Even so, records from Pompeii in the first century AD show a mule being sold at auction for just 520 sesterces and a slave for 6,252 sesterces.*

But the adult birds couldn't always be relied on to cooperate, as the same author warns:

> Now, the nightingale passionately loves its freedom; therefore when an adult bird is trapped and caged it refrains from singing and takes revenge for its slavery by its silence and so punishes the catcher. Consequently, men who have had this experience let the adult birds go and do their best to catch them young.
>
> Aelian, *On Animals* III 40

What particularly fascinated the ancients, however, was the ability of some birds to mimic other sounds, including human speech.* One particularly versatile performer was a barber's pet jay:

> There was a barber who had a shop in Rome opposite to the precinct called 'the Greek Market'. He reared a jay that was a real vocal prodigy, with a huge repertoire of sounds and voices. It could reproduce human speech, animal calls, and the sounds of instruments—under no compulsion, but making it a fixed habit and a point of pride to let no sounds pass without repeating and imitating them. Now it so happened that a rich man from that district was being buried to the accompaniment of many trumpets and as usual the procession halted at that spot while the trumpeters were applauded and encouraged to play on for a long time. From that day onwards the jay lost its voice completely and was mute, not emitting a single sound even for its daily needs. Regular passers-by who had previously marvelled at its voice now wondered even more at its total silence. Some suspected poisoning by rival bird-keepers, but most people supposed that the trumpets had blasted its eardrums and that its voice had been lost along with its hearing. In fact it was neither of these things, but an inner discipline and withholding of its mimetic skill while it adjusted and refashioned its voice like a musical instrument. For suddenly its voice returned and in place of its old repertoire of imitations there rang out the music of the trumpets, reproducing all its sequences and every variation in melody and rhythm.
>
> Plutarch, 'Cleverness of animals', *Moralia* 973c–e

The ability of various species of birds to mimic sounds they have heard—whether from other species of birds, animals, humans, music, or even machines—has continued to fascinate laypeople and scientists alike.[1] The most successful

---

[1] There is a splendid CD of bird mimicry published by the British Library Sound Archive (2006), which includes a jay mimicking a horse, a bullfinch singing German folk melodies, 'Sparkie Williams' the champion talking budgerigar, and a fawn-breasted bowerbird giving a perfect rendition of men at work on a tin roof in Port Moresby, Papua New Guinea.

performers tend to be members of the crow family (including jays, magpies, and ravens), starlings, hill mynahs, parrots, mockingbirds, and lyrebirds, but many if not most songbirds have the capacity to some degree if they are exposed to the sounds early enough and under the right conditions, since they learn their own songs largely by imitation anyway.* Famous individual mimics in history have included Mozart's starling, who seems to have memorized the theme from his Piano Concerto in G Major, K453 (and then had the compliment returned by Mozart in K522, the 'Musical Joke', which mimics a starling's rambling discordances).*

But the most celebrated mimics of all have been those who flatter their listeners by specializing in human speech. The extraordinary skills of parrots in this respect were already well known in the ancient world and that gave them a special status in some cultures:

> Parrots too are kept in these royal palaces, where they throng around the king. But no Indian eats a parrot, despite their great abundance. The reason is that the Brahmins regard them as sacred birds and esteem them even above all other birds. They say they are justified in this since the parrot is the only bird to give such a perfect imitation of human speech.
>
> Aelian, *On Animals* XIII 18

Greeks probably saw their first parrots in the course of Alexander the Great's India campaign in 327–326 BC. But the first actual mention of parrots in Greek literature is by the fifth-century author Ctesias, who was based in the Persian court, where he will have picked up various travellers' tales. In his (often credulous) book of 'Indian marvels' he seems to be describing a plum-headed parakeet (*Psittacula cyanocephala*):

> It has a human voice and speaks human language. It is about the size of a hawk; it has a purple head and a black beard; its body is dark blue, but round the neck the colour is that of red cinnabar. It speaks Indian like a real person, but if it is taught Greek it speaks that very well too.
>
> Ctesias, *Indica* 45a*

Not surprisingly, then, parrots attracted great devotion as pets, and there are two famous literary elegies on the deaths of favourite parrots, in the 'lamented pets' genre Catullus had made famous but without his simple immediacy of feeling.* Both are quite long so I have quoted only the beginning and end of the first and better of them. Ovid gives this mock lament for the parrot of his mistress, Corinna, in one of his *Amores* ('Loves'):

Her parrot, that winged mimic from the Indies,
is dead—come flock to his funeral, all you birds.
Come, faithful birds of the air, beat breasts with wings;
score tender cheeks with rigid talons;
rend ruffled feathers in place of mourners' hair;
and let your ringing songs serve for trumpets' sound.

The poet then describes the parrot's special friendship with the turtle dove and his unique powers of mimicry. His dying cry was 'Corinna, farewell' and he rests with other 'pious birds'[1] (phoenix, swan, peacock, dove) in a woodland grave in Elysium:

A mound covers his bones, one made just to his size,
and these lines of verse exactly fit the tiny stone:
SEE FROM MY TOMB HOW MUCH MY MISTRESS CARED.
MY SKILL IN SPEECH SURPASSED THAT OF ANY BIRD
    Ovid, *Amores* II 6.81–82

Statius, writing a generation later, offers his own parody of the genre in imitation of Ovid, which claims that his patron Melior's parrot outdid all other mimics—raven, starling, magpie, partridge, and nightingale.

Aristotle and Pliny somewhat deflate these high-flown eulogies, however, by noting that a parrot's performance tended to improve with the consumption of alcohol:

In general, all these crook-taloned birds [like owls] are short-necked and flat-tongued and are mimics, as is the Indian bird, the parrot, that is said to be human-tongued—and it becomes even more uninhibited after drinking wine.
    Aristotle, *History of Animals* 597b25–28

Most remarkable of all, birds can imitate the human voice, and parrots can actually hold a conversation. This bird comes from India, where it is called *siptaces*;[2] its body is green all over, broken only by a red circlet round the neck. It will greet its masters and repeat words it is told, being especially entertaining when in its cups.
    Pliny, *Natural History* x 117

---

[1] *Pius* here means the opposite of *obscenus* ('unclean', 'impure', and hence 'ill-omened', see p. 316).

[2] The equivalent of the generic Latin *psittacus*. The species referred to here is clearly the rose-ringed parakeet *Psittacula krameri*, an abundant species in India and now a familiar bird in the London parks (derived from escaped cage-birds in the 1960s), where they form the most northerly colonies of any parrot population.

3.6 Parakeets. Detail from a Roman mosaic from Pompeii (first century BC). A feral pigeon (*Columba livia*) and two parakeets (one to either side) perch on the rim of an urn; the bird on the left has features resembling the Alexandrine parakeet (*Psittacula eupatria*) while that on the right suggests the rose-ringed parakeet (*Psittacula krameri*), but the details are not accurately rendered and it may be a poor copy of another work. Parakeets were unknown in Greece before the eastern campaigns of Alexander the Great in 330–325 BC, but by Roman times they had become popular pets, largely because of their talent for mimicry.

Pliny later says that parrots were such highly valued performers as human mimics partly because they were exotic imports and he presses the claims also of native species including not only well-known mimics like the crow family and the starling, but also the thrush and nightingale:

> Agrippina, wife of Gaius Caesar, had a thrush with the ability to mimic what people were saying, something quite unprecedented. And at the time I was recording these cases the young princes [Britannicus and Nero] actually had a starling and also some nightingales that had learned to speak Greek and Latin; moreover, they practised assiduously and were speaking new words every day— and in ever longer constructions. The birds are taught in seclusion, away from any

interference by other voices, with the trainer sitting by them repeating the words
he wants retained and coaxing them with pieces of food.

Pliny, *Natural History* x 120

One may wonder if such feats are sometimes exaggerated by the proud
owners of the star performers, but Pliny's story of a famous city raven would at
least have been very widely attested. This was a young bird that attached itself
to a cobbler's shop in Rome:

It soon picked up the ability to speak, and every morning it flew off to the platform opposite the forum and greeted by name Tiberius, Germanicus, and Drusus
Caesar in turn, and then members of the public passing by before returning to the
shop. Remarkably, the raven performed this routine for many years.

The tenant of the next-door shoemaker's shop killed the bird, either from competitive rivalry or in a fit of anger because, he claimed, some of the bird's droppings had spattered his stock of shoes. This caused such a public uproar that the
man was first driven out of the district and then actually lynched, while the
funeral for the bird was celebrated with full rites. The draped bier was carried on
the shoulders of two Ethiopian bearers, preceded by a flautist, and with all kinds
of wreaths strewn along the way to the pyre that had been constructed on the
right hand side of the Appian Way at the second milestone, on what is called
Rediculus' Plain. The bird's genius seemed an entirely sufficient justification to
the Roman people for such a funeral procession and for the punishment of a
Roman citizen, and that in a city in which many leading men had been given no
funeral rites at all.

Pliny, *Natural History* x 121–23

But even that story is capped by another anecdote one very much wants to
believe—of a raven learning his lines of congratulation but delivering them to
the wrong person:

When Augustus was returning to Rome in triumph after his victory at Actium,[1]
among those who ran out to congratulate him was a man holding a raven that he
had taught to say, 'Hail Caesar, victorious commander'. Marvelling at this obliging
bird, Caesar bought it for 20,000 sesterces. The man's colleague, who had not
benefited at all from this munificent act, informed Caesar that his friend also had
a second raven, which Caesar asked to have brought out as well. When it was
produced it spoke the words it had been taught, 'Hail Antony, victorious com-

---

[1] The decisive naval battle in 31 BC in which Octavian (as he then was) defeated the combined forces
of Antony and Cleopatra, shortly after which he became the first Roman emperor, with the title Caesar
Augustus.

mander'. Unfazed by this, Augustus indicated that he would regard it as a satisfactory outcome if the first man divided his gift with his partner.[1]

Macrobius, *Saturnalia* II 29

Others then jump on this bandwagon and persuade Augustus also to buy a parrot and a magpie that have been taught to utter the same words.

That inspired a poor cobbler to train a raven to give the same salute; but after he had spent all his money on the bird and still it stayed mute the man kept muttering, 'all that work and money down the drain'. Eventually, however, the bird began to give the greeting it had been taught; but when Augustus heard it as he passed by he answered, 'I have enough birds at home to greet me like that.' But the raven retained a memory of his master's constant complaints and added, 'all that work and money down the drain', at which Caesar laughed and had the bird bought at a higher price than all the rest.

Macrobius, *Saturnalia* II 30

The emperor Caesar may have seen the joke here, but the prospect of being praised by a bird could easily go to the head of someone ambitious for an even greater status:

Hanno, the Carthaginian, got so far above himself that he was no longer content to accept the limitations of being human, but planned to get circulated reports about himself that indicated qualities superior to those allotted by nature. He bought a lot of birds of the singing kind and reared them in darkness, teaching them just one lesson, to say 'Hanno is a god.' When they had mastered this one phrase by listening to its repetition, he let them go off in all directions, thinking they would broadcast this chant about himself. But the birds, once they had stretched their wings and found their freedom, returned to their native haunts. There they sang their natural songs and made their bird music, saying a loud goodbye to Hanno and the lessons learned in their forced captivity.[2]

Aelian, *Miscellany* XIV 30

It seems appropriate to end this chapter by letting a bird have the last word, as in this mock epitaph:

---

[1] A performer who could make more tactful distinctions is recorded by the ornithologist Edward Armstrong: 'My wife had a parrot in Brazil which greeted the butcher, but never the milkman, with, "Is the meat tender today?" '*

[2] In another version of this story, the birds more actively subvert Hanno's intentions when they are taught by an enemy of his to say, 'He shut us up and forced us to say he was a god.'*

I am the jay who often before screamed back at
the shepherds, woodcutters, and fishermen,
and often struck noisy, mocking notes
of imitation from my mouth, just like an echo.
Now tongueless and voiceless I lie fallen
to the ground, renouncing my love of mimicry.
  Archias, *Greek Anthology* VII 191

*   *   *

These celebrations of pets, in life and in death, serve to illustrate the range of human responses that birds evoked, and still evoke. Some hover between affection and sentimentality. Some exhibit an innocent curiosity, some a deeper fascination, yet others a casual cruelty. Most seem moved by the combination of what is strange and of what is, or seems, familiar in our encounters with birds. Jointly, they thereby emphasize the ambiguous status of birds—apparently very like us in some ways and very unlike us in others. And that means that the relationships we may have with them are likely to be ambiguous and uncertain too. The next two chapters explore that thought further.

9

Sports and
Entertainments

Sometimes an absence can be as interesting as a presence. In his classic Sherlock Holmes story 'Silver Blaze', Conan Doyle has the following snatch of dialogue between the great detective and his Scotland Yard minder:

GREGORY Is there any point to which you would wish to draw my attention?
HOLMES To the curious incident of the dog in the night-time.
GREGORY The dog did nothing in the night-time.
HOLMES That was the curious incident.

There are many curious absences in what we know about the ancient world. Some are no doubt explained just by gaps in the record, since so much of ancient literature has not survived and we must have lost all sorts of wonderful works, and with them much interesting information.[1] Others may involve genuine absences—that is, aspects of life and culture we may have wrongly assumed will be present in particular societies because we are familiar with them in others. And there seems to be one surprising absence of the latter kind in the various sporting activities involving birds in the classical world. Why is there almost no mention of the ancient sport of falconry?

---

[1] To cite some examples from Greek drama: we have only seven of the eighty-one plays Aeschylus is supposed to have written, seven out of 123 for Sophocles, nineteen out of ninety-two for Euripides, eleven out of forty-four for Aristophanes, just one complete play out of 105 for Menander, and only fragments from the ninety-seven comedies of Menander's (now wholly forgotten) rival, Philemon.

3.7 Portrait of Frederick II, Holy Roman Emperor and King of Sicily. Frederick was devoted to falconry, employed some fifty falconers at court, and himself wrote the first (and very comprehensive) treatise on the subject, *De arte venandi cum avibus* ('The art of hunting with birds', *c.*1245–50). The bird by his side is probably a golden eagle, more a symbol of regal power in this context than a falconer's bird, though eagles are still used for hunting game in parts of Asia like Mongolia and Kazakhstan.

Falconry was certainly practised in Mesopotamia and further east in India, Mongolia, and China before the Graeco-Roman period, but it seems to emerge in Europe only from about AD 400 with the invasions of the Huns and Alans into the Roman Empire.* It then flourishes for over a thousand years in medieval Europe and achieves its definitive text in the remarkable handbook produced by Frederick II of Hohenstaufen (1194–1250), his *De arte venandi cum avibus* ('The art of hunting with birds'). But why did it not exist in Greece and Rome? There was no shortage of either predators or prey, after all. Aristotle lists eleven kinds of small raptor he classifies under the generic category of *hierax*, excluding eagles, vultures, and kites, and the implication is that these were all common at the time in the Mediterranean region, as indeed they are today.[1] In an interesting passage Aristotle then notes their different hunting behaviours:

> Some of them strike a pigeon when it is sitting on the ground and snatch it up, but do not take it in flight; others hunt it when it is sitting on a tree or some other perch, but do not take it in the air or on the ground; others do not touch it when it is sitting on the ground or perched elsewhere, but try to seize it in flight. And they say that the pigeons can recognize each of these different kinds of raptor as they approach, so if it is one of those that catch prey in the air they stay wherever they happen to be sitting, but if the approaching bird is one of those that strike on the ground they take to flight rather than waiting for it.
>
> Aristotle, *History of Animals* 620a23–33

It's hard to prove a negative, of course, but Aristotle and others would surely at least have mentioned something about falconry, if only in stray references, had it existed as a familiar pastime or pursuit. As we saw in chapter 5 on hunting and fowling, we do have a great deal of information about the many different means of catching and trapping birds for food, but although we hear a lot in these accounts about the hunting *of* birds we hear very little about hunting *with* birds. There is a systematic treatise by Xenophon entitled *On Hunting* and it makes no mention of falconry at all. The few references we do have suggest that raptors were sometimes used to flush birds so that they could then be killed by other means. Aristotle himself records examples of this kind of 'partnership' between men and birds in descriptions of hunting practices in the wild north-eastern part of Greece called Thrace, but he clearly regards these as exceptional:

> In the part of Thrace called after King Kedripolis, men hunt small birds in the marsh, working jointly with the hawks. They beat the reeds and undergrowth to make the birds fly up, and the hawks then emerge from the skies to hunt them down from above. In a panic they fly down again to the ground, whereupon the men club them with sticks, gather them up, and share them out with the hawks, throwing some of the birds in the air for the hawks to catch.
>
> Aristotle, *History of Animals* 620a33–b5

A similar story is recounted in a collection of 'reported marvels' (falsely attributed to Aristotle), which has an additional twist:

---

[1] Resident or regular migrant raptors in Greece today include four species of buzzard, two kites, six eagles, four vultures, osprey, four harriers, three hawks, and eight falcons.*

They say that in the part of Thrace above Amphipolis there is an extraordinary occurrence, which those who have never seen find incredible. Boys from the villages and places around there go out to hunt small birds together, taking hawks with them, which they employ as follows. When they reach a suitable place, they summon the hawks, shouting out their names. When these hear the boys' voices they come and spook the birds, which fly in terror into the bushes where the boys club them with sticks and catch them. But the most remarkable thing of all is this: when the hawks themselves catch any of the birds they drop them for the hunters, and the boys return the hawks a portion of the whole catch and then go home.

[Aristotle], *Reported Marvels* 118

In yet another version of the same story, Aelian says that the Thracians use hawks to drive wildfowl from the marshes into a circle of nets they have spread out, and again the implication is that this is worth noting as an unusual local practice in a remote region. Aelian says that hawks 'are by nature the tamest of birds and the most attached to humans' (*On Animals* 11 42), though he then goes on to make some absurd claims about how they demonstrate their devotion. And Pliny reports a similar hunting partnership between men and ravens, which were used to 'locate and flush the game' (*Natural History* x 124).

These anecdotes do point to some exceptional cases where ordinary people were keeping and training predators to help in hunting smaller birds—and even giving them personal names—but this is still a very long way short of proper falconry, and these were in any case examples from the periphery of the Greek world. It is possible, of course, that the anecdotes themselves are unreliable or misrepresent what was going on. It would make more sense, and would be more like some later forms of falconry, if the beaters were flushing the birds for the hawks to kill, rather than the other way round, but that isn't what these texts actually say.*

The only text that might be evidence for conventional falconry in the classical world before AD 400 is a tiny two-line epigram (just fourteen words in the Latin) by the poet Martial. This comes from a book of *Apophoreta* ('Gifts'), designed as a sort of gift-tag to go with personal presents (in this case a hawk):

Once a predator of birds, now a fowler's servant,
he takes birds and grieves they are not for him.

Martial, *Epigrams* xiv 216

That sounds promising, but the snippet is ambiguous, especially since there are two crucial textual uncertainties here. In line 1, is the hawk a predator *of* birds or *among* birds (a sort of epithet)? And more importantly, in line 2, should the key word *decipit* be understood as 'deceives' (as a decoy), 'distracts' (as in a flushing exercise), or 'seizes' (as in a stoop). Is it 'takes' or 'takes in'? Scholars are divided. Either way this riddling *jeu d'esprit* can scarcely stand the weight placed upon it by those determined to discern here solid evidence for a flourishing tradition of falconry in the Graeco-Roman period—perhaps because of their own enthusiasm for the 'noble art' and a consequent expectation that somehow it 'must have been there.'* Folklorists as well as falconers have helped to foster this assumption, tracing the etymology of hawkweed (*hieracium*) back to the Greek *hierax* (hawk) and linking it to the belief that moisture squeezed from the plant's juices was applied to hawks' eyes to improve their vision for hunting. The main source for this fancy, Pliny (*Natural History* xx 26), in fact reports—at nth hand—the quite different belief that hawks tear up hawkweed and apply it to themselves.

Why falconry was never fully adopted in mainstream classical culture is a mystery. Was it for some combination of social or political reasons? In Persia and the Middle East (as later in Christian Europe), it is associated mainly with those aristocrats who had the time, resources, and tastes to indulge their passion for it.[1] Perhaps the relevant connections with Greece occurred at a time when the political mood and structures were in some ways unsympathetic to such an oriental transplant, though such waves of xenophobia or prejudice tended to be short-lived and to have a very particular historical context.[2]

Or was there conceivably just no cultural space for it, if the privileged classes in Greece and Rome who might have adopted it already had better ways of occupying their leisure and parading their status? Aristocratic families in Athens, for example, were expected to perform 'liturgies' (literally 'work for the people') of public-spirited activities like funding dramatic festivals or triremes; while in Rome they sponsored events like the gladiatorial games at the Circus. But falconry would scarcely have made the same public impact. And among the lower classes there were evidently many other established means of obtaining meat and plenty of traditional popular entertainments, so perhaps there was no practical motivation at that social level either.

---

[1] Egypt, where the 'Horus falcon' was a sacred bird, was a different case, but the evidence for falconry there is also very slender.*

[2] For example, the hostility in parts of Greece to 'Medism' (the adopting of Persian lifestyles and political sympathies) after the Persian Wars of the early fifth century BC (see Thucydides I 95.5, 135.2).

Another possibility might be that because birds of prey were the birds of omen par excellence, as we shall see in chapter 14, it was judged inappropriate to deploy them as mere playthings. If they were among the principal channels of communication with the gods would it be an irreverence to try to tame and train them for such limited human purposes? This is pure speculation, but it might just connect with another possible inhibition we shall explore in chapter 17 to do with butterflies (see pp. 317–22).

There are many such mysteries in the histories of culture and science about which one simply has to confess honest perplexity. Take the case of technology. The Greeks and Romans performed marvels of construction in building the Parthenon, the monuments at Olympia, the lighthouse at Alexandria, and the Colosseum at Rome; they also invented many ingenious machines to support agricultural work—including mills, waterwheels, presses, and pumps, employing such sophisticated devices as the Archimedean screw—but they never designed a simple wheelbarrow.* Why not? Perhaps falconry is the wheelbarrow of sport?

So, none of these explanations quite satisfies. I shall return to the question of falconry at the end of this chapter after a comparison with a sport that *was* more wholeheartedly adopted, which may suggest a deeper cultural explanation.

Before that we should look briefly at another ancient skill, where the sporting connections with birds are also quite slender but are better attested. Archery was valued in the classical world, as in most pre-modern societies before the invention of firearms, for its effectiveness at long range in both warfare and the hunt.* It was also celebrated as a sporting accomplishment, and an archery competition is included in the earliest athletic festival we hear of in Western literature, the great 'Funeral Games' at Troy, held by Achilles to mark the death of Patroclus. The archers' target in this case was a bird, a dove tied to a ship's mast that had been set up as a mark a great distance away. The two principal contestants, Teucer and Meriones, draw lots and Teucer shoots first; but he has forgotten to promise a sacrifice to Apollo, the archer god, before letting fly:

> So he missed the bird, for Apollo grudged him that success,
> but he hit the cord by which it was tethered, near its foot,
> and the sharp arrow cut clean through the cord.
> The dove then took off into the sky, leaving the string
> dangling down towards the earth, and the Achaeans roared.
> But Meriones, who had long been holding an arrow ready
> while Teucer took aim, quickly snatched the bow from him

and promptly vowed to Apollo, the far-shooter,
that he would make him a fine sacrifice of firstborn lambs.
High up beneath the clouds he spotted the fluttering dove
and as she circled there he shot her in the middle
under the wing; the arrow passed straight through
and stuck in the ground by his feet; but the bird
settled back on the mast of the dark-prowed ship
with drooping head and her plumage flopping around her.
The life ebbed fast from her body, and she fell to ground
far away. The crowd gazed on and were lost in wonder.

    Homer, *Iliad* XXIII 865–81

At the other end of our period we have the Roman emperor Commodus show-ing off his archery skills on a very different target. Commodus was a megalomaniac, whose disturbed period of rule (AD 180–92) was identified by Edward Gibbon as the beginning of the 'decline and fall' of the Roman Empire. He sought to turn his slaughter of various megafauna into an art form, which is why the following extract comes in this chapter and not the one on hunting:

> Everyone was astounded at his marksmanship. For instance, on one occasion he took some arrows with crescent-shaped heads and used them to shoot at Mauretanian ostriches, birds that can move very fast because of their fleetness of foot and the way they fold back their wings. He decapitated them, cutting through the tops of their necks with his arrows, with the result that they went on running around as if nothing had happened even though their heads had been cut off by the impetus of the arrows.

    Herodian, *History of the Empire* I 15.7

But there were also more established forms of entertainment involving birds, principal among which were staged cockfights of a kind common to many cul-tures.* Cocks were renowned for their fighting spirit. The Greek name *alector* (or *alectruon*) is probably derived from the verb *alekso*, meaning 'repel' or 'defend',[1] and recognizes their aggressive instincts in defending their territories and mates against rivals. 'Brag away boldly, like a cock beside his hen', jeers the chorus to Aegisthus at the end of Aeschylus' *Agamemnon* (line 1671), knowing

---

[1] But there may be an older derivation from a cognate Sanskrit verb, which would be interesting given the bird's own origins as the Asian red junglefowl *Gallus gallus*.

that he will get his come-uppance later in the trilogy.[1] Pliny contrasts the behaviour of victors and vanquished in their contests:

> They acquire this domination by duelling with each other, as if knowing that the weapons on their legs grew for that purpose, and often the fights end with them both dying together. But if they win the palm they at once crow in victory and proclaim themselves champions, while the defeated bird hides away in silence and has to suffer the pains of submission. Even quite ordinary cocks strut around proudly, with necks held high and combs raised, and alone among birds they cast frequent glances skywards, holding their curved tails erect. Indeed, cocks are frightening even to lions, the noblest of all wild animals.
>
> Pliny, *Natural History* x 47

Aristophanes describes a defeated cock as 'a slave bird' (*Birds* 69–70), and Aelian elaborates the contrast:

> A cock that has been worsted in battle with another will not crow, for his spirits are cast down and he hides himself in shame. But if he is the winner he exults and holds his head high and seems very pleased with himself.
>
> Aelian, *On Animals* iv 29

Pliny goes on to explain that this natural tendency to aggression is exploited for human entertainment:

> Some cocks are therefore reared just for the purpose of constant wars and battles—through which they have even made famous their native homes, like Rhodes and Tanagra, while those from Melos and Chalcidice take second prize, thus demonstrating that the honour of the Roman purple[2] is awarded only to the worthiest birds.
>
> Pliny, *Natural History* x 48

Cockfights were generally associated with gambling, dicing, and other low-life activities. They came to have their own rituals and practices, which included staging the fights on special raised tables (*telia*), rubbing the birds down with garlic to

---

[1] The *Oresteia* trilogy comprises the *Agamemnon*, *The Libation Bearers*, and the *Eumenides*. In *The Libation Bearers*, Orestes, son of Agamemnon, takes his revenge on his mother, Clytemnestra, and her lover, Aegisthus, who had conspired to murder his father.

[2] Purple was worn by Roman magistrates and emperors to indicate their status. Its prestige derived partly from the expense of its production, the dye being extracted in a lengthy process from a Mediterranean sea snail, the spiny dye-murex.

3.8 Cockfight. Detail from a mosaic (perhaps first century AD) from the House of the Labyrinth, Pompeii. The incredible detail derives from the tiny size of the individual *tesserae* (tiles) used by the craftsman, some just a few millimetres square. The wand of Mercury on the table behind suggests some religious significance.

energize them, and accoutring them with spurs.* But from an early stage they also had some public, symbolic status. The cockerel was known as the 'Persian bird', having probably reached Greece from Persia in the seventh century BC (see pp. 36–38). And it was to celebrate the Greek victory over the Persians in 480–479 BC that Themistocles, the Athenian general who was one of the heroes of those wars, is reported to have founded an annual cockfight in Athens:

> After their victory over the Persians the Athenians passed a law that there should be a public cockfight in the theatre on one day each year. I will explain the origins of this law. While Themistocles was leading his military force against the barbarians[1] he saw some cocks fighting. He did not waste this observation, but made a point of halting the troops and addressing them as follows: 'These birds are not fighting for their country or for the gods of their fatherland; nor are they enduring this pain and suffering to defend the tombs of their ancestors or for their honour, their freedom, and their children; but each just wants to avoid defeat and not yield to the other.' These words gave heart to the Athenians, so he wanted to retain that symbol of courage as a reminder for future occasions.
>
> Aelian, *Miscellany* II 27

---

[1] The usual dysphemism for 'Persians'.

In what is probably the first reference to cockfighting in European literature, Aeschylus had made some metaphorical use of the same idea in his *Eumenides*, the third play in the *Oresteia* trilogy, produced in 458 BC. The goddess Athena is urging the chorus of Furies not to incite her people to civil war instead of facing the external enemy:

> So do you not cast into this country of mine
> whetstones for bloodshed, damaging to the hearts
> of the young, maddening them with a fury not of wine;
> and do not pluck the hearts out of fighting cocks,
> and implant them, as it were, in my people to incite them
> to internecine war and reckless deeds against each other.
> Let their war be against the enemy without, enough to satisfy
> whoever has in him a fierce passion for glory.
> But I will have nothing of birds battling within the home.
>   Aeschylus, *Eumenides* 858–67

And there is a direct reference to the effect fighting cocks can have on human behaviour in a fictional debate on sport by the much later satirist Lucian. In this skit Solon, the Athenian lawgiver, is defending his city's customs against a teasing Scythian, Anacharsis, who enquires why the Athenians do not employ actual physical combat instead of gymnastic exercises to train men for war:

> I wonder how you would feel if you saw our quail and cock fights and the great excitement they generate. You would laugh, no doubt, especially when you were told that they are required by law, and that all the young men of military age must attend and watch how the birds spar with each other until they are utterly exhausted. But this is no laughing matter; a spirit of resistance to danger is thus instilled into the men's souls, lest they appear less noble and courageous than cockerels and give in to wounds or weariness or adversity before they need. But as for testing our men in armed combat and watching while they butcher each other—get away with you.
>   Lucian, *Anacharsis* 37

Solon's opening remark here reminds us that there were also staged fights between other game birds, in particular partridges and quail,* and these provided more opportunities for moralizing and anthropomorphizing:

> Partridges are the most lascivious of birds, which is why they love the female birds with such passion and are constantly overcome by lust. So those who rear

partridges as prizefighters, when they are psyching them up to fight with each other, always make the females stand by their mates, since they have found this device to be an effective counter to any cowardice or reluctance for the contest. For the defeated partridge cannot possibly bear to show itself to either its loved one or spouse. He would rather die from the blows than flinch from his adversary and in his shame catch the eye of the female whose good opinion he desires.

Aelian, *On Animals* IV 1

There was also the bizarre sport of *ortygokopia*, 'quail-tapping', where one contestant's quail was placed on a board and the other contestant, the 'tapper', would prod it and tap its head; if the quail stood its ground the owner had won his bet, but if it ran away he lost it to the tapper. Aristophanes says that the nickname 'quail' was given to a man who always looked rather dazed, as though he had been hit on the head too hard by a heavy-handed tapper (*Birds* 1298–99); and excessive attachment to this pursuit was a recognized addiction known as *ortygomania*, 'quail madness', which the philosopher Chrysippus put on a par with *gynaikomania*, 'being crazy about women' (Athenaeus 464d). Marcus Aurelius even thought it worth warning against the malady in his book of philosophical reflections:

Don't waste time on nonsense. Don't be duped by miracle-mongers and sorcerers with their talk of incantations and exorcism and all the rest of it. Don't get obsessed with keeping quails or other crazes like that.

Marcus Aurelius, *Meditations* 1 6

The charismatic Athenian statesman Alcibiades, may have had a touch of this complaint. At any rate he was so attached to his pet quail that he would carry it around with him under his cloak and it was a 'wardrobe malfunction' involving the quail that gave him his entrée into politics as a young man:

They say that his first introduction to public life came about quite accidentally over a subscription of money to the state. Passing by the assembly one day he heard the Athenians applauding and asked what the reason was for the commotion. On being told that public subscriptions were being received he went up on the platform and made a donation himself. The crowd clapped and applauded enthusiastically—at which point he forgot about the quail he was holding inside his cloak. The bird took fright and flew off, whereupon the Athenians shouted all the louder and many of them leapt up to help him recapture the bird.

Plutarch, *Life of Alcibiades* 10

The Romans generally got their *sensations fortes* involving wildlife from the gruesome events at the Circus, in particular from the gladiatorial combats between men and animals called *venationes* ('hunts'), which were staged at Rome from 186 BC onwards. In these bloody contests professional fighters (the *bestiarii*) or sometimes disposable criminals (like Christian martyrs) were matched against large exotic beasts such as lions, bears, elephants, crocodiles, and hippopotami, to kill or be killed. Or sometimes one animal was pitted against another in an equally unnatural contest.

The scale of the slaughter was immense. The historian Cassius Dio documents the statistics in great detail: for example, in 2 BC 260 lions were killed in the Circus Maximus and 36 crocodiles in the Circus Flaminius; 400 bears and 300 lions were dispatched by Nero's bodyguard in AD 55; and then in a spectacle to mark the inauguration of Titus in AD 80, we hear of staged fights between both elephants and cranes (difficult to choreograph?) and the slaughter of some 9,000 animals.[1] But even that figure was outdone by Trajan's holocaust of 11,000 beasts to celebrate his Dacian triumphs in the early second century AD.

Ostriches were sometimes included in these events, as the only bird large and exotic enough to be worth exhibiting. They have already featured in the exploits of Commodus (see p. 157), who of all the bloodthirsty emperors took the palm for his personal feats of barbarity and expertise, on one occasion dispatching 100 lions that had been simultaneously released from subterranean traps with exactly 100 separate spears.[2]

The last emperor whose beast shows are recorded in literary sources was Probus (AD 232–82). The *venatio* to celebrate his triumph of 281 was an especially elaborate one. The Circus Maximus had been planted with uprooted trees to imitate a natural setting and he exhibited there a decidedly unnatural assemblage of some 1,000 ostriches, 1,000 stags, 1,000 boars, and various ibexes, sheep, and other gramnivores (*herbatica animalia*). The public was then admitted to the area and encouraged to help itself to the animals. On another occasion he put on a display of 100 Libyan and 100 Syrian leopards, 100 lionesses, and 300 bears, but the public apparently found this an anti-climax or were by then sated:

---

[1] This particular event had the further exotic touch of involving women in the slaughter ('but not any prominent ones', Cassius Dio LXVI 25.1).

[2] He apparently did this from a safe walkway and Herodian describes the feat as 'a better demonstration of accuracy than of courage' (1 15).*

It was agreed that all these wild beasts provided a spectacle more extensive than
it was pleasurable.

Historia Augusta, 'Probus' xix 7

3.9 Ostriches bound for Rome. Captured ostriches being loaded on to a transport ship
for a Roman circus. Detail from the mosaic of the 'Great Hunt' (early fourth century AD)
in the Villa Romana del Casale near Piazza Armerina in central Sicily.

The cruelties of the cockfight and the Circus still have their counterparts in
some countries in the world today. They have also had their parallels in the relatively recent histories of societies that would now find such things offensive and
immoral.[1] As we shall see in the next chapter, even in the ancient world some

---

[1] Cockfighting was finally made illegal in Britain in 1849, along with other proletarian 'cruel sports'
like bear-baiting and cock-throwing, though, as has often been noted, the gentlemen's sports of fox-
hunting, fishing, and shooting survived.*

voices were raised to protest against such things, in the context of exploring the similarities between human and animal capacities. But we should conclude this one by reflecting again not only how birds provided entertainment through sport, whether as partners or victims, but how in so doing they also provided symbols, metaphors, and moral exemplars for human behaviour.

In his classic essay 'Deep play: notes on the Balinese cockfight', the American anthropologist Clifford Geertz showed how the cockfight expresses and enacts some key features of Balinese social and political life. He remarks in his introduction:

> Bali, mainly because it is Bali, is a well-studied place. Its mythology, art, ritual, social organization, patterns of child rearing, forms of law, even styles of trance, have all been microscopically examined for traces of that elusive substance…the Balinese temper. But aside from a few passing remarks, the cockfight has barely been noticed, although as a popular obsession of consuming power it is at least as important a revelation of what being a Balinese 'is really like' as these more celebrated phenomena. As much of America surfaces in a ball park, on a golf links, at a race track, or around a poker table, much of Bali surfaces in a cock ring. For it is only apparently cocks that are fighting there. Actually, it is men.*

We should be alert to similar possibilities in understanding ancient cultures. If 'every people loves its own form of violence', as Geertz goes on to say, then some of the more violent forms of sport in the ancient world must presumably tell a story about the violence the perpetrators perceived and experienced both in nature and in human society; and the latter will be a story largely about male aggression, ambition, suffering, sacrifice, and above all competitiveness. The root of the Greek word for 'athletics' denotes variously 'struggle', 'contest for a prize', and 'misery'. The Romans took over or adapted much of this Greek vocabulary and many of their traditions in athletics, though they developed a particular taste also for the lavish spectacles of the Circus, which indulged much the same instincts on a grosser scale.

Another Greek word for a competition was *agon*, from which we get the words 'agonistic', 'antagonist', and indeed 'agony'. Sports were almost all direct competitions between two individuals and there was relatively little interest in cooperative team sports or in setting measurable records of the kind we are so concerned with today. But sport as a proof of excellence and a source of honour mattered very deeply. Indeed, the English word 'sport', with its connotations of a leisure diversion, is anachronistic in this sense and has no exact counterpart in

Greek. Poets in Greece were commissioned to write 'epinicean odes', that is 'victory songs', celebrating each of the winners in the great panhellenic festivals at Olympia and elsewhere. The greatest exponent of this genre was Pindar and we have forty-five of his victory odes extant, collected in four books. These are lyrical poems of great richness and complexity, weaving a narrative from strands of mythology, religion, and history to issue in moral precepts about the virtues and rewards of physical endeavour. Here are two typical endings:

> Success is the first prize in these competitions
> and honour among men the second reward,
> but the one who finds and grasps both—
> that man has gained the highest crown.
>
> Pindar, *Pythian Odes* 1.98–100

> Creatures of a day.
> What is a man, what is he not?
> He is the dream of a shadow.
> But when there comes to men
> a god-given gleam of splendour,
> there rests on them a radiant light,
> and life is sweet.
>
> Pindar, *Pythian Odes* 8.95–97

The games themselves and the victories of individual athletes were dedicated to the gods, so the 'agonies' of endurance and suffering can be seen as a kind of personal sacrifice in their honour. It is hard to imagine a more serious endorsement of the social standing and symbolic importance of competitive sport. What poet laureate today might be asked to eulogize our current sporting heroes in such terms?

Even the official chronology reflected the same preoccupations, since dates were always calculated by Olympiad, starting with the first Olympiad of 776 BC, which therefore effectively marked the start of recorded history for the Greeks. The Olympics were celebrated every four years thereafter, until they were finally banned as dangerous pagan rituals by the Christian emperor Theodosius in AD 393.

The notion of the *agon*, 'competition', thus permeated all Greek society. The word originally meant a 'gathering' and most gatherings had a competitive aspect to them.[1] The idea of an adversarial *agon* was crucial not only in sport but also

---

[1] The English word 'competition' is similarly derived from the Latin *competo* (a 'seeking together').

more generally in law, political debate, education, philosophical enquiry, even in medical practice, and perhaps in science; and there were institutionalized contests in music, drama, dance, and poetry recitations, as well as in athletics and equestrian events.*

The ultimate arena of competition was of course warfare itself, for which hunting and athletics were seen as manly tests and preparations, and the vocabularies of war and sport, then as now, provided each other with many easy metaphors. In both realms we regularly hear talk of attack and defence, tactics and strategies, victory and defeat, conquest and submission.* In his travel guide to the monuments of Greece, Pausanias even gives us a visual metaphor for this (*Description of Greece* v 20.3). He tells us that on the grand table made of ivory and gold at Olympia, where the winners' wreaths were set out, there are the twin statues of Ares, god of war, and Agon, personifying Contest.

Is there a clue here to the puzzle with which we began this chapter? Could these deep-seated instincts have been projected onto and expressed through birds that seemed to exhibit similar behaviour? Falconry and the cockfight were both foreign imports, but the latter seems to have tapped directly into something in traditional classical culture that the former did not. The falconer would maintain his birds in special quarters, train them in privacy, instil the necessary disciplines over a long period, and exercise his skills at long range and by remote control, as it were. Cockerels, on the other hand, inhabited the same communal spaces as humans, were part of the round of daily life, and openly revealed familiar kinds of attachments and rivalries. They displayed, competed, and when necessary fought with their fellows; in the extreme circumstances of the cockfight they would even kill them. Did the public intimacy and intensity of the cockpit in this way replicate the *agon* between two competing males or states?

These are only tentative suggestions. None of these sports involving birds was a defining feature of the Greek or Roman culture in the way Geertz tells us the cockfight is in Bali. Perhaps the surprise is rather that these foreign practices took root at all, since nations are often quite specialized and conservative in their sporting traditions. What is more relevant here, though, is that birds should feature somewhere in all this, symbolizing through their behaviour towards each other some of the traits we recognize in ourselves.

10

Relationships
and Responsibilities

Here is a 'Just So' story from Aesop's treasury of fables:

> When mistletoe first appeared as a plant, the swallow foresaw the danger it pre-
> sented to birds and, calling them all together, she strongly advised them to destroy
> the oak trees on which it grew; and if they couldn't manage that, she said, they
> should throw themselves on the mercy of mankind and beg them not to use the
> power of mistletoe juice to ensnare them.[1] The other birds ridiculed the swallow
> for talking such empty nonsense, so she went off herself to seek refuge with man-
> kind as a suppliant. They welcomed her, impressed by her prudence, and took her
> to live among them. So, while other species of birds are trapped and eaten by men,
> the swallow alone is regarded as having won sanctuary with them and makes her
> nest without fear, even in their houses.
>
> Aesop, *Fables* 39 (Perry)*

Birds could be pets and playthings, as chapter 8 illustrated, but they could
also be dependants, allies, or agents in various kinds of symbiotic relationship
with their human hosts and neighbours. Ecology is the study of the interactions
between organisms and their environment, and the term is derived from the
Greek word *oikos*, meaning 'home'. The same word gives us 'economics' ('household management'), which happily suggests—at a deep etymological level at any
rate—that the management of the economy should be connected to our stew-

---

[1] Bird-lime was made from mistletoe juice (see p. 74 n.1).

3.10 Aesop in conversation with a fox. Aesop created some 200 fables which had animals behaving and speaking like humans. He was traditionally portrayed as a cripple, and this man with a hypertrophied head is usually taken to be a caricature of Aesop, with the comic twist that the fox (one of Aesop's favourite characters) is here the one addressing the famous storyteller. Interior of an Attic red-figure cup, *c.*470 BC.

ardship of the planet. Birds have always been a familiar physical presence in our everyday lives and have often literally shared house and home with us too, especially in the ancient world where dwellings were usually simpler, towns and cities much smaller, and the economy more agrarian. And this sharing of spaces naturally led to other kinds of interactions, some beneficial and some harmful to one or other partner, which in turn led to various accommodations and relationships of a more collaborative kind. The idea of 'sanctuary' in the Aesop fable quoted above suggests a right as well as a relationship and we shall come back to ancient attitudes to what we now call 'animal rights' at the end of this chapter, after we have explored some less loaded kinds of relationship.

The familiar birds of town and country would have included many species common in the same habitats today, though several would not have been clearly distinguished by the ordinary person (any more than they are now). Aesop's swallow may well have been a house martin, for example, since both species nest in buildings and the same words—*chelidon* (in Greek) and *hirundo*

3.11 Swallow and sparrow. Detail from a wall-painting in a Roman villa near Naples, c.30 BC. Both species had long been regarded as domestic and temple familiars (sometimes mentioned together, see Psalm 84:3), though curiously the sparrow is rarely pictured in classical art, perhaps partly because the words for 'sparrow' (Greek *strouthos*, Latin *passer*) were also used as generic terms for any small bird.

(in Latin)—were used indiscriminately for all the hirundines (five kinds occur in the region –see 4.8). There are many references in ancient literature to the generic 'swallow' building its own little mud houses under the roofs of human dwellings.[1]

But there would also have been some differences between the distributions of species now and then. The 'crows' we hear about would have been hooded crows, jackdaws, or ravens, but would probably not have included the magpie or the rook;[2] and whereas the raven, after centuries of persecution, is now a rarity in most European towns, or at best a wary visitor, Aristotle grouped it with the crow as a regular city-dweller:

> As for the birds that are accustomed to live mainly in cities, the raven and the crow, these are always easy to see and they do not change their habitats seasonally or hide themselves away.
>
> Aristotle, *History of Animals* 617b12–15

[1] It is a minor curiosity that while we have many excellent visual representations of the barn swallow in ancient art we seem to have none of the house martin. Perhaps martins, which generally feed in a higher stratum of the air, were less closely observed.*

[2] See p. 98 and pp. 29–30.

Sparrows, starlings, and pigeons were all common too, along with various small *spiza* ('chirpers') that would have included finches, buntings, and other unidentified 'little brown jobs', as birders call them. But not all of these would have impinged on people to the same extent. One can derive a very rough list of the species that were prominent in the popular mind, or were at least well enough recognized and 'characterful' enough to lend themselves to literary purposes, from two authors who drew very heavily on everyday beliefs and experiences for their effects: Aesop the storyteller and Aristophanes the comic dramatist.*

The following birds appear among the principal subjects of Aesop fables:

Crow 22 times
Eagle 20
Cock / hen (chicken) 19
Pigeon / dove 11
Stork 9
Jackdaw 8
Swallow, nightingale, crane 7
Kite 6
Partridge, hawk, peacock 5
Goose, owl, lark 4
Heron, swan 3
Raven, gull, cuckoo 2
Wren, buzzard, vulture, kingfisher, ostrich, thrush 1

And the following appear more than once in the plays of Aristophanes:[1]

Cock / hen 22 times
Eagle 16
Swallow 14
Jackdaw, thrush 13
Crow, pigeon 11
Raven 10
Owl 9

---

[1] If you include all the single mentions, the total species count in Aristophanes is about seventy-five—see appendix, pp. 363–67.

Duck, goose, hawk, kite 6

Kestrel, dove, francolin 5

Blackbird, peacock, gallinule, stork, swan, kingfisher 4

Crane, cuckoo, coot, ostrich, partridge, quail, sparrow, woodpecker, vulture 3

Lark, nightingale, wren, gull, buzzard, corncrake, little grebe, heron, jay,
   warbler, stone curlew 2

It is hard to put together comparable figures from Roman literature. The more domestic 'comedies of manners' of Plautus and Terence have few references to birds. There are somewhat more in the satirical epigrams of Martial, but mainly in connection with birds for the table (see chapters 5 and 6), while most of those mentioned in the stories in Ovid's *Metamorphoses* occur in mythological contexts (and are therefore a better source for chapter 15 than for this one). The only references to birds in everyday Roman life on anything like the scale we have in Aristophanes and Aesop are in fact the *visual* representations that have been preserved from the Vesuvian area of Campania, following the destruction of Pompeii in AD 79. Some sixty-nine species can be reliably identified from the various wall-paintings, mosaics, sculptures, inscriptions, and graffiti that survived the holocaust.* These include many species from the native avifauna that must have been familiar in towns, gardens, and public places, as well as domesticated species like the goose and dove, plus a few exotic cage and aviary birds like parrots and peacocks, and one example of what appears to be an Indian common mynah (presumably kept because of its skills as a mimic).* There is a large overlap between these Vesuvian birds and the lists from Aristophanes and Aesop. The only species that appear in the latter but not the former are (perhaps surprisingly) crane, kite, lark, gull, and buzzard, and (perhaps less surprisingly) ostrich, francolin, stone curlew, and little grebe. In turn, the Pompeii images portray about twenty-five species that don't appear in either Aesop or Aristophanes and I give all three lists for comparison, together with some further comments about translation issues, in the appendix (pp. 363–67).

These are very shaky and unscientific statistics, of course, not least because of uncertainties about some of the identifications and generic categories. And it's hard to compare evidence from literary sources with that from artistic ones. But they do have an interest in giving some idea of the species with which (or perhaps with whom, in this case) it was thought one might in principle have some sort of relationship. Aesop's stories, Aristophanes' jokes, and the wall-paintings from Pompeii would lose much of their point if their audience was not pretty well acquainted with the appearance and behaviour of these species and had some feelings and attitudes towards them.

*   *   *

The attitudes in question could be quite various, of course. Sometimes birds were just nuisances. One consequence of sharing buildings with birds is that they tend to defecate on them—or on you, as the birds threaten to do here:

> But if you don't vote for us, you'd best make yourselves metal lids
> to wear over you, like those the statues have, because if you don't,
> then next time you're wearing your best white suit,
> that's just when we'll make you pay the penalty—
> with all the birds crapping on you.
>
> Aristophanes, *Birds* 1114–17

The Greek orator Gorgias turned this habit into a clever jibe:

> Gorgias' metaphor of the swallow, which hit him with its droppings when it flew overhead, was in the best tragic style when he said, 'Shame on you, Philomela.' For it wasn't shameful for a bird to do this, but it would have been for a girl; so he got in his insult by addressing her as what she once was, not as she is now.[1]
>
> Aristotle, *Rhetoric* 1406b15–19

Birds could also be thieves. Jackdaws were notorious for their taste in gold trinkets.* And kites were always ready to snatch up an unconsidered trifle, in Sophocles as in Shakespeare:

> He screamed like a kite that has snatched up a piece of meat.
>
> Sophocles fr. 767

> My traffic is sheets; when the kite builds, look to lesser linen. My father named me Autolycus; who being, as I am, littered under Mercury, was likewise a snapper-up of unconsidered trifles.
>
> Shakespeare, *A Winter's Tale* IV.3.23–25

---

[1] Philomela in the Greek version of the myth was changed into a swallow but in the later Roman version became a nightingale. (see pp. 279 n.1 and 410).

Pliny and Aelian thought kites were more discriminating than that:

Kites are members of the same family as hawks but differ in size. It has been noted that although this species is highly rapacious and always hungry it never takes anything edible from dishes of food at funerals nor from the altar at Olympia.

Pliny, *Natural History* x 28

The kite is remorseless in its rapacity. If they are strong enough to manage the chunks of meat on sale in the market they will swoop down and carry them off. But they will not touch any of the sacrifices offered to Zeus.

Aelian, *On Animals* II 47

But common sense and the evidence from elsewhere would suggest otherwise.* Ovid, in particular, has a vivid picture of kites circling around an expected meal:

The winged god [Mercury] noticed them as they were returning,
and instead of flying straight on he wheeled round in an arc;
just as when the acrobatic kite has spied a recent sacrifice,
afraid to come down while the priests crowd round the victim,
but not venturing to go far away, he circles around
twisting his wings and hovers greedily over his intended prey.

Ovid, *Metamorphoses* II 714–19

There are also plenty of grisly references to corvids feasting on both animal and human carrion and pecking out the eyes of their live victims (usually sheep and cattle).* 'Go to the crows' was a common curse, consigning someone to such a fate, and Aeschylus gives us this terrible image of Clytemnestra after the murder of her husband, Agamemnon:

Perched over his body
like a hateful raven
she croaks her song of triumph.

Aeschylus, *Agamemnon* 1472–74

And the stricken warrior Philoctetes, marooned and defenceless on a deserted island, fears that his former prey will now become the predators:

You winged birds, my prey, you bright-eyed
beasts that roam the hillsides here,
you need not now take fright and flee my home.
I no longer hold the bow that was my strength,

but am reduced to utter misery.
Flock here without restraint,
the place now holds no fears for you,
it's time to take your due revenge and sate
your mouths at will on my mottled flesh.

Sophocles, *Philoctetes* 1146–56

But the scavenger par excellence was the vulture, and all four European species—the Egyptian, griffon, black and bearded vultures—would have been
much commoner in the Mediterranean region in the classical period than they
are now. They are certainly referred to frequently in the literature from Homer
onwards, and their feeding habits were well known.* We have this vivid description of vultures around a carcass from the late writer Dionysius. He says that
vultures are quickly attracted to carrion from great distances because of their
acute sense of smell (an explanation only recently recognized as having a scientific basis),* and he then describes their feeding behaviour:

> Vultures are the most greedy and insatiable of birds and fight with each other
> over their food. The stronger bird drives the others away, extending one wing like
> a shield, while beating the rest of the birds off with the other. When he has had
> his fill and moved away, the rest of the flock leap in together to attack the feast,
> until one of them in turn drives off the weaker again.
>
> Dionysius, *On Birds* 1 5

Vultures would have been particularly conspicuous around battlefields and had
a reputation for following armies on the march:

> The vulture is the enemy of the corpse. At any rate, it swoops on it and devours
> one as if it were a foe and keeps a close watch on anyone who is in the throes of
> death. Vultures even follow behind armies on their foreign expeditions, knowing
> prophetically that these are marching to war and that every battle furnishes
> corpses, as they have discovered by experience.
>
> Aelian, *On Animals* 11 46

In this they were in fact performing a public service of a kind—by disposing of
bodies that would otherwise putrefy and spread disease—as was traditionally
the case in countries like India too, before the near extinction of vultures there.*
This hygienic function is also recognized in the generic scientific name of the
American turkey vulture, *Cathartes*, 'the purifier'. And the absence of vultures

from the scene was certainly noted when the terrible plague of Athens struck in
430 BC:

> Despite there being many unburied bodies the birds and animals that feed on
> human flesh either kept away from the corpses or if they started eating them died
> themselves. The evidence for this is that there was a marked absence of such
> birds, which were not to be seen around the bodies or anywhere else at all.[1]
>
> Thucydides, *The War of the Peloponnesians and the Athenians* II 50

Birds had an ambivalent role, too, as regards agricultural pests. They were
themselves pests to some extent—in raiding the fields and taking the newly
sown grain. Cranes were usually identified as one of the main culprits, though
other species could become victims of the countermeasures:

> The bird-catcher set his nets out in the fields, aiming to catch cranes. But there
> was also this stork who consorted with the cranes and got himself trapped along
> with them. He begged the man to release him, saying that not only did he never
> do the farmer any harm but that he was a great benefactor to him by killing all the
> snakes and other reptiles. The bird-catcher replied, 'But even if you're not so bad
> yourself you deserve to be punished for keeping such bad company.'
>
> Aesop, *Fables* 194 (Perry)*

But as that story suggests, some species could also be employed in the cause of
pest *control*:

> There are reports that in Thessaly live snakes are born in such quantities that if
> they were not eaten up by storks the people would have to leave their homes.
> Storks are therefore highly valued and it is unlawful to kill them. If anyone does
> so it is treated as a capital offence, just like murder.
>
> [Aristotle], *Reported Marvels* 23

Pliny tells the same story (*Natural History* x 62), and according to Cicero the
ibis performed a similar function in Egypt:

> Even the Egyptians, whom we mock, deified wild animals purely on the grounds
> of the practical utility they derived from them. For example, the ibis, being a tall
> bird with straight legs and a long horny beak, destroys vast numbers of snakes;
> they thereby protect Egypt from plague, since they kill and consume the flying

---

[1] It is still not known precisely what this plague was and whether or how it might have affected the
carrion eaters.*

snakes[1] borne from the Libyan desert by the African [south-west] wind and so save them from the bites of live snakes and the stench of dead ones.

> Cicero, *On the Nature of the Gods* I 101

Birds could also help suppress plagues of insects:

> The Thessalians, Illyrians, and Lemnians regard jackdaws as benefactors and have decreed that they actually be fed at public expense, since they do away with the eggs and destroy the young of the locusts which ruin their crops. The swarms of locusts are thereby considerably reduced and the seasonal produce of these peoples remains unaffected.
>
> Aelian, *On Animals* III 12

And Aristophanes catches the ambivalent roles of birds as both pests and pest-controllers in this nice exchange in *The Birds*, where the principal characters are telling the birds to consider how much harm or good they can do humankind, depending on whether or not they are granted superior status. First the damage:

> If in their ignorance they think you are worthless nobodies
> and that the true gods are on Olympus, then a cloud of sparrows
> and seed-pickers must arise and gobble up the seed from their fields.
> ...
> And to test them further the ravens can peck out the eyes
> of their sheep and the teams of oxen that till their land.

Then the benefits:

> For a start the locusts won't strip the vine-blossoms—
> one detachment of owls and kestrels will wipe them out.[2]
> Then again, the insects and gall-wasps won't be devouring the figs—
> one flock of thrushes will make a clean sweep of those.
>
> Aristophanes, *Birds* 577–92

One other class of incidental benefits is the various uses made of birds' feathers. For example, to scare game towards the hunters:

---

[1] The identity of the flying snakes is a mystery, though they are referred to also by Herodotus (III 107–08) and Pausanias (III 108) and recall the 'fiery flying serpent' of Isaiah 30:6. 'Locusts' might have made more sense in context.* See also Strabo on the ibis as a refuse consumer, pp. 199–200 below.

[2] An accurate observation about the diet of little owls and 'kestrels' (probably lesser kestrels, hobbies, and red-footed falcons, all of which do feed extensively on flying insects).

On one side they stretch a long, well-woven
rope of flax, just above ground level
with the cord at the height of a man's waist.
From this is hung a decorated line of many-coloured
bright ribbons, to scare the wild animals,
and dangling from those they attach thousands
of bright feathers, the wings of the birds of the air—
vultures, white swans, and long-legged storks.

    Oppian, *On Hunting* IV 385–92*

3.12 Ostrich-egg cup. Drinking-cup made from an ostrich egg, cut open at the top, with a mosaic band added at the rim and the base. Ostriches were common in the Near East in classical times, but the Arabian subspecies *Struthio camelus syriacus* was hunted out in the nineteenth century (see p. 87). This cup was discovered by Sir Leonard Woolley in a grave at the Royal Cemetery at Ur in Iraq and is dated to *c*.2600 BC.

or as a military crest:

The ostriches' eggs are extraordinary for their size and are used by some people as dishes, while their feathers adorn the crests and helmets of warriors.

    Pliny, *Natural History* X 2

or for those soldiers more concerned with home comforts:

> The demand for luxury has advanced to such a point that even the men insist on
> having goose-feather bedding under their necks.
>
> Pliny, *Natural History* x 54

or as a present of a toothpick:

> This pointed wing feather of a hook-billed eagle,
> carved with a knife and dyed with purple lacquer,
> adept at shifting with its gentle pick any morsels
> that remain hidden in the teeth after dinner—
> this small token of no small affection
> Crinagoras, your devoted friend, presents
> to you, Lucius, as a little souvenir of our feast.
>
> Crinagoras, *Greek Anthology* vi 229

or a fly-swat from a peacock's plume:

> This, which keeps the nasty flies from nibbling your lunch
> was once the proud tail of a noble bird.
>
> Martial, *Epigrams* xiv 67

or the luxury fan your demanding girlfriend wants:

> …[Now she's even asking me]
> for a fan, made from a proud peacock's tail.
>
> Propertius, *Elegies* ii 23.11

or for arrow-flights, though these could then be turned against their suppliers:

> An eagle was sitting on a high rock, keeping watch for hares to hunt. But a
> man took aim at the eagle and let fly an arrow, which hit him and stuck in his
> body. The eagle turned to look at the shaft of the arrow which was tipped with
> feathers and said: 'This is all the more painful because I'm being killed by my
> own feathers.'
>
> Aesop, *Fables* 276 (Perry)*

These examples of the utility of birds have so far all been cases where human beings have simply taken advantage of the birds' natural behaviour (and body parts); but there are also cases of closer forms of collaboration where birds are more deliberately employed to serve human purposes by doing things they are better at than we are. Geese, for example, offer a 24/7 security alarm and famously saved Rome in 390 BC from a commando raid on the citadel by Gauls:

> The Gauls ascended the cliffs so quietly that the sentries were quite unaware of them and even the dogs—which are so easily awakened by noises in the night—were not aroused. But they couldn't elude the attention of the geese—Juno's sacred geese, which despite the dearth of provisions had been spared. The geese were their salvation, for with their loud honking and the clatter of their wings they woke up Marcus Manlius, the distinguished soldier and consul of three years before [who then saved the situation] …
>
> Livy, *History of Rome* v 47

Birds also made good messengers. Pigeons and doves were the most usual carriers. 'Send off the pigeon with the news,' says a character in Pherecrates' comedy *Old Women*.* There were already good mythological precedents for this. In the ancient Greek version of the Great Flood story, Deucalion (like Noah) relied on a dove to tell him when the waters had subsided, and a dove guides Jason and the Argonauts through the dangerous passage of the Bosporus (see p. 326). But the earliest historical mention of a carrier pigeon is of one supposedly used in 444 BC to announce the Olympic victory of a wrestler to his home supporters:

> Some say that the victory of Taurosthenes at Olympia was announced the same day to his father in Aegina in a vision. But others say that Taurosthenes took with him a pigeon that left behind its nestlings still moist and featherless. And when he won he attached a piece of purple cloth to the bird and then released it. In its haste to return to its chicks, the pigeon got back to Aegina from Pisa the same day.[1]
>
> Aelian, *Miscellany* ix 2

Pigeon-fancying was clearly a popular hobby, especially at Rome, but it had its more serious military applications too.* Frontinus, the author of a textbook on military tactics, tells the story of how the consul Hirtius communicated by pigeon post with Decimus Brutus when the latter was being besieged at Mutina (Modena) by Mark Antony in 44–43 BC:

> Hirtius kept the pigeons shut up in the dark and starved them. Then he fastened letters to their necks by a hair and released them as near to the city walls as he could. The birds were desperate for both light and food, made for the highest buildings and were caught by Brutus, who by these means was kept fully informed

---

[1] Pisa was a town in the Peloponnese whose territory included Olympia. The distance from there to Aegina is about 100 miles, which might have taken a homing pigeon (a domesticated rock pigeon, *Columba livia*) just over two hours at their average flying speed of 50 m.p.h.

of everything, especially after he had deposited food in certain places and taught the pigeons to alight there.

Frontinus, *Strategems* III 13.8

Pliny tells the same story from Brutus's point of view (*Natural History* x 110). He also retails further anecdotes about swallows conveying sporting victories and military intelligence:[1]

> Caecina, a knight from Volterra who owned a four-horse racing chariot, used to catch swallows and take them with him to Rome; he would then dispatch them to take news of a win to his friends—when the birds returned to their nests with the winning colours painted on them. And Fabius Pictor records in his history that when a Roman garrison was being besieged by the Ligurians a swallow was taken away from her nestlings so that he could send a signal by means of knots on a thread tied to her foot, indicating how many days later reinforcements would arrive and when a break-out should be attempted.
>
> Pliny, *Natural History* x 71

Finally in this series of reports of birds as messengers, but now more in the realm of anecdote than reportage, a story about a remarkable crow:

> There was an extraordinary crow which belonged to the King of Egypt (the one called Mares) and was very tame. Any letters the king wanted to have delivered anywhere the crow would carry them there promptly. He was the speediest of messengers, and having listened to his instructions he knew where he had to direct his flight, which places he must pass by, and where to stop on arrival. In return for these services Mares honoured the bird on its death with a monument and a tomb.
>
> Aelian, *On Animals* VI 7

We are now well into the spectrum of relationships where birds can be thought of not only as the agents of humankind but also as their allies and friends. This was recognized metaphorically in the various pet names taken from birds and applied to loved ones. Two examples from comedy, one Greek and one Roman:

---

[1] Homing pigeons were regularly used to convey military intelligence in the twentieth century, too, and thirty-two pigeons were awarded the Dickin medal (the animals' Victoria Cross for 'conspicuous gallantry and devotion to duty') for service in the Second World War (as were eighteen dogs, three horses, and a cat).

OLD WOMAN Yes, my goodness, when he saw how depressed I was
he started calling me his ducky and dovey as nicknames.

Aristophanes, *Wealth* 1010–11

LEONIDA So, why don't you call me your little sparrow, hen, or quail,
or say that I'm your lambkin, kid, or little calf;

Plautus, *The Comedy of Asses* 666–67

The reverse process also occurred, particularly in relation to domestic pets. We
have records of fighting cocks being given names like Aeacus and Centaur, after
these virile mythical figures, and many of named dogs, though they are in this
case usually called after qualities (like Poleus, 'Rover') rather than people.[1]

There are also many sentimental stories of devoted pets who become attached
to, or even imprint on, their human owners and whose affections were sometimes returned. Aelian in particular relishes these sorts of anecdotes:*

Phylarchus records that a boy who was deeply attached to birds was given as a
present an eagle nestling, which he fed on a variety of foods and looked after with
every care. He reared the bird not as a pet to play with but more as a best friend or
younger brother, so concerned was the boy for the eagle's welfare. As time passed
there developed a strong mutual bond of affection between them. At some point
the boy fell ill, and the eagle remained by him and tended his former keeper: when
the boy slept the bird stayed quietly by; when he woke it was there at his side; if he
took no food it fasted too. And when the boy eventually died, the eagle accompanied
him to the tomb and as his body was burned it threw itself on the pyre.

Aelian, *On Animals* VI 29

The goose owned by Lacydes the Peripatetic philosopher[2] was an amazing creature. At any rate it was deeply devoted to its keeper—when he went for a walk the
goose walked with him, when he sat down it stopped too, and it wouldn't leave his
side for a moment. When the bird eventually died, Lacydes buried it with full
honours, as if he was burying a son or brother.

Aelian, *On Animals* VII 41

Pliny refers to some of the same anecdotes but has an interesting twist in his
tentative 'explanation':

---

[1] Xenophon is the best source, listing forty-seven different names for dogs in his treatise *On Hunting*
(7.5); interestingly, all of them have two syllables—to make it easier to call them. There are also lots of
horse names, but there seems to have been no tradition of naming cats in either Greece or Rome.*

[2] The Peripatetics were a school of philosophers active from *c.*300 BC to *c.*AD 200 in the tradition of
Aristotle, and were so named because Aristotle was said to have 'walked about' while lecturing.

There is also a story of a goose at Aegium that fell in love with the beautiful boy
Amphilochus of Olenus, and of the one that loved Glauce, the girl who played the
harp for King Ptolemy (and whom a ram was supposed to have fallen in love with
at the same time). Perhaps these birds could be thought to have some understanding of wisdom—for example, there is the story of the goose that attached
itself as the constant companion of the philosopher Lacydes, never separating
from him either in public or at the baths, and either by night or day.

Pliny, *Natural History* x 51

The interesting phrase of Pliny's here is *intellectus sapientiae*, which I have translated as an 'understanding of wisdom'. When philosophers like Aristotle were
debating the essential differences between human and animal species, a lot of the
debate turned on whether animals (including birds) could be said to have the
faculty called in Greek *logos* (in Latin *ratio*), which can be roughly translated as
'reason'. Most thought not, and they were followed in this by a long scientific
tradition that tended to downplay the idea of animal cognitive capacities; indeed,
the attribute of 'reason' or 'wisdom' came to be incorporated as the distinguishing
feature in the scientific name of our own species, *Homo sapiens*. But there were
dissenting voices, even in the ancient world, arguing that animals too have powers
of perception and memory, can experience emotions, and can often deploy real (if
limited) skills of inference and speech. So why deny them reason?*

We have in a sense already been primed for this by the references to mimicry
in chapter 8 (see pp. 143–49), but those were references to birds *imitating* human
speech without any comprehension of it. Indeed, the stories about the raven
who hailed 'Antony' when he should have said 'Augustus' and the scheme of
Hanno to release wild birds saying 'Hanno is a god' depend very much for their
humour on the birds' *lack* of comprehension of the human contexts involved.
But the philosopher Porphyry takes this a stage further. He suggests that hunters, herdsmen, and others who interact closely with animals must be able to
communicate with them to some degree, since they can understand some at
least of the animals' calls and can in turn give instructions that are compre-
hended and acted on. Owners of pets have the same experience, of course. More
controversially, however, Porphyry suggests that animals can on occasion adjust
their own vocalizations to communicate specifically with human beings, as in
the case of his pet partridge:[1]

---

[1] Presumably a rock partridge (*Alectoris graeca*), which is the common partridge of mainland Greece.
The chukar (*Alectoris chukar*) is the commoner bird in the Aegean islands and Turkey and is visually very
similar, but Aristotle and others were aware of the difference in their calls.*

I myself reared at Carthage a tame partridge, which would fly to me. As time passed and familiarity of habit made it very tame, I observed it not only making up to me and being attentive and playful, but even responding to our speech and, as far as it could, answering us, and doing so differently from the way that partridges call to each other. It did not speak when I was silent, but responded only when I spoke.

Porphyry, *On Abstinence* III 4

3.13 Partridges. Detail from the colourful frescoes in the Palace of Minos at Knossos, 1500–1100 BC, which have been heavily restored and reconstructed. These images resemble the red-legged partridge (*Alectoris rufa*) of Britain and western Europe, but are more likely to have been the chukar *Alectoris chukar* of the islands and the Near East, or possibly the rock partridge *Alectoris graeca* of mainland Greece.

Modern ethologists like Konrad Lorenz have made similar claims—in his case for ravens, and corvids would seem stronger candidates than partridges for such vocal behaviour, though partridges were common pets in the ancient world and were sometimes described as 'musical'.* We shall be looking more closely at reports of avian 'intelligence' in the next chapter; the relevance here is that this would represent one more step up the ladder of potential relationships between birds and people. Birds have moved in the course of this narrative from being objects of curiosity in aviaries and zoos, to participants (however unwillingly) in human entertainments, to domesticated pets and playthings in the home, and then to creatures with whom we might have mutual feelings of affection and with which we can communicate to some degree. Is there a further stage in this process in which one could claim some deeper form of kinship and hence some moral relationship involving rights and responsibilities?

There can be no doubt that despite many of the barbarities in the treatment of animals in the ancient world people could on occasion still feel a genuine compunction for their sufferings, amounting to sympathy for a fellow creature.

Pliny tells the story of some elephants under attack from gladiators in a circus sponsored by Pompey:

> But Pompey's elephants, when they had lost all hope of escape, supplicated the crowd to show them pity, entreating them with indescribable gestures and bewailing their fate with cries of agony. They created such distress in the watching public that they forgot the general and his acts of munificence so exquisitely designed in their honour, and in floods of tears rose as one and called down curses on the head of Pompey, for which he soon afterwards paid the penalty.
>
> Pliny, *Natural History* VIII 21

Cicero refers to the same incident in a letter to one of his friends (see p. 127) and explains that the public felt a sudden affinity or sense of fellowship (*societas*) with the animals. Oppian gives the further example of dolphins, which he says it is immoral or abominable to hunt—*apotropos* is his word ('to be shunned')—because they are 'like-minded' with men (*On Fishing* v 416–23, 519–20).

*   *   *

That brings this chapter full circle. We began with a parable from Aesop, suggesting that birds might enter into some kind of relationship of trust with humans, and so receive rights of refuge. It was just a fable, of course—in this case an aetiological one, explaining why swallows come to nest in and around our own homes. Aesop has another fable about refuge that represents a further stage in the progression of the claims a swallow might make on us. In this one the swallow is in public buildings not a private home, and she seems to be actually more concerned about the loss of her rights of refuge than she is about the loss of her children:

> The twittering swallow—which shares a home with men—
> built her nest in spring in the wall of the house
> where the senior arbiters of the law sit.
> In that court the mother gave birth to seven fledglings,
> not yet adorned with purple feathers.
> But then a snake came creeping from his hole
> and devoured them all one by one. The poor mother
> bewailed the untimely fate of her baby birds
> and said, 'Alas, for my unfortunate lot in life,

this is where humanity's laws and judgments are made,
but I, a swallow, have been wronged and must flee.'
  Aesop, *Fables* 227 (Perry)

The line of thought I have been tracing in this chapter is not a chronological one, though it takes us right back to the first reference to relationships between birds and people in European literature—Homer's account of Penelope and her beloved geese (see pp. 111–12). Nor is it a rigorously logical one either, in which each stage formally implies the next. But the progression is a humanly intelligible one, I think. Experiences lead to interactions, which lead to attitudes, and then to relationships, and finally to responsibilities. What this amounts to in the end is a more complex and interconnected universe of living creatures, and the exploration of that in the ancient world—the beginnings of zoology and ornithology—is the theme of the next part.

PART 4

Invention
and Discovery

It was from a sense of wonder that men were first inspired to seek knowledge, as they still are today. They initially wondered about immediate and everyday puzzles, and then gradually progressed to larger questions, for example about the moon, sun and stars and the origin of the universe. And a person who is puzzled and in a state of wonder realizes that they are ignorant—therefore, even a lover of myths is in a way also a lover of knowledge, since myth is grounded in wonders. So, if it was to escape ignorance that men sought knowledge, it is obvious that they were pursuing it for its own sake and not for any reason of practical utility.

Aristotle, *Metaphysics* 982b12–22

Nullius in verba ('Take no one's word for it').

Motto of the Royal Society (founded 1660), from Horace, *Epistles* 1 1.14–15

I cannot determine what I ought to transcribe, till I am satisfied how much I ought to believe.

Gibbon, *Decline and Fall of the Roman Empire* (1776–88), ch. 16

The most important characteristic of an intelligence officer has to be intense scepticism, such that he never believes anything he reads or is told unless there is some other reason for believing it.

F. H. Hinsley, *Intelligence in the Second World War* (1993), 40

4.1 Plato's Academy. Mosaic from the villa of T. Siminius Stephanus in Pompeii, probably from the first century BC. It is usually taken to be a portrayal of the Academy that
Plato founded in Athens in the mid-380s BC. The city is pictured at the top right and
there are further possible symbolisms in the laden olive tree (sacred to Athena, goddess
of wisdom), the sundial, votive columns and theatrical masks in the lush borders, and
the globe in the foreground. Plato is thought to be the figure third from the left, sitting
under the olive and lecturing his pupils, who may include Aristotle (far left, founder of
the Lyceum in 334 BC, holding a separate conversation) and Theophrastus far right
(Aristotle's successor at the Lyceum, with a more youthful head of hair). Another interpretation is that these are the Seven Sages of antiquity (traditionally Thales, Pittacus,
Bias, Solon, Cleobulus, Myson, and Cheilon, but membership of the group was fluid
and could later have been adjusted to include Plato).

Introduction

I begin with a quotation from a modern Greek rather than an ancient one. Melina Mercouri was a famous and charismatic Greek actress, who went on to become the first female minister of culture in Greece in 1981. This was seen as a brave appointment at the time, but Mercouri made a great success of the role and gained much respect for the manner in which she represented her country. When addressing one very august international conference she began her speech (in heavily accented English) as follows: 'Forgive me if I start by saying a few words in Greek.' The delegates groaned inwardly but sat back politely in their seats. She then began, 'Democracy, politics, philosophy, logic, theory, music, drama, theatre, tragedy, comedy, athletics, history, geography, physics, mathematics, astronomy ...'. Her point, of course, was that all these English words come from Greek and refer to subjects or activities the Greeks seem to have invented or pioneered. In this sense we all speak Greek all the time. She could have gone on, '... biology, zoology, *ornithology*'. These too are all derived from Greek, the last one from *ornis* or *ornithos*, meaning 'bird', and *logos*, meaning a 'verbal account' or 'study'. So, did the modern science of ornithology also have its origins in the ancient world, and if so in what sense?

We have already seen the various ways the Greeks and Romans interacted with birds—seeing them as indicators of natural phenomena like the weather and the seasons; interpreting the sounds they made; exploiting them as a resource through hunting and farming; and engaging with them as pets, agents, and friends. They could scarcely have had such close relationships with birds without also becoming curious about what kinds there were, how they behaved, and how they differed both from one another and from other animals (including human beings). And they did indeed record observations, thoughts, and theories about all these topics, which are the subjects of the chapters in this part.

The discussion will prompt various further questions. For example, how far did the miscellany of anecdotes, folklore, and traditional beliefs that every culture accumulates about such things get converted in the classical world into the more systematic set of disciplined observations and explanations we might want to call science? 'Science', however, was not one of the words Melina Mercouri laid claim to and in fact there was no one Greek or Roman word that meant just what we mean by 'science'. Is that significant? And what can we expect to learn from studying the history of subjects where we have progressed rapidly from what the Greeks started and have left them far behind, as opposed to subjects like drama, art, history, and philosophy, which don't 'progress' in quite the same way?

There is certainly an abundance of ancient material to examine. As a starting point, chapter 11 looks at anecdotal evidence—like travellers' tales about the various 'wonders' they encountered on their journeys—in order to get some sense of the range of popular beliefs about birds and how they came to be formed. And wonder is in a sense the theme of this whole part, involving as it does a sense of both fascination and curiosity, which motivated many of these enquiries. Chapter 12 considers the case of medicine, where birds crop up in medical tracts with such modern-sounding titles as Galen's *The Thinning Diet*, as well as in traditional remedies that owe more to folklore than to science. Chapter 13 then deals with the beginnings of a more scientific approach to observation and enquiry, and with the first steps in taxonomy and ornithology, looking in particular at the towering contribution of Aristotle.

11

Wonders

History is full of little stories that are more or less apocryphal, at least in their details, but make a memorable point. We think of Alfred and his cakes—a lesson in concentrating on the main issues—or Drake playing bowls before the Spanish Armada—a model of confident composure. Science has its own mnemonic myths too, in the form of *eureka* moments that dramatize a discovery. Some of these relate to a puzzle about a familiar experience— Archimedes displacing his bathwater, Galileo dropping the unequal weights from the Tower of Pisa, or Newton watching that apple falling from a tree. But some are supposed to have been stimulated by the observation of something exotic or unusual, as with 'Darwin's finches' in the Galapagos Islands. This was at least as apocryphal a *eureka* moment as the other examples, since Darwin himself did not initially see or record the significance of the variations in the finches that were later cited in support of his theory of natural selection. Indeed, he was more struck by the mockingbirds he had collected at the same time, whose differences between the various islands in the archipelago would, he thought, 'undermine the stability of Species'. The phrase 'Darwin's finches' was first popularized by David Lack in his book of that title in 1947 and has stuck ever since.* What is striking about all such apocryphal stories is their popularity and persistence, even when we (or some people) know better.

Indeed, science can sometimes inadvertently generate its own myths. There is a celebrated case involving spinach. Generations of families from the 1930s through to the present day have believed that they should administer large quantities of spinach to their protesting children because of its iron content. The Popeye cartoons, in which the hero gets superhuman powers from eating cans of spinach, did a great deal to popularize this belief and led to a massive increase in the sales of spinach. But this is a fallacy. Spinach does contain iron, but in a form that can't be readily absorbed into the intestinal system; indeed it may make it more difficult for us to absorb the iron we actually need. This scientific fact has been amply demonstrated but still no one believes it.

But there is a deeper irony in this story, too. Ever since an article about the case was published in a prestigious medical journal in 1981, it was believed that the source of the false belief about the efficacy of spinach was a misplaced decimal point in an earlier analysis, which thus exaggerated the iron content in spinach by a factor of ten. The 'discovery' of this mistake was eagerly reported many times and was even cited as a *locus classicus* of scientific myth-making in books with titles like *Follies and Fallacies in Medicine*. The reason for its popularity, of course, was (and still is) that it makes such a good story. Fancy a small typo having such huge social consequences. But it now appears that the explanation of the myth is itself a myth: the conclusion about the low nutritional value of spinach is correct, but the account of the source of the belief in a misplaced decimal point is false or at least unproven.*

The ancients had their own stories with dubious origins, which also survived because they made a memorable point that people wanted to believe. Myths and fables were of this kind, whether the 'Just So' fables of Aesop that we saw examples of in the last chapter or the even older myths involving magic and metamorphosis that we shall be looking at in chapter 15. What we are concerned with now, though, are the sorts of anecdotes, half-truths, and travellers' tales that fed into more mundane folklore and became part of a body of common beliefs that more serous investigators later drew on or reacted against. The encyclopedists Aelian and Pliny cheerfully retail many such unreliable reports as fact, and even Aristotle incorporates some of them into his more scientific analyses, though often prefacing them with a cautious 'some people have said that....'.

This kind of credulity—or at least the uncritical use of one's sources—is still common, of course. Some stories are endlessly handed down from one supposed 'source' to another, often with embellishments, as in Chinese whispers. A nice example is the account in a 1921 history of ornithology that Aelian reported kites 'snatching hair from men's heads' to line their nests. That anecdote was repeated in a famous study by David Lack in 1943, who added that it referred to an incident in London; it was then taken up in a major reference work of 2005, which two later monographs—in 2007 and 2014—cite as their authoritative source for the same story. In fact, Aelian made no such claim (he just says they snatch meat from market stalls, and of course he knew nothing of London), but the trail of misinformation continues.*

*   *   *

I start with some travellers' tales. War and trade gave the Greeks and Romans contact with many foreign places and cultures, and reports would come back of the various 'wonders' encountered, some of which got incorporated in special 'books of wonders', the genre technically known as 'paradoxography'.* These were accounts of strange sights, monsters, freaks, prodigies, and abnormal phenomena in the natural or human world, a sort of combination of the *Guinness World Records* and Sir Thomas Browne's *Pseudodoxia epidemica* (first published in 1646). There were also some great individual explorers, usually men of omnivorous curiosity, who described the peoples, customs, antiquities, natural features, and wildlife they encountered on their travels, including occasional reports of birds. I quote from three such figures in particular as sources of the kind of striking accounts of natural wonders that caught the public imagination and entered into the bloodstream of received opinion.

Herodotus was an early historian—'the father of history' according to Cicero—who set himself the task of exploring the lands around the Mediterranean, Asia Minor, and the Black Sea to help him understand the background to the great wars between the Greeks and the Persians in the early fifth century BC. Fortunately for us, he had very digressive interests, so we get fascinating, if sometimes credulous, accounts of all his findings along the way in places like Egypt, to which he devotes a whole book of his long history. He was fascinated by the crocodiles there and describes the relationship they have with some birds that seemed to be acting as their toothpicks:

> Since they live in the water the insides of their mouths are completely infested with leeches. All the other birds and animals keep their distance from the crocodile, except for the *trochilos*, which has a peaceful relationship with them because of the benefits it provides. Whenever the crocodile comes ashore out of the water and holds its jaws wide open (as it generally does to catch the west wind), the *trochilos* pops into its mouth and eats up the leeches; so the crocodile is grateful for this service and does the bird no harm.
>
> Herodotus, *Histories* II 68

The *trochilos* ('runner') here could be either the Egyptian plover (*Pluvianus aegyptius*) or the spur-winged lapwing (*Vanellus spinosus*). Other ancient writers repeat the story as fact, but none of them claims first-hand knowledge of such behaviour. In more recent times, another traveller prone to retailing questionable stories, the egregious Colonel Richard Meinertzhagen, claimed to have witnessed both species performing this service, but again there is no contemporary or subsequent supporting evidence.* In fact, a crocodile expert has cast doubt on the whole story, on the grounds that crocodile teeth are so constructed and so widely spaced that they have no need of toothpicks or any other form of dental hygiene. He thinks the story probably derives from the undoubted fact that various scavenging birds feed opportunistically around crocodiles, in the way that cattle egrets do around cattle. The crocodiles themselves gain no special benefit from this, but tolerate the birds' presence as harmless familiars that it isn't worth trying to catch. There is no real symbiosis. So, a story that has caught the imagination for over two millennia can be punctured by a few biological facts. But the story will doubtless live on…and there is even a faked image to support it.

4.2 Egyptian plover and crocodile. Faked photograph, illustrating a supposed example of the behaviour Herodotus was describing.

Then in Arabia we hear of intriguing 'cinnamon birds', which became a source of the valuable cinnamon that was otherwise very difficult for the local Arabs to find and harvest:

There are large birds that take these sticks (which we have learned from the Phoenicians to call cinnamon) and carry them off to nests of clay attached to steep mountain crags that are quite inaccessible to men. The Arabs have a clever way of overcoming this difficulty. They cut off huge chunks from the carcasses of dead oxen, asses, and other beasts of burden, take them to these places, set them near the eyries of the birds and then withdraw to a safe distance. The birds swoop down and carry the pieces of meat up to their nests; but these cannot support their weight and break up and fall to the ground. The Arabs then come to collect the cinnamon.

Herodotus, *Histories* III 111

Lots of later authors refer to these 'cinnamon birds', with minor variations in the story. They sound rather like vultures from their diet and their nesting sites, but a few authors connect them with the mythical phoenix, which was supposed to incorporate cinnamon sticks in its nest or its funeral pyre.* Herodotus, too, describes the phoenix in his section on creatures that the Egyptians hold sacred, though he is careful to disclaim any direct sightings:

There is another sacred bird called the phoenix. I have never seen one myself, except in paintings. For it is a rare visitor to Egypt, occurring just once every 500 years, according to the people of Heliopolis; and they say it makes these visits when its father dies. If the pictures are a fair representation of its size and appearance it looks like this: the plumage is partly golden but mainly scarlet, and it is most like an eagle in shape and size.

Herodotus, *Histories* II 73

Later writers elaborate on this story and give differing versions of the life, death, and cyclical resurrection of the phoenix, only one (asexual) member of which species exists at any one time. Some of the details are suitably fabulous: the ageing bird flies to Heliopolis and there bursts into flames, ignited by the sun's rays, and its successor is born from its ashes; its diet consists of the ethereal elements of sunbeams, dew, nectar, sea spray, and the winds; its song surpasses that of the nightingale; and so on.* No one has ever actually seen one, but everyone seems happy to believe in them. The only historical claim is one reported by Pliny, who simultaneously discounts it:

Cornelius Valerianus relates that a phoenix flew down into Egypt in the consulship of Quintus Plautius and Sextus Papinius [AD 36]; it was even brought into the city of Rome during the Censorship of the Emperor Claudius in AUC 800

[AD 47] and displayed in the assembly rooms. This is recorded in the official records, but no one doubts that it was a fraud.

Pliny, *Natural History* x 5

Pliny's younger contemporary, the historian Tacitus, who is usually a notably hard-nosed commentator, refers to what must be the same manifestation in Egypt (though he dates it two years earlier, to AD 34). He gives a very full, if sceptical, account of the bird's supposed characteristics, but ends by accepting its existence:

All this is full of doubt and legendary exaggeration. Still, there is no question that the bird is occasionally seen in Egypt.

Tacitus, *Annals* VI 28

It is fun to speculate about which species of bird might have inspired or been later used to sustain this myth. The following have all been suggested: flamingo (*phoinix* was the Greek for 'deep red', and *phoinikopteros*, the 'red-winged bird', was the flamingo); golden pheasant (for its Eastern origins and plumage); grey heron (for its supporting role in Egyptian religious symbolism); and lammergeier[1] (for its rusty plumage and soaring flight and the remote locations it frequents). This last was Meinertzhagen's suggestion, based on an experience in the mountains of Baluchistan which he claims to be describing in a characteristic diary note of 26 July 1914:

The finest view I ever had of a lammergeier occurred today. I came on him but a few feet away silhouetted against a gold-red sunset, magnificent against a horizon stretching for miles and miles into golden infinity. He was quite unconscious of my presence. He sat on a rocky pinnacle facing the setting sun, wings slightly drooping, and half-stretched head turned up towards heaven. Was this the phoenix of the ancients...? Was this lammergeier conscious of his sacred relationship with the sun? The phoenix of the ancients presaged peace everywhere in the land. What I saw this evening seemed to foretell war, a long bloody war. It was the finest, most beautiful and yet most terrible, the most romantic view of any bird I have seen at any time anywhere.*

But of course none of these species *was* the phoenix. The interesting question is not one of identification but one of belief: why did the myth survive and what purposes did it serve? We shall be looking more broadly at the symbolism of

---

[1] A kind of vulture, *Gypaetus barbatus*, also known as the 'bearded vulture'.

birds in chapter 16, but the obvious answer is that the phoenix reflected the human experience of natural regeneration and the never ending cycle of the year's turning, particularly evident in Egypt with the restorative flooding of the Nile each year, a topic that much interested Herodotus (II 5–34); it must also have expressed the craving for immortality that is satisfied for some by their religions. The idea of the phoenix still survives strongly, of course, and in that sense it has at least achieved its own immortality.

These three examples from Herodotus refer in turn to possible, unlikely, and impossible occurrences. The other two great travellers I shall quote in this chapter were on the whole less entertaining but also less credulous authors. Strabo produced a large-scale geography of the Roman world in seventeen volumes as a practical guide for statesmen and generals as well as various fringe readerships he mentions like hunters (*Geography* I 1.16). He too had an eye for interesting customs and natural phenomena in the many places he visited, which ranged, he said, 'from Armenia to Etruria, and from the Black Sea to the borders of Ethiopia' (II 5.11). Many of his observations can be verified today, including the meteorological remark that in Britain, 'The weather is more wet and rainy than snowy; and on clear days the mist can last so long that the sun is visible only around noon for about three or four hours of the whole day' (IV 5.2).

One avian wonder that caught his attention in Arabia was the ostrich:

> Situated above these there lives a small tribe called the *Strouthophagi*,[1] in whose area there are birds the size of deer that cannot fly but can run very fast, as ostriches do.[2] Some men hunt them with bows, while others conceal themselves inside the skins of the ostriches and insert their right hands into part of the neck; they then move it around in the same way as the live birds move their necks, while with their left hands they release a stream of seed from a pouch attached to their sides. With this bait they drive the birds into gullies where men armed with sticks jump on them and cudgel them to death. Their skins are used both for clothing and bed-covers.
>
> Strabo, *Geography* XVI II

Ostriches fascinated travellers not only because they were 'big game' that were difficult to catch and good to eat, but also because they seemed to be unclassifiable—neither quite bird nor mammal.[3] The peculiarities of the species would

---

[1] 'Eaters of ostriches'.
[2] A curious phrase, since these evidently *are* ostriches.
[3] See Aristotle's taxonomy on pp. 231–32.

have led naturally to various credulous misconceptions, and in recognition perhaps of their incongruity they came to be called *strouthokameloi* ('sparrow-camels'), the word Strabo uses here. The general Xenophon had also been struck by the sight of ostriches when he led his defeated army on their great retreat across the desert from Cunaxa near Babylon to the safety of the Greek world on the Black Sea coast, which the men famously greeted with joyous cries of 'Thalatta, thalatta' ('The sea, the sea!'):

> In this region [Arabia] the land was a continuous plain, as flat as the sea and full of wormwood. Any other plant or reed there was always fragrant, like spices. There was not a tree to be found, but there were all kinds of wild animals—huge numbers of wild asses, many ostriches, and also bustards and gazelles; and the horsemen sometimes chased these animals...But no one ever caught an ostrich; any horsemen who pursued one soon gave up the chase, for it would quickly out-distance them in its flight, not just using its feet to run but also raising its wings and employing them like a sail.
>
> Xenophon, *Anabasis* 1 5

4.3 Ostrich riders. Six youths ride ostriches towards a flute player on the right, whose presence suggests that this may be a chorus scene from an early comedy. On the other side of the vase is a corresponding picture of youths riding dolphins. Many early comedies had animal titles and themes (see p. 353). Attic black-figure vase, *c*.520–510 BC.

The later encyclopedists draw on such stories (usually without attribution) and garnish them with other anecdotal details:

> Our next subject is the nature of birds. The largest of these, which should almost be classified as an animal, is the ostrich of Africa or Ethiopia. This bird is taller than a mounted horseman and exceeds his speed too; it is provided with wings merely to assist it in running, but it is not otherwise a flying bird and does not rise above the ground. It has hooves like a deer and it uses these as weapons; they are cloven in two and are useful for grasping stones, which it throws back at its pursuers when in flight. It has a remarkable natural ability to digest whatever it has indiscriminately swallowed down, and a no less remarkable stupidity in thinking itself safely concealed when it has hidden its head and neck in some bushes, despite the great height of the rest of its body.
>
> Pliny, *Natural History* X 1–2

> The ostrich builds its nest low down on the ground, scraping away the sand with its feet. The centre of the nest is hollowed out, but it builds up a high rim all round, constructing it so that the sides keep out the rain and stop it from running into the nest and so deluging the young ostriches at a tender age. The ostrich lays over eighty eggs[1] but does not hatch them simultaneously: they do not all emerge into the light of day at the same time, but while some have already been hatched, others are still developing within the shell and others are being brooded.
>
> Aelian, *On Animals* XIV 7

This illustrates the beginnings of the process—slow, uncertain and often muddied with continuing misunderstandings—from first-hand anecdote or second-hand report through to the sort of body of common belief or received opinion with which more serious enquirers (and eventually scientists) could engage.

The next quotation from Strabo takes us back to Egypt:

> The ibis is a very tame bird. It is like a stork in shape and size, but there are two kinds of them and they have different colours—one like the stork and the other one completely black.[2] Every crossroads in Alexandria is thronged with them, and though they are useful in one way they are not so in another. They are useful in

---

[1] Sixty is a more likely upper limit, but Aelian probably didn't realize that several female ostriches contribute to that clutch size, laying their eggs in communal nests, and that the eggs are then brooded by both the male and the dominant female.

[2] The former will have been the sacred ibis, the latter the glossy ibis—or possibly the similar, but now much rarer, bald ibis; the glossy and bald ibises were not then distinguished and the bald ibis may once have been common, judging by its many representations in Egyptian art.

picking up all the pests and the discarded refuse from the meat shops and baker-
ies; but they are harmful in that they will eat anything, are themselves unclean,
and are difficult to keep away from what is pure and undefiled.
    Strabo, *Geography* xvii 2.4

4.4 Two glossy ibises in a Nilescape with wildfowl. The glossy ibis (*Plegadis falcinellus*)
is one of three species of ibis common in the ancient world (and often featured in Egyptian
hieroglyphs and art) but the only one still to be found there. The sacred ibis (*Threskiornis
aethiopicus*), which does have the feeding habits described by Strabo, had disappeared
from Egypt by 1930, while the hermit or bald ibis (*Geronticus eremita*) is now a highly
endangered species worldwide, with tiny relict colonies in Syria and Morocco. Detail
from a mosaic from the House of the Faun, Pompeii, one of the largest private residences
there, second century BC.

In this example some perfectly ordinary (and in this case accurate) observations
about bird behaviour feed first into practical concerns about hygiene and then
into larger prejudices about pests. But 'pest' (like 'weed') is an anthropocentric
category not a biological one. And it is one step on the way to demonization and
the quasi-religious ideas about impurity and defilement that we shall be considering in chapter 17.
    But none of these ideas is stable or neatly consistent. Strabo also emphasizes
here the ambivalent status of the ibis as both pest and pest-controller. Herodotus
had given a similar description and had made the further point that their

'service' in another kind of pest control—consuming the mysterious 'flying serpents' from Arabia—explains why the ibis is so 'greatly honoured' by the Egyptians and is indeed one of their 'most sacred' wild creatures (II 65, 75). The flying serpents themselves may be a complete fiction, or at least a transposition from some quite different species like locusts, but they later lead Herodotus into a very interesting digression on the biological mechanisms of *polygonia* and *oligogonia* (having many or few offspring) that control population numbers in different species (III 107–09).* Even bizarre or incredible travellers' tales can in this way provoke worthwhile speculations.

The third traveller I shall quote from is Pausanias. Whereas Strabo's work is a comprehensive guide to physical geography, Pausanias is the cultural Baedeker of his time (the second century AD), producing a detailed and reliable account of the antiquities of mainland Greece for tourists, which is still usable today. He also has an eye for natural wonders and comments on some strange birds reported from Mount Cyllene in Arcadia (a region of the Peloponnese):

> Mount Cyllene is also home to the following marvel. The blackbirds on it are entirely white. (The birds the Boeotians call blackbirds are some other species of bird that does not sing.) There are some swan-eagles,[1] which are as white as swans, that I have seen at Sipylos around the lake called Tantalus; and some private individuals have been known to own white wild boars and Thracian bears; there is also a white breed of Libyan hares and I have seen white deer in Rome to my great astonishment, though I didn't think to ask what land or island they came from. I mention all this because of the blackbirds on Cyllene, lest anyone doubt what has been said about their colour.
>
> Pausanias, *Description of Greece* VIII 17

Pausanias does not claim to have actually seen these white blackbirds but reports their presence as an established truth. In doing so, he is just following a long tradition, where one author after another repeats the same story, which most probably originated with the sighting of one or more albinos (a common enough aberration among individual blackbirds).*

The other anecdotes about albinism are a tangle of irrelevancies, half-truths, and mistakes, which provide the credulous with just enough hope to sustain their beliefs in the white blackbird story. Such myths die hard. Scholars have since

---

[1] The 'swan-eagles' are presumably Egyptian vultures *Neophron percnopterus*, which do look white and would not have been uncommon in mountainous areas.

climbed that mountain to look for themselves and in the nineteenth century one earnest German ornithologist, Dr A. Lindermeyer, even claimed to have found the white blackbirds there. It is just possible that the birds were actually snow finches, which are rare local residents in a few alpine locations in Greece (including Mount Cyllene), breeding mainly between 2,000 and 2,500 metres above sea level. These do show a lot of white, but they are a good deal smaller than black-birds (16.5–19 cm as against 23.5–29 cm).* A less likely candidate is the ring ouzel, which is closely related to the blackbird; but that is just a winter visitor to Greece and in any case shows white only in the crescent breast-band of the male. Neither of these species would have been specific to *that* mountain, of course, but once such stories gain momentum they can become unstoppable.

All these possibilities would be classic cases of euhemerism,[1] the rationalistic interpretation of mythology. On this view, mythological stories are distortions or exaggerations of actual historical events, and the 'white blackbirds' would have been based either on a variation in a real species or on a misidentification of another species. Mount Cyllene would have been a plausible site for such a myth, per-haps, because of its associations with Hermes, the messenger god (who was reputedly born in a cave there). Hermes was the intermediary between gods and men, a master of deception and invention, and the patron of travellers, thieves, and poets.

What all the cases considered in this chapter have in common, however, is that they all purport to be derived from observations. These birds are not like the purely imaginary creations or hybrid monstrosities of myth and poetry—such as the Sirens, the Stymphalian birds, or the Harpies, which we shall be looking at in chapter 17, 'Fabulous Creatures'. And the observations in question are reported by authors of the stature of Herodotus, Strabo, and Pausanias—all very serious and diligent enquirers, each of whom pioneered major areas of research. They report these phenomena as received opinion or common know-ledge, which they don't challenge, even if they don't themselves claim to authen-ticate it.

It is hard from this distance to know what status these authors would have given this kind of 'knowledge' or what distinctions they would have made, if pressed, between different kinds of knowledge and belief. What we do know

---

[1] Euhemerus was himself an appropriately shadowy figure. He was probably from Messene in Sicily, living in the fourth or third century BC. He wrote a book entitled *Sacred History*, essentially arguing that myths were 'history in disguise'.*

from our own times, however, is that myths, misapprehensions, and fantasies of this same general kind can persist and survive even after all the more scientific evidence we now have access to has decisively disproved them. This is the case with the 'urban myth' about spinach quoted above. There is also a contemporary example from the bird world. We all know, don't we, that magpies predate the eggs and young of songbirds? We also know that magpie numbers are increasing, while those of songbirds are declining. So it surely follows that if we control the numbers of magpies by culling we would be protecting the populations of songbirds? Wrong. Or at least, right about the premises but wrong about the conclusion. Research has shown that there is no general relationship between the numbers of magpies and the numbers of songbirds in a given area. You can have many magpies and many songbirds, or few magpies and few songbirds, or any combination of the variables. But we can't quite believe that. It goes against common sense, doesn't it? Newspapers fulminate against the wicked magpie, there are harrowing pictures on YouTube and elsewhere of magpies devouring the chicks of our much loved garden birds, and there have been national campaigns to exterminate this hateful enemy.* So we demonize the magpie and connive at its often illegal and irrational persecution. Culling domestic cats might be more to the point if we want to protect garden birds, but that wouldn't be such a popular move.

We also entertain beliefs about the possible existence of whole species unknown to science. There have been regular confident reports of such megafauna as the yeti, the bigfoot, the Loch Ness monster, and 'big cats' on the West Country moors. Indeed, there is a flourishing study of such possibilities called 'cryptozoology' (the study of 'hidden creatures'), a term first popularized by Bernard Heuvelmans in his book *On the Track of Unknown Animals* (1955). Heuvelmans made the point that many striking new species are in fact still being discovered, and he quotes the rash dictum of the famous French zoologist Baron Georges Cuvier, who in 1812 confidently announced: 'there is little hope of discovering new species of large quadrupeds'. In the next hundred years, Heuvelmans points out, the following species were among those first encountered and identified by Western scientists: tapir (1816), pygmy hippopotamus (1849), Père David's deer (1866), giant panda (1869), mountain gorilla (1901), okapi (1901), Komodo dragon (1912)...*

The process of scientific discovery goes on, of course, but cryptozoology is just a hopeful pseudoscience. Its current believers are quite uninterested in the many new beetles, ants, and other invertebrates that continue to be identified by zoologists. Their concern is wholly with the charismatic megafauna, despite the lack of any good evidence for them, because something in us *wants* to believe in the possibility of their existence. We feel our own lives would somehow be touched by such miracles. Shakespeare understood all this, of course:

> O wonder!
> How many goodly creatures are there here.
> How beauteous mankind is. Oh brave new world,
> That has such creatures in it.
> *The Tempest* v.1.182–84

'Wonder' is indeed the word.* It is a generous enough concept to encompass the notions both of wondering *at* something, in a sense of awe and discovery, and of wondering *about* something, in the kind of curiosity and wish to understand that inspires all true science. The reports of 'wonders' quoted in this chapter involve both kinds of motivation.

∿ 12 ∿

Medicine

Western literature begins with a disease and a birdwatcher. In the opening lines of Homer's *Iliad*, Apollo[1] inflicts a terrible plague on the Greeks to avenge Agamemnon's treatment of Apollo's priest Chryses, whose daughter Agamemnon has claimed as his concubine. The pestilence attacks humans and animals alike and 'the densely packed pyres of corpses burned unendingly' (1 51–52). To try and halt the outbreak, the Greeks turn not to their doctors, who were expected only to deal with battlefield wounds, but to a bird specialist:

> There stood up among them to speak
> Calchas, son of Thestor, by far the best expert on birds,[2]
> who knew things present, future, and past.
> Homer, *Iliad* 1 68–70

Calchas was an augur, whose job was to interpret the flight and behaviour of birds. He soon saw what the trouble was, took remedial action (involving a generous sacrifice to Apollo), and got the plague stopped.

Some 300 years after Homer things were very different. By the fifth century BC there was an emerging profession of medical practitioners, who had at their disposal a range of more rational modes of treatment than Calchas did. Not that they were always more successful. Thucydides describes another plague, this time a historically attested one, that attacked the population of Athens in 430–429

---

[1] Apollo, like other Greek gods, had a large portfolio, including light and sun, health and plague, truth and prophecy. He was the father of Asclepius, the 'healer god', whose daughters were Hygieia ('health') and Panacea ('universal remedy').

[2] *Oionopolos*, literally 'a man who busies himself with birds' (see p. 250).

BC during the early years of their great war with Sparta (and, interestingly, caused widespread deaths among animals as well as humans). But Thucydides makes a point of telling us that the doctors were powerless to deal with the epidemic, since they didn't properly understand its nature, and many of them caught the plague themselves from their patients (II 47.4). This may have been a deliberate dig at the doctors' scientific pretensions. Some were organized into local guilds, but they did not yet constitute a clearly defined group with recognized qualifications and standards. Nor were they the only ones out there recommending treatments. They were in competition with a varied assortment of herbalists, drug-sellers, and Magi,[1] who offered a range of prescriptions and therapies based more on traditional folklore than on science; indeed, to some extent the doctors were also in competition with one another in selling their services to the public.*

In this confused situation, however, real progress was being made in the science of medicine, if only partial and halting. And birds continued to be invoked, though now in a very different way. We saw in chapter 6 on cooking that birds regularly featured both as staple fare in ordinary household meals and as 'specials' on gourmet menus designed to titillate the appetite. The medical writers have comments to make on birds as food too, but here it is in the course of analysing diet and its effects on health.

The two great figures in the history of ancient medicine are Hippocrates and Galen, each of whom had a huge effect on the subsequent development of the subject in both the Islamic and Western traditions.

'Hippocrates' is a convenient single name for the various authors of extensive medical treatises produced between 430 and 330 BC. The original Hippocrates was a real historical figure, who came from the island of Cos and was an approximate contemporary of Socrates in the latter half of the fifth century BC, but we don't now know which of the many surviving works later ascribed to him he actually authored himself.* These include a remarkable range of treatises on physiology, epidemiology, anatomy, gynaecology, and pathology; practical manuals on diagnosis and specific methods of treatment; and some more general works on what we would now call 'medical ethics'. Indeed, medical students in a number of teaching institutions across the world are still required to commit to versions of the oath that goes under Hippocrates' name. In its original version (just one page long) the Hippocratic Oath still has an extraordinarily modern ring about it, in its requirements for confidentiality, respect for patients, and the amelioration and preservation of life.

---

[1] Pedlars of 'magic' through remedies and charms (see p. 267).

Hippocrates and his contemporaries were also responsible for pioneering a recognizably scientific methodology in their efforts to free medical practice from the realms of superstition, magic, and religion. Hippocrates produced, for example, a pioneering treatise on the 'sacred disease' (epilepsy), so called because of its alarming and mysterious symptoms, which it was supposed must have a divine origin. He begins his rebuttal of these assumptions with what must at the time have been a breathtaking assertion:

> I do not believe that the 'sacred disease' is any more divine or sacred than any other disease; on the contrary, it has its specific characteristics and a definite cause.
> Hippocrates, *The Sacred Disease* 1

He concludes with an even more confident assertion:

> This so-called 'sacred disease' has the same causes as all other diseases... Each disease has its own nature and power and none is beyond understanding or treatment... A man who knows how by means of a regimen to produce dryness and moisture or cold and heat in a person, could cure this disease, too, as long as he could tell the right moment to apply the remedies, without resorting to purifications and magic spells.
> Hippocrates, *The Sacred Disease* 21

The crucial move here was to insist that the causes in question were natural not supernatural ones. The gods were not involved in either the explanation or the cure. This is not to say that these medical writers, intellectually brave and innovative as they were, did not sometimes incorporate in their science untested notions taken over from earlier thinkers, as well as from their contemporary competitors in the healing business. The idiom remained that of rational explanation through physical causes, but the conclusions were sometimes based on dubious general theories about the nature of human physiology. For example, these references to elements like the wet and the dry were almost certainly derived from speculative philosophers like Empedocles (c.492–c.432 BC).*

Hippocrates wrote a book on the importance for health of diet and exercise, effectively an early text in preventive medicine, and this has a number of references to birds. He argues in particular that eating the wrong foods in the wrong quantities can disturb the balance of the natural constituents of the body:

> As far as birds are concerned the situation is as follows. Almost all birds are drier than mammals, since those creatures that have no bladder neither pass water nor

secrete saliva, on account of the hot temperature of the belly. For the moisture
from the body is used up in maintaining the heat, with the consequence that they
can neither urinate nor spit. It follows that whatever lacks such moisture must
necessarily be dry. The flesh of wood pigeons is the driest, then that of partridges,
and thirdly that of doves, cocks, and turtle doves; the moistest is that of geese.
Seed-eaters are generally drier than the others. Ducks and other birds that live in
marshes or on water are all moist.

Hippocrates, *Regimen* II 47

4.5 Hippocrates (left) and Galen (right). The two great figures from the history of
ancient medicine in an imagined conversation, from *De herbis et plantis* by Manfredus de
Monte Imperiali, *c.*1330–40.

Galen, writing in the second century AD, produced an even more astonishing
body of work, which dominated medical theory and practice through to the
Enlightenment.[1] He was born and educated at Pergamum in Asia Minor,
where the local stable of gladiators would have provided medical students with

---

[1] Unlike Hippocrates, Galen was one person and was probably the most prolific author in antiquity.
Only a third of his work survives, but that runs to some 3 million words, over half of it still untranslated
into English.*

plenty of practice in dealing with traumatic injuries; but he later moved to Rome and joined the imperial household, serving a succession of Roman emperors. Galen advanced the science of medicine massively through his extensive research, some of it based on animal dissection and vivisection, and he performed many famous feats of practical prognosis and surgery. He acknowledges Hippocrates as his predecessor and inspiration, and bases his own pathology on some of the same inherited ideas, like the doctrine of the four humours with their associated personality traits.[1] He also gives great emphasis to ecological factors—to the place of the human patient in the natural world of plants and animals, and to the environmental effects of climate, geography, and seasonality on species that form part of the human food supply. But Galen analyses the place of birds in a balanced diet in somewhat different terms:

> The whole class of winged birds is very much less nutritious than that of land animals, particularly pigs—in comparison with which nothing is more nutritious. But the flesh of birds is more easily digested, especially that of partridges, francolins, pigeons, and both cock and hen chickens. The flesh of thrushes, blackbirds, and sparrows, including the so-called 'house' sparrows nesting in buildings, is tougher than these, and even tougher still is that of turtle dove, wood pigeon, and duck. The flesh of pheasants is like that of chickens as far as digestion and nutrition are concerned but superior in terms of taste. The flesh of peacocks is tougher, harder to digest, and more fibrous than these. It is important to recognize a fact common to all winged creatures, as indeed it is to quadrupeds, that the flesh of growing creatures is much superior to that of those past their prime; the flesh of developed adults constitutes a middle case between these extremes; then again the flesh of the very young is bad, as in a different way is that of the aged ones; for the flesh of the latter is hard, dry, and sinewy and so is hard to digest and offers the body little nourishment, while the flesh of very young creatures is slimy and wet, and consequently contains bodily residues that more easily pass through the bowels.
>
> Galen, *On the Properties of Foods* III 18

He takes up the same theme in his very modern-sounding work *The Thinning Diet*, a book produced, ironically, at about the same time as Apicius was publishing his cookbook of waist-expanding gourmet menus (see pp. 106–07):

---

[1] The four elements of earth, air, fire, and water were connected with the humours (bodily fluids), respectively black bile, blood, yellow bile, and phlegm, and with their corresponding traits of the melancholic, sanguine, choleric, and phlegmatic.

The greatest and most abundant source of food you could wish to have for the thinning diet comes from rockfish and small montane birds. Birds of wetlands, creeks, and plains are moister and generate more waste. Creatures that live in the mountains are all drier and hotter in their make-up and their flesh is the least glutinous and produces less phlegm. In fact, everything that grows on the hills is far better than what grows in the lowlands. Montane birds, for example, are in my view far superior to those dwelling in the marshes and plains, not only from the thinness of the air but also as sources of nourishment. One should therefore eat starlings, thrushes, blackbirds, and partridges, along with other montane species, and avoid ducks and other such species. So one should steer clear of bustard, geese, and the other large birds called 'ostriches' and anything else of this kind if you are following the thinning diet. All these have flesh with waste products in it. The birds called 'tower-birds'[1] too, and the vineyard birds[2] and pigeons from towers are all better than those around ordinary houses.

    Galen, *The Thinning Diet* VIII 55–58

Galen has more specific comments to make about the edibility of different parts of birds, often in the form of warnings (my italics):

The *entrails* of birds have the same relation to their flesh as I explained in the case of animals. The *intestines* of all of these are completely inedible, though their *stomachs*, by contrast, are both edible and nutritious, and some of them are actually quite tasty—especially those of geese and next those of cockerels fattened on corn. The *wings* of geese, too, and more especially those of cockerels, are good for digestion and nourishment. And while there is quite a difference between the flesh of old and young birds generally, this is most marked in the case of the wings; similarly, as between skinny and plump birds. The best wings are those of young well-fed birds, the worst from the old skinny ones.

    The *feet* of virtually all birds are inedible.

    One can neither praise nor criticize the *combs* and *wattles* of cockerels.

    The *testicles* are the best part, especially of cockerels fed on grain, and even more so if they have been taking their food with milk whey, since they are then wholesome, nutritious, and easy to digest; however, they neither encourage nor inhibit excretion.

    Birds have small *brains*, but they are much better than those of land animals, to the extent that they are harder. And, among the different birds, the montane

---

[1] Apparently sparrows (not swifts, as one might have guessed). The modern Greek word for 'sparrow' (*pyrgites*) has the same etymology.

[2] This could be one of any number of species: black-headed bunting, black-eared wheatear, spotted flycatcher, several warblers (for example, Sardinian or olive-tree warbler, or a blackcap), all of which frequent vineyards.

species have better brains than the marsh species, to the same extent as with all their other parts.

Some people mistakenly swear by ostrich *guts* as a digestive medicine, while others praise seabird[1] guts much more highly. But these are neither easy to digest in themselves nor are they digestive supplements for other foods, as are ginger and pepper for example—and in another way wine and vinegar.

If I tried to say what everyone knows about the *tongues* and *beaks* of birds, I should rightly be assumed just to be waffling.

Eggs constitute another kind of food derived from birds and these differ from one another in three respects: first in terms of substance, hens' and pheasants' eggs being better than those of geese and ostriches; second, in the time they were laid, some longer ago and some more recently; third, some in being boiled for longer, some until moderately firm, and others only warmed up. These are respectively called hard-boiled, soft-boiled, and sucking eggs.

Some people consume the *blood* of hens and pigeons, especially those fed on grain, since it is just as good as the blood of pigs in respect of taste and digestion, although much inferior to that of hares. But however you prepare it, all blood is difficult to digest and is full of residues.

Galen, *On the Properties of Foods* III 20–22

Galen wrote in Greek, as did many other professional authors in the Roman era, like Strabo (geography) and Ptolemy (astronomy). Greek authors still provided much of the knowledge base and cultural inspiration for the Roman Empire in the first two centuries AD, despite the total domination of Roman military and political power, as Horace neatly described (quoted here in Latin as well as English, since the first five words are a famous and beautifully concise tag):

Graeca capta ferum victorem cepit, et artes
intulit agresti Latio.
Captive Greece took her fierce conqueror captive
and brought her arts into rustic Latium.

Horace, *Epistles* II 1.156–57

But there were correspondingly strong ideological reasons for Rome to establish its own empire of knowledge to match and support its political domination. Some of the forerunners in this Latinization of the Greek learned tradition were the agricultural writers Cato and Varro (quoted extensively in chapter 7).

---

[1] This seabird called an *aithuia* is referred to in literature from Homer onwards. Various identifications offered include diver, gull, shearwater, cormorant, and shag, of which the last two best fit most of the descriptions.

Celsus and Pliny, both writing in the first century AD, continued this process in various other fields, including medicine. They wrote as generalists rather than as specialists—educated gentlemen concerned to summarize Greek learning and recast it in terms of Roman values and traditions.

Celsus[1] wrote a large reference work on the *Artes*, which had separate books on such topics as agriculture, military science, medicine, and rhetoric, but only the eight books on medicine survive. He is most concerned with practical advice about the regimes that will best contribute to a healthy lifestyle and about the treatments of specific diseases through diet and drugs. Birds crop up in these recommendations from time to time, mainly to specify those yielding 'stronger food', that is those offering most nourishment:

> Those which depend more on their feet than their wings represent a stronger class of food; and of those that rely on flight, the larger birds constitute a more reliable source of food than smaller ones like the fig-bird[2] and the thrush. Moreover, water birds provide a weaker food than those that don't swim.
>
> Celsus, *De Medicina* II 18.6

Pliny's *Natural History* was an even more ambitious survey of 'the world of nature, that is, life' (Preface 13). No other writer, he says, Greek or Roman, has tackled the complete 'circle of learning'[3] that is his objective. Book I is entirely given over to the lists of contents of each book and the authorities consulted (with a running list of subtotals of the number of 'noteworthy facts' cited, giving a grand total of around 20,000), and there then follow the thirty-seven books of detailed exposition. He immediately makes it clear, too, that his method of research is literary rather than scientific, in that the facts are those culled and synthesized from the 2,000 volumes by some hundred authors he proudly tells us he has perused—'very few of them ever addressed by students because of their recondite subject matter' (Preface 17).

---

[1] This is Aulus Cornelius Celsus (*fl.* AD 50), not the later Celsus who launched the attack on Christianity answered by Origen in *Contra Celsum.*

[2] The *ficedula* (Greek *sukalis*) is probably a blackcap (*Sylvia atricapilla*) here, though other black-headed warblers of the region, like Orphean (*Sylvia crassirostris*), Sardinian (*S. melanocephala*), and Rüppell's (*S. rueppelli*) warblers, could have been confused with it.

[3] The *enkuklios paideia*, from which we derive the word 'encyclopedia'. It is, though, anachronistic to think of Pliny's work as an encyclopedia, with a consistent taxonomical structure in the modern sense: his work is really an accumulation of a vast number of separate items, loosely connected.*

The younger Pliny, nephew of the natural historian, describes in one of his letters the qualities of concentration and the work habits that made it possible for his uncle to combine this extraordinary industry with a busy public career. He managed on very little sleep and wasted not a moment of his waking hours. When he was not actually working at his desk he would have books read aloud to him, on which he made rapid notes—while sitting outside, while travelling, during meal-times, and even as he was being dried after his bath. 'He made notes on everything read, and he always said that there was no book so bad that you could not benefit from some part of it' (*Letters* III 5.7–16). This inclusive policy has the consequence that, although much of the information in the *Natural History* is hastily and uncritically assessed, it does represent, as Pliny himself claims, a veritable *thesaurus* or storehouse of popular beliefs. And that is its interest for us here, though some of the examples will be seen to be also relevant to later discussions of the development of science (chapter 13) and of magic (chapter 15).

After an extensive survey of the animal kingdom Pliny devotes several of the subsequent books (in particular xx–xxxii) to the medical applications of drugs and preparations derived from plants, mammals, and birds. It is reassuring, perhaps, to see that the complaints at least are familiar, even if the remedies are not:

Aches and pains
Goose grease is a celebrated medication generally…it should be mixed with cinnamon, cassia, white pepper, and the herb called 'commagene'[1] and placed in jars buried in the snow. It has an agreeable smell and is very useful for bad colds, cramps, sudden or unexplained pains, and all complaints treated by soothing salves, since it is equally good as an ointment and a medicine.
xxix 55–56

Snake-bite
Another remedy against snake-bite is the recently stripped-off flesh of doves and swallows and the feet of an eagle owl burnt with the herb plumbago.
xxix 81

Sores
Sores on the tongue and lips can be healed by a preparation of swallows cooked in honey mead; chapped skin by grease from a goose or a hen, by unwashed wool

---

[1] Commagene was named after a province in Syria, where it was a local remedy, but it can't now be identified with any certainty. Syrian nard (*Valeriana dioscoridis*) has been suggested as a possibility.

and oak-apple, and by the white webs of spiders and the little webs spun on rafters.

XXX 27

Facial problems
Vulture's blood beaten in with the root of the white chameleon plant I've already described and with cedar resin, and then wrapped in a cabbage leaf, heals leprous sores; just as do the legs of locusts beaten into goat grease. Poultry fat kneaded into onion cures pimples. Honey in which bees have died is good for the face, but the best thing for cleansing the complexion and smoothing away wrinkles is swan's fat.

XXX 30

Unwanted tattoos
Branding marks[1] may be removed by pigeon dung soused in vinegar.

XXX 30

Quinsy (acute tonsillitis)
Goose gall mixed with cucumber and honey gives speedy relief for quinsy, as does the brain of an owl and the ashes of a swallow drunk in hot water.

XXX 33–36

Lumbago
A hoopoe's heart is strongly recommended for pains in the side.

XXX 53

Tummy troubles
To settle the stomach try also: roasted liver of cockerel, or the skin from their crop (which is usually thrown away) moistened with poppy juice if old—though some people take it fresh and roast it to be drunk with wine; partridge broth with its crop separately ground up in dark wine; wild wood pigeon[2] boiled down in vinegar water; spleen of sheep, roasted and ground up in wine; dove droppings smeared with honey; or the gizzard of osprey, dried and taken in a drink—highly beneficial for those who can't manage their food, even if they only hold it in their hands while eating… The blood of drake mallard is also good for settling looseness in the bowels.

XXX 59–60

[1] These were the marks of ownership burnt on slaves, which they would try to have removed if given their freedom.
[2] I translate *palumba* here as 'wood pigeon' and *columba* in the next clause as 'dove', though it is unclear if the distinction matters, or indeed if it would have made any difference to the patient which droppings were used.

Flatulence and griping
Flatulence can be dispelled by eating snails. Treat griping with the spleen of sheep, roasted and drunk with wine, or wild wood pigeon boiled down in vinegar water, bustard fat in wine, or the ashes of a plucked ibis taken in a drink.

XXX 61–62

Kidney stones and bladder trouble
Take pigeon droppings with beans against kidney stones and bladder problems; also the ashes from wild pigeon feathers in vinegar, and three spoonfuls of the ashes from their intestines, some earth taken from a swallow's nest dissolved in warm water, the dried crop of an osprey, turtle dove droppings reduced in mead or the broth from the bird itself.

XXX 67–68

And so it goes on. We are recommended crested lark for colic, thrushes with myrtle berries to improve our urine, chicken broth as a laxative, or alternatively a suppository of swallow droppings mixed with honey, goose grease for a sore anus, and swan fat for haemorrhoids, along with the reliable old standby of pigeon droppings in honey.

Celsus has a similar list of unlikely cures for familiar complaints, as does the physician–traveller Dioscorides (first century AD), who compiled a study called *Materia medica* ('Materials of medicine'), a comprehensive catalogue of the medicinal uses of plants, minerals, and animal products. Dioscorides also recommended crested lark for colic and chicken broth for purging, but the remedy for which he was probably longest remembered is the application of 'swallow-stones' against epilepsy:

> At the time of the waxing moon, cut open the bellies of swallow nestlings from the first brood and you will find stones in their stomachs. Take two of these, one multicoloured and the other a pure one, and tie them in a bag of cowhide or deerskin before they can touch the ground. Apply that to the arm or neck as a relief for epilepsy and you will often get a complete recovery.
> Dioscorides, *Materia medica* II 56

That one was still being recommended as late as the seventeenth century by Thomas Willis (1621–75), 'the father of neuroscience', who was one of the founders of the Royal Society.*

Who knows what the origin of all these folk remedies might have been, and how often they were ever employed? One imagines that some of the ingredients might have been difficult to assemble at short notice anyway.

It is likely that the herbal and plant remedies Pliny records elsewhere might have been better attested than those involving birds, because with the former there were at least some recognized traditional practitioners. We hear from the fifth century BC onwards of various 'root-cutters' (*rhizotomoi*) and 'drug-sellers' (*pharmakopoloi*) who collected medicinal plants, and the work of such herbalists was taken seriously enough by the first great plant taxonomist, Theophrastus (*c*.372–*c*.286 BC), for him to submit it to critical discussion and analysis. The 'root-cutters' were in any case a sufficiently well-known fraternity to provide the title for a play by Sophocles (though only fragments of this survive).* Pliny rarely questions the material he accumulates so laboriously from his literary sources, but he does once or twice complain of the contemporary ignorance about herbs, except among the illiterate country folk who 'live among them' (*Natural History* XXXV 16). This is at least to ground the knowledge of plants in experience and recognize the need for some agreed method of investigation—what Pliny calls a *ratio inventionis*.

By contrast, many of the bizarre remedies involving birds seem to smack more of magic than medicine. The only analogous bird experts we hear about are either Magi or augurs and we consider them later, in chapters 14 and 15. Perhaps it was in any case harder to build up a reliable body of experience of the bird remedies. Some may have appealed precisely because they seemed so exotic—and were thus taken as evidence of an arcane and esoteric knowledge; others perhaps derived from a few chance successes and 'miracle cures', when the patient was consuming some part of a bird that had been caught for the pot and happened to recover for other reasons. 'Post hoc ergo propter hoc' can be a very persuasive fallacy in establishing the credibility of therapies, as it is in astrology and indeed in politics. And of course the placebo effect might apply as well, once there were at least some successes of this kind to report by way of encouragement.* Celsus and Pliny were very learned men, but they could nonetheless seem simultaneously both knowing and credulous about such superstitions. This comment from Celsus about a treatment for eye injuries, for example, seems to debunk one myth only to perpetuate another:

> Nothing is more efficacious than to anoint the eye with the blood of a dove, pigeon, or swallow. This for good reason, since if ever these species suffer some external blow to the eye their visual acuity returns after an interval of time to its original state. This has given rise to the story that the parents restore the vision with a herb, when in fact it comes back of its own accord. Thus it is that blood

from these birds offers our eyes, too, the best protection after some external
injury, in the following order of effectiveness, which applies in their case as well as
ours: swallow is best, then pigeon, and lastly dove.

Celsus, *De Medicina* VI 6.39

There may be some analogy with oracles, which also relied on strange rituals
(in some cases involving ecstatic priestesses, inebriated by the fumes of bay leaves),
but which were earnestly consulted and widely believed, and appeared often to
be uncannily accurate. Sceptical scholars have, of course, always been intrigued
by this phenomenon. One German professor duly consumed a large quantity of
bay leaves in the interests of research and solemnly pronounced that he didn't
feel any different afterwards (but perhaps he should have smoked them?).* Magic
and medicine can often coexist in a culture and the latter may replace the former
only gradually and incompletely.

13

Observation
and Enquiry

Some assumptions we make about the world seem so obvious and are so deep-rooted that it is hard to remember that they had a beginning and a history, and hard to believe, by implication, that things were once different. In fact, in the Western tradition it was only in the sixth and fifth centuries BC that various thinkers—never mind for now whether they are best called 'philosophers' or 'scientists'—began a series of enquiries that fundamentally changed human perceptions of the natural world. They assumed that the world was in principle intelligible and that they might be able to explain it. This was a momentous act of optimism and self-belief in the capacities of human reason, and seems to be something quite new. They assumed that the world's nature and workings could be understood by observing them and thinking about them in the right way, and that reason, stimulated by curiosity and wonder, could answer the sort of questions that had previously been the province of myth and religion: where did the world come from; why is it the way it is; how are natural phenomena and physical changes to be explained; and where do human beings fit in?

Some of the answers first offered were bizarre, hopelessly wrong, wildly speculative, or very obscure. And our sources for them are fragmentary, often inconclusive, usually second-hand, and always in need of careful interpretation. But some of these early ideas do seem to represent the first small steps in the long history of scientific discovery; some others suggest quite radical conceptual breakthroughs; and some sound startlingly modern at first sight. Consider the following early ideas:

Thales…says that water is the first principle (and for that reason claims that the earth rests on water), perhaps making this assumption from observing that everything derives its nurture from what is moist…and that the seeds of all things have a moist nature, water being the source of growth for moist things.

    Aristotle, *Metaphysics* 983b19–27

Anaximander says that the first living creatures were generated in moisture, enclosed by a prickly shell; and as they matured they came out on to drier land, and when the shell broke off they lived a different form of life for a short time.

    Aëtius, *Opinions of the Philosophers* v 19.4

Xenophanes thinks that the earth gets mixed in with the sea and is in time dissolved by the water. He cites as evidence the fact that seashells are discovered well inland and on mountains, and he says that in the quarries of Syracuse impressions of a fish and of seaweed have been found, in Paros the impression of a bay leaf deep in the rock, and in Malta flattened shapes of all manner of sea creatures. He says these things happened when everything was covered with mud long ago and the impressions then dried out in the mud.

    Hippolytus, *Refutation of All Heresies* 1 14.5

Heraclitus says somewhere that all things are in flux and nothing stays still. He compares existing matter to the stream of a river and says that you could not step into the same river twice.

    Plato, *Cratylus* 402a

[Empedocles says that] hair, leaves, the densely packed feathers of birds, and scales on sturdy limbs[1] are all the same sort of things.

    Aristotle, *Meteorologica* 387b4

Anaxagoras [and Empedocles] say that plants are moved by feelings of desire and are sentient and feel pain and pleasure. Anaxagoras says that they are animals, which feel joy and sadness, inferring this from the fall of their leaves…Anaxagoras [and Democritus and Empedocles] say they have mind and intelligence…and Anaxagoras says they have breath too.

    [Aristotle], *On Plants* 815a15–20, 815b16–17, 816b26

Archelaus says that when the earth was originally warming up in its lower region, where the hot and the cold were mixed together, many creatures began to appear, including humankind, all obtaining their means of nourishment from the slime. These were short-lived, but later on generation took place among them and they

---

[1] Perhaps he is thinking of crocodiles here.

were born from one another. Humans were distinguished from the other animals and established rulers, laws, arts and sciences, cities, and so on. Mind, he says, is inborn in all animals alike, for each animal makes use of it, some more slowly, some more quickly.

Hippolytus, *Refutation of All Heresies* I 9.1

Democritus sometimes rejects the evidence of the senses and says that nothing of what appears to be the case relates to the truth, only to belief. Reality consists only of atoms and the void. 'Sweet', he says, 'is just a matter of convention—also bitter, hot, cold, and colour; in reality there are just atoms and void.'

Sextus Empiricus, *Against the Mathematicians* VII 136

We call these men collectively the Presocratics, the philosophers 'before Socrates' (whose dates were 469–399 BC). Some of them were contemporary with Socrates, in fact, but the point of the distinction is that whereas they were largely concerned with the natural world, Socrates redirected philosophy to study the human world of ethics and politics. In the ancient world itself the Presocratics were known as the *phusikoi* or *phusiologoi* ('natural philosophers') and some of them wrote books with titles like *Peri phuseos* ('On nature').[1] As these quotations indicate, their interests ranged widely over subjects we would now distinguish as cosmology, physics, geology, physiology, biology, and zoology, as well as over other kinds of enquiry not represented in this small selection. In terms of subject matter, at least, this was 'philosophy' in its most general sense of 'love of knowledge'; and if it was 'science' it was more in the sense of the German *Wissenschaft* ('pursuit of knowledge') than in the narrower disciplinary meaning of the current English word.

Any assessment of these early speculations has to be heavily qualified and conjectural because of the nature of the evidence; but what they have in common is the assumption that there were *rational* answers to questions about the natural world. The workings of causes and effects in the world might be deeply puzzling, but they were not explicable only as the arbitrary interventions of divine beings. Indeed, Xenophanes pointed out that our perceptions of the gods might themselves be subject to rational explanation:

---

[1] Anaximander (died c.545 BC) is the first from this group definitely attested to have produced a book of some sort (and also a map).* Books, in the sense of written, non-fiction texts, were at a very early stage of evolution in what was still a largely pre-literate society; they could also take forms that may seem surprising now—those by Xenophanes and Empedocles, for example, were in verse not prose.

But if cattle and horses or lions had hands and were able to draw with their hands and act like men, then horses would draw the forms of gods to look like horses, cattle as cattle, and they would make their bodies look just like their own.

Xenophanes (quoted in Clement, *Miscellanies* v 109.3)

This was all hugely liberating, and various later scientists and philosophers have rightly hailed the Presocratic period as the first age of Enlightenment in the history of Western thought. Karl Popper thought scientists should go 'Back to the Presocratics' to recover their emphasis on problem-oriented theories and hypotheses rather than pursuing what he thought of as a deadening accumulation of observations and data through the sort of 'inductive' methods prescribed by Francis Bacon. In the same spirit, the physicist Erwin Schrödinger commended a definition of science as 'thinking about the world in a Greek way', and urged that we study these figures from a distant culture in order the better to understand and challenge our own, sometimes limiting, scientific assumptions. And modern cosmologists like Carl Sagan and Stephen Hawking have warmly saluted the Presocratics' creativity and intellectual courage, even if they then go on to patronize them somewhat as interesting but primitive ancestors.*

But whatever their originality, these Presocratic thinkers, like the contemporary medical writers we considered in the last chapter, were too unsystematic in their theorizing and too little reliant on structured observations and experiments to test their exciting ideas to be thought of as 'scientists' in any modern sense. The first person to whom that title might more plausibly be applied is Aristotle.

*   *   *

Aristotle (384–322 BC) was effectively a one-man university, whose interests extended over almost every field of academic enquiry: the physical, biological, and human sciences, ethics, politics, metaphysics, philosophy, logic, rhetoric, and literary criticism. In fact he founded a university to organize and expand his enquiries, the Lyceum at Athens, which had very much the function of a modern research institute. He was a sort of corporate author too, in that many of the works that come down to us under his name were probably drafted by him or his students as lecture notes, which were then further edited and expanded by various commentators after his death. We don't therefore know quite what degree of personal authority he would have given to all the details in the texts we now have.[1] But Aristotle was undoubtedly the creative genius behind this colossal output of work and in many subjects his influence persisted until the Renaissance—'the Master of those who know', as Dante dubbed him.

His importance for this chapter lies in his large corpus of writings on biology, which constitutes about a fifth of his surviving work and includes a great deal of descriptive and taxonomic zoological material on birds and other animals. This was evidently a strong personal interest and he seems to have gathered a lot of the data during fieldwork that he did in Asia Minor, and particularly on Lesbos, while he was away from Athens on his travels between 347 and 335 BC. Modern field biologists sometimes wonder if Aristotle ever 'got his hands dirty', but at least in this area of research he certainly did. He distinguished over 500 different animal species in his biological treatises, evidently dissected a good number of them, and made many remarkable discoveries, particularly in marine biology, based on close and detailed observations.* Some of his findings were long disbelieved, only to be confirmed centuries later.[2] He—or his editors—also made some strange mistakes, some of them absurd ones, and we shall be reflecting later on this disconcerting combination of sophistication and naivety.

Aristotle was the son of a doctor and that will have given him an early familiarity with some of the practical aspects of biology and medicine. He demonstrated his approach to zoological research not only by personally exploring the lagoons of Pyrrha in Lesbos, a 'local patch' he refers to a lot, but also by using a wide range of informants with direct experience of the different animals he was studying. Pliny tells us how Aristotle's most famous pupil, Alexander the Great, commissioned this assistance for him:

> King Alexander the Great was fired with a desire to learn natural history and delegated responsibility for this pursuit to Aristotle, who was the supreme authority in every branch of knowledge. Orders were therefore given to thousands of people throughout the whole of Greece and Asia—that is, all those who made their living from hunting, fowling, and fishing, and those who were in charge of animal enclosures, cattle farms, apiaries, fishponds, and aviaries—to

---

[1] Some other works were definitely not by him at all and these are indicated in the notes and references by putting his name in square brackets, as in [Aristotle], *Mirabilia*.

[2] For example, his discovery of the remarkable reproductive structures of the common smoothhound *Mustelus mustelus* (a small species of shark), which were 'rediscovered' and confirmed by Johannes Müller in 1842.*

respond to Aristotle's requests, so that he would not fail to be aware of any creatures from anywhere. His investigation of their findings filled almost fifty volumes of his famous work on zoology.

Pliny, *Natural History* VIII 44

There is a clear contrast in approach here between Aristotle and his teacher,
Plato, who is the other giant figure in Greek philosophy. Plato constructed an
elaborate theory of knowledge and metaphysics, based on abstract logical and
linguistic analysis, whereas both in precept and practice Aristotle placed great
emphasis on the collection of empirical data as a preliminary to theoretical analysis. A famous painting by Raphael, *The School of Athens*, shows the two great
philosophers engaged in earnest disputation, Plato pointing upwards to the
heavens and Aristotle downwards to the earth.

Unlike the Presocratics, Aristotle is explicit about his motives and methods.
At the end of his discussion of the reproduction of bees in *Generation of Animals*
he says:

> But the facts are incomplete, and if at any future time they are better established
> then more credence should be given to the evidence of the senses than to theories,
> and credence should be given to theories only if their conclusions agree with
> observed facts.
>
> Aristotle, *Generation of Animals* 760b30–33

He makes a similar point in another treatise on growth and change in the
natural world:

> It is lack of direct experience that diminishes our ability to take a comprehensive
> view of the admitted facts. Thus, those who have lived in a more intimate commu
> nion with the natural world are better able to propose principles to synthesize a
> wide field; whereas the limitations of those who rely on long abstract discussions
> without observing the actual facts are easily exposed.
>
> Aristotle, *On Generation and Corruption* 316a5–10

And the remarkable programmatic statement near the start of *Parts of Animals*
is worth quoting at some length. He starts by comparing our knowledge of the
forms of life on earth, which are subject to generation and decay, with that of the
unchanging but remote heavenly bodies:

4.6 Raphael's *School of Athens* fresco painted between 1509 and 1511 for the Apostolic Palace in the Vatican, one of a series representing the prin-cipal branches of knowledge: Philosophy (this one), Poetry (including music), Theology, and Law. The two central standing figures are Plato (left) and Aristotle (right), but identifications of the other figures are more speculative.

But concerning the things that are mortal, that is plants and animals, we have better sources of knowledge, since we live among them and anyone who is willing to take sufficient trouble can learn a great deal about each of their different kinds...Moreover, since they are nearer to us and have more affinity with our own nature, this is a compensating advantage compared to the study of heavenly things. And since we have already treated the latter and set out our views on them we can now turn to the discussion of animals, without omitting any of them if possible, but dealing alike both with those thought more, and those thought less, noble.

He then expands interestingly on this last point. Whatever moral or aesthetic reactions ordinary people may have to particular animals, from a scientific point of view they are all equally worthy of attention:

For although there are some animals which are more attractive to the senses, from the point of view of intellectual enquiry the craftsmanship of nature provides endless satisfactions to those who can recognize the causes in things and are naturally inclined to seek knowledge...

So, we must not recoil in childish aversion from the study of the less well-liked animals, since there is something to be wondered at in all of nature. There is a story that when some visitors of Heraclitus saw him warming himself at the kitchen stove as they were entering, they hesitated and held back; but he said, 'Don't be shy, come on in—there are gods even here.' Similarly, we should pursue our enquiries into every kind of animal without any sense of distaste, since each and every one of them is in some way natural and beautiful.

Aristotle, *Parts of Animals* 644b28–645a24

The point of this long preamble has been to establish that Aristotle was at least intending to study animals, including birds, in a quite different way from what had gone before. The hunters, farmers, and cooks of part 2 will also have acquired a good deal of practical knowledge about birds and their behaviour, but their motive was to exploit this for human consumption, not to study it for its own sake. The relationships between birds and people described in part 2 certainly suggest a more complex and interconnected universe of living creatures, but those involved did little to investigate it rigorously. Similarly, the medical writers in chapter 12 were interested only in using birds or parts of birds for their supposed medicinal benefits. Aristotle himself may not have always lived up to his own precepts about scientific enquiry but these did at least signal a new kind of endeavour.

Aristotle was above all a great systematizer and his taxonomies of the natural world were certainly applauded by some of the giants in the field who came later:

Aristotle from the beginning presents a zoological classification that has left very little to do for the centuries after him. His great divisions and sub-divisions of the natural world are astonishingly precise, and have almost all resisted subsequent additions by science.

Georges Cuvier, *Histoire des sciences naturelles* (1841), vol. I, pp. 148–49

Linnaeus and Cuvier have been my two gods, though in different ways, but they were mere schoolboys to old Aristotle.

Charles Darwin (Letter to William Ogle, 22 February 1882)

In the particular case of taxonomy, however, this adulation is disingenuous and somewhat misrepresents the true nature of Aristotle's influence. He offers several different ways of dividing up the world of animals but, as Cuvier and Darwin knew full well, none of them is a comprehensive hierarchical system like that of Linnaeus. He did make some basic distinctions between what we would now call 'species' (e.g. rook), 'genus' (e.g. crows), and 'class' (e.g. birds).[1] But these terms were not applied wholly consistently, do not correspond exactly to our distinctions, and, most importantly, do not form part of a full branching 'tree of nature' of the sort we find in Linnaeus's *Systema naturae* of 1735. Aristotle does not define sufficient intermediate categories—like 'order' (e.g. perching birds) and 'family' (e.g. corvids)—to complete these vertical hierarchies; nor does he enumerate anywhere a classified list of species. He does something different, but in its own way at least as interesting.

Aristotle organizes his zoological works not by species but by aspects of anatomy, behaviour, or attributes that have a larger biological significance for him. So, there are separate works on the *Parts of Animals* (morphology), *Generation of Animals* (reproduction and development), and *Movement of Animals* and *Progression of Animals* (both on locomotion); while his major work, the *History of Animals*, is subdivided by differences in external and internal parts, the senses, modes of reproduction, diet, habitat, disposition, distribution, and so on. True to his methodological programme, he distinguishes in the course of these analyses many particular species or groups of birds by way of furnishing the necessary

---

[1] Aristotle's usual terms are *eidos* ('species'), *genos* ('genus'), and *megiston genos* ('main kind').* The standard modern taxonomic sequence for a rook, however, would run: Kingdom (*Animalia*: Animals), Phylum (*Chordata*: With backbones), Class (*Aves*: Birds), Order (*Passeriformes*: Perching birds), Family (*Corvidae*: Corvids), Genus (*Corvus*: Crows), and Species (*Corvus frugilegus*: Rook).

II. AVES.

Corpus plumosum. Alæ duæ. Pedes duo. Rostrum osseum. Fæmina oviparæ.

4.7 The Linnaean hierarchy: Carl Linnaeus (1707–78) divided the natural world into the three 'kingdoms' of animals, plants and minerals. The animal kingdom in turn was subdivided into six 'classes': mammals, birds, amphibians, fishes, insects, and other invertebrates (*vermes*, literally 'worms'), each of which is further subdivided into orders, genera and species. This column dealing with the *Aves* (birds) is taken from the first edition of his *Systema Naturae* of 1735. Linnaeus progressively enlarged the work as new specimens were obtained and identified and the major tenth edition of 1758 included over 4,400 animal species and 7,700 plant species (still a massive underestimate, as it turned out, since there are now over 10,000 bird species alone, some 400,000 plant species, and possibly up to 30 million insect species).

empirical examples for his hypotheses,[1] but nowhere does he integrate all the descriptions of each individual species in one place. His interest is a functional one—what is the biological purpose of all these differences?

> Some birds have long legs and the reason is that they live in marshes. Nature makes the organs suit the work they have to do, not the work to suit the organs.
>
> Aristotle, *Parts of Animals* 694b13–15

It would not be unreasonable to go a little further and translate that as 'Nature *adapts* the organs to suit…', and one can see why Darwin would have responded to that. The line of thought is ecological. How are species suited to their environments?

Here are some other examples from the various differentiae Aristotle highlights. Beaks:

> Birds' beaks also vary according to their lifestyles. Some are straight, some curved—straight where they are just used for feeding, curved if they eat raw meat, since in that case they are needed for overpowering prey and these birds have to feed off living creatures, most often using force. Whereas marsh birds and herbivorous birds have broad beaks that are useful for digging and pulling up their food or cropping vegetation. And some of these have long beaks and long necks too, because they have to obtain their food from some depth. Most of these birds and also the partially or completely web-footed ones live by hunting various tiny water creatures, and the neck in these birds plays the part of an angler's fishing-rod, while the beak is the line and hook.
>
> Aristotle, *Parts of Animals* 693a11–23

Wings and legs:

> Again, some birds are well adapted for flight and have big strong wings—these are the birds with curved talons that live on raw meat and have to be strong fliers because of their lifestyles…But there are also other kinds of birds that can fly well—for example, those whose safety depends on their speed of flight and those with migratory habits. Some other birds, more heavily constructed, are poor fliers—these are the ones that live on the ground and are frugivorous, or those living on or around water…Some of these heavy-bodied birds have 'spurs' on their

---

[1] Probably about 140 species of birds are distinguished in the whole corpus, depending somewhat on how you count groups of birds and obscure cases.* See also the appendix, pp. 363–67, for some general remarks about naming and identification.

legs and use these as their means of defence instead of wings. But the same bird
never has both spurs and talons, the reason being that nature never makes anything superfluous.

Aristotle, *Parts of Animals* 693b27–694a15

Diet:

Other birds are grub-eaters, for example the pied and barred woodpeckers.[1]
Some people call both of these just 'woodpeckers', and they are similar to look at
and have similar voices, except that the greater has a louder voice than the lesser.
Both forage by fastening on to tree trunks. There is also the green woodpecker,
which is about the size of a turtle dove but green all over; that is a very vigorous
pecker of wood and feeds mostly on trunks; it has a loud voice and is mainly to be
found in the Peloponnese. Another species, called an insect-picker, is as small as
a finch; it is the colour of wood-ash and speckled; it has a soft voice and this bird
too is a pecker of wood.[2]

Aristotle, *History of Animals* 593a3–14

Nesting habits:

Wild birds devise their nesting sites to suit their modes of life and the security of
their young. Some are good parents and attentive to their young and some the
reverse; some are resourceful in providing the means of life, others not so. Some
make their homes around gullies, others round hollows and rocks—for example,
the so-called *charadrios*,[3] which is inconspicuous in coloration and voice and is
active at night but runs away from you in the daytime.

Aristotle, *History of Animals* 614b32–615a4

Habitat:

Some birds live by the sea, including the *kinklos*, which is a clever, mischievous
bird; it is hard to catch but captive ones can become very tame. It is defective in
that it can't keep its hind-parts still.[4]

---

[1] I have used these older terms because, although the identity of the barred (lesser spotted) woodpecker (*Dendrocopos minor*) seems clear from the reference to its size, the pied one was probably the
middle spotted (*D. medius*, common in Lesbos) rather than the great spotted (*D. major*, the familiar one
in Britain).

[2] This bird sounds like a treecreeper (but see pp. 234–35).

[3] Literally the 'ravine bird', probably a stone curlew *Burhinus oedicnemus* from this description.

[4] Probably, from this and other references, a white wagtail *Motacilla alba*. Aristotle refers earlier (*HA*
593b4–7) to this tail-wagging, which gave rise to a verb describing vigorous sexual thrusting.*

All the web-footed birds live by the sea, rivers, and wetlands, for nature itself selects what is best fitted. Many split-footed birds also live by water and wetlands—for example, the *anthos* that lives by rivers. This is a beautifully coloured species and a successful one.[1]

Aristotle, *History of Animals* 615a22–28

And voice:

All birds use their tongues for the purpose of communicating with one another, some more so than others, so that it seems likely that in some cases they are actually sharing information.

Aristotle, *Parts of Animals* 660a35–660b2

In some species the male and female birds have the same kind of calls, but in others they have different ones. Smaller birds tend to be more vocal and chatter more than do large ones, and every kind of bird is at its most vocal during the mating season. Some, like the quail, call when fighting; others, like the partridge, before fighting or, like cockerels, when they have won the fight…

Vocalizations and dialects vary by locality. Voice is distinguished mainly by pitch, high or low, but there is no distinction of kind between birds of the same sort. However, articulated voice, which one could call a kind of speech like dialect, does differ in different animals and also varies within kinds, according to locality. Thus, some partridges cackle, while others have a shrill call. And among small birds, some sing in a different way from their parents if they have been reared away from the nest and have listened to the songs of other birds.

Aristotle, *History of Animals* 536a23–27, 536b8–18*

Each bird can be described as a cluster of attributes derived from these various distinguishing features, but the process is a messy one with lots of exceptions, anomalies, and boundary crossings. That is, there is no neat and fully articulated hierarchy of attributes that uniquely defines each species. Indeed, some creatures are radical 'dualizers', which don't even fit into any one 'main kind': for example, the seal, bat, and ostrich, each of which has an unusual combination of features.* He says of the ostrich:

The Libyan ostrich has some of the attributes of a bird and some of a quadruped. It differs from a quadruped in having feathers, and from a bird in being

---

[1] This is probably the yellow wagtail *Motacilla flava*, which elsewhere is said to forage in agitated fashion around livestock, as indeed it still does (*HA* 609b15–20).

unable to take to the air and fly, having feathers that are more like hairs and are useless for flight. But it is like a quadruped in having upper eyelashes, and it is bald around the head and the upper neck, so that its eyelashes are correspondingly more hairy; and it is like a bird in having feathered lower parts. It is also like a bird in having two feet, but like a quadruped in having cloven hooves (for it has hooves, not toes). The explanation of these features comes from its bulk, since it is the size of a quadruped not a bird. For speaking generally, a bird has necessarily to be of very small size, because it is difficult for a body of any great bulk to become airborne.

    Aristotle, *Parts of Animals* 697b14–26

Whatever the mistakes in details here,[1] it is to Aristotle's credit that he emphasizes the approximate and provisional status of these taxonomic labels, and perhaps one could even say their arbitrariness.[2] He was more interested in similarities and differences than in definitions.

    In some other examples Aristotle reproduces popular confusions between superficially similar species—for example, between swifts and swallows, which actually belong to quite different families.[3] In this passage the generic and the specific seem to get mixed up, since at the start they are all lumped together as *apodes*[4] ('footless' birds—that is, birds bad on the ground but good in the air), while later the *drepanis* and the *apous* are distinguished:

> Some birds are ill equipped with feet and for this reason are called *apodes*. The little bird in question is a very good flier, and almost all those species like it are also good fliers but with deficient feet—for example, the swallow and the *drepanis*. All these have similar behaviour and wing structure and a similar appearance. The *apous* can be seen throughout the seasons, but the *drepanis* when it has been raining in the summer—that's when it is observed and is caught, but in general it is a rare species.
>
>   Aristotle, *History of Animals* 487b14–31

The *drepanis* ('sickle bird') sounds like the alpine swift, which has very much that silhouette and is the rarer swift in the region; while the *apous* in the last sentence could in this context refer to the crag martin, the only hirundine that

---

[1] The hairs over the eyes are not actually eyelashes and each foot has two large toes (which look like but are not actually hooves).

[2] A loaded expression, to be sure, but Darwin himself says that 'species' is a term 'arbitrarily given for the sake of convenience' (1859), ch. 2.

[3] Three kinds of swifts and five of hirundines occur locally.

[4] This etymology survives in the current scientific name of the swift genus, *Apus*.

can be seen the year round in parts of Greece (including Lesbos). However, the confusion spreads in a later passage (618a30–b2) where Aristotle says that the *apous* (now also called a *kupselos*) is hard to distinguish from the swallow, except by its 'shaggy legs' (which strongly suggests a house martin).*

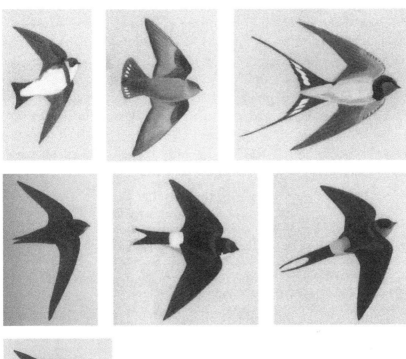

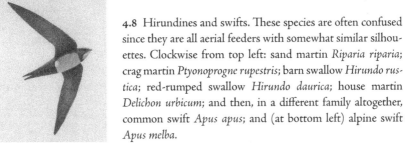

4.8 Hirundines and swifts. These species are often confused since they are all aerial feeders with somewhat similar silhouettes. Clockwise from top left: sand martin *Riparia riparia*; crag martin *Ptyonoprogne rupestris*; barn swallow *Hirundo rustica*; red-rumped swallow *Hirundo daurica*; house martin *Delichon urbicum*; and then, in a different family altogether, common swift *Apus apus*; and (at bottom left) alpine swift *Apus melba*.

Other passages include some more obvious mistakes.[1] In the extract on 'voice' (above) Aristotle goes on to say that female as well as male nightingales sing

---

[1] Darwin complains about some of Aristotle's 'grossest mistakes' in a less often quoted passage from the highly complimentary letter cited above (p. 227).

(in fact the females of European robins and a few other temperate-zone species do, but not those of nightingales).* In a passage on colour (*History of Animals* 519a) he says that the crane is the only bird whose plumage changes with age (but this happens in many species, if you count juvenile plumages; and in some, such as gulls and raptors, the full adult plumage takes several years to develop); but he adds that many species change their plumage with the seasons and in particular that some dark birds turn white (the ptarmigan does, but not his examples of raven, swallow, and sparrow). He also perpetuates a number of hoary myths about swans singing before they die (615b), nightjars milking she-goats and causing them to go blind (618b), swallows hibernating (600a), and the kingfisher breeding in winter during the 'halcyon days' (542b). Aristotle was by no means the first or the last to retail these fallacies, of course, many of which have survived for centuries.*

But he does also record some very nice observations and distinctions, including some whose possible significance was not seen at the time—a good test of anyone's field notes:

> Some scops owls are resident throughout the year and are called 'Always-scops'. These are not eaten because they are considered inedible. Others appear some time in the autumn and are present just for a day or two at the most. These are edible and are a highly regarded dish. They are virtually identical with the 'Always-scops', except in regard to their fatness; and they are silent whereas the other kind are vocal. Nothing has been ascertained about their genesis except that they evidently appear with the westerly winds.
>
> Aristotle, *History of Animals* 617b33–618a8

We now know that there are in fact two subspecies of scops owl in Greece: *Otus scops scops*, mostly found on parts of the mainland and the Ionian Islands, and *Otus scops cycladum*, mostly in Crete and the Cyclades. Some but not all of these different populations are partially migratory, and in autumn these migrant birds would have fattened themselves up for their flight to their winter quarters in Africa and would just pause for a few days on passage, when they would generally have been less vocal.*

We should remember that observers in the ancient world had no optical equipment and the small distinctions of plumage so finely discriminated in modern guides would often have gone unnoticed in the field. Aristotle does, however, describe some bird calls that might mark interesting points of identification. In the passage on diet quoted above, he refers correctly to the 'soft voice' of the treecreeper; but in a later passage (616b28–31) he says the *kerthios* (which is clearly a treecreeper of some sort from the description) 'has a clear voice'. Could the latter be the short-toed treecreeper (*Certhia brachydactyla*), whose voice the best modern field guide highlights as a distinguishing feature, being 'strong… with a clear and penetrating quality'? And in the passage on voice (p. 231 above), notice that Aristotle distinguishes two different partridge vocalizations, one 'a cackle' and the other 'a shrill call'. Could that be a distinction between two visually very similar species: the chukar *Alectoris chukar* (common in Lesbos, the Aegean Islands, and Asia Minor) and the rock partridge *Alectoris graeca* (common in mainland Greece and to the west)? The onomatopoeic Greek verb *kakkabizo*, translated here as 'cackle', does indeed sound very like the chukar's call, which the field guide transcribes as 'ga ga ga ga cha chakera-chakera-chakera', while the other verb, *trizo*, is usually defined as to 'utter a shrill cry' (citing bats or young birds).*

What are we to make of this rather mixed performance from one of the world's greatest intellects? There is such a wealth of good observations and original theory that one should not be too defensive about the occasional weaknesses, some of which are no doubt due to circumstantial factors like the following:

1. These texts are probably just lecture notes, not all of them compiled by Aristotle himself. His more literary works prepared for wider publication are all lost.
2. In particular, it is thought that Books VII–X of the *History of Animals*, the source of most of the references to birds and many of the cruder mistakes, are not by Aristotle at all but are later compilations by his less critical successors.
3. All the genuine texts were in any case subject to later additions and interventions over which Aristotle had no editorial control.
4. Aristotle's practice of assembling the observational data (*phainomena*) as a preliminary to explanatory theory will have led to the incorporation of many second-hand reports from his wide range of informants, not all of whom will have been fully reliable.
5. And he needed this help because he had no real predecessors, either in the collection of data other than that preserved in folklore or in taxonomic theory.

Aristotle was the first in his field. He will also have brought to it his own *idées fixes* and prejudices. After all, many other great scientists have harboured beliefs that most people would now dismiss as mere superstitions: one thinks of Newton (alchemy), Linnaeus (creationism), Darwin (hydrotherapy), Alfred Russel Wallace (spiritualism), Fred Hoyle (panspermism),[1] and all the hopeful adherents of such fancies as phlogiston, phrenology, and astrology.

In assessing Aristotle's shortcomings one should, in any case, distinguish between defective observational data, whether simple gaps in knowledge (ignorance) or failures of interpretation (mistakes), and larger beliefs in, or failures to challenge, the prevailing consensus of thought at the time. The latter are generally the more interesting aberrations, and a key example here would be Aristotle's anthropocentrism, his understandable belief that the human species is at the apex of a 'ladder of nature', ranked by a progressive complexity of structure and function.

Aristotle was quite explicit about this. He conceived the natural world as a continuum of increasing complexity. Nature, he says, in a phrase irresistibly recalling Darwin, 'proceeds by small steps':[2]

> Nature proceeds from the inanimate to the animate by small steps, so that because of the gradual progression we fail to notice where the boundaries of demarcation or the middle points in the continuum are.
>
> Aristotle, *History of Animals* 588b4–6

The continuum runs through the inanimate to plants, to simple forms of marine life, and so on through animals, which are ranked by criteria like vitality, capacity for motion, and sensibilities; and that leads to differences in 'habits of life', principally modes of reproduction, feeding, and habitat. He then launches into the analyses of his 'main kinds' of animals—insects, fishes, and in due course birds and mammals. The key differences between all these lower animals and humankind are those of intelligence, language, and culture. That is why he famously defined a human being as 'by nature a political animal' (*Politics* 1253a2). And that is why the human species is also the supreme one—the model and paradigm for all the others.

---

[1] The physicist Fred Hoyle stoutly maintained to the last that all the world's viruses and bacteria came to us from outer space.

[2] Darwin borrowed the Latin tag 'Natura non fecit saltus' ('Nature does not make jumps') from Linnaeus and he uses it no fewer than seven times in *The Origin of Species*, though it has since become a controversial claim.*

At this point Aristotle is clearly making value judgements as well as zoological ones. That is in itself neither surprising nor unusual. Aristotle's ladder of nature became the *scala naturae* of medieval and Renaissance thought, which extended the ladder upwards to include God at the top, and belief in that system was seriously challenged only in the eighteenth century. Indeed, the existence of such a hierarchy would still represent the unquestioned belief of most of the world's human population today.

What is interesting is how Aristotle himself partly undercuts this idea, not only in his scientific manifesto (quoted on pp. 224–26 above: *Parts of Animals* 644–45) but also in some of his actual descriptions, as if the scientist in him was struggling to free himself from his cultural norms. He sees that there are in the animal kingdom many examples of behaviour that look very similar to human behaviour. For example, bees too are 'social animals' (*History of Animals* 623b25–627b22); various animals share human qualities of character and disposition (*History of Animals* 608a8–b18); they have their own friendships and enmities (*History of Animals* 608b19–610a34); birds have voice, which he describes as a 'kind of speech' (p. 231 above); and they also display many notable skills, which certainly amount to a kind of intelligence (the key differentia).

The swallow, for example, constructs a nest on sound building principles:

> Consider first in the case of birds the nest-building of the swallow. She keeps to the same order in mixing mud with chaff. She interweaves mud with stalks, and if the mud runs out she moistens herself and rolls her feathers around in the dust. Moreover, she builds the nest in just the way humans do, placing the stiffer materials down first as a foundation and adjusting the size to match her own.
>
> Aristotle, *History of Animals* 612b18–27

Similarly, cranes manage demanding migratory movements and flock coordination:

> Cranes seem to exhibit many signs of intelligence too. They migrate over great distances and fly at a great height in order to be able to survey the far distance; and if they see clouds or bad weather ahead they fly down and pause in their journey. Moreover, they have a leader and others who are assigned to call out signals, flying on the edge of their flocks so as to be heard by all. And when they are roosting, the others sleep with their heads tucked under the wing and standing on each foot in turn, while the leader keeps a lookout with head uncovered and if he sees anything he signals that with a cry.
>
> Aristotle, *History of Animals* 614b18–26

4.9 The medieval *scala naturae*. Drawing of the 'Great Chain of Being' from Didacus Valades, *Rhetorica Christiana* (1579).

And the cuckoo has cunning reproductive strategies:

> The cuckoo, as noted elsewhere, does not make a nest of its own but lays in those of other birds, mostly pigeons and ground-nesting wheatears[1] and larks, or the tree-nesting bird known as the greenfinch. The cuckoo lays one egg but does not sit on it herself. Instead the bird in whose nest it is laid hatches it and rears the young; and they say that when the cuckoo chick grows larger it expels the young of the host and so kills them.[2]
>
> Aristotle, *History of Animals* 618a8–16

This, he says, is a sign that the cuckoo 'manages its reproduction intelligently...by making its own offspring into substitutes of a kind, in order to ensure their survival' (618a26–29).

In giving such examples of avian 'intelligence' Aristotle isn't always himself sure whether any differences between humans and animals in this respect are best described as ones of degree or of kind. Are these capacities one can ascribe to animals only metaphorically and 'by analogy'?* A later writer, Plutarch, who wrote an interesting essay titled 'The cleverness of animals', was quite impatient with all these academic distinctions. Anyone who works or lives with animals, he says, just *knows* that they have a large range of emotions and cognitive abilities and we should plainly describe them accordingly:

> There are those who stupidly assert that animals do not feel pleasure or anger or fear, or make preparations for the future or remember the past, but say that the bee 'as it were' remembers, the swallow 'as it were' makes preparations, the lion is 'as it were' enraged, and the deer is 'as it were' frightened. But I don't know how they would deal with assertions that animals can only 'as it were' see and hear, that they can only 'as it were' give voice, and can only 'as it were' live. For the first set of denials is as absurd as the second.
>
> Plutarch, 'Cleverness of animals', *Moralia* 961e–f

And that takes us right back to the 'wisdom of folklore' in Aesop, and the famous story of the crow and the pebbles:

---

[1] The black-eared wheatear *Oenanthe hispanica* is a guess based on the etymology of *hypolais* ('under-stone'). This does nest in a depression in stony ground or under stones and is a regular host species to the cuckoo in Greece today.

[2] This observation about the cuckoo expelling the host's young was largely ignored for the next 2,000 years and the behaviour was 'rediscovered' only in 1788 by Edward Jenner, who now takes the credit.*

A thirsty crow saw a huge water jar and noticed that there was a little water just at the bottom. For a long time the crow kept trying to spill some water out so that it would pour on to the ground and enable him to slake his raging thirst. But after he failed to find a way despite his best efforts, the crow became frustrated. So he summoned up all his cunning and found an ingenious solution. He dropped little pebbles into the jar, whereupon the water level rose of its own accord and he was able to take a drink. The moral is that intelligence can triumph over brute strength, since that is what enabled the bird to complete his task.

Aesop, *Fables* 390a (Perry)

4.10 The crow and the water jug. A favourite story, often repeated in slightly different forms.* The thirsty crow's feat has now been many times tested experimentally and confirmed (you can watch a performance on YouTube). This picture was drawn by Milo Winter for his illustrated edition of *Aesop's Fables* (1919).

Aristotle represents a high point. He had no serious predecessors in the ancient world. His immediate successor was Theophrastus, who had shared in Aristotle's fieldwork in Lesbos and became the next head of the Lyceum. Theophrastus continued Aristotle's scientific work in many fields, though practically all that survives is his remarkable work on botany (which he can be said to have founded as a proper subject in Western thought). The interesting difference here was that there were not the same temptations to anthropomorphism in botany. Theophrastus never tried to devise a hierarchy of plant species, with just one form nominated as the paradigm to which others were aspiring. But that temptation was all but impossible to avoid in the case of the animal kingdom. Aristotle's later successors in the Roman world, like the self-styled 'natural historians' Pliny and Aelian, largely contented themselves with recirculating versions of Aristotle's work (now arranged by species rather than function), combined with their gleanings from other sources and from popular wisdom. The resulting potpourri in effect envisaged the natural world as an extension of the familiar human one, enlivened by curiosities and satisfying parallels. Aristotle himself continued to exert an enormous influence on the later history of taxonomy, for which he was not always thanked, though the criticisms would more fairly have been directed not at him but at those who failed to build on his work and allowed it to ossify into dogma.

His work was not wasted, though. Some of Aristotle's categories proved very insightful and were directly influential on such sixteenth-century taxonomists as Edward Wotton, Conrad Gesner, Pierre Belon, and Ulisse Aldrovandi; his basic distinction between land and water birds recurs in the foundational early modern text of Francis Willughby and John Ray (1676); and his fourfold division of birds into hook-taloned raptors, web-footed swimmers, waterside 'split-feet', and terrestrial 'poor fliers' is later recognizable in four of Linnaeus's six orders, as the Accipitres, Anseres, Grallae, and Gallinae.*

It is traditional to recognize such achievements in the eponyms that later taxonomists confer on the species they name. But it is hard to know if Aristotle would have been more touched than disappointed to discover that the only bird named after him was *Phalacrocorax aristotelis*, 'Aristotle's bald-raven' or the common shag, a resident around Lesbos.

PART 5

Thinking
with Birds

If you abolished mythology throughout Greece, all the tourist guides would starve to death, since foreign visitors have no wish to hear the truth, even when they can have it for free.

Lucian (second century AD), *The Liar* 4

Every creature in the world is for us like a book, a picture and a mirror.

Alain de Lille (twelfth century AD), *De incarnatione Christi*, 579a (Migne)

Les espèces sont choisies non comme bonnes à manger, mais comme bonnes à penser.

Claude Lévi-Strauss, *Le totémisme* (1962), 128*

5.1 Metamorphosis myth. Ovid's stories caught the imagination of many later writers and illustrators, and the *Metamorphoses* was a very popular book in the Renaissance. This seventeenth-century engraving, from a work perhaps by Cornelis Bloemaert (1603–92),* portrays Cygnus being changed into a swan, and the inscription below the engraving quotes from the line in Ovid, *Metamorphoses* II 377, 'Fit nova Cycnus avis' ('Cygnus became a new bird'). Cygnus is approaching the dead figure of Phaethon on the bank, who crash-landed in the river after his fiery flight through the sky and whose death Cygnus has been grieving; Phaethon's weeping sisters, the Heliades (daughters of the sun god, Helios), become poplar trees; and the reclining figure on the left is the river god Eridanus, here (unusually) in the form of a bull. See also p. 279.

Introduction

The last part considered progressive attempts to understand the place of birds in the natural world—their classification, characteristics, and behaviour—and the gradual and partial development of what could be called a science of ornithology. In this part we shall be looking not so much at thinking *about* birds as thinking *with* them: that is, at the part they played as metaphors and symbols in the ways people represented the natural world and engaged with it. Birds were among its most conspicuous inhabitants. They were found throughout the world of human experience, strikingly visible and audible in the realms of land, sea, and air alike. Wherever you were, there were birds—feeding, displaying, fighting, vocalizing, mating, and engaging in a whole range of social behaviours that would seem instantly recognizable to human observers. No surprise, then, that birds did not just present themselves as physical objects of curiosity and study, but also populated people's minds and imaginations and then re-emerged in their language, legends, and patterns of thought in some symbolic form.

This, I take it, is what Lévi-Strauss was indicating in his much quoted dictum that supplies the part title. In discussing the phenomenon of totemism, Lévi-Strauss says that natural species are chosen not so much because they are *bonnes à manger* as because they are *bonnes à penser*. That doesn't translate neatly into English, since although we talk about things being 'good to eat' it is unidiomatic to say that birds, for example, are 'good to think'. 'Good for thinking' won't quite do either, since that suggests some sort of intellectual workout, like doing crosswords. The phrase is therefore usually translated as 'good to think with', which well enough captures the questions we want to consider here. 'Think birds' might be the modern vernacular equivalent.

The point here, at any rate, is that birds were clearly considered to have a *significance* that went well beyond their place in the inventory of natural species that could be studied, identified and classified. Why did the army generals in

Homer's *Iliad* study the flight of eagles to help them make military decisions, why did the Romans keep a collection of sacred chickens and appoint a college of experts to interpret their feeding behaviour, why would a small woodpecker be pinned to a wheel as a love-charm, what was a wagtail dance supposed to achieve, and why do so many of Ovid's delightful fairy stories concern men and women changing into birds? Why birds particularly rather than other animal species, and why some birds more than others? It is striking, for example, that in the ancient folklore about the metamorphosis of people into other forms of life there are far more stories involving birds (around fifty of them) than mammals or other creatures. Owls and raptors feature especially strongly, as they do also in an ancient handbook on the interpretation of dreams, which we shall analyse in chapter 16. So what were the qualifying traits for these symbolic roles?

In any case, just to say that these curious (to us) practices and stories were 'symbolic' doesn't get us very far. What did people actually say and believe about them? Were they taken literally and at face value? Were there those who criticized them as mere superstitions, or did some people at least think they might be performing another kind of social or cultural function? And how can we make any sense of this today? It was once supposed that such belief systems were evidence of a kind of primitive, proto-science from which we have now moved on; but of course there are ample examples of metaphorical and symbolic uses of birds in our more 'advanced' societies today. Our own language is still rich in figures of speech derived from familiar birds like swallows, nightingales, swans, crows, and owls, as well as more exotic ones like peacocks, ostriches, albatrosses, and the dodo; we all understand the associations implied by references to political hawks and doves, commercial vultures, and military eagles; and we still have a shared resource of myths and folk memories on which poets, artists, musicians, and writers have drawn for imaginative purposes in their evocations of such species as the raven (Edgar Alan Poe), crow (Ted Hughes), nightingale (Keats), thrush (Browning), skylark (Shelley, Vaughan Williams), goldfinch (Raphael, Fabritius), swan (Rubens, Leonardo), and so on.*

What follows, then, should perhaps be less surprising, or at least less likely to provoke the reaction 'How on earth could they think that?'. The first two chapters in this part deal respectively with omens and auguries and magic and metamorphosis. Between them they illustrate a variety of attempts to interpret the workings of the natural world, to rationalize them, and to influence or accommodate to them. These purposes are not always clearly distinguished, but taken jointly they help to explain why birds became so important as 'signs' that were then projected back on to the world in the form of metaphors and symbols—the topic of the last chapter in this part.

At this point in the book the number of internal cross-references and interconnections between chapters is multiplying fast. Magic has an obvious relevance to chapter 12 on medicine, and metamorphosis to the fables about bird–human relationships in chapter 10, while the discussions of omens and dreams point forwards to the idea of birds as messengers and intermediaries dealt with in the next and final part.

~ 14 ~

Omens and Auguries

Translators regularly face the problem that the words and expressions of one language do not always translate exactly into those of another. In fact a literal translation can sometimes seem incomprehensible, particularly where the beliefs or behaviour of people from another culture are involved. Consider the following passage from Aristophanes' play *The Birds*, where the chorus of birds is trying to explain to their human visitors all the benefits they bestow on humankind, principal among which is acting as special consultants:

> We are your oracles—your Ammon, Delphi, Dodona, and your Apollo.[1]
> You don't start on anything without first consulting the birds,
> whether it's about business affairs, making a living, or getting married.
> Every prophecy that involves a decision you classify as a bird.
> To you, a significant remark is a bird; you call a sneeze a bird,
> a chance meeting is a bird, a sound, a servant, or a donkey—all birds.
> So clearly, we are your gods of prophecy.
> Aristophanes, *Birds* 716–24

That just sounds like a bizarre mistranslation. But it begins to make sense when you remember that the Greek word for a bird, *ornis* or *oionos*, was also the word for an omen. Birds were thought of as 'signs'. They were the principal agents through which the gods revealed their will to humans, so they could reasonably describe themselves as the gods' messengers and privileged intermediaries, who should

---

[1] Delphi and Dodona were the sites of the principal Greek oracles, while Ammon was the oracle in the Libyan desert, later made famous when Alexander the Great made a detour to visit it. Apollo was the prophetic deity presiding over oracles.

be consulted about future plans and important decisions. And all those items called 'birds' towards the end of the extract turn out to involve common super-stitions, rather like our habit of saying 'bless you' when someone sneezes.* So, to call something 'a bird' was simultaneously to say that it might be significant and that birds might be the clue to what that significance was.

That may help explain the linguistic confusion, but what about the larger cultural ones? Just how were birds supposed to fulfil these roles, and was it all birds or only some of them? Who believed in all this and on what basis? How could the societies that effectively invented Western science, philosophy, medi-cine, engineering, and mathematics entertain such curious superstitions?

Let's start with the practicalities and nomenclature. If birds were in some sense 'signs' that helped to explain the workings of the world and the will of the gods, the first thing you would need were some experts to decode bird behaviour.* Early practitioners of this skill were variously known as *oionoskopoi* (bird-watchers), *oionistai* and *oionomanteis* (bird interpreters), or *oionopoloi* (bird experts), and they appear regularly in classical literature from Homer onwards to advise on matters of state at critical moments. In Homer they are consulted particularly on military strategy. In the *Iliad* you have on the Greek side Calchas, 'by far the best expert on birds, who knew things present, future, and past' (I 68–70), while on the other side Helenus was 'by far the best birdman in Troy' (VI 76); and in the *Odyssey* Halitherses 'surpassed all men of his generation in his knowledge of birds and in expounding omens' (II 157). The seer Teiresias even had a special 'bird observatory' from which to practise his art, located in some place 'where every kind of bird finds refuge' (Sophocles, *Antigone* 998–1002), and this *oionoskopeion* was famous enough to be mentioned much later as a tourist attraction by the travel writer Pausanias (IX 16.1). Most of the augurs in Homer are men, but Helen too inter-prets a complicated bird omen in the *Odyssey* (xv 160–78), and female priestesses and diviners were central to the operation of most oracles.*

These interpreters of bird signs were among the exponents of the skill known more generally as *mantike* ('divination'), though that was an umbrella notion that also included interpreters of oracles, entrails, lots, the throw of dice, and dreams.[1] The 'ornithologists' tended to base most of their judgements on observations of the flight and calls of birds. They were then not usually making predictions as such, but rather establishing whether the prospects for particular courses of action

---

[1] The technical terms for these (often coined much later) are 'haruspicy' (entrails), 'cleromancy' (lots), 'astragalomancy' (dice), and 'oneiromancy' (dreams). For a discussion of dream divination, see pp. 285–89.

were good ones. The other exponents of *mantike* were more likely to be asked to
make prophecies as well, for which they might need a little divine inspiration;
and as the root of the word *mantike* suggests they were likely to be touched by a
little 'mania' to help them perform. The Roman word for the profession was
divinatio while a bird interpreter was called an *augur* or *auspex*, from which we
get the words 'augury' and 'auspicious' (literally 'watching birds' again). The Romans,
as you might expect, put all this on an organized basis, with an official body to
codify the rules and set professional standards, and we shall be looking at these
institutional arrangements later.

But the point to make first is that though there were recognized experts in ornithomancy or 'bird augury', this was by no means thought of as an occult or mysterious skill; it was a common one that everyone believed in and practised to some
degree, rather like forecasting the weather, where the basic lore of what constituted
good or bad signs was widely understood. It provided a sort of framework of implicit belief of the kind most people had to help them make sense of the world.

There is a different kind of example in Hesiod's long poem *Works and Days*,
which is largely a manual of good practice for farmers, organized by the agricultural calendar. At the end of this Hesiod makes an explicit connection between
bird augury and the belief in propitious and unpropitious days:[1]

> These [fortunate] days are a great blessing to men on earth,
> but the other ones are fickle, vapid, and offer nothing.
> Some praise one day, some another, but few understand them.
> Sometimes a day is a stepmother, sometimes a mother.
> Happy and fortunate the man who knows all these things
> and goes about his work without offending the immortals,
> interpreting bird signs rightly and avoiding transgressions.
>
> Hesiod, *Works and Days* 822–28

Here are also a few examples from Homer of augury in action, where everyone witnessing the signs could see what they portended. Towards the end of the
Iliad the old king of Troy, Priam, prays to Zeus to send him a favourable omen
for his dangerous mission to plead with Achilles. The god obliges:

> At once he sent an eagle, most significant of winged birds,
> the dark hunter whom they also call the 'dusky eagle',
> his wings stretched as wide on either side as

---

[1] A belief that survives in modern superstitions like those around 'Friday the 13th'.

the well-bolted doors of a rich man's lofty hall.[1]
It appeared on the right as it swooped through the city,
and those watching rejoiced and their spirits were raised.
    Homer, *Iliad* XXIV 315–21

An example of an *unfavourable* omen occurs earlier in the *Iliad*, when Hector is pressing the attack against the Greek ships:

A bird had appeared to them as they were eager to advance,
a high-flying eagle, skirting the army on the left,
holding in its talons a monstrous blood-red snake,
alive and still writhing. Nor had the snake given up the fight,
but it twisted back on itself and struck the eagle gripping it
on the breast by the neck; and the eagle in sharp pain
dropped it to the ground, so that it fell among the throng,
while with a loud cry he soared away on the currents of air.
The Trojans shuddered when they saw the gleaming snake
lying among them, a portent from almighty Zeus.
    Homer, *Iliad* XII 200–08

Hector is advised by his augur, Polydamas, to hold back, on the grounds that the Trojans will eventually be repulsed like the eagle. But Hector is distinctly unhappy with this advice and impatient with all this ornithology:

Polydamas, I don't now want to hear this sort of message.
Surely you can come up with a better story than that?
If you are really serious in what you are saying
the gods must have scrambled your brains,
since you are telling me to forget the advice Zeus,
lord of the thunder, gave me as a solemn promise himself.
You tell me to follow the flight of long-winged birds,
creatures that do not interest me at all. I do not care
whether they fly to the right towards the morning sun
or to the left into the murky western gloom.
We must listen to the advice of almighty Zeus,
who is king of all mortals and immortals alike.
One omen alone is best—to fight for one's country.
    Homer, *Iliad* XII 231–43

---

[1] We still talk of eagles, especially sea eagles, as having wings 'as wide as barn doors'. Homer's 'dusky eagle' could have been a lesser spotted eagle (*Aquila pomarina*) or maybe even a black vulture (*Aegypius monachus*), commoner in Greece then. The eagle in the next extract is behaving more like a short-toed eagle (*Circaetus gallicus*), which specializes in catching snakes and is still common in the region.

As illustrated here, the omens were thought to be favourable when birds flew by on the right, unfavourable when on the left. But this prognosis would seem rather arbitrary since it depended very much on the way the observer happened to be facing at the time. The Hector example perhaps suggests that it was the *direction* of flight that mattered, which might make rather more sense, since the east—associated with light, morning, and the sun—was regarded as the auspicious quarter. The Romans thought left was favourable and right unfavourable, which seems to be because they faced south when conducting auguries while the Greeks faced north, so that east was on the right for the Greeks and on the left for the Romans. This confusion is reflected in their left / right etymologies. There is a marked predisposition in favour of right-handedness in most cultures and the word for 'right' tends to have a range of other uses with strongly favourable connotations, as it does in English (the *right* course of action, the *right* answer, a legal *right*, and so on). In the same way the Latin *dexter* means 'right', 'opportune', and 'dextrous'; but the Latin word for 'left', *sinister*, has to do double duty as both 'favourable' (as a sort of euphemism) and 'unfavourable' (more literally). No wonder, said Cicero, that there was scope here for 'a little error, a little superstition, and a great deal of fraud' (*On Divination* II 83).*

5.2 Eagle coin. Silver tetradrachm (4 drachmas) from Agrimentum in Sicily, 411 BC, bearing the image of an eagle with a hare in its talons.

Some omens required a more complex interpretation anyway. In Aeschylus' *Agamemnon* (112–20) two eagles, one 'black' and one 'white-tailed' (representing Agamemnon and his brother, Menelaus), appear on the side of the spear hand (the right, auspicious side) and are devouring a hare (Troy) that is pregnant (inauspicious, suggesting eventual retribution). And in another play (probably also by Aeschylus) we are told some of the technicalities that need to be mastered by the serious ornithoscopist:

I took pains to determine the flight of crook-taloned birds,
marking which were of the right by nature,
and which of the left, and what were their ways of living,
each after his kind, and the enmities and affections that were
between them, and how they consorted together.[1]
    Aeschylus, *Prometheus Bound*, 488–92

Poor old Aeschylus had a particularly intimate connection with raptors, having
reputedly died after being hit on the head by a tortoise dropped from a great
height by a lammergeier (the bearded vulture), who mistook his bald pate for
the sort of rock on which the bird regularly dropped tortoises to smash their
shells.*

Another problem was deciding which birds were significant. Just as Hector
had objected to a prophecy from his augur, Polydamas, when it didn't suit his
military plans, so in the *Odyssey* the famous seer Halitherses makes a prediction, based on the flight over the town of Ithaca of two aggressive eagles, that
Odysseus is returning to take his revenge on the suitors. They, of course, don't
want Odysseus' son or wife to believe this and sneer at the forecast:

Off with you, old man, go home now and prophesy
to your children to save them from future troubles.
On this matter, I am a far better prophet than you.
Many are the birds that fly back and forth under the sun's
rays and not all are fateful. As for Odysseus, he died
far away and you should have perished with him.
    Homer, *Odyssey* II 177–84

Raptors, and particularly eagles, were the species most often referred to in
military contexts needing interpretation. There are many other examples, not only
in Homer but also in the wars and campaigns reported by Herodotus, Xenophon,
and Arrian.* No doubt this was because raptors were predators, who conveyed
the necessary sense of power and physical violence; and since they were also
often carrion eaters they had a literally visceral relationship with animal entrails,
whose interpretation (haruspicy) constituted another branch of the discipline.
Raptorial birds (defined more generally) tended to have special relationships to
the gods, too, perhaps for related reasons: the eagle was the bird of Zeus (king

---

[1] This is the translation cleverly devised for his own purposes by the historian Lewis Namier on the
title-page of his famous study *The Structure of Politics at the Accession of George III* (1929), which is actually about party politics in England.

of the gods), the falcon and raven were the messengers of Apollo (god of prophecy), while the little owl (*Athene noctua*) was the eponymous bird of Athena (goddess of war).

*   *   *

War wasn't the only context in which omens were consulted, however, and eagles weren't the only significant birds. Birds were also weather forecasters, as we saw in chapter 1, and they might be asked about any number of difficult problems to do with journeys, business affairs, marriage, or other private matters, as listed in the quotation from Aristophanes' *Birds* at the start of this chapter.

Any bird could be ominous in the right circumstances, it seems. In the *Iliad*, again, Athena sends a heron to encourage Odysseus and Diomedes on their clandestine night mission to penetrate the enemy camp, and the bird calls out in the darkness as a comforting omen. By contrast, the travel writer Pausanias tells us that it was a crested lark that guided settlers from Attica to found a new colony (always an important venture, needing a good send-off). And it was a swallow that flitted insistently round the head of Alexander the Great while he was taking a nap in his tent, to warn him of a plot against his life.* These seem to be special cases, however, and apart from eagles, the other 'ominous' species that crop up most often in Greek literature are ravens and crows (not always reliably distinguished) and owls.

Ravens were generally bad news. They were often portents of death or disaster. Pausanias tells the story that when the Athenians were preparing for their calamitous military expedition to Sicily in 415 BC 'an uncountable flock of ravens descended on Delphi' and vandalized all the precious images the Athenians had dedicated to the god there. Pausanias reports all this with a straight face, but makes the worldly comment, 'I put the blame on human rogues and thieves myself' (*Description of Greece* x 15.5). Ravens could also act as guides, though, as they did to Alexander and his troops:

> When the guides became confused over the landmarks and the travellers got separated, lost their way, and started wandering about, ravens appeared and took over the role of guiding them on their journey. They flew swiftly in front for them to follow, but then waited for them if they slowed down and lagged behind. What was most remarkable of all, we're told, was that they called out to those who strayed away at night and by their croaking set them back on the right track.
>
> Plutarch, *Life of Alexander* 27.2–3

It was their croaking, in fact, that was especially significant:

> As for the raven, that is said to be a sacred bird, and one in the service of Apollo. That is why it is generally regarded as good for divination, and those who can interpret the positions of birds in the sky, their cries, and their flight patterns, whether on the right or the left hand, pay special attention to its croaking in their divination.
>
> Aelian, *On Animals* 1 48

Ravens were also thought to have unusual powers of sharing information. After a particularly grisly massacre at Pharsalus in Thessaly in 395 BC, ravens were said to have gathered there in great numbers, 'having deserted all their usual sites in Attica and the Peloponnese, suggesting that they had some sense through which they could communicate with one another' (Aristotle, *History of Animals* 618b13–17). Ravens have been the subject of many such anecdotes throughout history, but it is now known that some scavenging species (seabirds as well as raptors) have an exceptionally well-developed sense of smell.* Pliny, referring to the same incident, remarks that 'ravens seem to be the only birds to have an understanding of their own signs in auguries' (*Natural History* x 33). That is, they recognize the signs that they themselves represent—a rather sophisticated thought, if that is what he meant.

Crows were less often specifically mentioned and were sometimes distinguished only to their disadvantage, as in this Aesop fable:

> The crow was jealous of the raven's ability to reveal omens to humans, since it was the raven who was always consulted about future prospects and he wanted to have the same status. So, when the crow saw some travellers passing, he flew up into a tree and sat there, croaking loudly. The men turned to the cry in some alarm, but then one of them said, 'Let's go on, friends. It's only a crow and his squawking doesn't signify anything.'
>
> Aesop, *Fables* 125 (Perry)

In any case, they seem to be more ambiguous signs, depending on context. Their reputation for matrimonial fidelity meant that they might be invoked at weddings, for good or ill:

> Crows are extremely faithful to each other and when they enter into a partnership they display intense affection. You wouldn't catch one of these creatures acting promiscuously. Those who know about these things say that when one of them

dies the other remains a widow. There is also an ancient tradition of 'singing the
crow' after the bridal hymn as a pledge of union between those coming together
for the procreation of children. However, those who observe the flight of birds
and the quarters of the sky say that to hear a single crow is a bad omen for a
couple at a wedding.

Aelian, *On Animals* III 9

This is a typical example of hedging one's bets in the soothsaying business.

Owls could be interpreted both ways, too. Plutarch tells us that at the battle
of Salamis in 480 BC, a famous Greek victory over the invading Persians, 'an owl
was spotted flying in through the fleet from the right to settle in the rigging,[1]
and it thereby encouraged the troops to respond to Themistocles' call and prepare for a sea-battle' (*Life of Themistocles* 12). And when Agathocles, the Syracusan
leader, was urging his troops into battle against superior odds in the war with
the Carthaginians in 310 BC, he encouraged them with a tactical release of owls:

> Seeing that his men were terrified by the barbarians' huge force of cavalry and
> infantry, he let loose at various points in the army owls, which he had gathered
> well beforehand in case he needed to stop the common soldiers from becoming
> discouraged. The owls flew through the phalanx and settled on their shields and
> helmets. This boosted their morale, with everyone interpreting this as a favourable
> omen because the owl is the creature sacred to Athena. This sort of thing might
> seem to some an empty device, but it often proves very successful, as it was on this
> occasion.
>
> Diodorus, *Bibliotheca historica* XX 11.3–5

The owl 'sacred to Athena' was the little owl, a familiar and popular enough denizen
of the city to be pictured on the Athenian coinage. The Romans, however, tended
to think of owls as mysterious and frightening creatures of the night. They
probably had in mind here more particularly the eagle owl (*Bubo*) and the barn
owl (*Strix*), though it's hard always to be sure which species is intended, or indeed
whether the reference is just generic:[2]

> The eagle owl is regarded as a bird of death and abomination, especially in public
> auspices. It inhabits desert places that are not only desolate but also terrifying and

---

[1] It was September—could it have been a migrant?

[2] The tawny owl (which now, confusingly, has the generic name *Strix*) is also a possibility. But the
Romans and (more particularly) the Greeks had over forty different folk names for owls, which are often
unidentifiable as to species.

remote. It is a monster of the night, and its voice is not so much a song as a deep groan. So if it ever appears in a city by day it is a dire portent.

Pliny, *Natural History* x 34–35

Pliny does go on to say, in a more matter-of-fact tone of voice, 'I know of several cases, however, where one sat on a private house without any ill effects occurring'; but common sense is no match for superstition in such situations and owls of all kinds have been regularly thought of as omens of disaster in many cultures.* Here are a few other examples from Latin literature.

At the Battle of Cannae in 216 BC Hannibal inflicted one of the worst ever defeats on a Roman army, before which 'many an owl frequented the gates to the camp' (Silius Italicus, *Punica* VIII 634); and in the great Civil War between Caesar and Pompey (49–48 BC), 'the call of an owl on the left' should have warned the augurs to override the more favourable omens from other birds (Lucan v 395–96).

Ovid's *Metamorphoses*, too, has many cautionary references to owls: Ascalaphus[1] was changed into a bird as a punishment and became 'an abomination, a prophet of doom, a slothful owl, a dire omen for mortal men' (Ovid, *Metamorphoses* v 543–550); at the ill-omened wedding of Tereus and Procne[2] 'a profane owl brooded like an incubus on the roof of the wedding chamber' (VI 431–32); an owl called thrice to avert an act of incest (x 452); and, most famously, there were

5.3 Owl of Athena coin. Silver Athenian tetradrachm (4 drachmas), fifth century BC, depicting a little owl with a sprig of olive, both sacred to Athena (whose head is on the other side), and symbols of the city. The abbreviated inscription ATHE means 'belonging to the Athenians'; such coins were known colloquially as 'owls'—hence the proverb 'owls to Athens' (= 'coals to Newcastle')—and the coins are still called 'owls' in the numismatics trade. The modern scientific name of the little owl is *Athene noctua*.

[1] See pp. 280–81.
[2] See p. 279.

ample warnings of the death of Caesar when 'the owl of death gave its mournful cries in a thousand places' (xv 791), an image that Shakespeare adapted as:

And yesterday the bird of night did sit
even at noon-day upon the market-place,
hooting and shrieking. When these prodigies
do so conjointly meet, let not men say
'These are their reasons; they are natural',
for, I believe, they are portentous things
unto the climate that they point upon.

> Shakespeare, *Julius Caesar* I 3.26–32

Two other species crop up regularly as omens in the Roman period. The first is the woodpecker, already associated with other ominous species in the early Roman comedy writer Plautus. The speaker here, one Libanus, is looking for guidance, and incidentally illustrates the confusion between Greeks and Romans about whether left or right meant good luck:

Ah, an omen, an omen from the birds—I can go in any direction!
The woodpecker and the crow on the left, and the raven and owl
on the right recommend it. I'll certainly follow your advice.
Hang on, though. A woodpecker's tapping an elm. That must be
significant. As far as I can see from this woodpecker omen,
one of us is in for a beating now.

> Plautus, *The Comedy of Asses* 259–64

Pliny identifies the woodpecker as 'the bird of Mars', which is specifically the mighty black woodpecker, whose scientific name is indeed *Dryocopus martius* ('tree-banger of Mars'), and he gives a little etymological history:

Woodpeckers themselves have been the most important omens for augury in Latium ever since the time of the king [Picus] who gave his name to the bird.[1] I must mention one example of their prophetic power. When the city praetor, Aelius Tubero, was giving judgments from the bench in the forum on one occasion, a woodpecker alighted on his head and was so tame that he could catch it by hand. The seers declared that if the bird were released disaster was portended for the empire, but if it was killed then it was disaster for the praetor. He straightaway tore it to pieces and not long afterwards fulfilled the prediction.

> Pliny, *Natural History* x 40–41

---

[1] In mythology Picus was the father of Latinus and was changed into a woodpecker by the sorceress Circe, whose advances he had spurned.

Woodpeckers crop up as omens in many other classical references and in the folklore of many other countries in Europe, North America, and Asia, often as 'thunder birds' or 'rain birds'. The association with thunder would have presumably arisen from the birds' loud drumming, and perhaps the association with rain was a natural inference from that, though neither of these attributes seems to be claimed in the classical sources.*

5.4 Woodpecker of Mars. Engraved ring-stone of carnelian (c.200–c.100 BC), portraying a Roman warrior by a column, which is entwined by a serpent and has a bird on top, probably the woodpecker of Mars, who is being consulted as the voice of the oracle. There is an intriguing reference supporting such an interpretation by the historian Dionysius of Halicarnassus (first century BC), who says that a place called Tiora in Umbria is home to 'the messenger of the gods, whom the aboriginals call *picus* but the Greeks call 'oak-pecker'…delivering an oracle from a pillar of wood' (*Roman Antiquities* I 14.5).

Woodpeckers are born charismatic, one might say; but it was another, much less striking bird that had charisma thrust upon it. The Romans gave a central role in augury to the domestic chicken, which played a crucial part in the relevant rituals. As we have seen, Greek modes of augury were somewhat opportunistic and informal, even though there were some generally recognized experts and procedures. The Romans, by contrast, established an official body to oversee and regulate the practices of augury and put it all on a professional footing. That body was the College of Augurs, whose origins were traced back to the time of Romulus and which went on to acquire great status and authority among the institutions of state. The augurs had the responsibility of delivering authoritative interpretations of omens, and, as Livy makes clear, they had the power of intervening in (literally 'inaugurating') a wide range of civic activities:

Who is not aware that this city was founded after taking auspices, and that it is only after taking auspices that all activities are carried out, whether of war or peace, and whether at home or on the battlefield?

Livy, *History of Rome* VI 41.4*

Livy also recounts a story about the famous augur Attus Navius, which demonstrates the power of the augur and his chickens even when pitted against a king. King Tarquin[1] had determined to add some new military units to strengthen his cavalry:

But since Romulus had had recourse to the auguries before creating the existing units, Attus Navius, the distinguished augur of the time, declared that no such change or innovation could be made, unless the birds signified approval. That angered the king, and to mock the augur's art, as the story goes, he retorted, 'All right then, prophet, use your augur's art to tell us if what I'm now thinking of can come to pass.' Navius duly took the auspices and announced that whatever it was would indeed come to pass. 'Well,' Tarquin replied, 'what I was thinking of was your cutting a whetstone in half with a razor. So get the birds and perform the task they say is possible.' Whereupon, they say, without a moment's delay Navius cut the whetstone in two.

To commemorate this feat they erected a statue to Navius on the site and deposited the whetstone there too, and Livy goes on to draw the historical moral:

Such great honour was brought to the auguries and their priesthood by this that afterwards no action was ever undertaken, in the field or at home, unless the auspices had been consulted: assemblies of the people, war levies, great affairs of state—all would be put off if the birds withheld their approval.

Livy, *History of Rome* I 36.2–6

The Romans also systematized the theory and practice of augury and gave it a technical vocabulary. Most Greek augury had consisted in interpreting unsolicited omens—the sudden and chance appearance of birds whose flight or whose calls were judged significant. Such birds were designated by the Romans as either *alites* ('flying birds') or *oscines* ('songbirds'). But the Romans placed much greater emphasis than had the Greeks on omens they themselves sought out deliberately and could control to some extent (technically the 'impetrative' as opposed

---

[1] Tarquin the Elder, who according to legend ruled Rome from 616 to 579 BC.

to the 'oblative' signs). These could again be divided into two kinds. Signs solicited *ex caelo* ('from the sky') depended on marking out a quadrant of sky and then observing it from a designated *templum* ('sacred space') to see what birds appeared in it. The city of Rome had a permanent observatory of this kind on the Capitoline Hill and armies established temporary ones in the field. Signs solicited *ex tripudiis* ('from beating on the ground'), on the other hand, involved having the *pullarius* ('chicken-keeper') put out grain for the sacred chickens and watching their feeding habits. If they ate greedily, dropping some grain on the ground as they fed, the signs were positive, special attention being paid to the sound and force of the grain as it hit the ground; but if they refused to feed or moved away, the signs were negative and whatever initiative was being contemplated would be postponed.*

Augury was not an exact science, however, and being a chicken-keeper was a high-risk profession, especially when one was delivering bad news, or at least news the commander didn't want to hear. Livy tells the story of one unfortunate *pullarius* who had expressed doubts about launching a particular assault, so was put in the front line where he was straightaway killed by a stray javelin. At this, the bullish commander, Spurius Papirius, declared, 'The gods are with us in this battle, and the guilty man has paid the penalty' (Livy x 40.9–13). On this occasion the commander was right and the Romans routed the enemy. What mattered most to the generals in such situations, of course, was the morale of the troops. If the omens were judged favourable, the men would believe that luck and the gods were on their side and they would fight with more spirit and confidence, so the prophecies were to some extent self-fulfilling.

This was well understood by the authorities. In another such case, the Roman general Pulcher 'took the auspices' before an important battle[1] in which he had hoped to make a surprise attack on the Carthaginians and was furious that the chickens refused to perform. So he famously shouted, 'Bibant, quoniam esse nolunt' ('If they won't eat, let them drink') and had them thrown into the sea. He went into battle anyway, but this time the general who had backed his own judgement lost. Pulcher was subsequently tried back at Rome and condemned, not for losing the battle, nor even for disbelieving in augury, but for demoralizing his troops by destroying *their* confidence in it. A nice twist.[2]

This illustrates how enlightened scepticism about such superstitions could coexist with an acceptance of them. There were always those who challenged the

---

[1] The Battle of Drepana (249 BC).

[2] The declared motive for the prosecution appealed to Machiavelli as an example of shrewd political behaviour (*Discourses* I 14).*

5.5 Augury by chickens. The sacred chickens of Rome feeding on grain in their coop, from an engraving of military insignia and instruments of war by Nicolas Beatrizet (1551).

omens. As we saw, Hector in the *Iliad* objected to an augury that didn't suit his military purposes, just as Papirius and Pulcher did; but the playwright Euripides goes further and has a character bitterly accuse augurs not just of obstruction but also of incompetence and corruption:

> … as for the lore of diviners, ,
> I see now how empty that was, how full of lies.
> No sound judgement could be based on sacrifices
> or the cries of birds; sheer folly it is even
> to suppose that birds could help our humankind.
> …
> Dispense, then, with divination,
> that was just a bait devised to make someone a living,
> and no idler ever prospered through his faith in sorcery.
> Good judgement and good counsel are the best of seers.
>
> Euripides, *Helen* 744–57

The accusation of venality was not uncommon.* Plenty of commentators remarked, too, on the slipperiness of the various 'judgements' made, which—like modern horoscopes offered in the popular press—were often sufficiently vague to enable the credulous to believe what they wished. Cicero, referring here specifically to divination by oracles, makes this devastating critique:

> Concerning your predictions: some in my view were false; some proved true by chance, as often happens even in ordinary conversation; some were so complicated and obscure that their interpreter needs an interpreter and the oracle itself must be referred back to an oracle; and some were so ambiguous that they need a logician to deconstruct them.
>
> Cicero, *On Divination* II 115

This whole dialogue, *On Divination*, debates at great length the arguments for and against a belief in divination, and this extends naturally into a philosophical discussion about the existence of the gods and their possible interventions in the human world. Cicero, in fact, embodies in his own career the ambivalence of the culture about such practices. He had been a member of the College of Augurs and had written earlier in favour of maintaining the rites of augury for reasons of social cohesion. He starts this dialogue by recognizing the prevalence of the belief:

> I know of no people, however enlightened and educated or however brutish and savage, that does not believe the future is revealed in signs and can be read and foreseen by certain individuals.
>
> Cicero, *On Divination* I 2

And he goes on to present the argument that in the present state of knowledge it is 'more important to examine the results than the causes of divination' (I 12), given the many demonstrable benefits it has brought over the years. He makes the comparison with herbal medicine, where 'reason has never explained the potency or nature of the remedies, but through their efficacy both the art and its inventor have our approval' (I 13).[1] But Cicero ends with a robust rejection of divination as 'a superstition, widespread throughout the world, that has invaded the mind of almost every person and exploited their weaknesses'. He now sees it

---

[1] Ironically Hippocrates had made the same analogy centuries earlier, but with the precisely contrary purpose of complaining that because physicians sometimes disagree in their prognoses 'the public thinks they are no more scientific than bird augurs' (*Regimen in Acute Diseases* 8).

as his duty 'to tear up this superstition by the roots' (*On Divination* II 148). At various points in Roman history the authorities had their own reasons for extirpating such *superstitio* (in which they came to include Christianity), but it always proved both difficult and impolitic to eradicate it entirely. Tacitus offers the characteristically pithy comment that 'the class of astrologers … will always be banned and always retained in our city' (*Histories* I 22).*

Anthropologists regularly encounter this kind of cultural ambivalence. Indeed, there is the celebrated case of the Azande of the Sudan, who also employed chickens as their agents of divination. In a classic study of their 'poison oracles', the Oxford anthropologist Sir Edward Evans-Pritchard described how every Zande household kept a supply of poison. This was administered in a small dose to their domestic chickens whenever a difficult question had to be answered, such as 'Should I make this journey, start this war, divorce this person?' or whatever. They would then ask, 'If so, let the poison kill the fowl.' The rules and rituals of this consultation were very carefully prescribed and the results were taken seriously. Like the Romans, the Azande must have got through a lot of chickens, but these were no doubt chosen for this purpose for the sensible practical reasons that they were readily available and relatively dispensable. Evans-Pritchard realized that people back in England would ask all sorts of sceptical questions about how the Azande could believe in such things, but says that these were the wrong questions to ask. He was analysing behaviour, not belief. The Azande had very little theory about their oracles and their behaviour had to be understood from the inside not the outside.

In fact, if one views such practices not as primitive and mistaken forms of explanation about how the world works but as modes of dealing with it, they have their parallels in our own, different conventions. After all, we have our ceremonies and rituals too. We mark the start and end of special events: we raise and lower flags; we have ceremonies for the signing of treaties, coronations, graduations, the opening of buildings, and the naming of ships; and we have religious or quasi-religious services and prayers for births, marriages, and deaths. We also commemorate things in ritual ways where it is important to observe the right details: Christmas and New Year celebrations, anniversaries, processions, and services. We wear special clothes for special occasions (wigs, gowns, suits) and may be required to behave in particularly formal ways such as kneeling, bowing, and saluting. Then there are all the conventions of politeness and social interaction: shaking hands, presenting gifts, sending flowers, making toasts, giving apologies and good wishes, greetings and farewells, cheering and clapping, waving and smiling. None of this is strictly *rational* behaviour and it would quite miss the point to demand that it should be. Should we therefore think of the ancient oracles and auguries more as rather elaborate rituals for ensuring (and so reassuring) that people were doing things in the right way?

The Oxford professor entered into the spirit of things, at any rate:

> I never found great difficulty in observing oracle consultations. I found that in such matters the best way of gaining confidence was to enact the same procedure as the Azande and to take oracular verdicts as seriously as they take them. I always kept a supply of poison for the use of my household and neighbours and we regulated our affairs in accordance with the oracles' decisions. I may remark that I found this as satisfactory a way of running my home and affairs as any other I know of.*

15

Magic and Metamorphosis

'Magic' is another word we owe to the Greeks. It derives etymologically from the practices of the Magi, who were thought to be a tribe or priestly caste of Persian origin, exercising some kind of religious authority through their interpretations of dreams and other 'signs'. That sense persists in the Bible, where the *magi* who follow a sign in the sky to visit the infant Christ are in the Authorized Version respectfully described as the 'Wise Men from the East'. But in the classical period as a whole Magi are usually 'magicians' of a more dubious kind, dispensing all manner of charms, spells, horoscopes, and curses on a commercial basis, and they are often thought of as frauds and tricksters. We saw in chapter 12 how the early medical scientists like Hippocrates tried to counter their influence and expose the superstitions on which they traded. But whatever criticisms were made of their practices by a few enlightened intellectuals, the popular belief in magic remained widespread and persistent over the centuries. Nor is this a phenomenon restricted to the ancient world. Indeed, in his classic study *Religion and the Decline of Magic*, Keith Thomas shows how similar beliefs still flourished at all social and economic levels in sixteenth- and seventeenth-century England, perpetuated by a sense of human helplessness in the face of disease, natural disaster, and existential uncertainty. Thomas concludes:

> If magic is defined as the employment of ineffective techniques to allay anxiety when effective ones are not available, then we must recognize that no society will ever be free from it.*

Magic was not marginal to ancient beliefs and behaviour, but was pervasive throughout the whole social and cultural structure, even though attempts were occasionally made at an official level to ban what were perceived as its more pernicious forms.* Nor did science smoothly displace magic as it progressively provided better explanations of natural phenomena—witness the fact that most ancient astronomers were also astrologers.[1] The examples that follow should not therefore be thought of just as quaint and curious survivals from a more primitive period, but as part of a loose web of beliefs about the world in which rational and irrational elements coexisted together, often untidily and in some tension. In any case, the function of magic was not so much to understand the world as to intervene in it, through whatever powers could be summoned or exploited.

Magic drew widely on the resources of the natural world for its suite of offerings. The two most famous literary witches, Circe and Medea, both made extensive use of drugs concocted from herbs and plants, as did all the early healers and pharmacists (the 'root-cutters', see p. 216). Circe was the sorceress in Homer's *Odyssey*. She laced the wine and snacks she offered to Odysseus' companions with a particularly potent psychotropic drug before turning them into pigs with a touch of her wand. She was going to pull the same trick on Odysseus, but he was forewarned and craftily protected himself with the antidote from another plant, whose 'nature'[2] had been explained to him. Circe was so impressed by his powers of resistance that she thereupon invited him to go to bed with her. He also resisted that offer for a while, until she had restored his companions to human form.

Medea, too, specialized in plant drugs, though according to the account in Ovid the rejuvenating brew she gave Jason of the Argonauts also included various animal parts—owl wings, wolf entrails, snakeskin, and 'the eggs and head of a crow nine generations old' (*Metamorphoses* VII 268–74). But the *chef d'œuvre* in this line of cuisine was produced by a Thessalian superwitch, Erichtho, who could actually reanimate a corpse with her preparations.[3] Moreover, she administered her spells with an extraordinary vocal performance, also drawn from the natural world:

Then, her voice, more potent than any herbs to summon
the spirits below, first uttered a cacophony of discordant

---

[1] As indeed they were in the medieval and Renaissance worlds—Tycho Brahe, Kepler, Galileo, and Bruno among them.*

[2] See p. 4.

[3] Lucan's description of Erichtho's powers was probably the inspiration for Mary Shelley's *Frankenstein*.

notes, quite unlike those from any human tongue,
a babel of the barking of dogs and the howl of wolves,
the eerie plaints of the horned owl and the nightly screecher,[1]
the cries and bellowing of wild beasts and the serpent's hiss.
There too were sounds of the beat of waves crashing on rocks,
the noise of the forest and the crack of thunder from a cloud.
In that one voice could all these things be heard.

      Lucan, *Pharsalia* VI 685–93

This was necromancy—calling up the spirits of the dead—but Thessalian witches
like Erichtho were best known for the equally difficult feat of 'drawing down the
moon', which was a common literary trope in erotic attraction magic.*

Not surprisingly, there is often an erotic context to the use of magic charms
and spells more generally. We hear of magic potions to smear on one's genitals
to improve sexual performance (the recipe, in case of interest, includes crow's
egg, plant juice, and bile of electric ray, mixed in with honey), and various aphro-
disiac animal products (boar gall, ass suet, goose fat, stallion semen, powdered
lizard—the usual stuff).* But the item most fully described in the inventory of
erotic aids is a bird—the wryneck, a small migratory woodpecker. Aristotle gives a
short (and accurate) description of the unusual features of the species that may
help to explain how it acquired its reputation:

> Most birds have three toes in front and one behind like a heel, but a few have two
> toes in front and two behind, as the wryneck does. This bird is not much larger than
> a sparrow and is mottled in appearance. The arrangement of its toes is peculiar, and
> it has a tongue like that of a snake, in that it can protrude its tongue to the breadth
> of four fingers and then retract it again. Moreover, it can twist its head round back
> to front, while keeping the rest of its body motionless, again like a snake. It has large
> claws, like those of woodpeckers, and it has a shrill, high-pitched call.
>
>   Aristotle, *History of Animals* 504a10–19

Wrynecks do indeed have long tongues, longer in relation to their body size
than those of any other bird, and they use them to lick up ants from the ground
or from within crevices. They also hiss loudly and writhe their very mobile necks
when threatened, and these reptilian characteristics, combined with their
cryptic plumage and their seasonal appearances and disappearances, might well

---

[1] *Bubo* ('horned owl' = eagle owl) and *strix* ('screecher', presumably = barn owl, still known by the
common name 'screech owl'); but see also p. 257 n.2.

have made them seem uncanny birds. The Greek name for the wryneck was *iunx*, from which we get the word 'jinx',[1] and the bird's fate was to be bound spread-eagled on the spokes of a revolving wheel to form a mechanical love-charm. This was spun rapidly to make a whistling noise and was intended to excite a sexual response from the object of one's desire.

There are two classic texts on the wryneck's unhappy role in this. The earliest comes in an ode by the early lyric poet Pindar (fifth century BC), where Aphrodite (goddess of erotic love) is making Medea fall in love with Jason of the Argonauts:

> Aphrodite, queen of the sharpest arrows,
> first brought down to men from Olympus
> that bird of madness, the mottled wryneck,
> bound fast to the four spokes of the wheel,
> and taught Jason the lore of spells and charms.
>   Pindar, *Pythian Odes* IV 213–17

The second comes in a remarkable poem by the Hellenistic author, Theocritus. In 'The Sorceress', which is the second in his anthology of *Idylls*, the lovelorn Simaetha is performing erotic magic to recover the affections of her errant lover, Delphis, and she goes through a series of attraction procedures familiar from other accounts of sympathetic magic, like melting wax images and burning fragments of a loved one's garment. Each of the first ten stanzas describing these rites is followed by the same incantation:

> Wryneck, draw my man here to my house.

It is unclear whether it is the bird, the wheel, or the bird-on-a-wheel that is being invoked here, since the name *iunx* came to refer to the wheel itself, by a kind of transference or 'metonymy'. In this anonymous little epigram it is the wheel that evidently serves as the charm:

> Nico's wryneck charm that can draw a man back
> from overseas and charm boys from their rooms,
> chased in gold and carved from transparent amethyst,
> this is for you, Cypris, to have and to hold.
> Here it is, hung on a soft thread of purple wool,
> a present from the witch of Larissa.[2]
>   *Greek Anthology* V 205

[1] The wryneck's scientific name is *Jynx torquilla* (literally 'little twister, bringing bad luck', though the spell or charm could be lucky for some, of course).

[2] Larissa was the capital city of Thessaly, the traditional home of witches.

There may have been good practical reasons for this extension of meaning, too. As one commentator drily pointed out, disappointed lovers were no doubt commoner than wrynecks and the supply might not have met the demand.* The bird does, however, feature on plenty of ancient vases and wall-paintings, suggesting that it was more familiar to the general public then than it would be now.[1]

5.6 Wryneck wheel. *Pyxis* (a box often used by women to store cosmetics or jewellery) decorated with the scenes and symbols of an impending marriage, including a woman spinning a *iunx* wheel as a love-charm. Attic red-figure pottery, 440–415 BC.

Other forms of sympathetic magic involved imitating the songs and dances of birds.* We hear about crane dances, owl dances, and even a wagtail dance that sounds a bit like the hokey-kokey in one description:

---

[1] There may be fewer than 200 breeding pairs left in Greece, while in Britain it was last recorded as breeding in 2002 and is now only a rare passage migrant, after suffering a dramatic decline in the twentieth century.

Shake the old man's loins about,
shake them all about,
just like the wagtail,
and work a powerful spell.

But it sounds more graceful when performed by girls:

As dear maidens, daughters of Lydia,
sport and play,
leaping lightly and
clapping their hands
for fair Artemis at Ephesus,[1]
now bobbing down and then springing up,
like the dancing wagtail.

> Aelian, *On Animals* XII 9 (quoting Aristophanes and Autocrates)

We encountered a 'swallow song' in Athenaeus (see pp. 15–16), and the same author records a 'crow song' sung by *koronistai* ('crowers') at weddings. The role of these celebrants was to make a collection and wish the happy couple success in procreating children. Crows were invoked presumably because they were good scavengers and were thought to be faithful partners.*

Good sirs, give the crow, the child of Apollo,
a handful of barley or a dish of wheat,
or a loaf of bread, half an obol, or what you will.
Sirs, give the crow whatever you have to hand.
She'll accept a lump of salt—she really likes
to dine on that. Whoever gives salt today
will give her a honeycomb some other time.
Open the door, lad, Wealth just knocked;
and let a maid bring figs for the crow.
You gods, let this woman be ever faultless,
and may she find a rich and famous husband,
and may she lay a son in her old father's
arms and a girl on her mother's lap,
a child to raise as a wife for her kinsmen.
…
Come, sirs, hand over some wealth from your store.
Give a donation, my lord, and you too, my young lady.

---

[1] Ephesus (in the ancient kingdom of Lydia) was the site of the famous temple of Artemis, whose roles as the goddess of virginity, fertility, and childbirth (and much else) included the care of young girls.

When the crow asks, the law requires a handful.
That's my refrain. Whatever you give will do.
Athenaeus, *The Intellectuals' Dinner Party* 359e–360a

Other magical practices are more to do with avoidance than attraction—
apotropaic rather than sympathetic magic. There are human enemies to be
repelled or harmed, but there are also natural pests, ranging in scale from fleas
to whole weather systems:

There's this wonderful fact about the cuckoo. If at the spot where you first hear
one, you mark round the outline of your right foot and dig out the earth, then no
fleas will breed wherever it is sprinkled.
Pliny, *Natural History* xxx 85

I know for a fact that flocks of sparrows and starlings—the plague of millet and
grain crops—can be driven away if a certain plant (whose name is unknown to
me) is buried in the four corners of the field. This has the remarkable consequence
that no bird will then enter the field.
Pliny, *Natural History* xviii 160

I was particularly struck at Methana by this custom. When the vines are just shooting, the Sirocco blows violently from the Saronic Gulf and scorches the shoots.[1]
As the wind gets up, two men take a cockerel covered in white feathers, tear it
apart, and run round the vines in opposite directions, each with half the bird.
When they get back to the place they started from they bury it there. And that is
their device to counter the Sirocco.
Pausanias, *Description of Greece* ii 34.3

As we saw in chapter 12 (pp. 209–17), birds and parts of birds were also used
in a wide range of cures and concoctions that were more a matter of magic than
medicine. Pliny is again a main source for these, and so reveals and represents
the ambivalence of the culture towards such superstitions. He begins his inventory with a devastating condemnation of 'the empty deceptions of the magic
arts' (*Natural History* xxx 1), but goes on to suggest that magic has held such
sway over humankind because it has embraced and incorporated the three other
most potent influences on human emotions: medicine, religion, and astrology.

---

[1] The geography is as bad as the horticultural science here: the Sirocco is indeed a hot southerly wind
from Africa, but the Saronic Gulf is north of Methana (though south of Athens, where Pausanias was
writing this).

Between them these cater for the natural and universal human concerns about health and the prediction and control of one's future. But Pliny then goes on to detail the cures offered by magical practices at such length—in what is supposed to be an objective encyclopedia—that one suspects he is motivated by more than just anthropological curiosity.*

Astrology, as Pliny points out, was another of the 'magic arts', and birds are involved here too. Early on in human history, the perennial fascination with the night sky had led to attempts to identify patterns in the scatter of stars. This had practical applications for navigation (for celestial maps) and farming (for calendars to chart the agricultural year), but it also lent itself to speculation about astral signs, expressed in the form of 'catasterisms', which explained in mythological terms how the particular constellations or combinations of constellations came to be so arranged. About half of the constellations identified were named after animals they supposedly resembled, including three birds—the Swan, the Eagle, and the Crow.[1] The myth surrounding the Crow is a typical example.

The crow (raven) was the bird of Apollo and was sent to fetch some pure water for a sacrifice Apollo was conducting. But the bird was distracted by the figs growing by the spring and waited some days until those ripened so he could eat them, which made him seriously late with the water. He then lied to Apollo (big mistake with the god of prophecy). The crow's punishment is described in one of the collections of constellation myths as follows:

> So, each year while figs are ripening the crow is unable to drink, because it has a sore throat during that season. In order to illustrate the crow's thirst, the god arranged the bowl among the constellations, placing the water snake beneath it to hold back the thirsty crow. And the Crow seems to be pecking at the base of the Water Snake's tail, in order to be allowed to get to the Bowl.
> Hyginus, *Astronomy* II 40

Compilations like those of Hyginus became popular in the Hellenistic period (late fourth to first century BC) and reached their canonical form in the *Almagest* of the Alexandrian polymath Ptolemy (second century AD), which catalogued 1,022 individual stars and forty-eight constellations. But the form of astrology that critics like Cicero and Pliny were specifically objecting to rested on the belief that the stars also influenced human fortunes, in ways that could be predicted

[1] 'Crow' by convention, though the Greek *korax* and the Latin *corvus* more specifically denote the raven, which makes better sense of connected myths about the bird's hoarse voice and swollen bill.*

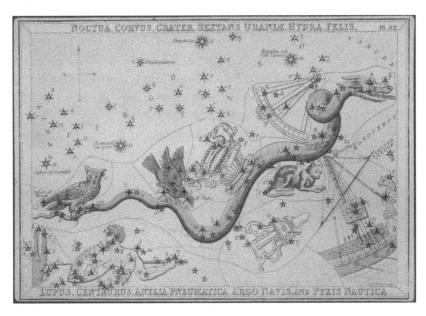

5.7 Crow constellation. The two adjacent constellations of Corvus (the Crow) and Crater (the Bowl) on the back of Hydra (the Water Snake), as depicted in the *Uranographia* by Johann Bode (1801). The star we know as Alpha Corvi marks the crow's beak, while Beta Corvi marks its feet.

from a knowledge of their conjunctions. This too was a Hellenistic development (one with Babylonian origins), which gathered momentum and flourished at Rome, leading to several (largely ineffective) measures to ban most forms of it. The habit of consulting personal horoscopes was tolerated, however, and even practised by some emperors eager to find reasons to hope for their future success, or at least their survival. But there was plenty of rational scepticism about the predictive value of horoscopes, as in this attempted knockdown argument in a second-century AD commonplace book:

> If in the case of human beings the time, the manner, and the causes of life, death, and all their affairs were written in the heavenly stars, what would these people say about the case of flies, worms, and sea-urchins and the many other tiny creatures of land and sea? Were they born to live and die under the same laws as humankind? Either frogs and gnats have their fates assigned at birth by the movements of the constellations or, if they don't believe that, there is no reason why the stars should be thought to have the power to influence humankind but not the rest of creation.
>
> Aulus Gellius, *Attic Nights* XIV 1.3

Magic thus insinuated itself into almost every sphere in which human beings were trying to understand the workings of the world and manage their own destinies. No wonder that it was regarded as socially and politically subversive—a *superstitio* not a *religio*—by some of the Roman emperors, who were themselves supposed to have a god-like status and so saw it as a competing attraction. Nor is it surprising that magic was thought to achieve its effects through manipulating the properties of particular plants and animals, including birds. These are, after all, other forms of life, which share in some but not all human characteristics, so they might reasonably be supposed to have direct effects on us and lessons for us, if their potential could only be understood and harnessed. For the same reason they could readily acquire great symbolic significance, and that leads us on to the second theme of this chapter, the more radically transformative situation in which human beings are not just affected by other animals but are imagined to *become* them.

*   *   *

Metamorphosis is the process through which one's physical form changes completely but one's original identity in some sense persists. This moves us from the physical world to the world of the imagination, for whereas magical practices were expected, however improbably, to have some actual effect on people's daily lives, the notion of a human metamorphosing into an animal of some kind is a literary invention that initially presents itself as no more than an entertaining story. That will turn out to be too literal an interpretation, however—or at least an incomplete interpretation. What magic and metamorphosis have in common, and the reason for treating both in one chapter, is that in their different ways they both raise the same question. Why do birds feature so prominently in these beliefs and fancies? Why are birds so good to think with?

'Metamorphosis' is another word with an interesting history. Aristotle describes the biological phenomenon whereby an insect like a butterfly metamorphoses from caterpillar to chrysalis to fully formed imago, but he doesn't actually use the word *metamorphosis* to describe this process. That noun, derived from Greek words meaning 'change of form', occurs in Greek only much later and it remained a rare usage.* The current scientific meaning of the English word 'metamorphosis' dates principally from its use by William Harvey in his study *On the Generation of Animals* (1651), which is in large part a reaction to Aristotle's work and so introduced into English a coinage never used in that sense in the language from which it is derived.* Not an uncommon linguistic phenomenon, but a mildly paradoxical one.

The term eventually became well known in a literary context rather than a scientific one, when two Latin authors—Ovid (43 BC–AD 17) and Apuleius (c.AD 124–70)—each used it as the title of a famous book of mythological tales and fairy stories about the transformations of humans into animals.

Ovid's *Metamorphoses* (completed in AD 7) was to become one of the most admired books of antiquity. It is a beautiful and sustained feat of storytelling, whose influence can be traced through many different strands in Western art, literature, and culture. Chaucer, Milton, and in particular Shakespeare all borrowed heavily from Ovid for their own literary purposes; and more recently the poet Ted Hughes has followed them with his best-selling *Tales from Ovid* (1997), which is a retelling of twenty-four favourite stories from Ovid. Hughes finds in them an authentic guide to human passion, 'Not just ordinary passion either, but human passion in extremis—passion where it combusts, or levitates, or mutates into an experience of the supernatural.'* Hughes's comment hints at a darker side to these fanciful tales, and of course we also have the example of Franz Kafka's nightmarish short story entitled 'The Metamorphosis' (*Die Verwandlung*), in which a man wakes up to find he has changed into a monstrous cockroach. The idea of a transformation between natural species seems to tap into some deep fears as well as light fancies.

Such stories also excite our curiosity and exercise the imagination. We are invited to wonder what it would be like actually to *be* some other species, and so perhaps to reflect more consciously on what we are ourselves. Apuleius explicitly announces that as his theme at the outset of his own book of *Metamorphoses*:

> I want you to wonder at the spectacle of the figures and fortunes of men being transformed into alien forms and then being restored again to their own by a chain of interconnections.
>
> Apuleius, *Metamorphoses* I 1

This book is often better known by its alternative title, *The Golden Ass*. The hero, Lucius, is eager to experience life as a bird, but his girlfriend Photis gives him the wrong magic potion by mistake and he is turned into an ass instead. He describes vividly what the process actually felt like:

> I spread out my arms and flapped them up and down alternately, desperate to become a bird. But no plumage appeared, not a single feather. Instead, my body

hair thickened into bristles and my soft skin hardened into a hide. At the ends of
my hands my fingers were becoming fewer and were being compressed into single
hooves, while from the base of my spine a great tail sprouted. By now my face was
enormous, my mouth elongated, nostrils were gaping and lips drooping. My ears
too grew huge and bristly. The only consolation in this wretched transformation
was that my penis was growing—though I could no longer get to embrace Photis.

    Apuleius, *Metamorphoses* III 24

The rest of the novel deals with his picaresque adventures in this new form and
his eventual redemption, but birds play little further part.

    By contrast, birds feature throughout Ovid's *Metamorphoses*. Here they are
regularly the subjects of 'Just So' stories, explaining how particular species of birds
came to acquire their characteristic attributes, and sometimes also their names,[1]
from figures of legend. There are two respects in which these bird metamorphoses differ from nearly all the (few) metamorphoses involving mammals. Firstly,
they are terminal—that is, one-way and permanent transformations. Picus is
turned into a woodpecker as his punishment and there is no going back; he has
been destroyed as a person. Secondly, they are aetiological—that is, explanatory
of the distinctive features not just of one individual but of the whole species; so
we learn why Picus the woodpecker has the habit of loudly drumming on trees.*
Here are some examples.

    Picus, who had dared to reject the approaches of Circe, felt the full force of
revenge from a woman scorned and was changed into a woodpecker:

He saw his body sprout wings, and indignant
at suddenly becoming a new bird in the forests
of Latium, drilled the wild oaks with his hard beak
and angrily scarred their long branches.

    Ovid, *Metamorphoses* XIV 390–93

Perdix was a boy genius, an inventor whom Daedalus came to resent as a
potential rival and threw off a tower; but just before he hit the ground he was
caught by Athena, who smartly changed him into a partridge:

His native wit passed intact into his wings and feet,
though his name remained the same as it was before.

---

[1] In some cases these personal names still survive in the current generic names of related species:
Perdix perdix (grey partridge), *Picus viridis* (green woodpecker), *Ardea cinerea* (grey heron), and *Cygnus
olor* (mute swan).

The bird does not fly up high or nest in trees and lofty crags,
but glides close to the ground and lays its eggs in hedgerows,
remembering that fall of old, and now fearful of heights.

VIII 256–59

Cycnus (Cygnus) lamented the death of Phaethon, who had been dashed
from the sun's chariot in a ball of fire:

As he went, his voice became high-pitched, white feathers
hid his hair and his neck grew long, stretching far out from
his chest, while a membrane joined his reddened fingers,
wings clothed his sides and a blunt beak enclosed his mouth.
Cygnus became a swan, a new kind of bird...
whose favoured haunts were the marshes and wide lakes,
and hating fire, he chose to live on water, its very opposite.

II 373–80

Tereus raped his wife's sister and cut out her tongue to silence her, but the
two women take a gruesome revenge on him when they serve him up his son for
supper. Tereus pursues them in fury, but is changed into a bird:

... on whose head a crest of feathers appears,
with a long protruding beak instead of a sword—
his name is the hoopoe, and he looks armed for battle.

VI 668–74

Meanwhile, the women escape 'on wings of flight'. Procne flies to the roof as a
swallow, 'whose breast still bears the marks of murder, her feathers stained with
blood', while her sister *Philomela* escapes into the woods as a nightingale.[1]

Arne, Queen of Siphnos, who had been bribed by Minos to betray her country, was given an appropriate new form:

After receiving the gold she had in her greed demanded,
she was changed into the bird which even today covets gold,
a black-footed, black-winged jackdaw.

VII 465–68

The Pierides (the daughters of King Pierus of Pella) challenged the Muses to
a song contest and lost, but unwisely objected to their decision, so were changed
into birds:

[1] In the Greek version she became a swallow.*

Magpies, a rackety presence in the woods, which even now
in feathered form keep their former gift of speech,
their harsh chattering and their insatiable desire to talk.
    v 676–78

In most of these cases the features thus 'explained' are broadly accurate and
would have been readily recognizable; but in the case of the kingfisher one myth
just leads to another. The grieving Alcyone and her shipwrecked husband Ceyx
are both changed into kingfishers, though the 'halcyon days' and the nesting site
they then enjoyed are a purely literary invention:[1]

    … and at last the gods took pity on them and both
    were changed into birds; so they shared the same fate,
    but their love survived, nor did their conjugal bonds loosen,
    and even as feathered birds they still mate and rear their young;
    and for seven days of calm seas in the winter season
    Alcyone broods on her nest, which floats upon the waters.
        XI 741–48

This transformation was intended as an act of mercy, and there is a similar
case involving the grieving daughters of Meleager, who are finally put out of
their misery and turned into *meleagrides*, that is guinea-fowl, an African species
widely domesticated in ancient Greece and Rome.[2] There are also a few other
metamorphoses where becoming a bird offers a means of escape from some dire
threat.* To be given wings is to be freed from earthly constraints; and that, of
course, was the ambition that inspired Daedalus and Icarus, as well as the 'flying
dreams' that Freud found so revealing.

It is noticeable that most of the examples above are portrayed as forms of
punishment or revenge. Sometimes there was an additional, spiteful twist to
this, as when the Queen of the Pygmies was changed into a crane and so 'was
made to wage war on those she once ruled' (VI 90–92). The 'war between the
cranes and the pygmies' was a traditional piece of folklore, much rehearsed and
embroidered both in art and literature.*

Being changed into an owl seems to have been regarded as a particularly
'ominous' fate. Ascalaphus was an informer, who had spied on Persephone and

---

[1] See p. II.

[2] The classical Latin name was *gallina africana* ('African hen') and the current scientific name is
Numida meleagris. The Greek name may be a reference to the female bird's call (sometimes rendered as
'melek') or may be derived from a Semitic name.*

5.8 Crane and pygmy. The traditional enmity between the pygmies and cranes was first mentioned in Homer. The source of the folklore is unknown, but Herodotus and Aristotle both reported the existence of races of very small men in the cranes' wintering areas. Detail from a red-figure bowl from Volterra in Tuscany, fourth century BC.

so thwarted her return to the upper world, for which Ceres turned him into a *profana avis*, an 'ill-omened bird':

> Dispossessed of himself, he is now clad in tawny wings;
> he grows a head and long, hooked talons, and finds
> it hard to raise the feathers growing on his sluggish arms.
> He has become an abomination, a prophet of doom,
> a slothful owl, a dire omen for mortal men.
>   v 546–50

Similarly Nyctimene,[1] who was sexually abused by her father, is forced to feel a victim's sense of guilt:

---

[1] *Nyctimene* (meaning 'nocturnal') survives as the name of a genus of an Australian fruit bat and of an asteroid.

She is now a bird, to be sure, but conscious of her guilt
she flees the sight of men and the light of day, and in darkness
hides her shame, driven by all the birds from the open air.
       II 593–95

But this case is more complex, since as an owl Nyctimene has been adopted by
Pallas Athene as one of her attendants, so has an honorific status too; in fact she
displaces Coronis, who has been turned into a crow to help her escape the attentions of Neptune (II 562–88). It is typical of figures in myth to attract subsidiary
anecdotes and accrete new roles in this way, but the symbolic messages can then
get blurred and confused—or, to put it more generously, you can take whatever
you need from them.

There are also other interesting kinds of metamorphoses involving birds in
Ovid's epic fantasy. Sometimes it is the birds themselves that are transformed in
respect of some quality. The raven's plumage, for example, is changed from white
to black as a punishment for being a gossip:

For he had once been a silvery-white bird,
with snowy wings to match the spotless doves
and rival the geese, which saved the Capitol
with their watchful cries, or the swans of the river.
His tongue was his undoing—thanks to its chattering,
this once white bird was now the very opposite.
       II 536–41

And on three occasions birds are born dramatically from the ashes of a fire.
Strange birds rise from Memnon's funeral pyre:[1]

Black ashes whirled aloft. Compressed densely into one
body they took on form and drew heat and the spark
of life from the fire, whose lightness gave them wings;
this first resembled a bird, but soon became a real bird,
which flew on whirring wings, joined in noisy flight
by countless sisters born from the same source.
       XIII 604–09

The birds then fight around the pyre. Descriptions elsewhere of these 'birds of
Memnon' led to an ingenious possible identification of the mystery birds. The
French zoologist George Cuvier (1769–1832) suggested that the myth might have

---

[1] Memnon was an Ethiopian king, killed by Achilles in the Trojan war.

originated with displaying ruffs, gathering at a traditional site near ancient Troy on their spring migration north.* In another case, Ovid performs the identification himself. The city of Ardea fell in war and was torched:

> Amidst the chaos, a bird of a kind never seen before
> flew out, shaking the ashes from its beating wings.
> The bird took on the sounds, the haggard looks, the pallor,
> and all the marks of a captured city, indeed even its name,
> Ardea,[1] and beats itself in lamentation with its own wings.
>
> XIV 576–80

But the bird that most famously 'rises from the ashes' is an entirely mythical one, the phoenix. Ovid is at this point in the fifteenth book of the *Metamorphoses* bringing his great work to an end. He is explaining that metamorphosis is not merely a theme for engaging literary stories, but a natural process underlying all physical change. Frogs appear from spawn, bees from larvae, and birds from eggs. But the phoenix is the exception that proves the rule:

> All these creatures derive their beginnings from other forms,
> but this one bird reproduces and regenerates itself all alone:
> the Assyrians call it the phoenix.[2]
>
> XV 391–93

*   *   *

These stories are pure fantasy, of course. Ovid is not attempting anything like an argument or investigation here, and these different passages illustrate how the imaginative and the factual are intermingled in such a way that the boundaries between them are deliberately blurred. His main theme in this last book, however, remains the universal phenomenon, which spans the natural, human, and spiritual worlds alike:

> Nothing retains the same appearance for ever, but nature,
> the great innovator, keeps creating new forms from old.
> Nothing in the whole world perishes, you can be sure,
> but things vary in appearance and take on new aspects.
> What we call 'birth' is but a new beginning, and 'death'
> just a cessation of what was before.
>
> XV 252–57

---

[1] Heron, whose current scientific name is *Ardea cineria* (literally 'ash-grey heron').
[2] See pp. 195–97 for travellers' tales about the phoenix.

There is an implication here for the idea of personal identity, and Ovid presents this as part of a discourse by the mathematician and mystic Pythagoras about the transmigration of souls:

> All things change, but nothing dies. The spirit wanders
> and passes now here, now there, occupying whatever frame
> it chooses: from beasts it crosses into human bodies,
> and from humans back into beasts, but never perishes.
>
> XV 165–68

Religion and the idea of birds as intermediaries is a topic for the last part of this book, but we end this chapter on a more worldly note. Like the consummate storyteller he was, Ovid leaves us with a contemporary twist and a mystery. The final 'transformation' in the *Metamorphoses* is that of the emperor Julius Caesar, elevated into a star after his murder, and the work ends with a prudent paean of praise to Caesar's adopted son and successor, Augustus. Now, Augustus was also Ovid's patron, but before Ovid had given the *Metamorphoses* its final revision Augustus abruptly expelled him from Rome. We don't know what the real reason was—Ovid just says it was for 'a poem and a mistake'. Scholars have guessed that the 'mistake' was some sexual indiscretion involving the imperial household, but at any rate he was forced to leave Rome in AD 8 and reinvent himself as a poet in exile, his personal metamorphosis. And in a final dramatic gesture, he threw the manuscript of the *Metamorphoses* on to the fire, declaring it unfit for publication. But this too rose from the ashes, in a manner of speaking, since Ovid knew there would be other copies still around…

∽ 16 ∾

Signs and Symbols

The discussions of omens, auguries, and magic in the last two chapters were mainly about the interpretation, and in some cases the manipulation, of events in the external world. But what about the internal world of our imaginations? What about the play of ideas and impressions there? Freud was in no doubt about the best source for the study of these:

> The interpretation of dreams is the Royal Road to a knowledge of the unconscious activities of the mind.
>
> Freud, *The Interpretation of Dreams* (1899)

Freud regarded this as one of his most original discoveries ('Insight such as this falls to one's lot but once in a lifetime'), but he was gracious enough to acknowledge (albeit briefly) that he had an ancient Greek predecessor, Artemidorus of Daldis, who produced a massive work of *Oneirocritica* ('Dream interpretations') in the second century AD.

There had already been a long tradition in the ancient world of writing about dreams. There are famous dream sequences in Homer's *Iliad* and *Odyssey*, for example; Herodotus spices his *History* with many vivid dream anecdotes involving dramatic prophecies; and Theophrastus in his sketch of human character types pokes fun at the 'Superstitious Man', who is always rushing off anxiously to dream analysts for guidance on his latest nightly experiences.* Artemidorus was one such analyst, but is best thought of as part of a medical rather than a literary tradition.

The interpretation of dreams was one of the recognized arts of divination and attracted many practitioners. Most of these were no doubt trading on the credulity of their customers, but the phenomenon of dreaming attracted more serious investigators too. A Hippocratic author (probably fourth century BC) had written a tract on dreams as symptomatic indicators, and Galen (a contemporary of Artemidorus) incorporated the investigation of dreams into his massive programme of empirical research. Books of dream interpretations go back to the fifth century BC, but Artemidorus' own work is our earliest surviving collection of actual case studies (ninety-five of which are described in Book v of his *Oneirocritica*), and he was scathing about what he thought of as the pseudo-sciences of divination. He contrasts the 'false prophets' who rely on palmistry, necromancy, and readings from horoscopes, physiognomy, dice, cheese, sieves, and other bizarre sources with 'true prophets' like bird augurs, weather-watchers, and dream specialists (II 69). The methodological distinctions here may seem unclear, but at any rate his own work attained great celebrity as a diagnostic text in later history. It was translated into Arabic in the ninth century AD and into all the main European languages in the sixteenth century, and the tradition he represented is said still to be alive in the eastern Mediterranean.*

Freud and Artemidorus share some important assumptions about the study of dreams. Both men believed that one could interpret dreams by deciphering the symbolic significance of their contents, and both thought that for an accurate reading the analyst needed to know as much as possible about the personal circumstances and character of the dreamer. Context was key. The fundamental difference between them, however, was that whereas Freud was concerned with dreams as a means to understanding the past history and present pathology of his patients, for Artemidorus they were studied in order to predict future outcomes. Artemidorus was especially interested in the logic of the imagery of dreams, which he saw as offering suggestive analogies. He summarized his method of interpretation as 'the juxtaposition of similarities' (II 25). That in fact marks another, perhaps more fundamental, shared feature between Artemidorus and later dream analysts. There is a great show of technical vocabulary, but the interpretations themselves often seem either obvious or obviously false, or else vague enough to be hard to verify either way.

Birds, at any rate, regularly feature in these case histories, supporting the hypotheses favoured by the analyst. Here are some examples from Artemidorus, based on interviews he had conducted.

> Gulls, cormorants, and other maritime species portend great peril for sailors but not their death, since all these birds can submerse without drowning in the sea...

They also indicate that things lost will not be recovered, since these birds gulp down whatever they get hold of.

Artemidorus, *Oneirocritica* II 17

To see in a dream an eagle sitting on a rock or a tree or some lofty perch is a good sign for those initiating some activity, but spells trouble for those who are fearful. Similarly, to see an eagle flying in a leisurely and undisturbed way signals good fortune for a man, though this will tend to come about slowly. But an eagle that settles on the dreamer's head portends his death, for whatever an eagle grasps in its talons is doomed to die.

II 20

A vulture signifies the same things as an eagle, but some vultures are good for potters and tanners because they live outside city limits[1] and take corpses. But they indicate serious trouble for doctors and the sick, since they revel in dead bodies. And they can also signify enemies and those who are cursed and defiled and live outside the city, and in other respects they represent troubles to come.

II 20

Hawks and kites signify robbers and bandits—hawks those that attack their victims openly, and kites those that attack by stealth.[2] A raven represents an adulterer and a thief, both through its appearance and through its frequent changes of voice. A crow indicates a long duration and delay in one's affairs; it also signifies an old woman on account of its longevity, and winter storms since it is a herald of that season.

II 20

Cranes and storks observed in flocks and dense gatherings indicate an attack by pirates and enemy forces, and they portend a storm when they appear in winter and a heatwave when in summer. When they appear singly and on their own, cranes and storks are good signs for travelling abroad and for one's safe return, on account of their own comings and goings as the seasons change. They are also auspicious for marriage and child-bearing because of their own habits in this. In

---

[1] In ancient Athens, for example, the district where the potters and tanners worked was outside the city limits by a river because both trades needed ready access to a water supply. 'Some vultures' evidently refers to a different species from the first 'vultures' in this sentence, since different terms are used (*aigupios* and *gyps*); similarly he says that 'different kinds of eagles indicate different outcomes' (II 20); but the various names used for big raptors by Artemidorus and other classical authors are often impossible to translate convincingly into specific English equivalents.

[2] Presumably a reference to the well-documented habit of kites (in this region the black kite *Milvus migrans*) snatching items from market stalls and from temple altars during sacrifices.*

particular, the stork is propitious for bearing children on account of the support
the offspring give their parents.

    II 20

One gets the idea. But these passages also reveal that Artemidorus is vague
and inconsistent about the kind of agency operating in such examples. The overall
sense is that the birds *portend* these consequences, but his terminology runs
together the very different notions of *signifying* them and *causing* them.* At any
rate, there are similar diagnoses involving starlings (disorderly crowds of poor
people), falcons (good and regal wives), doves (mistresses), pigeons (whores),
swallows (reminders to work on the home), quails (warnings of fractious immi-
grants), and of course flying (freedom). What is interesting about these claims
is not their predictive value (almost zero), but the species selected and the knowledge of their behaviour that is being assumed. All these birds must have been
familiar to the dreamer, analyst, and reader for the 'interpretations' to make any
sense at all, even as stories. And the species referred to must have been sufficiently
abundant and conspicuous to be part of a shared experience. But how many of
Freud's patients, or how many people now, would know from personal observation about the migratory habits of cranes and quails, the different predatory strategies of hawks and kites, or the vocal range of ravens? How many would even
have seen a vulture or an eagle or have witnessed a cormorant's feeding habits?

    Folklore dies hard, however. Beliefs about the fertility and parental devotion
of the stork, for example, have easily outlasted the actual decline of the species
throughout most of Europe, and the continuing human affection for the species
has even inspired successful reintroduction programmes.* Analogous points
could be made about the swallow as a domestic familiar and a herald of spring.
Such folklore has its origins, no doubt, in specific experiences, but it long survives them in symbolic form. Artemidorus makes an interesting point in this
connection about the persistence of swallow myths, which he seeks to disprove
by testing them against his correspondents' actual reports:

> It is said that this creature [the swallow] signifies both untimely death and grief
> and great sadness, since there is a story that this bird came into being from such
> unhappy events.[1] ...And it is said that even if a legend like this is basically ficti-
> tious, the fact that it is *believed* to be true means that the imagination brings the
> legend to the forefront of the mind when one seeks to make a prediction involving

---

[1] The Philomela and Procne myth, see pp. 172, 279, and 410.

the bird in question. I have myself discovered that this argument works in the case of most legends, but by no means all. Hence my policy is in every case to follow not plausible arguments but the evidence of actual experience. And on this basis I say that the swallow is not a sign of trouble—unless, that is, it is suffering some strange symptoms or changing colour in an unnatural way. For its song is not a lament but a prelude and inducement to work ... and as soon as spring arrives the swallow is the first to appear so, one might say, points to the tasks to be undertaken. And when it appears it never sings in the evening but does so at dawn when the sun rises, as a reminder to any mortals it encounters of the work they should begin.

II 66

That may not make one feel any more confident in Artemidorus' own interpretations, but it does at least recognize the power of symbolism to shape our thoughts. Once a creature like a bird has been established in our minds as a symbol it becomes hard to see it in any other way. The connotations we have invested it with become part of its perceived identity, while characteristics inconsistent with our image of it are ignored or denied. The robin would be a case in point in British culture. It is regularly voted as Britain's national bird, much loved because of its trusting, friendly presence in our gardens, its plump profile and pert manner, the bitter-sweet song almost all the year round, and of course that bright red breast which conjures up ideas of Christmas cheer and adorns a million greeting cards. In fact, however, the robin is an aggressive and highly territorial species and the habits we find confiding are the merest cupboard love.*

*   *   *

Certain species of birds recur as symbols of one sort or another throughout classical culture—in language and art and as the physical insignia of private and public life. Figures of speech are one fruitful source. Homer's great epics are full of extended similes, some two hundred of them in the *Iliad* and forty or more in the *Odyssey*, and many of these are taken from the natural world, with birds prominently represented.[1] The gathering of the Greek armies preparing for battle is like clamouring flocks of cranes and wildfowl on migration (*Iliad* II 459–68); the disloyal maidservants are strung up like thrushes caught in a snare (*Odyssey* XXII 48–72); Odysseus' bowstring sings to his touch like a swallow

---

[1] In the *Iliad* the top categories for similes are lions (40), birds (22), fire (19), cattle (18), wind and waves (18), and boars (12).*

(*Odyssey* XXI 410–11); and Penelope nightly mourns her absent husband like a wailing nightingale (*Odyssey* XIX 512–23). But the birds most often invoked in such images are eagles and other raptors, particularly in the context of war:

> Nor did Hector remain among the crowd of mail-clad Trojans,
> but as a fiery eagle swoops down on a flock of winged
> birds that are feeding along the banks of a river—
> wild geese or cranes or long-necked swans—so Hector
> rushed on, making straight for a dark-prowed ship.
>   Homer, *Iliad* XV 688–94

> So saying, the fair-haired Menelaus departed, glancing
> warily all around him like an eagle, which men say
> has the keenest sight of all the birds of the air
> and from high in the sky can spy the swift hare
> crouched under cover of leafy vegetation. He swoops
> down and seizes it and swiftly robs it of life.
>   *Iliad* XVII 673–78

> Patroclus was striken by grief for his fallen comrade
> and charged through the front ranks of fighters, like
> a swift falcon scattering flocks of jackdaws and starlings.
>   *Iliad* XVI 581–83

> Just as vultures[1] with crooked talons and curved beaks,
> descend from the mountains to prey on smaller birds.
> These shrink from the clouds and scud across the plain,
> but the raptors pounce on them and destroy them,
> and they have no means of defence or escape,
> while men enjoy the spectacle of the chase.
> So did the attackers set upon the wooers throughout the great hall
> and strike them down as they turned this way and that.
>   *Odyssey* XXII 302–08

Homer excels in the use of such vivid similes, which have their force through a 'juxtaposition of similarities', rather as Artemidorus described in relation to dreams. Birds feature regularly in metaphors too, where they convey a more direct and compressed form of identification, in which people are said not just to be *like* birds but in some sense to *be* them.* It was a common form of shorthand, especially in the colloquial exchanges in comedy and satire, to call someone by the name of a bird that embodied the qualities you wanted to emphasize. That could either be by way

---

[1] These vultures (*aigupioi*) sound more like eagles, in fact, since vultures are largely carrion feeders.

of endearment: 'ducky and dovey' (Aristophanes and Plautus), 'my little sparrow /
hen / quail / swallow / jackdaw' (Plautus), and 'my little spadger' (Juvenal); or it
could be a form of abuse: 'gossiping jackdaws' (Aristophanes), 'public cockerel'
(Athenaeus), 'grasping vultures' (Euripides), 'greedy hawk' (Plautus), and 'plucked
ostrich' (Seneca).* In his play *The Birds*, Aristophanes takes this to comic extremes
with a long list of punning metaphors in which he describes how the Athenians all
go ornithomanic with excitement and become literally ornithomorphic:

> They are all bird-mad now and are only too pleased
> to imitate everything the birds do.
> They rise with the lark from their beds
> and fly down to enjoy a diet of laws;
> then they brood on their books
> and peck away at the bills.[1]
> And the height of this ornithomania is
> that many of them get given bird names too.
> There's the tradesman with a limp called
> 'Partridge', Menippus is called 'Swallow',
> and Opuntius 'the one-eyed Raven';
> Philocles is 'Crested Lark', Theagenes 'Sheldrake',
> Lycurgus 'Ibis', Chaerephon 'Bat',*
> and Syracosius 'Jay'; while Meidias here
> is called 'Quail'—he does look like a quail
> that's had a bang on the head from a flipper.[2]
> And these bird-lovers are all singing songs
> that mention birds—a swallow or wigeon or goose
> or a pigeon—or wings, or even a shred of feather.
> That's the news from earth, and I can tell you this:
> there'll soon be thousands of them heading this way,
> all wanting wings and the kit for living like birds.
> So you'd better lay in supplies for a wave of immigrants.
>
> Aristophanes, *Birds* 1283–305

Ancient proverbs furnish another range of extended metaphors, most of
them self-explanatory and some familiar in our own culture:

> Go to the crows
> One swallow doesn't make a spring
> A true friend is a rare bird

---

[1] There are some untranslatable puns in this passage, which I have replaced with (equally feeble)
English ones. We can only guess at how most of these individuals earned their nicknames.*
[2] See p. 161 for the game of quail-tapping.

A cuckoo in the nest
You're teaching an eagle to fly
Eagles do not bring forth doves
A vulture / jay / owl could sooner imitate a nightingale*
Until the crows turn white
Only a fool lets slip a bird in the hand for one in the bush
Eggs today are better than chickens tomorrow

But a few need a little explanation:

One jackdaw is always found near another (birds of a feather...)
Owls to Athens (coals to Newcastle)
From a bad crow, a bad egg (like father, like son)
When birds are silent in spring (never)
Bird's milk (a great luxury)
Further than a kite roams (a huge distance)
Going after the crows (on a wild goose chase)
Birds love figs but will not plant them (no pain, no gain)
Every lark must have his crest (some things are unavoidable)
A sitting pigeon (a simpleton)
To throw a vulture (an unlucky cast at dice)
Son of a white hen (with a silver spoon in his mouth)
Under good birds (good omens)
An eagle doesn't catch flies (don't bother with trifles)
Owls say one thing, crows another (a natural enmity)

Aesop's fables are full of similar moralizing sayings, often presented as the punchline to a story. A list of the species most often invoked in Aristophanes and Aesop is included in the appendix, and chapters 14 and 15, on omens and magic, have shown other ways in which certain birds can carry a symbolic freight of meaning.

Rather than elaborating further references to particular species it may be more revealing to look at the general aspect of bird behaviour that was most often invoked metaphorically—that is, the capacity for flight, the key distinguishing feature of birds in the animal kingdom and the one that most appeals to human aspirations. Homer uses the expression 'winged words' well over a hundred times in describing human utterances. It is one of his formulaic phrases, almost a cliché, but the metaphor is still live enough to conjure up the idea of words flying like birds from the mouth, as in a cartoon bubble.[1] The metaphor comes even more alive in its less common, contrary form: 'unwinged words' are those that cannot be got out, but stay imprisoned behind the 'barrier of the teeth'.*

The metaphor of flight had other practical applications too, at least in folklore. We saw in chapter 15 on omens that the flight of birds was observed with great attention as a guide to the interpretation of divine will. There was also an ancient belief that the flight formations of cranes were the source of the shapes of several capital letters adopted for the Greek alphabet: lambda Λ, delta Δ, possibly also upsilon Υ and psi Ψ, and so on to less easily imagined examples:*

> Just as the cranes leave their summer home of Thrace
> clamouring, when they exchange the Strymon for the warmer Nile,
> the letter traced by their formation stands out against the clouds
> and the air is inscribed with the characters made by their wings.
>
>   Claudian, *The War against Gildo* 475–78

The tragic playwrights often invoke our longing to fly, whether to escape from a troubled situation or to realize some other form of liberation.

> O to become a high-flying eagle,
> and soar beyond the barren waters
> over the swell of the grey sea.
>
>   Sophocles, *Oenomaus* fr. 476

> O for the wings of a swift dove,
> to be borne upwards on eddies of air
> and gaze down from the clouds on the fray.
>
>   Sophocles, *Oedipus at Colonus* 1079–81

> O to fly like a bird on the ocean of air
> far from Greece to the stars of the west.
>
>   Euripides, *Ion* 796–97

> Would that I could wing my way
> through the skies to where
> the Libyan cranes, fleeing
> winter weather, fly in formations
> obedient to the piping
> of their elder, their shepherd,

---

[1] In his 1997 translation of the *Iliad*, Stanley Lombardo renders the first occurrence of this phrase at 1 201 as 'words flew from his mouth like winging birds'.

who cries out as he leads them to
fertile lands free from storms.
    Euripides, *Helen* 1478–86

I wish I were under the steep cliffs
so that a god might make me a winged bird
joining the flying flocks
and I might soar over the swell
of the Adriatic sea.
    Euripides, *Hippolytus* 732–37

In *The Bacchae* there is a darker image, when Euripides portrays the Maenads (the female followers of Dionysus) racing in an ecstatic frenzy across the plains 'like birds borne upwards in flight by their speed' and then 'swooping down on their prey like hostile predators' (748–53).

It is noticeable in several of these examples that the flights of freedom most often take place over the sea, which was such a crucial but dangerous element in ancient travel. And, by extension, boats were awarded the same metaphorical mobility and were thought of as being 'winged', whether by oars or sail.*

Flight was invoked in psychological and spiritual metaphors too. Personified emotions like Love and Fear hover, swoop, and wing their way around the world. In death, human souls 'fly' from the body, and in the two great classical allegories of visits to the underworld, Homer's *Odyssey* and Virgil's *Aeneid*, the heroes of each encounter the souls of the dead 'flitting and fluttering' there like birds or bats. In the myth of Pandora, too, all human ills escape from the great jar she has rashly opened and she only just gets the lid back on before the last of its contents, Hope, can 'fly out'.*

*　*　*

Visual metaphors also abound, in which birds actually embody physical symbols. The eagle is a prime example, most famously as the standard (*aquila*) of the Roman legions. Pliny dates the formal inauguration of this practice to 104 BC:

The eagle was adopted as the special symbol of the legions by Gaius Marius in his second consulship. Even earlier it had been their principal standard, along with four others—wolves, minotaurs, horses, and boars—carried in front of the respective ranks. A few years before then it had already become the custom to carry the eagle alone into battle, leaving the rest behind in camp, but Marius discarded these others altogether. From that time onwards it was noted that scarcely a single winter camp was set up without there being a pair of eagles in the area.

Pliny, Natural History x 16

5.9 Eagle standard. Detail from the statue of Augustus (probably from the reign of Tiberius, 14–37 AD) found in the House of Livia near Rome, portraying a Parthian soldier returning the Roman Eagle to a young officer.

Roman legionaries were subsequently expected to fight, and if necessary to die, for the *aquila* that was their regimental standard. There is a rather melodramatic account by the epic poet Silius Italicus of the standard bearer Bruttius doing just that in the Second Punic War (218–201 BC):

Thus in every battle he won glory and guarded the sacred
bird. But that very honour proved his fatal undoing.
He faced certain death, and when he could no longer stop
the enemy capturing the Eagle, seeing his side's fortunes
slipping away and the battle turning into a great disaster,
he tried to hide it a while by burying it in the ground.
But overcome by a sudden blow he threw his failing

limbs upon it and covered it with his dying body.
When consciousness returned after a dreadful night of
darkness, he raised himself from the ground with a spear
from a nearby corpse, and exerting all his strength dug
a hole with his sword in the earth, drenched as it was in
blood and easy to pierce. Then to honour the buried effigy
of the unlucky Eagle he smoothed the sand over it with
exhausted palms. His last, dying breath expired into thin air
and delivered his great soul to the underworld.

  Silius Italicus, *Punica* VI 25–40

In another such disaster in AD 9 the Roman armies under their commander Varus suffered their worst ever defeat at the Battle of the Teutoburg Forest. A band of German tribes, united by their resourceful leader, Arminius, destroyed the flower of three proud legions, killing some 15,000–20,000 men. 'Varus, give me back our legions,' the Emperor Augustus is reported to have cried when he heard the news back in Rome. In the television version of *I, Claudius* this becomes, 'Give me back my Eagles,' and that was perhaps just as important. The loss of the three legionary standards was a terrible blow to Roman pride and to their self-image of invincibility. They launched a massive force to exact retribution and try to recover the Eagles. They recaptured two of them in AD 16 and they persisted until they finally found the third in AD 41, some thirty-two years after the original disaster.* In a later comment on the quasi-religious veneration of the Eagles by the military, the Christian author Tertullian (*c.* AD 155–240), remarked:

  Roman religion is wholly a religion of the camps. It venerates the standards,
  swears by the standards, and esteems the standards before all the gods.

  Tertullian, *Apology* XVI 8

In his long section on eagles (he distinguishes six kinds), Pliny suggests the reason why they enjoyed this status. Eagles were thought to be pre-eminent 'in honour and in strength' (x 6). And for similar reasons many of the world's armies have since marched under the standard of an eagle.* The ideas of strength and honour are closely related in a warrior culture, of course. This is why the eagle was 'the bird of Zeus'. The king of the gods employed eagles on various royal missions. They were the instruments of the gruesome punishment employed against Prometheus, who had stolen fire from heaven and given it to humankind:

  Zeus bound clever Prometheus fast with bonds,
  drove a stake through his middle and set on him

5.10 Eagle motifs in national emblems, clockwise from top left. Albania, based on the seal of the national hero, Gjergi Kastrioti Skanderbeg (1405–66). Mexico, a golden eagle based on the Aztec eagle symbol of the sun god, Huitzilopochtli. Russia, a complicated genealogy traceable from the double-headed eagle of the late Byzantine Empire (East and West) through Ivan III (1462–1505), Peter the Great (1672–1725), and the Imperial Empire, and then restored as a symbol of the Russian Federation in 1992 after the collapse of the USSR. Egypt (from 1985), supposedly based on the Eagle of Saladin (1137–93), and later adopted as a symbol of Arabic nationalism by Iraq, Palestine, and Yemen. USA, the first United States seal, adopted 20 June 1782, depicting a bald eagle, clutching arrows in its left foot and an olive branch in its right; its head is inclined to the olive, indicating a preference for peace over war; in its beak is a scroll bearing the words 'E pluribus unum' ('Out of many, one').

> a long-winged eagle, which fed on his immortal liver;
> but by night the liver grew again and replenished
> all that the long-winged bird had devoured by day.
>
> Hesiod, *Theogony* 521–25

There is a similar violence in many other associations and images. Eagles and vultures would have been a familiar sight scavenging and ripping the human flesh they found readily available on battlefields, where corpses were left to 'glut the dogs and birds', as Homer puts it. Eagles were therefore easily imagined as the terrifying agents of Zeus, who would devour Prometheus' liver or rape Ganymede, the object of his sexual desire. These archetypal fears have deep roots.

The power of eagles gave them other, less threatening, symbolic functions, too. We saw that as omens they were the messengers of the god's will, and they also acted as his emissaries on one particular project of great importance—that is, establishing the supremacy of the oracle at Delphi. Pindar told the story that Zeus wanted to discover the centre of the world, so he dispatched a pair of eagles, one heading east and one west and both flying at the same speed. After flying in opposite directions they met again at the oracle, and thus marked the *omphalos* (literally the 'navel') of the world.*

Pindar's choral odes in honour of the winners in the great athletic festivals at Olympia and elsewhere are full of references to eagles as symbols of power and success, and there is a particularly realistic evocation of a sleeping eagle at the start of an ode invoking the power of music:

> The eagle sleeps, perched on the sceptre of Zeus,
> his swift wings let to fall slackly on either side.
> The king of birds, over whose curving head you have
> poured a black cloud, a sweet seal for his eyelids,
> and while he dozes he ripples his supple back.
>
> Pindar, *Pythians* 1.6–9

Other visual symbols include birds on coins (most famously the owls of Athena), rings, seals, pottery, mosaics, and wall-paintings, many of which are featured in this volume. There were some more bizarre representations, too. There are phallus-birds, like those illustrated in 5.11, and there is a bird perched on the erect member of a herm (a kind of little statue on a squared base, which had a head, torso and often male genitals carved into the block). And there are many other representations of birds in surprising (to us) erotic contexts.* The meaning of these images is not always clear, nor is their identification always certain. The scholar Kenneth Dover, who published a pioneering book on Greek homosexuality in 1978, confesses that in researching the visual evidence for homosexual practices in Greek art he began after a while 'to see penile imagery everywhere'.

An even more curious bird-related image comes in the 'egg poem' composed by Simmias, a scholar–poet of the third century BC. This was one of a genre called 'pattern poems' or *jeux d'esprit* (*technopaignia*), remarkable more for their technical ingenuity than their literary merit. The poem was probably inscribed on an actual egg, with the line lengths gradually increasing towards the middle of the egg and then decreasing again. To read the poem as a sequential text, one has to take the

5.11 Phallic tintinnabulum. Bronze amulet or wind-chime from Pompeii, first century AD, depicting a phallic quadruped with a bird's wings, a scorpion's tail, and a couple of insects (perhaps cicadas) on its back.

shortest line at the top, then the shortest at the bottom, then the second shortest at the top, then the second shortest at the bottom, and so on to the longest lines in the middle. The consequence of this layout is that the reconstructed text doesn't itself mirror the shape of the egg, so a translation is (fortunately) besides the point. The theme begins with a nightingale (code for the poet himself) and becomes some sort of self-referential riddle about the complex metrical pattern of the poem.[1] It has no purpose beyond its own virtuosity of composition. A post-modernist joke?

* * *

Similes, metaphors, proverbs, fables, allegories, and myths—each with a different scope and scale—all have similar analogical functions. They use what is

---

[1] This progresses, a scholar tells us, from 'a trochaic monometer catalectic to a complicated decameter of dactyls, anapaests, paeons and spondees.'*

Κωτίλας
τᾷ τόδ’ ἄτριον νέον
πρόφρων δὲ θυμῷ δέξο· δὴ γὰρ ἁγνᾶς
τὸ μὲν θεῶν ἐριβόας Ἑρμᾶς ἔκιξε κάρυξ
ἄνωγε δ’ ἐκ μέτρου μονοβάμονος μέγαν πάροιθ’ ἀέξειν
θοῶς δ’ ὕπερθεν ὦκα λέχριον φέρων νεῦμα ποδῶν σποράδων πίφαυσκεν
θοαῖς ἴσ’ αἰόλαις νεβροῖς κῶλ’ ἀλλάσσων ὀρσιπόδων ἐλάφων τέκεσσιν·
πᾶσαι κραιπνοῖς ὑπὲρ ἄκρων ἱέμεναι ποσὶ λόφων κατ’ ἀρθμίας ἴχνος τιθήνας,
καί τις ὠμόθυμος ἀμφίπαλτον αἶψ’ αὐδὰν θὴρ ἐν κόλπῳ δεξάμενος θαλαμᾶν μυχοιτάτῳ
κᾆτ’ ὦκα Βοᾶς ἀκοὰν μεθέπων, ὅγ’ ἄφαρ λάσιον νιφοβόλων ἂν’ ὀρέων ἔσσυται ἄγκος.
ταῖσι δὴ δαίμων κλυτᾶς ἴσα θοοῖς δονέων ποσὶ πολύπλοκα μετίει μέτρα μολπᾶς.
ῥίμφα πετρόκοιτον ἐκλιπὼν ὄρους εὐνάν, ματρὸς πλαγκτὸν μαιόμενος βαλίας ἑλεῖν τέκος
βλαχαὶ δ’ οἴων πολυβότων ἂν’ ὀρέων νομὸν ἔβαν τανυσφύρων ἐς ἂν’ ἄντρα Νυμφῶν·
ταὶ δ’ ἀμβρότῳ πόθῳ φίλας ματρὸς ῥώοντ’ αἶψα μεθ’ ἱμερόεντα μαζόν,
ἴχνει θένων . . ταν παναίολον Πιερίδων μονόδουπον αὐδάν,
ἀριθμὸν εἰς ἄκραν δεκάδ’ ἰχνίων κόσμον νέμοντα ῥυθμῶν.
φῦλ’ ἐς βροτῶν, ὑπὸ φίλας ἑλὼν πτεροῖσι ματρός·
λίγειά μιν κάμ’ Ἴφι ματρὸς ὠδίς·
Δωρίας ἀηδόνος
ματέρος

5.12 Simmias, egg poem. *Greek Anthology* xv 27.

known and familiar to illuminate some aspect of experience, and they do it by comparison rather than by direct description. On the face of it this seems very unlike the procedures of science, with its emphasis on precisely defined terms and exact descriptions. But scientists too make good use of metaphorical expressions to promote understanding. 'Black holes', 'selfish genes', 'hardwired instincts', and 'genetic codes' are still recent enough formulations to retain something of their original expressive force; but in cases like 'electric currents', 'radio waves', and 'magnetic attraction' the original metaphors have long been deadened in their effects, though they may still have consequences for the way we view these phenomena and seek to explain them. Our language is unavoidably a human language, so when we apply this to the physical world we naturally take our analogies from human experience. Even a hard-nosed scientific ornithologist, fully aware of the dangers of anthropomorphism, will routinely use terms like 'courtship', 'display', 'aggression', 'song', and 'migration' to explain bird behaviour. In the same way we may refer to birds 'searching', 'choosing', 'deciding', 'cooperating', and (more controversially) 'intending', 'thinking', 'feeling'—and therefore 'suffering', by which time we have entered difficult ethical as well as scientific territory and we may start wanting to make some distinctions.*

It is this careful making of distinctions—the marking of similarities and differences, of sameness and otherness—that is surely at the heart of most serious

enquiries, of whatever discipline. In the case of analogies, the imagination provides the link. When these symbolic representations are apt they can be incred-
ibly powerful in enlarging, enriching, and reinforcing our perceptions. And then
by a process of transference we can become deeply attached to the symbol itself.
Freud's successor and critic Carl Jung had his own dictum about this: 'Between
the dreams of night and day there is not so great a difference.'*

PART 6

Birds as Intermediaries

In ancient times it was birds, not gods, that ruled over men.

Aristophanes, *Birds* 481–82

Nature! We are surrounded and embraced by her: powerless to separate ourselves from her, and powerless to penetrate beyond her.

Goethe *Maxims and Reflections* (quoted by Thomas Huxley in the Preface to the first issue of the journal *Nature*, 4 November 1869)

We do not know what the dragon *means*, just as we do not know the meaning of the universe, but there is something in the image of the dragon that is congenial to man's imagination, and thus arises in many latitudes and ages.

Jorge Luis Borges, *The Book of Imaginary Beings* (1967), Preface

6.1 Bird-dancers. Two men in full-body bird costumes, including feathered wings and coxcombs, followed by a piper, on an Attic black-figure wine-jug, 500–490 BC. Similar bird-dancers reappear on fifth-century red-figure vases (see also **6.15**), leading to the suggestion that these might have referenced performances of the many Greek comedies with bird titles and choruses, perhaps even that of Aristophanes' *The Birds* itself (though the date of *The Birds* in 414 BC is a difficulty for that tempting thought). These bird-men also share some features with satyrs and suggest the connections of Greek drama with the cult of Dionysus, not least in the ithyphallic imagery.

Introduction

This final part aims to be both an extension of the themes so far addressed and a pulling together of them. It would be wrong to think of it as any kind of completion, however, since by the end of the book we shall still have encountered only a fraction of the abundant material on birds available in ancient texts and pictorial representations. Moreover, the structure I have adopted to present this selection is only one of several possible ones, so there can be no single final and definitive account. It has been more a question of building up a composite picture of a landscape seen from different angles, in different lights and seasons, and over a long time period.

The previous chapters have all been filling out this dynamic picture and continuously modifying it. Part 1 began by exploring how birds came to stand as markers for various natural phenomena like seasons, weather, and time, and were evidence of the close and deep relationships the ancients had with the physical world. Part 2 looked at the way that relationship was exploited for human purposes, as birds were hunted, cooked, and farmed as an abundant natural resource. In part 3 the attention turned to social attitudes and the treatment of birds as entertainments and domestic pets, while in part 4 birds were considered as the objects of curiosity, wonder, and eventually science. Given their ubiquity and their interest and importance to humankind in so many different areas, it is not surprising that birds also came to feature in people's dreams, imaginings, and symbols, and that was the theme of part 5.

This final part now extends that idea and explores the status of birds as intermediaries—creatures in some ways like us and in others unlike us. Where were they (and we) thought to fit into the mental maps of the natural and supernatural worlds? Did birds serve some spiritual or symbolic function as winged guides or messengers between different realms of existence? The gift of flight certainly made them the natural intermediaries between men and gods, moving freely between earth and heaven.

The sources here need careful interpretation. Religion in the ancient world, as has often been pointed out, was at least as much a matter of practice as of belief. The round of communal rituals, festivals, and sacrifices was what constituted religious commitment for most people, rather than the adherence to specific doctrines, creeds, or theological positions embodied in some sacred text (they didn't have one). When Socrates was put to death by the Athenian court in 399 BC the two official reasons given were: firstly, that he was a corrupting influence on the young (through his disturbing, or as governments might now say, radicalizing conversations with them); and, secondly, that he was committing offences against state religion. The latter charge is usually translated as 'not *believing in* the city's gods', but the verb *nomizein* that was used in the court's judgment would be better translated here as 'not *observing* (or *acknowledging*) the city's gods'. Socrates preferred to follow the promptings of his personal *daimon* or 'conscience' and acted accordingly.

Many people did have their beliefs, of course—which were often challenged by sceptics. But these may often have been largely implicit and it is difficult or misleading to extract them as a set of consciously held theories about the world that can then be compared with other bodies of belief like those represented by magic or science.

I end by summarizing and contrasting some modern and ancient responses to the natural world, and asking why it should in particular be *birds* that served all the different roles and functions the preceding chapters have explored? This is explained partly by their attributes and partly by the human reaction to those. It turns out that the book as a whole is as much about us as it is about the birds themselves.

⮿ 17 ⮾

Fabulous Creatures

James Frazer took the title of his famous work *The Golden Bough* (1890) from a passage in Virgil's *Aeneid* where the hero Aeneas is searching for a magic 'Golden Bough' as a gift for Persephone, goddess of the underworld, to win him passage down to her realm and (most importantly) back again to the world of the living.* Birds have both a positive and a negative role in the story. His mother, Venus, sent Aeneas two doves to serve as his messengers and they led him through the deep forest right to the tree he needed, near a volcanic crater that was believed to be the entrance to the underworld. That place was called Avernus, which Virgil explains comes from the Greek *a-ornos* and literally means 'birdless', so named because any birds flying over it were brought down by the poisonous fumes issuing from the crater.[1] When Aeneas crosses the threshold, he is immediately confronted by various grotesque and terrifying monsters, including some Harpies (winged women). The hero draws his sword at these, but then realizes that they are just 'flitting creatures of the imagination, without bodily form' (*Aeneid* vi 292–93). We shall come back to these imaginary hybrids.

Frazer and the assorted school of anthropologists, folklorists, and classical scholars most influenced by him—which included such figures as Robert Graves, Jane Harrison, Gilbert Murray, F. M. Cornford, and E. A. Armstrong*—were very struck by some puzzling references to birds and other animals in classical art and literature. These seemed to them to be evidence that 'animal gods' were a key feature in the world view of Greek and other early societies. They

---

[1] The present day Lago d'Averno, west of Naples in Campania. Aristotle noted prosaically that it wasn't actually birdless, since there were often swans there.

seized on passages like those in Aristophanes' *The Birds* (462–522), where it is proclaimed by the human visitors to the kingdom of the birds that the birds are the oldest beings in the world and were once themselves the ancient gods and masters of the universe, only to be later dispossessed by the Olympians. In particular, they drew attention to lines like these:

> Zeus will not quickly yield the sceptre to the oak-pecker.
> It's easily proved that in ancient times it was birds,
> not gods, that ruled over men and were lords of the world.
>   Aristophanes, *Birds* 480–82

This was taken to be a folk memory of ancient bird cults, involving here the woodpecker ('oak-pecker') and in other sources also the cuckoo. But this was to rest a large hypothesis about animal gods on very slender supports that were, as a later scholar has said, 'reconstructed from ambiguous surviving fragments in a search for lost origins.'* A rather desperate search, one might add. *The Birds*, after all, is a comedy, not a religious text, and the lines in question are spoken by one of the Athenian interlopers, who is scheming to flatter the birds into accepting their approaches. The speaker later reveals that his name is Peisetaerus or 'Comrade-persuader'—not necessarily the most reliable witness, therefore. In any case, anthropology itself moved on and came to reject as naive the notion that so-called 'primitive' societies all moved through the same determinate phases of development from magic to religion and on to science. It is now accepted from the classical evidence as well as from that of other cultures that these different modes of engaging with and understanding the world can coexist at any one time in the same society and perform somewhat different functions.*

But if birds were never actually thought of as gods nor became the object of bird cults in the sense Frazer supposed, the gods themselves were certainly sometimes believed to have bird-like attributes. The various metamorphoses we looked at in chapter 15 were mostly of legendary humans who were turned into birds, but gods could turn themselves into birds too, when it suited their purposes. In Zeus' case the purposes tended to be aggressively sexual, and at different times he became a swan to seduce (or rape) Leda, a cuckoo to inveigle himself into Hera's embrace, and an eagle to abduct the boy Ganymede.

Very often, though, in such references to gods as birds, it is unclear whether we are dealing with transformation, illusion, or metaphor. In Homer, in particular, gods are often said to be behaving *like* birds: Athena and Apollo sit on an oak 'like vultures' to watch a battle (*Iliad* VII 58–60), but were they actually in bird form or

6.2 Leda and the swan. The myth of Zeus in the form of a swan seducing (or raping) Leda was a popular subject in ancient art from about 450 BC, but it became an even more potent source of inspiration from the Renaissance onwards for artists like Leonardo, Michelangelo, Correggio, Rubens, and Delacroix, as well as for poets, most famously W. B. Yeats. This painting is thought to be a sixteenth-century copy of a lost painting by Michelangelo.

in human form (the latter improbable, surely, up an oak tree)? Similarly, Athena flies up to sit on a beam of Odysseus' house 'like a swallow' to watch the slaying of the suitors (*Odyssey* XXII 239–40). And then again Athena abandons her human disguise and leaves Pylos 'in the likeness of a vulture'[1] (*Odyssey* III 371–72). These sound like temporary transformations; but there are other cases that read more like traditional Homeric similes, as when the gods need to travel swiftly over land or sea and 'skim the waves like a seabird'[2] (*Odyssey* V 51–53), 'dive like a cormorant' (*Odyssey* V 352–53), 'soar like a raptor' (*Iliad* XIX 349–51), or 'stoop like a falcon' (*Iliad* XV 236–38). Perhaps no sharp distinctions between the literal and the metaphorical are, in any case, intended here, and the ambiguity serves other poetic purposes.

* * *

[1] *Phene*, which in other references seems to be either a black vulture or a lammergeier (bearded vulture).
[2] *Laros*, which usually means a gull, but sounds here more like a shearwater of some kind.

Hybrids and other fabulous creatures challenge conventional distinctions of category, anyway. The full list of the 'monstrous forms' Aeneas encounters at the entrance to the underworld divides into hybrids—centaurs (man–horse), Scylla (cephalopod–shark–woman), Chimaera (lion–snake–goat), Gorgons (snake-haired women), and Harpies (winged women)—and freaks—the beast of Lerna (a water serpent or hydra, with the capacity to grow several heads when one was pruned), Briareos (a giant with many arms and heads), and Cerberus (a huge dog with 'triple throats').

Elsewhere in classical literature we also find hybrids like griffons (eagle–lion), Pegasus (winged horse), satyrs (man–goat), Echidna (snake–woman), the Sphinx (woman–bird–lion), Medusa (snake-haired woman), and Furies (snake-haired women, usually winged).* In the combinations involving humans, the human part tends to be the face, presumably as our most distinctively expressive feature; but before one is seduced by some large cultural generalization about this, it should be remembered that the minotaur (bull–man) is one exception in Greek mythology and that birds and other animals provide the heads in many ancient Egyptian hybrids.

Before reviewing the classical bird hybrids, we should look at two other fabulous birds with equally alarming attributes. Ovid describes some ghastly 'vampire birds', which he explicitly distinguishes both from owls (whose name they share, as 'night-screechers') and from Harpies (from whom 'they take their descent'):

> These are greedy birds with …
> huge heads, goggle eyes, and beaks designed for butchery,
> feathers frosted grey and talons barbed with hooks.
> They fly by night and seek out untended children,
> whose bodies they snatch from their cradles and defile.
> They are said to rend the flesh of suckling babes
> with beaks that fill their throats with swallowed blood.
> 'Screechers' they are called from their horrid nightly screams. Whether, then, they
>   are born as birds, or are creatures
> of fiction, hags conjured into birds by wizards' spells,
> they entered Proca's chamber, where the child just five days old
> became the birds' fresh prey. With greedy tongues they sucked
> at his infant breast, while the poor child screamed for help.
>
> Ovid, *Fasti* VI 131–46

The 'Stymphalian birds' were also thought to be man-eaters, but in this case were possibly real birds of Arabian origin. Heracles had to clear them from Lake Stymphalus in Arcadia for his sixth labour, as the travel writer Pausanias describes:

6.3 Heracles and the Stymphalian birds. Heracles killing the man-eating birds of Lake Stymphalos in Arcadia. No natural species fits the various descriptions and depictions of the Stymphalian birds, and various speculative identifications like egret, lammergeier, swan, and great crested grebe can be firmly ruled out.* Attic black-figure *amphora*, *c.*540 BC.

There is a legend about the Lake of Stymphalus that man-eating birds once bred there; and the story is that Heracles shot them down with arrows (though in another account Peisander of Camira says that Heracles did not kill the birds but drove them off with the noise from castanets). Now among the wild-life of the Arabian desert there are some birds called 'Stymphalian', which are just as aggressive towards humans as lions or leopards. They fly at those who come to hunt them, wounding or even killing them with their beaks. The birds can pierce through any bronze or iron armour men may put on; but if you clothe yourself in thick bark the birds' beaks get held fast in the bark, just as the wings of small birds get stuck in bird-lime. These birds are the size of a crane and resemble ibises, except that their beaks are stronger and are not curved like those of ibises. Whether the current birds of this name in Arabia are the same species as these Arcadian birds, I don't know; but if there have always been Stymphalian birds in the way there have always been hawks and eagles, then these birds would appear to be of Arabian origin and a flock of them could have flown to Arcadia at some point and found their way to Stymphalus.

Pausanias, *Description of Greece* VIII 22

Pausanias goes on to describe the temple of Artemis at Stymphalus, which had some images of these birds on the roof, but these have not survived, alas.

The vampire birds and Stymphalian birds seem to be straightforwardly the stuff of nightmares, exaggerated and distorted versions of actual birds on which one could project the sort of fears many people have of birds' beaks, claws, and beating wings—fears that Alfred Hitchcock exploited so cleverly in his 1963 horror film *The Birds*. The hybrid monsters, on the other hand, seem to have a more complex symbolism. They too can be aggressive and threatening, but they are also frightening because they are so *weird*, being composed of a disturbing combination of bodily parts that belong to quite different natural species. The three hybrids most relevant for this chapter are the Sirens, the Scylla, and the Harpies—all female.

The Sirens are often referred to in classical literature, but for their appearance we are more reliant on artistic representations, where they are usually pictured as either birds with large female heads or women with feathered bodies and birds' legs. In Homer they are the 'siren voices' that bewitch passing sailors and lure them on to the rocks. Odysseus wanted very much to hear them, so he safeguarded himself and his boat by blocking his sailors' ears with wax and hav-ing them tie him hand and foot to the mast with strict instructions not to release him, however much he begged them to, until they were safely out of earshot.

6.4 Sirens. Odysseus' boat passing the Sirens, who are imagined as birds with women's heads. Odysseus is lashed to the mast and Sirens are singing from either side, while one of them apparently plunges to her doom (perhaps because he has broken their power by defying them). Attic red-figure vase, *c*.480–470 BC.

Circe, who was something of an enchantress herself with her own designs on Odysseus, had warned him what the risks were:

> First you will come to the Sirens, who bewitch all men
> that approach them. Whoever in his ignorance
> comes near them and hears their siren voices,
> never again will he have his wife and young children
> cluster round and welcome him on his return home.
> Instead, the Sirens will beguile him with their sweet songs,
> as they sit in a meadow among a great pile of bones
> from decaying men whose skins shrivel around them.
> Homer, *Odyssey* XII 39–46

Thanks to these precautions, Odysseus survives his close encounter with the Sirens, but then he has to avoid the twin perils of Scylla and Charybdis, located on either side of a narrow sea channel. Charybdis is a whirlpool, and Scylla was once a beautiful woman, but Circe changed her into a multi-limbed sea-monster in a fit of jealousy.

Scylla's speciality was snatching sailors from passing ships to devour them:

> Within this cave dwells Scylla, squealing terribly.
> Her voice may be no louder than a young whelp's,[1]
> but she herself is an evil monster. Anyone would flinch
> from the sight of her, even any god that encountered her.
> For she has twelve legs, all writhing like tentacles,
> and six very elongated necks, and on the end of each
> a ghastly head armed with six rows of teeth,
> all jammed tight together, laden with black death.
>
> Homer, *Odyssey* XII 85–92

Circe advises Odysseus to avoid Charybdis at all costs and if necessary risk losing a few sailors to Scylla. That is just what happens when his attention is briefly distracted by Charybdis:

> Scylla meanwhile snatched from the hollow ship
> six of my strongest and most able-bodied comrades.
> Looking back at my swift ship for my companions,
> I saw their feet and hands already hoisted high above me.
> They cried out aloud to me in anguished despair,
> calling on me by name, for that one last time.
> Just as an angler from his rock casts bait to trap
> the little fishes and with his long rod lowers the ox-horn[2]
> into the sea, then flings his struggling catch ashore;
> so they were drawn struggling up the rocky cliffs.
> Then at her cave's entrance she devoured them, shrieking
> and reaching out their hands to me in their mortal fight.
> That was the most piteous sight my eyes ever witnessed
> in all my troubled journeys across the ocean's ways.
>
> Homer, *Odyssey* XII 244–59

The third of these female hybrids are the Harpies, literally in Greek the 'raptors'.[3] They too are mentioned in Homer as dangerous body-snatchers, but

---

[1] There is a pun or implied derivation here between *skulax* (whelp) and *Skulle* (Scylla).
[2] No one knows what this 'ox-horn' was—a weight, a float, or a cover for the hook?
[3] The harpy eagle (*Harpia harpyja*) of Central and South America is called after this mythological creature.

there is a fuller description in Virgil. He pictures them as winged women, behaving rather like scavenging kites:

> Birds with maiden faces, filth spewing from their bellies,
> talons for hands, and faces ever haggard with hunger.
> …
> But suddenly the dread Harpies appear, swooping
> down from the mountains in a clamour of wing-beats
> to plunder the feast—foul creatures, polluting everything
> they touch; then that terrible scream amid the stench.
>
> Virgil, *Aeneid* III 216–28

6.5 Harpies. Two Harpies depicted on an Attic black-figure vase, fifth century BC.

Here we have a new theme emerging. The Harpies with their 'maiden faces' not only steal the food but also *pollute* it—with their excretions and their filthy claws and mouths. 'Even the little food they left behind', explains the mythographer Apollodorus, 'stank so badly that no one would touch it' (*Library of Greek Mythology* I 9.21).

The idea of pollution, *miasma* in Greek, is a deep theme running through many ritual practices in the ancient world, and one that untidily connects a whole range of beliefs about food, hygiene, medicine, religious observance, and physical relationships. The risks of defilement were most present at the terminal life events of birth and death, in serious disorders like madness, in sexual activity, and in extreme social aberrations like incest, murder, and cannibalism. The notions of sacrilege and the 'obscene' (Latin *obscenus*) were correspondingly broad, and the need for socially agreed forms of 'purification' correspondingly important.

Birds were implicated in this, first in a direct way as potential polluters of both sacred sites and domestic buildings with their excretions, but also more metaphorically as ominous and potentially unlucky or obscene presences.* Women were also implicated, at least in male perceptions, through the impurities associated with fertility, menstruation, conception, and birth, and through the 'inner' characteristics associated with women's bodies and lives. May there even be, as one scholar has suggested, some implicit general analogy here between the female interior and the underworld?*

What are we to make of these depictions of bird–humans and other hybrids like Scylla? To the extent that the most prominent (and dangerous) ones are female, should we put that down to cultural misogyny, or at least gynophobia— the fear of the combined seductive power and destructive potential of the female? The origins and processes of myth formation in traditional societies continue to be much debated, and there is no clear agreement about the key factor or (more likely) factors.* But if one function of myth is to express and explain social norms by relating them to an imagined past, this interpretation might be plausible as at least part of the story.

Monsters are quite frightening enough anyway, however gendered, and they would have served as convenient fictions on which to project all kinds of fears about the dangers of the physical world and its inhabitants. The fears were understandable ones, in any case. The population then was largely rural and was exposed to threats from weather, terrain, wildlife, and darkness, from which modern city-dwellers are largely protected. There were real wildernesses and uncharted areas, both on land and at sea, concealing who knew what mysteries and surprises. We saw in chapter 11 on 'wonders' the fascination travellers had with exotic creatures and the tall stories they conjured up about them. If it is still easy now for some inhabitants of suburban Britain to believe in the existence of 'big cats' roaming Exmoor or plesiosaurs lurking in Loch Ness, how much easier would it have been then to imagine strange beings living in remote times and places?

'Strange' may be an important clue here. Monsters, and especially the subgroup of hybrids, pose a problem for the way we see the natural world and the patterns and regularities we expect to recognize within it. They seem to defy classification and to challenge our usual categories in ways that are both physically and intellectually threatening. Confronted with a Scylla or a Siren the natural reaction for us as well as for Odysseus would be one of both fear and horrified curiosity. The medieval bestiaries, the illustrated compilations of weird and wonderful creatures, traded on both these reactions. They had their source in the Greek text *Physiologus*, produced some time between the second and fourth centuries AD. This was a very influential work that deployed animal stories and depictions to preach moralizing Christian messages—for example, the fanciful account of the pelican that kills its offspring and then after three days revives them with its own blood. The bestiaries included both real and imaginary animals in their bizarre menageries, but we now know that the products of natural selection are quite remarkable enough in themselves to provide us with all the symbols and surprises we need.*

Anthropologists and linguists have long taken particular interest in the ways that traditional societies classify the natural world and how the distinctions they make are reflected in their cultures through their myths, rituals, and symbols. The famous quotation from Lévi-Strauss that 'natural species are good to think with' is the mission statement for this approach, and in part 5 we looked at a range of examples from the ancient world of how birds were used as signs, metaphors, and symbols. Zoologists prefer to think *about* animals rather than *with* them, but from Aristotle onwards they too have been much concerned with questions of classification and taxonomy—that is, with sorting out the hierarchies of relationships and affinities between different natural species. Aristotle himself was puzzled by what he called the 'dualizers', creatures like seals, bats, and ostriches that seemed to cross boundaries or combine characteristics from quite different natural groupings like fish, bird, or mammal.[1] The bird–human hybrids, on this line of thinking, would have been dualizers writ very large indeed, and painted red for danger.

* * *

I want now, though, to look at a much gentler, more attractive, and more familiar class of anomalous creatures that pose a puzzle in cultural interpretation, not by their presence but by their absence. Butterflies.

[1] See notes to p. 231.

Aristotle knew about the life cycle of butterflies and gives the first scientific account of their metamorphosis[1] from caterpillar to chrysalis to fully formed imago:

> Butterflies, as they are called, come from caterpillars. These live on plants with green leaves, especially the *raphanos*, which some people call the cabbage. At first they are smaller than a grain of millet, then they grow into tiny larvae, and then after three days into little caterpillars. After growing further, they become immobile and change their form. They are now called chrysalises and have a hard casing, moving if this is touched. They cling on by means of filaments like cobwebs and have no mouth or other organ visible. After a short time the outer covering bursts open and out fly the winged creatures we call butterflies.
>
> Aristotle, *History of Animals* v 551a

He knew that butterflies were insects and was clearly setting out here some familiar, observed facts. The surprise, and the mystery, is that no one before Aristotle had ever mentioned butterflies. This is most odd. Butterflies, like birds, would have been at least as abundant in the Mediterranean countries then as they are now. They are colourful, conspicuous, and widely distributed and would have been a familiar, and presumably an attractive, sight to everyone. Why would no one have mentioned them in all the literature we have from Homer (eighth century BC) up to the time that Aristotle wrote his account in about 340 BC? They would have been perfect, surely, for one of those Homeric similes about the fragility of life and would have had a natural place in descriptions of the countryside in other poetry and prose. Birds, after all, are mentioned all the time in Greek literature, as are many kinds of flowers, mammals, and fish, and indeed other insects like bees, wasps, and cicadas. But butterflies appear nowhere in all the lyric or pastoral poetry, in tragedy or comedy, in the travelogues of Herodotus and Xenophon, or in the works of the early natural scientists. How could they have overlooked something so obvious?

We can rule out a few possible explanations straightaway, I think.

Firstly, we can discount the idea that the environment then was so different that it couldn't support butterfly populations in the way it does now. There is no evidence at all for that in the archaeological or geological record, and even if there had been it would also have affected the birds, flowers, and other insects that we hear so much about. If anything, the situation is the reverse. Butterflies

---

[1] Though he doesn't actually use that word (see p. 276), and he omits to mention the egg stage.

are under pressure now in most European countries from environmental degradation, intensive farming, and urban development and are declining in both abundance and diversity everywhere. But even now there are something over 230 species of butterfly in Greece (the exact number depends on how you count sub-species and migrants), compared with fifty-nine in Britain.* There would have been at least as many kinds then and they would almost certainly have been pre-sent in greater numbers.

Secondly, only a fraction of classical literature has survived (see p. 151 n.1 above). Might butterflies have been mentioned in some of the works we have lost, so ending the mystery? Well, it's true that it is dangerous to argue from an *absence* of evidence, but in this case we do still have a large amount of the relevant lit-erature and you really would have expected at least some references to a creature so physically striking and so ideal for a whole range of metaphorical and sym-bolic exploitations. After all, we hear all the time about gods changing them-selves or humans into other physical forms like birds, trees, mammals, and even a shower of gold, so why not into butterflies?

Thirdly, it might be tempting to pick up on a few stray references in much later authors where butterflies are quaintly described as 'little birds'.* Could it be that butterflies were not identified as a separate class of creatures at all, but were thought of as small colourful birds? That seems an unlikely mistake in itself, and anyway it still wouldn't explain why they were not mentioned as one kind of 'bird' among others in appropriate contexts, since so many species of birds *are* so dis-tinguished and described.

A more promising line of thought might be to start from the name. The Greek for a butterfly is *psuche*, but the same Greek word also means 'soul' or 'spirit' (from which we get 'psychic', 'psychology', and so on).[1] But, to use a distinction from linguistics, are these two senses of *psuche* ('butterfly' and 'soul') just homonyms— two words that sound the same and are spelled the same but have two quite unrelated meanings (like the bark of a tree and the bark of a dog)? Or are they polysemes—two words with related meanings (like the mouth of a river and the mouth of a human)? You can see why the latter interpretation might have seemed attractive. The 'winged souls' of the departed were thought to fly from the body at the time of death and Aeneas encounters them 'flitting restlessly' in the underworld after he has run the gauntlet of the monsters with which this

---

[1] The etymology of *psuche* in this sense is from the verb 'to breathe', hence it also comes to stand for life itself and the centre of consciousness.

chapter began. Butterflies, too, are insubstantial, flitting creatures. They have an ethereal, fragile beauty about them, which is both emphasized and symbolized by their extraordinary life cycle and their final, fleeting epiphany. If you wanted a physical emblem of a soul you could hardly do better, as the later history of butterfly imagery demonstrated. Early Christian writers like St Basil (fourth century AD) and other Church Fathers saw the polyseme 'butterfly / soul' as too good a metaphorical opportunity to pass up and turned it into an allegory of the Resurrection. And the butterfly continued to be the image of choice for artists representing Christian beliefs about death and the afterlife throughout the Middle Ages to the Renaissance.

6.6 *Memento mori.* An allegorical mosaic from Pompeii (30 BC–AD 14), representing death (the skull), equally balanced by wealth (purple cloak, left) and poverty (beggar's scrip, right). Below is a butterfly (soul) over a wheel (of fortune). The butterfly is identifiable as a lesser purple emperor (*Apatura ilia*).

On this account, the relationship between *psuche* as butterfly and *psuche* as soul would be analogous to the relationship between *ornis* as bird and *ornis* as omen, whose implications we explored in chapter 14. That seems most likely, but how might it bear on our original problem of the centuries of silence about butterflies before Aristotle? Some scholars have wondered if this association of butterflies with the souls of the dead made it somehow taboo to refer to them directly. As D'Arcy Thompson put it, 'I think the Greeks found something ominous or uncanny, something not to be lightly spoken of, in that all but dis-embodied spirit which we call butterfly, and they called by the name of *psuche*, the Soul.'* That's the sort of solution people tend to find seductive. It offers a vague but sweeping explanation of an odd puzzle; it gives us all a piece of recon-dite knowledge (the ambiguity of the word *psuche*); and it appeals to our sense of the exotic. It reminds one of the way people happily repeat the linguistic 'urban myth' that unlike us the Inuit have fifty different words for snow.*

D'Arcy Thompson's suggestion may possibly be true, but I am sceptical, for several reasons. Briefly: (1) There seem to be few inhibitions in Greek culture about discussing anything. Comic writers like Aristophanes felt free to satirize conventional mores on sex and family, politics and politicians, religion, race, and foreigners, and the plays are full of outrageous obscenities and irreverent jokes. (2) The fifth century BC was the first great European Enlightenment, in which rational, scientific, and humanistic ideas were being applied to all manner of questions that were once the preserve of myth and religion. In particular, ques-tions about life and death and about the soul and a possible afterlife were vigor-ously discussed and debated throughout this period. There's no evidence that the word *psuche* itself was taboo at all—indeed, the conventionally pious author Xenophon recommends it as a good name for a dog. (3) The Latin word for 'butterfly' was *papilio*, and that wasn't ambiguous in the same way as *psuche* ('soul' in Latin is *anima*), though *papilio* too is an infrequent usage, which some-times occurs in funereal contexts.* (4) *Psuche* in Greek included moths as well as butterflies, though as creatures of the night these might have been expected to have different associations.

Finally, (5) if there was some kind of inhibition why didn't it apply to the visual arts, where butterflies (or moths) seem to be depicted in various contexts from the Minoan period onwards? Here too, however, there is a timely warning against over-interpretation. There is a Greek vase of the sixth century BC in the Pergamon Museum in Berlin which has a dramatic image of a naked man with a butterfly apparently dancing in a jet of his sperm. This has sometimes been eagerly cited as evidence of the connection of butterflies with psyche as 'life force'. But the curators of the museum have recently revealed that the 'butterfly' was just an accidental smudge on the surface that they have now had cleaned off in a restoration....

The silence over butterflies in the literature remains a mystery, but it is not unique. Butterflies are not mentioned in the Bible either (though moths are, usually as symbols of decay and corruption). And they are mentioned surprisingly rarely even in Shakespeare, though he famously makes imaginative use of many species of birds, flowers, and other insects.

*   *   *

I leave that hanging. The point of this apparent digression from monsters to butterflies is to show how hard it is to decode the myths of another culture when dealing with anomalous categories. It is often tempting to seize gratefully on a theory that seems intuitively simple and satisfying—that is, satisfying to us, now. But myths are not neat, coherent, and systematic accounts. They have a history of their own and over time they usually accrete alternative versions and contradictory elements. When one is dealing with animal symbolism it is also well to remember that projections can go both ways. Zoologists are schooled to avoid the professional sin of anthropomorphism—that is, projecting human capacities, sensibilities, and values on to the animals they are studying. But there is also the opposite risk of theriomorphism—of basing explanations of human culture and behaviour too closely on models that apply more to other animals. The point of many animal myths, fables, allegories, and metaphors, as illustrated in part 5, is to use animals to think with, and so by imaginative transference see things in ourselves we might need to recognize. This can be very illuminating, but we shouldn't assume that we can extract literal truths from these other forms of expression or translate them back into more transparent descriptions. Nor should we assume that in this case the myths are just false. We often use the English word 'myth' in a pejorative sense to mean 'false belief', but the original meaning of *muthos* in Greek is simply 'story'. The stories may be revealing or otherwise, but they are not simply either true or false.

18

Messengers
and Mediators

Our notion of 'making a sacrifice' is now far removed from what sacrifice represented in the classical world. This is one of those sideways shifts in semantic history that is not so much a case of something being lost in translation as of a radical difference in social practice. If we 'make a sacrifice' we are deliberately giving up something valued. It's often an individual choice, maybe of a quite ordinary kind, and it may have no larger cultural significance. For the Greeks and Romans, on the other hand, sacrifices were an established public ritual and a key part of religious observance. Moreover, they sacrificed in order to *gain* various benefits, not to forgo them. The purpose was to establish a channel of communication with the gods, whether to honour, thank, or propitiate them, or to seek some specific advice or future advantage. Most sacrifices in the ancient world involved the ritual killing of animals, often on a large scale, and were conducted in accordance with carefully prescribed rules and regulations to ensure the success of the operation. The resulting gifts to the gods were the inhalations they received from the cooking of specific body parts from the slaughtered animals, as the savours drifted upwards to the heavenly realm. The Greek word for 'sacrifice' was *thuein*, which literally means 'to make smoke' or 'to burn' (not 'to slaughter').

The meat did not go to waste, however, and so was not 'sacrificed' in our sense. On the contrary, most of the edible parts of the cooked animals were consumed by the celebrants, and such public sacrifices were a major source of meat and protein in the diet of ordinary people. Access to this supply of meat also served both to define and strengthen the social fabric of which people were a part; indeed, Aristotle goes so far as to say that communal sacrifice is one of the key activities constituting membership of a civil society.* Roman sacrificial practices were broadly similar, though the Latin term *sacrificare*, from which the English word derives, doesn't map exactly on to the Greek one, but means more generally 'to make sacred', that is, to put the offering into the possession of the gods.*

The animals most often sacrificed in this way were domestic animals such as cattle, sheep, pigs, and goats. There were a few exceptions to this involving birds— for example, the special case of the cockerel, which was a standard offering to Asclepius, god of healing, and was famously invoked in the reported last words of Socrates, 'Crito, we owe a cock to Asclepius. Please don't forget to pay it to him.' (Plato, *Phaedo* 118a). Chickens and geese were also sacrificed, sometimes to foreign gods like Isis; and there were perverse and exotic sacrifices of flamingoes and other birds made by (and to) the mad emperor Gaius.* But birds generally represented a cheaper and less common option for personal or public sacrifice.

Sacrifice to the gods provides the central hinge of the plot for Aristophanes' comic fantasy play *The Birds*. The two adventurers who are seeking to escape from the high taxes and oppressive city life in Athens hatch a plot to join the birds and establish a bird city ('Cloud-Cuckoo Land') in the skies. From this intermediate kingdom they hope to establish border controls and start charging the gods transit fees for the smoke of sacrifices passing up to them from earth (lines 172–93). The birds build a wall to starve the gods out (1118–69), and eventually the gods submit to this blackmail (1685–87). This is a comic inversion of the usual assumption that humans are the intermediate category between the animals and the gods—in both zoological and cultural terms. Aristophanes thus turns sacrificial ritual on its head and says that since the birds are now in charge (and are in any case the original masters of the earth) humans must change their habits and adjust their sacrificial gifts accordingly:

> I suggest you send another bird to take the message to the human race
> that since the birds are sovereign they must sacrifice to them,
> and only secondarily to the gods; and they match each god
> with whichever bird is most appropriate.

He then gives some punning examples, ending with the sacrifices that might once have gone to Zeus, king of the gods:

And if it was going to be a sacrifice of a ram to Zeus,
well, the wren[1] is the king bird, so you should slaughter
a victim for him first, ahead of Zeus, an uncastrated...gnat.

  Aristophanes, *Birds* 561–66

Such fantasies work dramatically only if there is a cultural assumption that
makes them paradoxical, and this chapter explores the idea of birds as intermediaries of a privileged kind.

We saw in chapter 10 how birds were sometimes used as physical messengers, in an early exploitation of the innate directional skills of carrier pigeons
in particular. It was natural, therefore, that pigeons (or doves—neither a precise term) would become the metaphorical messengers of choice too. In the
ancient Greek version of the Great Flood story, Deucalion (like Noah) relied
on a dove:

The storytellers relate that Deucalion released a dove from the ark, and as long as
she returned it was a sign that it was still stormy, but when she flew away it her-
alded fair weather.

  Plutarch, 'Cleverness of animals', *Moralia* 968f

6.7 Noah's Ark coin. Bronze coin from the reign of Gordian III (AD 238–44), depicting
Noah and his wife in the (very small) Ark with a dove above them. The coin comes from
Apameia in Phrygia, which was near a mountain identified by local people as the place
the Ark came to rest.

---

[1] *Orchilos* is a name for the wren, while *orchis* is 'testicle', so the only way of preserving this pun might
be to translate the bird as 'nuthatch' (or 'nutcracker').

Jason and his Argonauts also rely on a dove to guide them through the 'Clashing Rocks' that guarded the perilous passage from the Bosporus to the Black Sea:

> These were gigantic rocks, which were dashed together by the power of the winds, blocking the passage by sea. Thick mists swirled around them, they crashed with a tremendous noise, and it was impossible even for birds to fly between them. So he advised them to release a dove to fly between the rocks and if they saw it pass safely through to sail through themselves with an easy mind, but if it perished not to try and force a passage. After hearing this advice they put to sea and when they drew near the rocks they released the dove from the prow. It flew off and the rocks just snipped off the tip of its tail as they clashed together. So they waited until the rocks had drawn apart again then rowed hard and, with some help from Hera, made it through, though the tip of the ship's poop was shorn off. Ever after that the Clashing Rocks stood still, since it was fated that once a ship had succeeded in passing through they should become completely stationary.
>
> Apollodorus, *Library of Greek Mythology* I 9.22

The historian, Herodotus, tries to make sense of another piece of mythology. He recounts the story of the role doves played in establishing the famous oracles at Dodona (in Greece) and the shrine of Ammon (in Libya) as the authentic 'voices' of the gods:

> Two black doves flew over from Thebes in Egypt, one to Libya, the other here to Dodona. The latter perched on an oak and spoke to us in a human voice, declaring that this must be the site of Zeus's oracle. The people of Dodona understood that this was a message to them from the gods and they duly established the shrine there.
>
> Herodotus, *Histories* II 55

The priestesses at Dodona came to be called the Peleiades ('Doves') and Herodotus goes on to give his rationalization of this:[1]

> I imagine that the people of Dodona called these women 'Doves' because they were foreigners and people first thought their voices sounded like those of birds. After a time they said the dove was speaking with a human voice because by then they could understand what the woman was saying. As long as she spoke in a

---

[1] A further part of the 'explanation' might be that the wild rock dove *Columba livia* is common on the rocky cliffs around Dodona.*

6.8 Sacrificial hammer from Dodona. Bronze hammer (seventh century BC), incorporating doves in its design, thought to be used in the ritual sacrifice of animals (presumably to stun them before their throats were cut). Dodona, in the remote region of Epirus in north-west Greece, was the site of the oldest Greek oracle and was second only to Delphi in prestige.

foreign language, however, they thought her voice sounded like that of a bird. After all, how could a dove speak like a human being?

Herodotus, *Histories* II 57

This last question Herodotus raises was one that later inspired both literary invention and intellectual debate. In *The Birds*, Aristophanes has Tereus, the hoopoe, act as interpreter between the human interlopers and the birds with whom they want to negotiate. Tereus was once a human, 'so understands everything a human does and everything a bird does too' (*Birds* 119); moreover, he explains, 'I have lived with the birds a long time, so they are no longer the barbarians they were before I taught them to speak properly' (199–200). And the later satirist Lucian has a fantasy in which a cockerel amazes his owner Micyllus by suddenly addressing him in Greek:

MICYLLUS By Zeus, the god of miracles, and Heracles, our protector from evil, what the hell's going on? The cockerel just talked like a human being!

COCKEREL Why should you think it a miracle if I speak the same language as you all do?

The cockerel then reminds Micyllus of some of the mythological precedents for species crossing linguistic boundaries, like the horse of Achilles (which even managed to do it in hexameter verse) and the oak at Dodona (with its whispering leaves). No surprise in this case, then, given also the cock's close relationship with the Messenger God:

> I am an associate of Hermes, the most talkative and articulate of all the gods, and besides I've been brought up with you men and lived alongside you, so it was never going to be hard to learn your language.
>
> Lucian, *The Dream* 1–2

The cockerel further reveals that he was once actually a man—the famous Pythagoras, in fact. This is a nice twist because Pythagoras, who is probably best known now for his mathematical theories, was also associated with quasi-religious doctrines about the transmigration of souls. Only 'associated with', since Pythagoras himself wrote nothing, but was the sort of charismatic figure around whom legends later clustered and whom others claimed as the inspiration for their own beliefs; and some these included various ritual abstinences such as vegetarianism…and a prohibition on sacrificing cockerels.*

One later philosopher much influenced by Pythagoreanism, if not by Pythagoras himself, was Empedocles (*c*.492–*c*.432 BC), who clearly believed in the cycle of reincarnation, linking humans to all other creatures:

> For I have already once been a boy and a girl,
> a bush, a bird, and a leaping fish going on its way.
>
> Empedocles fr. 117

Plato is drawing on a similar tradition when he has Socrates, in a discussion of immortality, make the grossly anthropomorphic suggestion that souls will pass from humans to animals of like character:

> And presumably the souls of those who have chosen lives of injustice and tyranny and robbery pass into the bodies of wolves and hawks and kites. For where else should we suppose they might go?
>
> Plato, *Phaedo* 82a

A belief in this metempsychosis (transmigration of souls) might naturally engender some mutual sympathies between humans and other species, an idea Shakespeare played with in *Twelfth Night*, when he has the Fool catechize Malvolio in his cell to test his right-mindedness, in a parody of religious inquisitions:

> FOOL What is the opinion of Pythagoras concerning wildfowl?
> MALVOLIO That the soul of our grandam might haply inhabit a bird.
> FOOL And what thinkest thou of his opinion?
> MALVOLIO I think nobly of the soul, and in no way approve his opinion.
> FOOL Fare thee well. Remain thou still in darkness. Thou shalt hold the opinion
> of Pythagoras ere I will allow of thy wits, and fear to kill a woodcock lest thou
> dispossess the soul of thy grandam. Fare thee well.
>
> William Shakespeare, *Twelfth Night* iv.2.39–46

Such beliefs might dispose one to believe in the potential for communication between species. But there might also be other reasons to do so, quite independently of such religious or mystical doctrines. We saw in chapter 8 the ancient fascination with the capacity of birds to mimic human voices. Mimicry in itself does not, of course, imply *understanding*, since it may be just mindless repetition, indeed a mere 'parroting'. But the possibility of more genuine forms of communication with animals was considered by some later philosophers, in connection with the related question of whether animals could be said to be *rational* in any real sense.[1] After all, animals can evidently communicate with each other in various efficient ways; and people who have close relationships with animals— like hunters, herdsmen, and pet owners—would certainly want to say that they can themselves correctly interpret at least some animal vocalizations:

> No one doubts that some peoples even now have the affinity to understand the speech of certain animals: the Arabs can hear what ravens are saying, the Etruscans eagles, and perhaps we and all humans would be able to understand all animals, if a snake cleaned out our ears too.[2]
>
> In any case, the complexity and diversity of their speech demonstrate that it is meaningful. Animals can be heard making different sounds when they are afraid, when they are calling out, when they are begging for food, when they are friendly,

---

[1] That is, to have *logos*, the Greek word for both 'speech' and the faculty of 'reasoning'. See also Aristotle on animal intelligence, pp. 237–40.

[2] A reference to the superstition, common to many folklores, that snakes could be important intermediaries in accessing hidden knowledge, in this case by licking one's ears clean at night to improve one's powers of perception.*

and when they are being aggressive. The diversity of their repertoire is so great that even those who have spent their lives observing animals find it difficult to distinguish between all the different variations, just because there are so many of them. Experts have interpreted a certain number of the calls of crows and ravens, but have had to leave the rest as being too difficult for humans to comprehend.

So, given that animals can communicate and make good sense to each other, even if we can't all understand them, and given that they can evidently also imitate us, can learn to speak Greek, and can understand their owners, who then would dare deny them the faculty of reason, just because he cannot himself understand what they are saying?

> Porphyry, *On Abstinence* III 4

Even if we do not understand the utterances of the so-called 'irrational' animals, it is surely probable that they are conversing, but that we just don't comprehend them. After all, when we listen to barbarians talking we don't understand them either—it just sounds like undifferentiated noise. Similarly, we hear dogs making one sort of sound when they are driving people away, another when they are howling, another when they are beaten, and a quite different one when they are fawning. And to generalize, one would find on examination that all other animals, too, utter sounds that vary according to the particular circumstances, so one can fairly conclude that the so-called 'irrational' animals do in fact participate in reasoned spoken communication.

> Sextus Empiricus, *Outlines of Scepticism* I 74–75

These philosophical musings are in effect a sort of rationalization of traditional beliefs in birds as omens. In one of the early 'Homeric Hymns' Hermes, the messenger god, explains that in dispensing advice he will favour those who listen to the right birds and can interpret their calls correctly:

> Whoever comes to me guided by the calls and flight
> of prophetic birds, will be helped through my voice
> and not deceived; but whoever trusts birds that merely chatter
> emptily, and seeks to invoke my prophecy against my will,
> in order to try and know more than do the eternal gods,
> that man, I can tell you, will come on a fruitless mission,
> though I would still accept his gifts.
>
> *Homeric Hymn* (to Hermes) IV 541–49

This 'Hymn to Hermes' became well known to English readers through Shelley's verse translation, claimed by one scholar as 'better than the original', which renders the reference to the gods rather differently:*

6.9 Hermes. Roman statue, second century AD, based on a Greek original of the sixth century BC, featuring the usual accoutrements of the messenger god: the herald's staff, and the traveller's cloak and wide-brimmed hat.

... but he who comes consigned
by voice and wings of perfect augury
to my great shrine, shall find avail in me.
Him will I not deceive, but will assist;
but he who comes relying on such birds
as chatter vainly, who would strain and twist
the purpose of the Gods with idle words,
and deems their knowledge light, he shall have missed
his road—whilst I among my other hoards
his gifts deposit.
    P. B. Shelley, 'Hymn to Mercury'[1]

More prosaically, the stolid historian Xenophon defends Socrates against the charges of impiety by comparing Socrates' reliance on the voice of his personal *daimon* with the reliance others have on diviners:

---

[1] In his poem Shelley switches between the Greek and Latin names of the god (Hermes / Mercury), as the rhyme and prosody require.

Socrates was no more introducing strange gods than were these other practitioners of divination, who rely on bird omens, oracles, coincidences and sacrifices. For these people do not believe that it is the birds or chance encounters that reveal what will benefit those consulting them, but that they are just the instruments through which the gods signify these things. And that is what Socrates believed too; only whereas most people say that they are warned or encouraged by the birds and those they meet, Socrates said just what he meant—that his *daimon* gave the sign.

Xenophon, *Memorabilia* 1 3

And Ovid, in the *Fasti*,[1] his long verse treatise on the Roman calendar and its associated customs, has an entry for 9 January on the sacrifices due to the god Janus on that day. Towards the end of this he explains that the birds no longer enjoy their immunity from the risk of sacrifice, since they stand accused of conspiring with humans:

You birds were once inviolate. You, the solace of the countryside,
you denizens of the woods, you harmless race of creatures
that build your nests and warm your eggs with downy breasts,
and with such facility sing sweet measures of song.
But this now avails you not at all. You stand accused of crimes
of speech, and the gods think that you are revealing their minds.
Nor is this untrue; for the closer you are to the gods,
the more accurate are the signs you give, whether by flight or call.
Safe for so long, the race of birds was then at last cut down,
and the gods gloated over the guts of the informer.

Ovid, *Fasti* 1 441–50

So henceforth the dove, the goose, and the cockerel in particular, despite their great services to humanity, all become vulnerable to sacrifice on this festal day (lines 451–56).

*   *   *

And this, in a sense, brings us back full circle to Aristophanes and to the speculations of James Frazer and others about animal gods, with which we began chapter 17. The chorus in *The Birds* has been quite clear that humans, by contrast with birds, have only a feeble grasp of the eternal verities. They explain this with a portentous gravity that descends into bathos:

---

[1] It is no surprise that James Frazer was drawn to this repository of folklore. He produced a five-volume edition of it in 1929 and his translation was later incorporated into the Loeb edition of 1931.

Come, then, you men, you diminished creatures, mere leaves,
puny incompetents, made of clay, a shadowy feeble tribe,
you earth-bound ephemera, pathetic dreamlike mortals—
pay attention to us, the true immortals, living lives eternal,
ageless creatures of the air, whose counsels never perish.
From us you'll hear the correct account of all higher matters,
and you'll know the real nature of birds, the origins of gods, rivers,
space, and darkness, and then you can tell Prodicus from me—
to get lost.

Aristophanes, *Birds* 685–92

Prodicus was one of the new wave of intellectuals known collectively as the Sophists, who were a key element in the extraordinary humanist Enlightenment in Greece in the fifth century BC. They challenged traditional thinking and values on various fronts, including the religious. The term 'Sophist' didn't then have the pejorative connotations it later acquired, but the issues were of course sensitive and controversial ones. Prodicus was particularly associated with the view that a belief in the gods could be explained (and hence explained *away*) by the primitive habit of deifying those features of the natural world that were most important and beneficial to mankind—the sun (Apollo), water (Poseidon), fire (Hephaestos), and life-sustaining food and drink (Demeter and Dionysus).*

Aristophanes would have relished the chance to poke fun at the more celebrated Sophists and their radical ideas, but as a free spirit himself he probably had some sympathy with them too. Other critiques of religion located its origins more in the human fear of natural phenomena than in any gratitude for their benefits, and would seek to explain the workings of the world in purely scientific terms that allowed no space for divine intervention—and therefore no need for placatory sacrifices. Lucretius, in his massive didactic work *De rerum natura*, makes the fullest attack of this kind on religious practice and belief, though even he allows a place for the gods in his cosmic scheme, on the understanding that they don't interfere in a world they did not create and cannot influence. Ironically, what finally (and much later) displaced the beliefs in omens, animal sacrifices, and all the associated superstitions was not the assault of rationalism but another, much more powerful religion, Christianity.

The question that remains is why *birds* in particular were thought such suitable intermediaries between humans and whatever supernatural powers were believed in, and why they remained such good vehicles for metaphor even when those religious beliefs no longer had any literal appeal. That will be the topic of the final chapter. Before then, though, we explore the idea of Mother Earth as the creative and sustaining source of the whole natural world, as a preliminary to larger comparisons between ancient and modern responses to the environment.

19

Mother Earth

The idea of a personified 'Mother Earth'[1] has deep roots in many ancient cultures. It was gratefully adapted and exploited by James Lovelock in propounding his 'Gaia hypothesis' in 1979—the idea that the earth is a complex, self-regulating system that maintains the conditions for life on this planet.* Classical names and precedents are often invoked in this way to offer historical depth. And the Greeks and Romans did indeed originate many of our current ideas about what constitutes 'nature', though their key terms, *phusis* and *natura*, had a rather different range of meanings. They also had, in general, a more direct and robust engagement with the natural world, which tended to exclude some later European sensibilities and sensitivities. These differences in vocabulary and culture may have contributed to the common belief that the ancients did not really share our aesthetic appreciation of nature. Schiller expressed this doubt in his essay 'On naive and sentimental poetry' (1795):

> We find very few traces in Greek poetry of the sentimental interest with which the modern world looks on the scenes and characters of nature. The Greeks, to be sure, are accurate and faithful in their descriptions of nature, but they show no more special enthusiasm than in describing a tunic, a shield, a suit of armour, a piece of furniture or any mechanical product…They do not cling to nature with the emotion, spirituality or sweet melancholy of the moderns.*

What the following extracts suggest, however, is that there are important continuities and similarities as well as differences.

[1] The words for 'earth' and 'nature' in both Greek and Latin are all feminine in grammatical gender (Greek: *ge, gaia, phusis*; Latin: *terra, tellus, natura*).

6.10 Gaia, the earth mother. The primordial goddess who bore the sky, mountains, and sea. Gaia (or possibly Pandora, the first woman) here rises up from the earth, surrounded by a pair of dancing Panes (goat-headed Pan-figures symbolizing fertility and wild nature). Attic red-figure vase, c.450 BC.

The first quotation is the 'Homeric Hymn' to the goddess Gaia (whose name Lovelock borrowed):

Earth, mother of all, I will sing of her.
She is our firm foundation and eldest being.
She nourishes all the creatures that are in the world,
all that walk the wondrous land, all that travel the seas,
and all that fly; she feeds all these from her rich store.

Through you, Queen, men are blessed in their children and harvests.
It is you who can give life to mortal men or take it away.
Happy is the man you are gracious enough to honour.
He has everything he could want freely given him:
his fields are fertile with corn, his pastures abundant with cattle,
and his home is filled with good things. Such men
rule with law and good order in their cities of fair women;
and great fortune and wealth attend their lives.
Their sons exult in youthful high spirits,
and their daughters skip and play with light hearts,

dancing with posies over the softly flowered fields.
Thus do you honour them, holy goddess and bountiful spirit.

    Homeric Hymn (to Gaia) xxx 1–16

There is a parallel 'Hymn to Aphrodite', emphasizing that the power of love and sexual passion drives and connects the whole world—natural, human, and divine:

Muse, tell me the deeds of golden Aphrodite of Cyprus,[1]
who incites the stirrings of sweet passion in the gods
and overpowers the tribes of mortal men,
and all the birds of the air and all creatures,
all that the land and the oceans nurture;
every one of them takes Aphrodite to their hearts.

    Homeric Hymn (to Aphrodite) v 1–6

The idea of 'Mother Earth' is cleverly run together with the patriotic idea of 'Mother Country' in a literary funeral oration attributed to Aspasia, the mistress of the Athenian statesman Pericles.* She is arguing that we must love and honour the land that has nurtured us as we would a mother, and by so doing honour also the natives of that land, in this case the Athenians. The word 'land' here thus combines the two senses it has in both Greek and English: the earth that generates life and the country that supports us as its citizens.

We have the strongest proof of this argument [for the special claims our country has on us] in that this land of ours has given birth to all our generations past. For every creature that gives birth provides the nourishment appropriate for its offspring. Indeed, this is the test of whether a woman is a true mother, as she would not be if she has no sources of nourishment for her children. In this case our land, which is also our mother, gives ample evidence that she has brought forth men; for she was the first and only land of that time to provide humankind with the grain of wheat and barley, which is the finest and best form of nourishment for the human race, and thus showed herself to be the true mother of this creature. And one ought to give more weight to such proofs in the case of a land than of a woman. For it is not the land that imitates the woman in this matter of conception and birth, but the woman the land; and this produce the land did not begrudge to others but shared it with them too.

    Plato, *Menexenus* 237e–238a

---

[1] Paphos in Cyprus was the traditional birthplace of Aphrodite, goddess of love and sexual passion, and was one of the centres of her cult.

The Jewish writer Philo (first century AD), who became an explicit link between these Greek philosophical ideas and later Christian theology, extends the analogy:

> The earth is also a mother, as we know, which is why the first humans called her 'Demeter', connecting the name of mother with that of earth.
>
> For, as Plato said, earth does not imitate woman, but woman imitates earth; and poets as a class are actually in the habit of calling earth 'mother of all' and 'bearer of fruit' and 'giver of all' [Pandora], since she is the cause of birth and continuing life for every animal and plant alike. This is why nature had good reason to bestow on earth, that most ancient and fertile of mothers, as her counterpart to breasts, the running streams of rivers and springs so that plants might be watered and all creatures might have water to drink in plenty.
>
> Philo, *On the Creation* 133

Cicero, however, connects this line of thought rather with the Stoic view of the natural world as one vast organism with its own governing principles of order and design. He sees the wonders of nature as evidence of this 'intelligent design':

> First let us consider the earth as a whole, situated in the middle of the universe, a solid sphere held together as a globe by the concentric gravitation of all its parts, and clothed with flowers, grasses, trees, and fruits of incredible abundance and endless variety. Add to these the icy, everlasting springs, the pure rivers flowing clear between banks of the brightest green, deep vaulted caves, craggy rocks, towering mountain heights, and the vast spaces of the plains. Then add the hidden veins of gold and silver and the infinite quantities of marble.
>
> Consider too all the different species of animals, both tame and wild, and the flights and songs of birds, the pastures filled with cattle, and all the life in the woods and forests. And what about the race of men? They are appointed, as it were, to cultivate the land and prevent it becoming a wilderness of savage beasts or a wasteland of thicket and scrub. It is through their human labour that the fields, islands, and shores are adorned with all our different houses and cities. If we could only see all this as we can picture it in the mind's eye, no one who contemplated the earth in its totality could doubt the existence of a divine intelligence.
>
> Think, too, of the great beauty of the sea—the vision of its whole expanse; the number and variety of its islands; the delights of its shores and coastlines; the quantity and diversity of marine creatures, some dwelling in the ocean depths, some floating or swimming on the surface, and yet others clinging on to the rocks in their individual shells. Indeed, the sea itself so longs to embrace the earth that it sports with her shores, and the two elements seem to fuse into one.

Then there is the air that borders on the sea. It alternates between day and night; at one time it rises up rarefied and expanded; at another it condenses and is compressed into clouds, and as it becomes humid it waters the earth with enriching showers; while at another time it flows here and there generating winds. Moreover, the air produces the seasonal variations of cold and hot every year; it also supports the flight of birds and is the breath inhaled to nourish and sustain all animate life.

Cicero, *On the Nature of the Gods* XXXIX

Aristotle, too, made the connection between understanding the natural world in all its complexity and variety and admiring its beauty, though in his theory the beauty of the design consists in the exquisite adaptation of all life forms, however humble, for particular structural purposes. In his inspiring manifesto for the study of natural history at the start of his work on physical morphology, he remarks:

Similarly, we should pursue our enquiries into every kind of animal without any sense of distaste, since each and every one of them is in some way natural and beautiful. For in the works of nature the idea of purpose and not accident is of key importance. The purpose or end for which these works are constructed or formed belongs in the category of the beautiful.

Aristotle, *Parts of Animals* 645a23–27

The beauty of the natural world is also celebrated by many poets, both Greek and Roman. But they are more concerned to express a strong 'sense of place' than to advance any philosophical theory. In Homer's *Odyssey* we get this lovely description of Calypso's island, where the goddess is seducing Odysseus to stay. The gods' messenger, Hermes, is dispatched there to instruct her to let him resume his journey home:

Hermes sped over the waves like a seagull,[1]
which dips its feathered wings in the salt spray,
hunting fish over the dread troughs of the restless sea.
Just so did Hermes travel across the countless waves.
But when at last he reached the distant isle,
he then left the violet sea to go ashore
and made his way to the mighty cave where the nymph

---

[1] *Laros*, which might also be a tern, though Aristotle distinguishes a white and an ashy-coloured species of the *laros*, which fits gulls rather better (corresponding presumably to their adult and juvenile plumages). 'Cormorant' (the Loeb translation) seems ruled out at any rate.

with the beautiful hair lived, and he found her inside.
A huge fire was blazing on the hearth and the fragrance
of split cedar logs and citronwood wafted
over the island as they burned. She was within, singing sweetly
as she worked the loom, weaving with a golden shuttle.
Surrounding the cave was a flourishing forest
of alder, black poplar, and fragrant cypress,
in which long-winged birds made their nests:
owls and falcons and chattering sea crows,[1]
who make their livelihoods out in the ocean.
And there around the hollow cave was stretched
a cultivated vine, luxuriant and laden with clusters of fruit.
Four springs in a row, flowing with bright water,
were close by each other, running in different directions;
and all around bloomed soft meadows of violets and wild celery.

6.11 Calypso's cave. Odysseus' 'imprisonment' on Calypso's island, as imagined by Jan Brueghel the Elder (1568–1625). Despite ingenious efforts by both ancient and modern commentators, Ogygia, which Homer describes as Calypso's home, has not been convincingly identified with any existing island and is best thought of as the sort of literary fantasy Brueghel evokes in this genre painting of a 'paradise landscape'.

---

[1] Here (and at *Odyssey* XII 418–19) these 'sea crows' must be cormorants, which do nest in trees near water, creating very noisy colonies.

In this place even an immortal god who chanced by
might gaze in wonder and refresh his spirit;
and here too stood the messenger god and marvelled.
>   Homer, *Odyssey* v 51–75

Sappho is best known for her love poetry, but in these fragments from a lost
poem she is also evoking a beautiful natural scene:

Come here to me from Crete to this holy
temple, to your lovely apple grove
where the altars smoke
with incense.

Here cold water plashes through apple leaves,
the place is all shadowed by roses,
and from the shimmering leaves drifts down
deepest sleep.

Here too is a meadow where horses graze,
spring flowers bloom, and the winds
waft gently.
>   Sappho, fr.2

In this next extract[1] the dramatist Sophocles is describing the charms of
Colonus (in Attica), his birthplace. Oedipus, now a blind old man, has just
arrived there, looking for sanctuary:

Stranger, you have come to white Colonus,
earth's fairest home in this land of fine horses,
favoured haunt of the clear-voiced nightingale
who for ever warbles in the green glades,
keeping to the wine-dark ivy
and the untrodden groves of the god,
thick with leaves and fruit,
untouched by sun or the winds of any storm,
where Bacchus, the god of ecstasy,
treads the ground in revels and ever roams
with the nymphs who fostered him.

Fed by the dew of heaven each day
the lovely narcissus blooms there in clusters,

---

[1] See also p. 50.

6.12 The poet Sappho reading from a papyrus scroll, perhaps to a group of students in the school she is said to have founded. Despite her great celebrity (ancient and modern), her work survives for the most part only in fragments. Attic red-figure vase, 440–430 BC.

> the ancient crown for the two great goddesses,
> along with the gold-gleaming crocus.
> Nor do the sleepless, wandering streams
> of the river Cephisus ever fail,
> but each and every day
> they flow across the plains
> to give quick increase of life
> with their undefiled waters over
> the broad bosom of the earth.
> Nor do the dancing Muses ever shun this place
> nor Aphrodite of the golden reins.
>   Sophocles, *Oedipus at Colonus* 668–93

Euripides was the third of the great Athenian tragedians, after Aeschylus and Sophocles, and he strikes a very different note in this passage from his *Bacchae*, where the chorus of women, possessed by the god Dionysus, is celebrating the power and 'otherness' of nature. The description of the fawn enjoying the 'green pleasures' of the meadow is a particularly striking image, irresistibly recalling Marvell's 'green thought in a green shade':*

> Shall I ever again set my bare feet
> to dance the whole night through
> in Bacchic frenzy, throwing back my head
> to the dewy air of heaven?
> Like a fawn revelling in the green
> pleasures of the meadow,
> when she has escaped the terrifying
> hunt, beyond the ring of watchers,
> over the well-woven nets, while
> the huntsman roars on the hounds,
> stretching them to their fastest speed?
> In her distress, the fawn runs like the wind
> and bounds over the river plain,
> rejoicing to have found solitude from men
> in the young growth of the shady-leaved wood.
>
>   Euripides, *Bacchae* 862–76

Pastoral poetry represents a different kind of response to landscape, in this case often an idealized one evoking a *locus amoenus*, a 'pleasant place' in which to enjoy the peace of natural surroundings in contrast to the distractions of the city.* The creators and best-known exponents of the pastoral tradition were the Hellenistic Greek poet Theocritus and the Latin imperial poet Virgil, but they may have found an unlikely inspiration in an earlier passage in Plato, where Socrates is extolling the delights of a spot just outside the city to which he and his companion have retreated to find a quiet place for a philosophical discussion:

> By Hera,[1] what a fine spot to pause at. There's this lofty, spreading plane tree, and that tall willow offering lovely shade—in full bloom too, which makes the whole place really fragrant. And a charming little spring runs under the plane, icy cold— as my foot testifies! It seems to be a place sacred to some nymphs and to Acheloüs,[2] judging from the figurines and statues. Then again, if you will, how very pleasant

---

[1] The wife of Zeus, invoked here for her traditional 'loveliness', reflecting the beauty of this place.

[2] Acheloüs was the river god, named after the longest Greek river (some 150 miles long, rising in Epirus and flowing into the Corinthian Gulf).

and agreeable it is to have this saving breeze. The place resounds too with the shrill summer music of the cicadas, and most delightful of all is the grass growing on this gentle slope, just thick enough to rest your head on. You've been the perfect guide to bring us here.

    Plato, *Phaedrus* 230b–c

Whatever the irony intended here—since Socrates goes on to declare that he learns far more from conversations with people in the city than he ever does from nature—this is surely an *aesthetic* response of the kind Schiller thought absent in the ancient world?

The pastoral poets themselves lauded rural life and landscapes much more wholeheartedly than Socrates did, even if they were still writing for a sophisticated urban readership. They often connected the attractions of the countryside with an imagined golden age of natural abundance and plenty:

Over our heads many an aspen and elm stirred
and rustled, while nearby the sacred water
of the nymphs murmured, welling from their cave.
In the shady foliage of the trees the dusky
cicadas were busy chirping, and some songster murmured
his laments, high up in the thorny thickets.
Lark and finch were singing, the turtledove crooned,
and bees hummed and hovered, flitting about the springs.
All around, the smell of high summer, the smell of ripe fruit;
Wild pears lay at our feet, with apples beside,
rolling about in profusion; and slender branches
were weighed to the ground, laden with wild damsons.

    Theocritus, *Idylls* VII 135–46

For you, child, shall the earth pour forth unworked
her first little gifts of straggling ivy, foxgloves,
and the Egyptian bean mingled with smiling acanthus.
Uncalled, the goats will bring home milk from
swollen udders, and herds will have no fear of huge lions;
unasked, your cradle will pour forth sweet flowers.
The serpent shall perish, along with the false poison-plant,
and everywhere will spring up Assyrian spices.

    Virgil, *Eclogues* IV 18–25

And in his *Georgics* Virgil makes the further connection between enjoying the fruits of nature, understanding its workings ('the causes of things'), and living the good life:

6.13 *The Dream of Arcadia.* A romanticized vision of a Greek landscape by the American painter Thomas Cole (1801–48). The distant temple signifies the spiritual significance of the natural landscape, while the human figures are a reminder that this is not an entirely wild and untouched countryside.

Happy the farmers—more than happy, if only they knew
their luck—on whom, far from the clash of arms,
the just earth lavishes an easy living as their due.
  Virgil, *Georgics* II 458–60,

Theirs is a life of secure peace, free from deceits,
rich in its many treasures and the ease of their broad lands;
they have caverns, living lakes, and cool vales,
lowing cattle and soft slumber under the trees;
all these are theirs.
  II 467–71

Blessed the man who can know the causes of things
and has mastered his fears of inexorable fate
and the howls of the hungry underworld.
Happy too the man who knows the country gods—
Pan, old man Silvanus, and the sister nymphs.
  II 490–94

These ideas of natural abundance lead us naturally to various invocations of Venus, personified as the life-giving, creative force in the physical world. The first comes in Lucretius' preface to his long didactic poem about the actual operation of nature's laws. His appeal to the deity needs to be read metaphorically here, as a standard literary convention, since the whole point of the poem was to explain and celebrate a world *without* gods.

> Nurturing Venus, mother of Aeneas and his race,
> the source of pleasure for gods and humans,
> you it is under the gliding constellations of the sky
> who fills with life the ship-bearing seas and the fruitful earth,
> since through you every kind of living thing is conceived
> and arises to look on the light of the sun.
> Before you, goddess, the winds take to flight
> and the clouds flee the skies at your coming;
> for you the wonder-working earth puts forth
> its sweet flowers, for you the expanses of ocean laugh,
> the skies are calmed and glow with radiant light.
> For as soon as the day takes on the aspect of spring
> and the west wind is freed again to bring life,
> first the birds of the air proclaim you and your advent,
> goddess, pierced to the heart by your power.
> Then herds wild and tame, frisk over the rich pastures,
> swimming rapid rivers—captured by your charm
> and driven by desire to follow wherever you may lead.
> Then throughout seas and mountains, rushing rapids,
> the leafy homes of birds, and verdant fields,
> you breathe seductive love into every breast
> and cause their passion to procreate, kind by kind.
>
> Lucretius, *De rerum natura* I 1–21

Lucretius goes on to make it clear that these instinctive urges are shared not just across all species but also by both sexes:

> Nor does a woman always fake her passion in sighing
> when she embraces her mate, body joined to body,
> and holds his lips in a deep moist kiss.
> Often she does it from the heart, and seeking mutual
> pleasures rouses him to run the full course of love.
> Nor otherwise could birds, cattle, wild beasts,
> sheep, and mares submit to the male, if their own
> nature was not overflowing with passion in season
> and gladly welcomed the advances of their mates.
>
> Lucretius, *De rerum natura* IV 1192–200

The next comes from a remarkable and mysterious poem, the *Pervigilium Veneris* ('The vigil of Venus'), whose date and authorship are quite unknown but which reads as a sort of link between classical and medieval Latin poetry. The poem celebrates the procreative power of nature, though it also ends with a sorrowful note as the poet asks when *his* (or perhaps *her*) spring will come. I have included here just the first and the last four of the twenty-two verses, all of which end with the same refrain.[1]

> The spring is new, spring is now singing, spring is the world reborn.
> In spring the loves are united, in spring birds mate,
> and the woodland loosens her hair under fertile showers.
> *May whoever has never loved, love tomorrow,*
> *and may whoever has loved, love tomorrow.*
>
> The countryside is fecund with desire and feels the stirrings of Venus.[2]
> Love himself, the child of Dione, is believed born in the country.
> While the field was giving birth she herself took him to her bosom
> And herself nurtured him with the tender kisses of flowers.
>
> Look, now the bulls stretch out their flanks in the broom,
> each company held together in a conjugal bond.
> And look, the bleating ewes with their husbands under the shade,
> And the tuneful birds whom the goddess has not made silent.
>
> Now the noisy swans splash loudly over the pools,
> and the daughter of Tereus sings forth under the shady poplar
> such strains that you would think this the very music of love
> and not a sister's complaint about a barbarous husband.
>
> She sings, we are silent. When is *my* spring coming?
> When shall I be like the swallow and find *my* voice?
> I have lost my muse in silence, and Apollo neglects me.
> Thus it was that through its silence Amyclae[3] was destroyed.

---

[1] The great economy of Latin means that this refrain consists of only nine words (*cras amet qui nun-quam amavit / quique amavit cras amet*). English versions seem very wordy by contrast and inevitably lose the epigrammatic force of the original.

[2] See also pp. 17–18. Venus is the Roman equivalent of Aphrodite.

[3] The silence of Amyclae was proverbial, perhaps deriving from the story that Amyclae (on the coast of Latium, the region that contains Rome) had passed a law forbidding further reports of threatened enemy attacks, since there had been several false alarms. So when the enemy did come no one gave a warning and the city perished.

May whoever has never loved, love tomorrow,
and may whoever has loved, love tomorrow.
    Pervigilium Veneris I, XIX–XXII

Finally, a lyrical celebration of nature by the late (fourth century AD) Latin poet Tiberianus (who may possibly have been the author of the *Pervigilium Veneris* too):

The broad stream flowed through the fields in the chilly valley,
smiling with its sparkling pebbles and adorned by flowery grasses.
Above it, the turquoise laurels and grass-green myrtles
swayed gently in the sweetly murmuring breeze.
And below, the soft turf teemed with blooming flowers;
the ground blushed with crocuses and gleamed with lilies,
and the whole grove was fragrant with the scent of violets.
Among these gifts and jewelled favours of the spring
stood out the queen of all perfumes and the day-star of all colours,
the flame of Venus, the golden-flowered rose.
The dewy grove was thick with moist grasses,
little streams murmured here and there, fed by a running spring;
within the caves moss and myrtle were tightly intertwined,
where the wandering streams shone with bright spray.
In the shadows every bird—musical beyond belief—
voiced their spring songs in gentle tones;
and the quietly chattering stream made harmony with the leaves,
to which Zephyr's muse added the melody of the breeze.
So, whoever passed through the greenery, beauty, scents, and music—
the birds, stream, breeze, wood, flowers, and shade all combined to please.
    Tiberianus, 'The River'

That surely seems familiar enough.

20

Epilogue

If anthropomorphism is the eighth deadly sin for zoologists, then anachronism is its equivalent for historians. But it is easier to remark on this professional hazard than altogether to avoid it. Just as zoologists often find it helpful to compare human and animal behaviour, and sometimes to describe one in terms of the other, so political and cultural historians are irresistibly drawn to compare ancient and modern practices and beliefs. That, after all, is part of the interest. And no matter how carefully the necessary distinctions and qualifications are made in such comparisons there is always the risk of some contamination in the language. Scientists talk about bird courtship, song, display, family relationships, and migratory strategies, fully aware that in human contexts these terms may have different connotations and implications as self-conscious activities, but nonetheless finding them useful analogues through which to describe avian behaviour. Similarly, historians may talk of ancient 'science', 'religion', 'art', and 'democracy', with or without the scare quotes, well aware of the differences that may be lost in translation but concerned to explain some of the continuities and similarities too.

The first five parts of this book were all concerned in their different ways with the place of birds in the natural world and the range of human perceptions and responses they aroused. Many of these still seem broadly familiar, and we can identify with the various interactions between people and birds illustrated in these ancient texts and images. Indeed, in some ways the very different historical context makes the sense of underlying familiarity seem the more striking. We can thrill to the Minoan 'Spring fresco' and the figures in the vase-painting welcoming the return of the swallow; we can almost hear the sounds of drowsy high summer Theocritus is evoking in his shepherd's idyll; we recoil from the gluttony of Trimalchio's feast of thrushes and the cruelties of the cockfight and the Circus; we are charmed by Lesbia's pet 'sparrow' and amused by the talking parrots and ravens; we are fascinated by the wonders of exotic birds and are intrigued by the feats of bird 'intelligence'; and we too sometimes find birds to be ominous, charismatic, or suggestive as symbols. In all these cases the local colour and circumstances of the ancient examples are very different from anything we can experience directly, but they serve to highlight the perceived similarities of response rather than to conceal them. 'Yes, just so,' we instinctively say, in an impulse of sympathy and recognition.

Perceptions can deceive, of course, and there can be gross misunderstandings of cultures distant in time or place. So I conclude by briefly (and therefore riskily) summarizing some of these similarities and differences in the responses to birds between our different worlds.

For a start, in the hackneyed phrase, the ancients lived closer to nature. Birds would have been more abundant and must have been even more conspicuous then than they are now. It is estimated that in modern Britain we have lost more than half of all our wildlife in the last fifty years, a staggering statistic.* This can largely be explained by relatively recent factors: intensive agriculture, urban development, environmental pollution, population growth and density, and to some extent climate change. A few species have flourished, but in most cases the story is one of a sharp decline, affecting many much-loved species of great significance in our cultural history, such as nightingale, skylark, cuckoo, turtle dove, curlew, and even house sparrow.

These destructive trends took effect mainly from the mid-twentieth century onwards in the Western world. The only significant environmental damage in the ancient world that might have been attributable to such human ('anthropogenic') interventions was a degree of localized erosion from deforestation. But the extent of that has proved a controversial issue among scholars of ecological history. Timber was certainly used in great quantities for shipbuilding and other construction projects, and we now know some of the potential dangers from extensive clear-felling. However, in the case of the classical world the claim that this of itself caused serious erosion relies heavily on a single passage in Plato's *Critias*, where he is contrasting the imagined primeval fertility of his native region, Attica, with its relative impoverishment in his own day:

Since there were many great deluges in the 9,000 years between that time and this,[1] the earth's soil has leached away from the high ground in the course of these periodic disasters and has not built up any significant sediment, as it has in other places, but has kept running off and disappearing into the sea. And just as happens in the case of small islands, what now remains, compared to what once was, is like the skeleton of a sick man, all the soft fat having wasted away, leaving only the bare bones behind.

  Plato, *Critias* 111a–b

And that, says Plato, is why the land no longer supports the same abundance of trees and vegetation and why the rain runs off instead of being absorbed into the soil.

This account probably sounds more modern than it really is. The redoubtable Oliver Rackham, in his joint study with A. T. Groves of the ecological history of the Mediterranean, complains that 'this much-abused passage has passed into the folklore of erosion'.* Rackham interprets Plato actually to be saying that catastrophic deluges were the cause of soil erosion and that loss of soil was the cause of the deforestation, not vice versa. In any case, if you attend to the literary context of this oft quoted (and variously translated) extract, Plato is not offering a scientific analysis here, but evoking an earlier golden age as part of his mythological account of the rivalry between Athens and Atlantis.

This is not to suggest that human activity did not affect both the abundance and the diversity of bird life in the ancient world. Hunting for sport and for the table will have affected the populations of some species of birds, though not as much as it did big game animals, which were procured from north Africa and elsewhere in vast numbers for the Circus and other entertainments in the Roman period.* The drainage of marshes, heavy grazing by goats, and the clearance of woodland and scrub for agricultural development will have had their effects locally too, but the last at least might easily have been in the direction of greater not less biodiversity, since by modern standards the agriculture was so much more organic and less intensive. Lucretius, in his survey of human evolution and the development of civilization in Book v of *De rerum natura*, noted how the forest line had retreated before the advance of cultivation. But the kinds of nature-friendly cultivation he describes will have actually added to the habitats and food sources available to birds:

---

[1] If this is interpreted as a reference to the great erosion of the last Ice Age it is a remarkably accurate guess at the time-scale.

So they tried various ways of cultivating their treasured plots
and they watched the wild fruits grow in the earth,
tamed by their kindly treatment and gentle management.
Day by day they kept forcing the woodland ever further
up the mountain-sides, yielding the lower ground to tillage,
to extend over hill and plain their meadows, pools, and streams,
their crops and their fertile vineyards, with belts of grey olives
stretching out over mounds, hollows, and level ground alike.
And now you can see the whole area in its variegated charm,
interspersed with sweet orchards and set with rich plantations.

Lucretius, *De rerum natura* v 1367–78

As for urban development, cities were comparatively small and even there, in the
absence of modern standards of public sanitation and municipal tidiness, a wide
range of birds evidently flourished in the sprawl of houses, shops, markets, stables,
smallholdings, and public spaces. As we have seen, these species included not
only such regular city scavengers as kites, corvids, pigeons, and sparrows, but
other more surprising ones like ibises (see pp. 199–200); owls were common in
towns; swallows, martins, and swifts nested in the buildings; nightingales could
be heard singing in the suburbs of Athens and Rome (see p. 50);[1] and one would
have encountered cuckoos, wrynecks, and hoopoes within the city limits as well
as a host of warblers, finches, buntings, and other passerines.*

It is at any rate clear from the literary references quoted throughout this volume, as well as from the many representations of birds in art and on domestic
artefacts, that there was a direct and often intimate familiarity with far more
species than is the case today. In a recent survey of first-year biology students at
Oxford University, researchers made the startling discovery that 42 per cent of
the sample could not name even five species of British birds.[2] By contrast, in
chapter 10 and in the appendix I list some twenty-eight species of birds featured in Aesop's *Fables*, seventy-five in the plays of Aristophanes, and seventy-
five on the wall-paintings of Pompeii.* Such literary and visual representations
do not necessarily translate directly into common knowledge, of course, but
they are surely some indication of it. The references have to be familiar enough
to be appreciated.

---

[1] As imagined also in Respighi's *I pini di Roma* (1924), though his recording was made from captive
nightingales.*

[2] The figures for naming butterflies were even worse—only 18 per cent of the students managed to
name five species of those, but here the ancients may not have done any better (see pp. 317–21).

6.14 Garden scene from Pompeii. Detail from a fresco with birds in a garden setting with oleanders and strawberry trees, in the House of the Gold Bracelet, Pompei, AD 30–50. Some birds are readily identifiable: barn swallow, magpie, house sparrow (or maybe the closely related Italian or Spanish sparrow since it is so bright), wood pigeon, and various domesticated doves. Some are less obvious: a possible corvid in flight (top right) and perhaps a golden oriole (or a jay) perched lower down.

Aristophanes' *Birds* has been a natural source of examples in this book, but it is by no means the only ancient Greek play whose title references animal species. Aristophanes himself wrote plays entitled *Frogs*, *Wasps*, and *Storks* (this last not extant), while lost plays by other authors include *Nightingales* and *Ant-men* (Cantharus), *Bees* (Diocles), *Nanny Goats* (Eupolis), *Fishes* (Archippus), *Birds* and *Fruit Flies* (Magnes), and *Beasts* (Crates). These will have had their choruses in the appropriate costumes, and there are some famous images on contemporary vases of bird-dancers and other human–animal combinations that may have influenced some of these.*

As for bird names, Aristotle distinguishes about 140 separate species and a modern lexicon of ancient bird names lists no fewer than 730 different Greek names for birds, many with further variant spellings or dialectal forms and most with their Latin equivalents, but not all of them identifiable as to species.[1]

---

[1] The Greek letters with by far the largest number of headwords in this list are *Kappa* (137) and *Pi* (94), the equivalents of our plosives K and P, suggesting perhaps that many of the names are onomatopoeic in origin, as indeed are more of the common English names of birds than is often realized.*

6.15 Costumed bird-dancer. A 'bird-man' with coxcomb, feathered wings, and spurs, possibly in a costume for a Greek comedy performance (see also **6.1** and p. 353). Attic red-figure vase, *c.*425 BC.

There may seem to be a paradox here. 'The environment' is invoked on all sides today. There are government ministers with named responsibilities for it; there are environment agencies that monitor its condition; there are countless conferences, books, and courses on the subject; and there are environmental businesses, taxes, organizations, and charities. In this sense, more people know and care about the environment now than ever before. By contrast, in the ancient world there was not even a word for it, either in Greek or Latin. But why would there be? By contrast with modern highly urbanized Western societies, people then could largely take for granted what we now see as a sustaining but threatened resource—the interconnected totality of our natural surroundings, whose dynamics we are only just beginning to understand properly.

The history of the English word 'environment' demonstrates how recently this concern has arisen. It first occurs as a rare seventeenth-century usage, meaning just 'the act or state of being encircled'; by the nineteenth century it had come to mean 'the things or the area surrounding something'; but it was not until the mid- to late twentieth century that it began to carry its present conservationist connotations. 'Environmentalist' and 'environmentalism' date from the late 1960s and the 1970s: both the UK Department of the Environment and the US Environmental Protection Agency were established in 1970; international awareness was first properly mobilized by the UN Stockholm Conference on the Human Environment of 1972; and only in the late 1980s did phrases like 'global warming' and 'climate change' begin to enter common discourse.

What probably did more than anything else to stimulate popular receptivity to such ideas were the spectacular 'Earthrise' photographs from the Apollo 8 mission of 1968, which first showed us the earth from a distance in all its wonder and vulnerability, and so seized the public imagination in a way no scientific or governmental pronouncements could ever have done. Meanwhile, the 'environmental sciences' have evolved from what used to be the separate disciplines of biology, zoology, botany, geography, geology, and so on (all names that have classical etymologies and subjects with classical antecedents), and the environmental sciences may themselves start to morph into other subjects or combinations of subjects (like 'earth system science') in due course—a reminder that modern scientific disciplines have their own histories and evolving vocabularies too.[1]

But even though there were no analogous terms and institutional frameworks in the ancient world, various authors were certainly beginning to reflect on what we would now call environmental questions about the causal relationships between the human and natural worlds. Herodotus and the other ethnographers, who delighted in retailing stories of 'natural wonders' of the kind represented in chapter 11, were always looking for possible links between geography, climate, and ethnic characteristics. Herodotus, for example, suggests connections between the heat of the sun in Egypt, the dark skin and (more dubiously) the skull thickness of its inhabitants.* And it was an explicit presupposition of the emerging medical science we considered in chapter 12 that all illnesses had natural causes. Indeed, in some of these discussions there is a strong if naive sense of environmental determinism. The author of a fifth-century BC Hippocratic text, for example, speculates about the effects of climate on ethnic differences:

---

[1] As an example of the institutional mortality of professional disciplines, the first chair of botany was established at Oxford in 1669 and the last students of the subject in Britain graduated from Bristol University in 2013. Botany is not now taught as an undergraduate degree in the UK, though plant science is.

The other peoples of Europe differ widely from one another in size and form as a result of the violent and frequent changes in their seasonal climates—hot summers and severe winters, heavy rainfall followed by long periods of drought, causing many changes of different kinds. So it is to be expected that these changes also affect reproduction through variations in the coagulation of the semen, so that it too changes between summer and winter and between periods of rain and drought. This, I believe, is the reason for the greater variation in physique among Europeans than Asians and why their stature varies so much even within a single city.

The author goes on to apply this to differences in character as well. He acknowledges that culture can be a causal factor here, though he suggests that culture too is ultimately formed by physical geography:

You will find as a general rule that both the physique and culture of a people are shaped by the nature of the place they live. Where the soil is rich, soft, and well-watered, and where the water is near the surface, so as to be warm in summer and cold in winter, and where the situation is favourable in relation to the seasons, there the people will be fleshy, with joints obscured and of a watery character. They will be of a lazy disposition and generally weak-spirited. You can see that they are indolent and sleepy people, and as far as the arts are concerned they are clumsy, lacking subtlety and sharpness. But where the land is bare, waterless, and rough, oppressed by winter storms and seared by summer heat, there you will find people hard and spare, raw-boned, sinewy, and hairy. They will by nature be hard-working and alert, stubborn and independent in character and temper, more wild than tame, keener and more intelligent in the arts, and braver in war. And other things that grow in the earth all adapt to the earth they live in.

[Hippocrates], *Airs, Waters, and Places* 23–24

The comparisons in this text tend to be to the general disadvantage of the non-European races, as also in a preceding passage (22), where the writer earnestly suggests that the reason Scythian men often suffered from infertility and impotence was that they wore trousers and spent too much of their lives riding horses.

Such speculations do at least reflect a more explicit recognition of the interconnectedness of things, which was implicit from the start of the classical period in the broader notion of what constituted 'nature'. All the major systematic philosophies of the classical world made the same assumption, whatever their other, often radical, differences. Plato in his one excursion into cosmology (which is probably to be read more metaphorically than literally) describes how his imagined demiurge ('divine craftsman'):

First set all the elements in order and then from these constructed the present universe, as one living creature containing within it all other living creatures, both mortal and immortal.

Plato, *Timaeus* 69c

Aristotle's professed purpose was to offer a systematic empirical account of the entire natural world and its inhabitants. That was the programme set out at the start of *Parts of Animals* (quoted above, pp. 226, 339) and largely delivered in the *History of Animals* and his other extant biological works.

And later, the two great competing Hellenistic philosophies of Stoicism and Epicureanism both saw the natural world as an interdependent whole. The Stoics described it as a single, vast organism, whose governing principles of order are evidence of 'intelligent design' by a benign creator (as Cicero described in the long passage quoted above, pp. 338–39). Within this integrated whole, human ethics are thus perfectly aligned with human nature:

Living well is equivalent to living in accordance with our experience of the course of nature; for our individual natures are parts of the nature of the whole; and that is why the end is to live in sympathy with nature—that is, in accordance with our own nature and with that of the universe as a whole.

Chrysippus, *De Finibus* (third century BC)*

The Epicureans by contrast saw the unity of the cosmos in the chance inter-actions of atoms in the void, which give rise to 'innumerable worlds'. One of these worlds is the earth we happen to inhabit together with the rest of animal life, but all of them are on this account governed by the same purely physical principles, which exclude any form of divine intervention.*

*   *   *

The notion that the natural world was an interrelated whole has been a theme running through this volume, with birds as the connecting thread. What it now remains to ask is 'Why birds?' Why did *birds* in particular—of all life forms—seem then, as they have continued to seem, such good vehicles for exploring and expressing our relationships with the natural world?

The sheer ubiquity and abundance of birds must have been one factor. For anyone at all aware of their surroundings, there they were—visible and audible at most times of the day; occupying all the domains of land, air, and sea; in urban, cultivated, and wild areas alike. Mammals by contrast were both less numerous and less conspicuous, more likely to be shy or nocturnal, and always earth-bound. Fish were found in just one domain, while the multitudes of insects were not much differentiated and didn't prompt the same kind of human response.[1]

Birds are on a convenient physical scale as well—large enough to be easy to see clearly and small enough to act as convenient miniature models for human comparisons. In structural terms too, the similarities must have seemed striking. Like humans they stand upright on two legs. They can walk, run, hop, and jump. Plato famously defined man as 'the featherless biped', prompting the dissenting philosopher Diogenes to pluck a chicken and march into the lecture room brandishing it and announcing 'Here is Plato's man.'* Ovid, too, saw the metaphorical force of this characteristic when in the first book of his *Metamorphoses* he describes the creator fashioning the world and its creatures:

> While all other animals are prone and gaze at the earth
> He gave humans an erect stance and bade them look to heaven
> and raise his eyes to the stars.
> Ovid, *Metamorphoses* I 84–86

Birds were an *active* presence too. They were prominent in the foreground of people's experience, interacting with them as both parties went about their daily lives. They used humankind's buildings for nest sites and perches, they scavenged around their towns and villages, they fed in their fields and predated their crops, they followed armies on the move and fishermen in their ships, and in some cases they shared human dwellings as family pets and entertainments.

Bird behaviour provides ample examples and analogues for a sympathetic rapport, now as then. We observe their social gatherings and can watch them eating, playing, courting, displaying, homemaking, competing, and fighting. We can hear them singing, communicating, and communing. We think we know what they are up to and can relate to their perceived purposes and activities.

Above all, birds have the gift of flight, a perennial topic of human fascination, and at some level a deep aspiration too, expressed in all kinds of metaphorical and symbolic ways, as we explored in chapter 16. 'Winged birds' was the Homeric phrase, which emphasizes this identification of birds with the power of flight. Wingless birds like ostriches were 'wonders', but mainly because they were

---

[1] Except for a select group that have an honorary place in literature and myth for their social arrangements (bees and ants), perceived nastiness (wasps), or sounds (cicadas and bees).*

freaks that crossed categories and seemed to have more in common with the big mammals.

Mammals, insects, flowers, trees, and fish were all important presences in the landscape too, but they each lacked this combination of characteristics that made birds seem so familiar and such suitable subjects for stories, myths, fables, allegories, and other human imaginings. That in the end was surely why birds featured so strongly as omens and metaphorical messengers in the ancient world. They were ideally constructed, both physically and symbolically, to be the bearers of signs and meanings, and the links between gods and men. Plutarch saw this and explains why it is birds not other animals that constitute the principal branch of divination and give it its very name of 'ornithomancy':[1]

> It is their quickness and apprehension and their speed of response to any phenomenon that makes them such suitable instruments for the gods, who direct their movements, their cries and calls, and their formations, which like the winds are sometimes contrary and sometimes favourable.
> Plutarch, 'Cleverness of animals', *Moralia* 975a

Is this all so different, *mutatis mutandis*, from the significance birds are perceived to have in the modern world? Our known world is much larger than the ancient one, but whatever the environmental changes and losses in the last 2,500 years, birds are still to be seen and heard almost everywhere today. They span the globe from the most inhospitable regions of the Arctic and Antarctic, across oceans and seas, through desert, mountain, and plain, forest and jungle, right into the domesticated landscapes of our cities, farms, and back gardens. But they spread further still. Birds are not only out there in the physical world, they have also entered human heads and hearts. They populate our minds and imaginations, arouse our emotions, become intimately associated with our memories of particular times and places, and so intervene continuously in our daily lives. They enter our language as figures of speech—we talk about craning our necks, larking about, and swanning around; we make verbs of gull, rook, quail, snipe, and crow; we enlist owls, swallows, and storks in proverbial sayings; we identify our political leaders as hawks or doves; and we know just what we mean when we call someone a magpie, vulture, dodo, or gannet, or think of them as a bit cuckoo.

---

[1] Fish by contrast, Plutarch says, are all 'deaf and blind' as far as conveying omens and predictions was concerned.

Many of our perceptions of birds are seen through the prism of such associations. And once we have internalized these conceptions of birds we then project them back on to the world in the form of symbols—on national flags, stamps, and coins; on our street and pub names (some 3,000 of the latter in Britain); in churches (eagles as lecterns) and bookshops (Penguins, Pelicans, Puffins, Ospreys); and on sports logos (the Toronto Blue Jays, Arizona Cardinals, Norwich Canaries). We brand and decorate all manner of commercial products with birds: wallpaper, cards, mugs, clothing, and ornaments. And throughout history many of the world's armies have marched under the standard of a bird (usually an eagle)—as they still do. Some of the assumptions and beliefs behind these characterizations are as misplaced as their equivalents in the ancient world, but what they demonstrate is the continuing engagement with birds, both in our daily experience and our imaginations.

6.16 Phoenix pub signs. An ancient one from Pompeii (left), which has the inscription PHOENIX FELIX ET TU (literally 'The phoenix is happy and you', meaning 'good luck to you as well'); and a modern English one at Ebenezer Place, York.

In the climax to *The Birds*, Aristophanes describes how everyone is now asking for a set of wings in order to join the birds in their new city in the skies. The comic hero, Peisetaerus, is the man in charge of the supplies and he admonishes the last applicant, who wants wings just to fly round the cities more quickly on his dubious legal business. Peisetaerus then has a riff on the idea that language itself has the power to 'take wing':

INFORMER I don't want your advice, good sir, I just want wings.

PEISETAERUS That's just what I'm trying to give you now, through my words.

INFORMER How can you give a man wings through words?

PEISETAERUS Didn't you know? Words can help everyone take wing.

Peisetaerus gives him some examples of winged hopes and ambitions, and how drama itself can cause the heart to flutter, then concludes:

> Yes, it's by words that the mind is uplifted
> and humankind soars aloft.
>   Aristophanes, *Birds* 1436–49

Flight was the prerogative of birds and a good part of their fascination for earth-bound mortals. Language, meanwhile, was supposed to be the unique distinguishing feature of humankind. But here, in an artful metaphor, Aristophanes forges a connection between the two faculties and with them the two realms of birds and humanity. The birds have successfully challenged human domination, and through winged words the power of imagination has transcended the limitations of human experience.

6.17 The Cambridge Greek Play, 1903. The splendidly costumed cast of Aristophanes' *The Birds*, performed 'in the original Greek' at the New Theatre in Cambridge in 1903. The chorus of twenty-four different birds is arranged on either side of the two Athenian visitors to Cloud-Cuckoo Land, with Tereus, the hoopoe, behind them. The Cambridge Greek Play is a famous tradition, begun in 1882, which continues to the present day. The early performances enjoyed great prestige as part of the nineteenth-century enthusiasm for Hellenic culture, and attendance at them clearly had some social cachet—a special train was put on from King's Cross and back for performances of the inaugural 1882 play (Sophocles' *Ajax*). The 1903 performance of *The Birds* had music by Sir Hubert Parry and was attended by figures like Prince Albert Victor and the Postmaster General. It attracted very favourable reviews in the national press (though *The Times* sniffily complained that some members of the audience who didn't understand Greek were laughing in the wrong places), and also in the provincial press (including the *Yorkshire Daily Post*, the *Liverpool Post*, and the *Blackburn Weekly Standard*, which gave it two and a half columns), and even internationally (in *Le Figaro*). *The Birds* was a regular favourite and was performed in 1883 (probably the first complete production since antiquity), 1903 (as illustrated here), 1924, 1971, and 1995, its success evidence both of the colourful dramatic possibilities the play offers and the continuing fascination with its avian fantasies and embedded symbolisms.*

APPENDIX

Some Bird Lists from Ancient Sources

I have referred at various points in this book to the number and kind of species that might have been distinguished in the ancient world (for example, pp. 168–72, 352). The compilation of species lists of this kind is a modern habit rather than an ancient one, and even the early zoological taxonomists like Aristotle and Theophrastus don't seem to have produced them, at least not in this summary form. The purpose here is just the interpretative one of seeing what species were known to and distinguished by some of our principal sources of information.

The lists that follow are extracted from the literary works of Aesop and Aristophanes and from the visual representations that survived the destruction of Pompeii in AD 79. Direct and detailed comparisons between them are not straightforward, firstly because in all three cases only a selection of the work that once existed has survived; and secondly, and perhaps more importantly, because the two literary works often just use generic terms like 'hawk', 'finch', 'goose', or 'eagle', while we can ourselves now identify in the painted representations from Pompeii individual species like chaffinch, greenfinch, and hawfinch that may not have been distinguished consistently, if at all, in these literary references. Nonetheless, the lists have their interest in showing what species were recognized and thought worth noting by these different authors and artists for their audiences.

The lists follow a modern taxonomic sequence. I have drawn heavily on the secondary sources cited in the endnotes to chapter 10, but have not followed them exactly and have queried the more uncertain identifications.* In the case of the two literary works, I have given the Greek terms most commonly used by the respective authors.

Aesop uses the following twenty-eight species as principal characters in the Greek versions of his *Fables*:

ostrich (*strouthos*)	kite (*iktinos*)
swan (*kuknos*)	hawk (*hierax*)
goose (*chen*)	buzzard (*triorchos*)
partridge (*perdix*)	crane (*geranos*)
cockerel / hen (*alektor / ornis*)	gull (*laros*)
peacock (*taos*)	pigeon / dove (*peristera*)
heron (*erodios*)	cuckoo (*kokkyx*)
stork (*pelargos*)	owl (*glaux*)
vulture (*gyps*)	kingfisher (*halcyon*)
eagle (*aietos*)	jackdaw (*koloios*)

crow (*korone*)
raven (*korax*)
lark (*korydalos*)
swallow (*chelidon*)

wren (*basiliskos*)
starling (*psar*)
thrush (*kichla*)
nightingale (*aedon*)

Aristophanes refers to all of the above in the corpus of his eleven surviving plays, except for the starling (a surprising absence). He also mentions at least twice the following species, all of which can be identified with some probability from his and other authors' descriptions:

mallard (*netta*)
teal / garganey (*baska*)
wigeon (*penelops*)
ruddy shelduck (*chenalopex*)
francolin (*attagas*)
quail (*ortyx*)
grouse (*tetrax*)
pheasant (*phasianos*)
ibis (*ibis*)
white pelican (*pelekinos*)
Dalmatian pelican (*pelekan*)
flamingo (*phoinikopteros*)
little grebe (*kolymbos*)
lammergeier (*phene*)
Egyptian or griffon vulture (*nertos*)
tern (*katarrakte*)
wood pigeon (*phaps*)

hoopoe (*epops*)
woodpecker (*dryops*)
jay (*kitta*)
tit (*aigithallos*)
warbler (*eleas*)
blackbird (*kopsichos*)
blue rock thrush (*laios*)
sparrow (*strouthos*)
wagtail (*kinclos*)
finch (*spinos*)
osprey (*haliaetos*)
kestrel (*kerchines*)
corncrake (*krex, ortygometra*)
gallinule (*porphyrion*)
coot (*phaleris*)
stone curlew (*charadrios*)
plover (*trochilos*)

Then there are the further species that he mentions only once (and most of these only in *The Birds*); these are not identifiable from other sources, so here I list them the other way round, giving the Greek terms first, with their literal meanings in parentheses, followed by speculative identifications. The etymology of the Greek sometimes provides clues, and may pick out what struck people as the salient features, but of course these features are often common to a range of unrelated species, and different translators or commentators have cheerfully proposed some wildly varying identifications:

akalanthis ('thistle bird') goldfinch / linnet
ampelis ('vine-bird') black-headed bunting / warbler / spotted flycatcher
elasas ('driver') arctic skua / harrier
erythropous ('red-foot') redshank / chough / stock dove / red-footed falcon
hypothumis ('under thyme') bunting / pipit / wheatear
keblepuris ('fiery-head') firecrest / goldfinch / woodchat shrike
keirulos ('barber') sparrow / kingfisher
krex (onomatapoeic) corncrake / black-winged stilt / ruff
kumindis (unknown origin) eagle owl / nightjar / cuckoo
mĕlanokoruphos ('black-crown') great / sombre or coal tit; or black-headed bunting; or blackcap / Sardinian warbler

phlexis ('fiery'?) marsh harrier / lesser spotted eagle

Phrygilos ('Phrygian bird') chaffinch / cattle egret

spermologos ('seed-picker') rook / jackdaw / starling / maybe generic 'pest'

triorches ('three-testicled') buzzard

One could argue that in translations it might often be better to render occurrences of this last list of unknown species with versions derived from these etymologies, like 'red-head', rather than arbitrarily choosing one of the bizarre alternatives, like 'chough' or 'redshank'. That might more faithfully represent the understandings and intentions of those using these terms.

This makes twenty-seven species that Aristophanes shared with Aesop, plus thirty-four others that can probably be identified, and then a further fourteen that are separately named but not identifiable—seventy-five species in all.

For comparison, the following seventy-five species appear in the Jashemski and Meyer catalogue of the birds that they believe can be identified from depictions in the various remains from the Vesuvian area of Pompeii in AD 79.* I have put a query against those where the identifications seems to me uncertain and have enclosed in square brackets those that refer only to skeletal remains or are very speculative indeed:

helmeted guinea fowl?

Indian peafowl (peacock)

common quail

rock partridge

red jungle fowl (chicken)

common pheasant

capercaillie?

swan

greylag goose

Egyptian goose

shelduck

[garganey]

wigeon

mallard

common teal

flamingo

rock dove / feral pigeon

wood pigeon

turtle dove

[collared dove]

cuckoo

water rail?

purple gallinule

moorhen

coot

white stork

sacred ibis

glossy ibis

cattle egret

grey heron

[purple heron]

little egret

[snipe]

sandpiper (common?)

little owl

tawny owl?

griffon vulture

golden eagle

sparrowhawk?

kingfisher

European bee-eater?

wryneck

parrot (grey?)

parakeet (rose-ringed?)

great grey shrike

woodchat shrike

magpie

jay

[jackdaw]

hooded crow

raven

tit species

barn swallow

blackcap (or Sardinian warbler)

warbler species (reed?)

nuthatch?

wren?

common mynah

robin

nightingale

common redstart

black-eared wheatear

northern wheatear?

house sparrow

chaffinch

greenfinch

goldfinch

hawfinch

[bunting species]

starling?

golden oriole

blue rock thrush

blackbird

song thrush

redwing

There are various points of interest in this list. Several of the species listed occur mainly or exclusively in particular artistic contexts: for example, wigeon and mallard in hunting scenes, glossy ibis and Egyptian goose in the 'Nile mosaic', greylag goose in a domestic setting, and sacred ibis in the 'Sanctuary of Isis'. We should not therefore assume that all the species depicted are familiar visitors to the city of Pompeii or its nearby countryside. Some may have been depicted just as talking points or as exotic travel souvenirs, like holiday photos. There are also some striking omissions: one might have expected such colourful and obtrusive birds as hoopoe, bee-eater, and roller to feature more often, unless the distribution of these birds has changed considerably, as it may possibly have done in the case of the roller (which is identifiably mentioned nowhere in classical literature and may therefore have been a later arrival from the east).*

Some of the species I have put queries against are hard to identify with confidence because the surviving images have been in some way damaged or degraded over time. That applies to the wren, nuthatch, and starling, all of which were undoubtedly common and well-known.

The image of the species pictured in 7.1 represents a different sort of problem, however. Here the image is strikingly clear and the depiction vividly realized. One can identify laurel, roses, and Solomon's seal among the plants in the background, and the artist evidently had a good eye for detail. The posture of the bird perched on a cane and the coloration of its back and underparts might suggest a reed warbler, and though this would be an unusual breeding habitat for them they do occasionally turn up in gardens and elsewhere on migration. The tail shape, however, looks more like that of a *Locustella* warbler or perhaps a Cetti's. On the other hand, the habitat, the stout legs and bill, and the eye-ring might fit better with a melodious warbler. One can happily play this game but we can't actually know the answer, and maybe in a deeper sense there isn't one. Even if the artist had painted the bird more carefully so that the distinguishing features of a reed warbler were absolutely clear, would we then be right to say he had painted a reed warbler if he had not himself known what it was and if there was not even a local name for it?

In this case we can't be sure of the bird's identity, but there are other wall-paintings where we can recognize from the excellent depictions species like woodchat shrike, hawfinch, and black-eared wheatear, though these are nowhere distinguished in ancient literature. This is a problem for translation and interpretation, but is it also one of perception?

7.1 'Little brown job': an identification challenge from the garden fresco in the House of the Gold Bracelet, Pompeii, AD 30–50.

The literary and the visual records compared in this appendix thus present two precisely contrasting uncertainties in our understanding of the naming of birds in the ancient world. In the Aristophanes case we may often understand the connotations of the terms employed (the description) but not their precise denotation (the species they refer to); in the Pompeii case it is the reverse, we can see exactly which species is being depicted but we don't know whether the artist or viewer was making the same discriminations as we do.

BIOGRAPHIES OF AUTHORS QUOTED

This section contains brief biographies of authors whose works are quoted in the main text; in a few cases entries cover collective works, such as the *Greek Anthology*, and those whose author is unknown, such as the *Pervigilium Veneris*. The length of the entries is determined more by their relevance to the themes of this volume than by the larger historical importance or reputation of their subjects: so Aratus gets a longer entry than Plato, for example.

Aelian (*c*.AD 165–235).   Roman teacher of rhetoric, who wrote in Greek. His main surviving work is the large and rambling *De natura animalium* ('On animals'), running to seventeen books, which is an encyclopedic collection of anecdotes, folklore, and moralizing stories about the natural world, mixed in with some personal observations. There is little attempt to sift fact from fiction in any critical way, however, and he is very reliant for his more interesting material on other authorities like Aristotle. Unlike Aristotle and Pliny, Aelian does not attempt to classify birds but he does describe or refer to 109 different species. He wrote a second large collection of *Varia historia* ('Miscellany') or, in its Greek title, *Poikile historia* ('Colourful enquiry'), which also contains a few items about the natural world and is as random as the title suggests.

Aeschylus (*c*.525–*c*.456 BC).   One of the greatest Greek tragic poets and the earliest whose work has survived. He wrote some seventy to ninety plays but only seven of these survive, mostly grouped around particular themes or myths, as in the *Oresteia* trilogy. His plots tend to develop slowly but inexorably, and the main dramatic exchanges are between the principal actors and the chorus, who meditate on the significance of the events unfolding. The plays are characterized by the profundity of the themes and a matching grandeur in the language.

Aesop (sixth century BC).   Shadowy figure named as the author of a collection of some 200 fables. These usually involve the adventures of mammals or birds, behaving and speaking like humans, and they take the form of short narrative stories ending with a moral or *bon mot*. Many are famous enough to have become proverbial in other cultures: the boy who cried wolf, the dog in the manger, the fox and the sour grapes, and so on. The historical Aesop was said (by Herodotus) to have been a slave who won his freedom through his gifts as a storyteller. He may, however, just have been a figure of legend to whom traditional oral tales were later attributed—so himself a convenient fiction. The published versions of the fables come down to us through two main anthologies, one in Latin verse by the Roman poet Phaedrus (early in the first century AD), the other in Greek verse by Babrius, a Hellenized Roman (probably late first century AD). There are various subsequent collections based on these, in English, French, and other languages, and the stories have been many times retold, imitated, and adapted.

Aëtius (first or second century AD).   Author of a doxography (a survey of ancient 'opinions') on questions of natural philosophy. The work itself is lost but survives in later compilations by others and is an important source for the Presocratic philosophers.

Alcaeus (late seventh century BC).   Greek lyric poet, contemporary with Sappho and from the same island of Lesbos. 'Lyric' poetry was that composed for singing or recitation at social gatherings, with musical accompaniment from the lyre. Only fragments of his extensive output survive but they range over such topics as war, politics, wine, love, myth, and the gods.

Alcman (seventh century BC).   Early Greek choral lyric poet, whose birthplace is uncertain (Sparta and Sardis both claim him).   His work survives only in fragments and through quotation by other authors, but he clearly derived much of his imagery from animals and the natural world.

Anaxagoras (*c.*500–*c.*428 BC).   One of the early group of Greek 'natural philosophers' who wrote a prose work *On Nature*, of which we have only fragments preserved in quotation. He originated from Clazomenae in Ionia, but settled in Athens and became part of the humanist 'Enlightenment' there.

Anaximander (died *c.*545 BC).   One of the earliest of the group of Presocratic 'natural philosophers', from Miletus in Ionia. He wrote a work of some kind *On Nature*, produced an early map of the known inhabited world, and seems to have pioneered many highly original ideas about the origins of the earth and humankind, though we know of these only secondhand and through one quotation (which thus constitutes the earliest surviving fragment of European philosophical prose).

Antipater (1) (late second century BC).   Greek poet from Sidon, who spent his later years at Rome. He was the author of some seventy-five epigrams included in the *Greek Anthology*, but there is some uncertainty how to assign authorship of several epigrams between the two Antipaters.

Antipater (2) (*fl.* II BC–AD 12).   Greek poet from Thessalonica, whose work was included in the collection of *Greek Epigrams* edited by Philip of Thessalonica (*The Garland of Philip*; see below) and published some time in the first century AD.

Antiphon (*c.*480–*c.*411 BC).   Greek orator and politician, much involved both in the fifth-century intellectual 'Enlightenment' in Athens and the political turmoil of 411, which led to his execution. He composed many speeches for litigants, which were regarded as models of rhetoric and prose, though only fragments of these survive.

Apicius (first century AD).   Cognomen of various Roman gourmets, in particular one M. Gavius Apicius, a contemporary of the emperors Augustus and Tiberius. He is said to have invented several new dishes and cooking techniques and to have written a guide to sauces. A volume of recipes was published under his name very much later, in the fourth century AD, designed as a practical cookbook for staff working in wealthy households. One whole section of this (Book VI) is devoted to recipes involving birds, including such exotic fare as cranes, flamingoes, and peacocks.

Apollodorus of Athens (second century BC). Distinguished scholar who studied in Athens and later worked at Alexandria. He was credited with a wide range of works, but the *Library of Greek Mythology* ascribed to him was probably written later, in the first or second century AD. It is a rather routine compilation of the stories in Greek heroic mythology, but has proved a useful source book for other writers on these topics from ancient times through to Robert Graves.

Apuleius (*c*.AD 124–70). Latin author and intellectual, born in Madaurus (Numidia) and educated at Carthage, Athens, and Rome. His two best-known works are: the *Apologia*, a speech in his defence against the charge of practising magic, which includes valuable information on magical rites and rituals; and the *Metamorphoses* (also known as *The Golden Ass*), which is the only Latin novel surviving whole, and contains within it such famous set-pieces as the story of Cupid and Psyche.

Aratus (*c*.315–*c*.240 BC). Greek poet of the Hellenistic period, who seems to have studied in Athens and later spent time as court poet in Macedonia and Syria. His best-known (and only surviving) book is the *Phaenomena* ('Appearances'), mainly on astronomy and meteorology. This became one of the most widely read works in the ancient world after Homer's *Iliad* and *Odyssey*, but was presumably valued more for its mythological tales than its scientific content. It deals with both celestial and terrestrial phenomena, and there is a large section on *diosemeiai* ('weather signs'), which may have been published separately; it records supposed examples of bird and animal behaviour as predictors of weather patterns. Aratus is an important source for the accumulated folklore on all this. Theophrastus (see below) produced a similar work on weather signs, but it is unclear whether one of them was copying the other, or whether they were both using some common source.

Archelaus (*fl. c*.450 BC). One of the Presocratic group of 'natural philosophers', probably an Athenian and a pupil of Anaxagoras, but very little is known for sure about his life. We hear of various reported theories of his in cosmology and zoogony.

Archias (*fl. c*.100 BC). Greek poet from Antioch and the likely author of at least some of the epigrams ascribed to an Archias in the *Greek Anthology*.

Argentarius (probably first century AD). Greek poet and epigrammatist whose work was included in the collection of *Greek Epigrams* edited by Philip of Thessalonica (*The Garland of Philip*) and published some time in the first century AD. He was considered among the most elegant and witty of the authors in that anthology.

Aristophanes (*c*.446–*c*.386 BC). Greek comic dramatist and the author of over forty plays, of which only eleven survive. He was not himself an active political figure, but all his plays have a political dimension and they were controversial enough to have twice landed him in the courts. The plots tend to be farce, the dialogue is spiced with slander and obscenity, but at a deeper level the ideas expressed are radical and subversive. *The Birds*, for example, is a political fantasy about two Athenians, fed up with taxes, over-regulation, and life in the city generally, who negotiate with the leader of the birds (a hoopoe) and the chorus of twenty-four different species of birds (all identified) to establish a 'Cloud-Cuckoo Land' in the sky.

The birds welcome this approach and make their own distinctive contributions to the building work. The experiment is declared a great success and all their fellow Athenian citizens go ornithomanic in excitement and want to join in. The play was produced in 414 BC, at the time of the disastrous Athenian imperial expedition against Sicily, and the timing can scarcely be accidental. The selection and descriptions of the species of birds in the play assume an easy familiarity with them on the part of the audience, and the play as a whole is a *locus classicus* in literature for the symbolic potential of birds. There are several incidental references to birds in his other plays too, especially as items of food for the table.

Aristotle (388–322 BC).   One of the most important figures in the history of Western thought. He was a pupil of Plato, but after a spell in Macedonia as tutor to Alexander (later 'Alexander the Great') he returned to Athens to found his own school, the Lyceum. His writings represent an enormous, systematic output covering virtually every field of human knowledge, though what survives is mostly in the form of lecture notes and student texts, edited after his death. He was a pioneer in zoology, collecting much of his material during time spent on the islands of Lemnos and Lesbos (a favourite destination for birdwatchers today, too). His major work in ornithology, which he effectively founded as a subject, is in Book IX of his *History of Animals*, though the Greek word *historia* in this title just meant 'enquiry' (hence our expression 'natural history'), not 'history' in our later, more restricted sense. He classified birds on the basis of their anatomy and environment and distinguished about 140 different species (not all precisely identifiable from his descriptions now). He also examined questions of seasonal plumage change, migration, embryonic development, and morphology, and the relationship between size and climate. His work in biology and zoology more generally is always teleological in character—relating form and behaviour to purpose and function. Aristotle's three main biological works are *Parts of Animals* (on morphology), *Generation of Animals* (on embryology and reproduction), and *History of Animals* (on taxonomy, description, and behaviour). Two minor ones are *Movement of Animals* and *Progression of Animals* (both on locomotion) and there are also a few other compilations like the *Reported Marvels* falsely attributed to Aristotle. His work does contain some inaccuracies and exaggerations and a few rank absurdities (possibly added to his texts by later editors); but his corpus of work as a whole formed the basis of many later treatises like those of Theophrastus, Pliny, and Aelian and had an unequalled and largely unchallenged influence through to the Middle Ages.

Arrian (AD 86–160).   Greek historian, man of letters, and 'public intellectual', who saw himself as the heir to Herodotus, Thucydides, and more especially Xenophon. His only surviving works are the *Anabasis*, his celebrated and eulogistic account of the campaigns of Alexander the Great, which is now our best source on Alexander, and the short companion piece, the *Indica*, an ethnography of India and a travelogue of the voyage of Alexander's fleet from India to Persia.

Artemidorus (late second century AD).   Although he came from Ephesus he styled himself 'Artemidorus of Daldis' after his mother's birthplace in Lydia. He was the author of the only extant dream book from the ancient world, a series of case studies and their analyses in Greek entitled the *Oneirocritica* ('Interpretation of dreams'). Birds were prominent among the dream motifs he collected. His work was later influential both in the Arab world and in Europe from the Renaissance onwards, and Sigmund Freud acknowledged it as an important influence in his own work of the same title.

Athenaeus (*fl. c.*AD 200). Prolific Greek author who came from Naucratis in Egypt. His main, and only surviving, work is the fifteen-volume *Deipnosophistae* ('The intellectuals' dinner party'), set in the form of an extended series of dinner-party conversations between the twenty-nine learned and loquacious guests, whose topics range across literature, history, philosophy, grammar, medicine, law, culture, manners, and in particular food and drink. The volumes constitute a huge body of valuable source material about the ancient world and about the other ancient authors cited and quoted.

Aurelius, Marcus (AD 121–80). Author of the famous book of philosophical reflections *Meditations*, written in Greek. He became emperor of Rome in 161 at the height of its power and has been hailed as the 'philosopher–king' Plato had hoped for. The *Meditations* were notes written for himself, not originally for publication (the title was invented later), and the text survived in just one later manuscript copy; but the work became one of the best-known works of popular philosophy and is said to have been among the favourite reading of Frederick the Great, Alexander Pope, Goethe, and Bill Clinton.

Ausonius (*c.*AD 310–95). Latin poet from Burdigala in Aquitaine (modern Bordeaux), who became tutor to the Emperor Gratian. He wrote a range of undemanding poetry that was more popular in his own day than it has been later. Edward Gibbon dismissed it as follows: 'the poetical fame of Ausonius condemns the taste of his age.'

Babrius. See under Aesop.

Caesar, Julius (100–44 BC). Roman general and statesman, who enjoyed a career of great military and political success, culminating with his victory over Pompey in 48 BC and his appointment as 'dictator for life' in 44 BC. But his further ambitions for kingship and deification led to his assassination on the Ides of March (the 15th) in 44 BC. He was also a distinguished orator and the author of two large-scale histories—of the Gallic and the Civil Wars—much of which survives. They are written in a simple, direct style that made them the standard first texts for generations of reluctant students of Latin.

Cassius Dio (born *c.*AD 164). Roman historian. Born in Nicaea in Bithynia, he enjoyed a distinguished political career in Rome but is best known as the author of an eighty-book history of Rome (written in Greek) from the foundation of the city to AD 229. Of this monumental work only the books covering the period from 69 BC to AD 46 survive complete or in substantial part. He is the sole narrative source for much of this period, but it is unclear what his own sources were or how critically he used them.

Cato the Elder (234–149 BC). A defining figure of the early Roman Republic, who after a very successful military and political career was elected censor in 184 BC, on a programme of reversing the decline in traditional morality. He effectively founded Latin prose writing with his historical survey *Origines* and various shorter essays, but the only work of his we have intact is his *De agri cultura* ('On agriculture'), the first technical manual of its kind, describing how to run a small estate whose primary products were wine and olive oil. This also contains a lot of somewhat miscellaneous information about the management of slaves and about recipes, domestic animals, and farmyard poultry.'Cato was the first to give agriculture a Latin voice', acknowledged Columella in his survey of earlier writers on the subject.

Catullus (*c*.84–*c*.54 BC).   Latin poet and a leading representative of the 'new wave' of writing in the later republic, which looked to Greek rather than traditional Roman models. He died young and produced only one 'slim volume', as he put it himself, of 114 poems, but these are very varied in form and topic as well as strikingly innovative as a body of personal poetry. They include love poems (addressed especially to a married woman, Lesbia), epigrams, social satires, political invectives, obscene skits, elegies, and two long wedding poems. His work is characterized by great elegance, wit, and facility.

Celsus, Aulus Cornelius (first century AD).   Roman encyclopedist (not to be confused with the later Celsus who launched the attack on Christianity that was answered by Origen in *Contra Celsum*). He wrote a large reference work of practical *Artes*, which had separate books on such topics as agriculture, military science, medicine, and rhetoric, but only the eight books on medicine survive. These include a few references to birds as part of a healthy diet.

Chrysippus (*c*.280–*c*.206 BC).   Greek philosopher who was the third head of the Stoic school of philosophy (after Zeno and Cleanthes). He systematized the whole of Stoic philosophy, but his voluminous writings are all lost and his work is known to us only through quotation and summary by others.

Cicero (106–43 BC).   Famous statesman and author. He was an influential and active participant in the violent last phase of the Roman Republic. Born in Italy, he was educated at Athens and Rhodes, and returned to Rome to make an illustrious public career as an orator and politician, but was eventually killed in Mark Antony's proscriptions. He was the author of many celebrated speeches and wrote important works on rhetoric and philosophy, which were particularly influential in the Renaissance; but he is best known now for his voluminous personal correspondence, which is a major source for the political and social history of the period.

Claudian (*c*.AD 370–404).   Egyptian poet from Alexandria, who wrote initially in Greek but later went to live in Italy and became a respected Latin poet at the court of the Western emperor Honorius at Mediolanum (Milan). He wrote a number of stylish epic and mythological poems, panegyrics, and invectives.

Columella (first century AD).   Roman agriculturist. We know little of his background, except that he was born in Spain and spent most of his life at Rome. His major surviving work is the very long and systematic treatise in twelve books, *De re rustica* ('On agriculture'), which is aimed particularly at the owners of large estates and gives detailed instructions on everything to do with farming, from the location and layout of farms to the management of arable crops, viticulture, and animal husbandry (including a very long section on poultry, ducks, and geese), and the duties of the bailiff and his wife. This is a highly professional handbook, but there is also a moralizing strain throughout, urging a return to traditional Roman values; and the tenth book in the series (on horticulture) is written in hexameter verse, hoping to broaden its appeal to literary landowners, who will have been familiar with Virgil's famous *Georgics* (see below).

Crinagoras (*c*.70 BC–*c*.AD 18).   Greek poet from Mytilene (Lesbos), the dates of whose epigrams range from 45 BC to AD 11. He lived in Rome as a court poet to Augustus. Many of his fifty-one well-turned epigrams in the *Greek Anthology* are included in the collection known as *The Garland of Philip* (see under Philip of Thessalonica).

Ctesias (fifth century BC).   Greek physician employed at the Persian court, who also wrote histories (like his *Persica*) and accounts of the customs, 'wonders', and beliefs of distant cultures (his *Indica*), though the latter in particular is an often credulous and unreliable compilation of current stories in circulation featuring such prodigies as pygmies, dog-headed men, and the unicorn. His work survives only in fragmentary form and in quotations by other authors.

Democritus (*c*.460–*c*.370 BC).   Greek philosopher from Abdera (Thrace). He wrote some seventy works, ranging through science, mathematics, ethics, and politics, but none of these survives and his writings are known only through short quotations and summaries by others. He and Leucippus are jointly credited with propounding a highly original atomic theory of matter, which was taken up by Epicurus as the basis for his materialistic physical theories. In a much later recognition of his interest, he was the subject of Karl Marx's PhD thesis.

Diodorus Siculus (first century BC).   Greek historian, named 'Siculus' ('the Sicilian') to distinguish him from various other figures also called Diodorus. He wrote a massive 'universal history', which was in fact mainly about Greece and his native Sicily and which concluded at 60 BC. Only fifteen from the original forty books of this *Bibliotheca historica* ('Historical library') survive, but they are an important source for the history of the fifth and fourth centuries BC.

Dionysius (1) of Halicarnassus (*fl. c*.30 BC).   Historian and literary critic who lived at Rome but wrote in Greek. His major work was a twenty-volume study of the early history of Rome (*Roman Antiquities*) but he is best known now for his rhetorical and critical essays.

Dionysius (2), known as Periegetes, 'the Guide' (probably second century AD).   Obscure figure who wrote a geography of the known world and also a lost work, his *Ornithiaka* ('On birds'), of which we have only a much later prose paraphrase. The original work seems to have been a poem in Greek, containing a mixture of factual material and folklore, and may indeed have been by a quite different but also obscure Dionysius (of Philadelphia).

Dioscorides (1) (third or second century BC).   Greek poet, probably living in Egypt, and the author of some forty epigrams in the *Greek Anthology*.

Dioscorides (2) (first century AD).   Physician and traveller, who compiled a large work in five books, the *Materia medica*, on the medicinal uses of plants, minerals, and animal products. This lists some 700 plants and over 1,000 drugs. Some of his remedies were still being recommended as late as the seventeenth century.

Empedocles (*c*.492–*c*.432 BC). One of the Presocratic group of 'natural philosophers', from Acragas in Sicily. He was reputed to be a statesman, mystic, and thaumaturge, as well as a philosopher. Two hexameter poems, 'On nature' and 'Purifications', are ascribed to him, and his theories of the four elements (of earth, air, fire, and water) and the cosmic forces of Love and Strife were very influential on later scientific and medical thought. His ideas also had links with Pythagorean and Orphic beliefs, including those on reincarnation.

Ephippus (fourth century BC). Greek comic poet from the period of Middle Comedy (404–321 BC) whose work is known only through fragments, one of which is quoted by Athenaeus.

Euenus (fifth century BC). Greek poet and sophist from Paros, eight of whose poems survive in the *Greek Anthology*, though they may be the work of one of several other figures with the same name.

Euripides (*c*.480–*c*.406 BC). The third of the three great Athenian tragic dramatists (after Aeschylus and Sophocles). He wrote some ninety plays, of which nineteen survive, but enjoyed less success in the annual theatre competitions than either of the other two. He left Athens, possibly in disgruntlement, *c*.408 BC and spent the rest of his life in Macedon. He is often thought to be the most 'modern' of the great tragedians in his realism, social iconoclasm, and theatrical innovations in treating themes like the brutality of war and the darker complexities of human (especially female) psychology. Aristotle reports the judgement that 'Sophocles presented men as they ought to be and Euripides presented them as they are.' One of his last plays was *The Bacchae*, a classic confrontation between the rational and irrational elements in human motivation; this was produced posthumously and, ironically, won first prize for the year 406.

Frontinus (died AD 103/04). Senior Roman public figure, who held a number of political and military positions (including governor of the province of Britain in 73–77). He wrote a series of practical handbooks on such topics as the aqueducts of Rome and land surveying, and a major work on military tactics, the *Strategemata*.

Galen (AD 129–?217). Greek physician and polymath. He was born and educated in Pergamum (Asia Minor), but gravitated to Rome in 162 where he spent most of the rest of his life as court physician to Marcus Aurelius and his immediate successors. He wrote widely on philosophy, logic, and philology, as well as medicine, believing that 'the best physician is also the best philosopher'; but it was his voluminous scientific writings on anatomy, physiology, pathology, and diet that established his very great reputation and ensured that his medical corpus had an authoritative status both in the Islamic and the Western European worlds at least up to the time of the Enlightenment.

Gellius, Aulus (first century AD). Roman scholar and the author of a learned commonplace book of miscellaneous material, published *c*.AD 180 and entitled *Attic Nights* to commemorate its drafting through the long winter nights of a sojourn in Athens. It is an important source of quotations from and information about other ancient authors whose work is now lost.

Greek Anthology. Collection of occasional poems in Greek, largely epigrams (that is—in its original sense—poems worthy of 'inscription'), which evolved from the 'garlands' of Meleager and Philip of Thessalonica (who first used the term 'anthology'). It was later expanded to include Byzantine compositions, and took its definitive form in the edition of Constantine Cephalus in the 10th century AD. The poems are all short but span serious commemorations, light satire, and erotic fancies. There have since been many other selections, translations, and imitations. See further under Meleager and Philip of Thessalonica.

Heraclitus (*fl.* 500 BC). Greek philosopher, born at Ephesus, and one of the early 'Presocratic' thinkers speculating about the origins, constituents, and principles of causation in the natural world. He produced a book *On Nature*, though only tantalizing and often puzzling fragments of this survive, such as his famous pronouncement that everything is in a state of flux ('you can never step into the same river twice'). His vivid, oracular style tends either to fascinate or repel, but philosophers as eminent as Hegel claim to have taken their inspiration from him.

Herodian (third century AD). Greek historian. Perhaps from Antioch, he became a minor official at Rome. He wrote a vivid but rather unreliable history of the Roman emperors in eight books, covering the period from Marcus Aurelius to Gordian III (AD 180–238).

Herodotus (*c.*490–*c.*425 BC). Greek historian, born at Halicarnassus in Asia Minor. He travelled widely throughout the Greek world, collecting material for his monumental history of relations between the Greek and non-Greek ('barbarian') peoples up to and including the Persian Wars. His *Historiai* ('Enquiries', usually known as his *Histories*) is the earliest surviving prose work in Greek literature and led Cicero to call him 'the father of Greek history', though his critics (ancient and modern) have found him lacking in rigour and objectivity in his treatment of his sources. The work has at any rate enjoyed an enduring popularity for its easy narrative style and its engaging mixture of observations, anecdotes, and digressions about the people and places he is describing.

Hesiod (*fl. c.*700 BC). Countryman and shepherd, who came from the small village of Askre in Boeotia (central Greece), which he describes as 'awful in winter, miserable in summer, and no good at any time'. He is one of the very first authors in Greek literature, and in what was still predominantly a non-literate culture his work was very likely performed, and may even have been composed, orally. *Works and Days* is a poem in the genre of 'wisdom literature', a celebration of the life of honest, god-fearing labour, including some mythological material, various maxims, and much practical as well as moral advice on religious observances, seafaring, and in particular agriculture. The descriptions of the natural world are often vivid and always unsentimental. There are several references to birds in relation to the cycles of the farming year, and the work originally had a sort of appendix (now lost), an *Ornithomanteia* on bird omens.

Hippocrates (fifth century BC).   Reputed by Galen to have been head of a medical school in the Aegean island of Cos, but almost no biographical facts about him are known with certainty. He has given his name to a remarkable corpus of about sixty medical treatises that are now thought to have been composed by various different writers between 430 and 330 BC. They span quite technical works on anatomy, surgery, dietetics, and gynaecology, and also more general studies about the nature, objectives, and ethics of medical practice, including the original 'Hippocratic Oath'. This body of work constitutes an important example of early scientific writings, with its insistence that illness and disease have natural and not religious causes and require treatment based on evidence rather than on superstition or magic.

Hippolytus (c.AD 170–236).   Theologian in Rome who wrote a *Refutation of All Heresies* in nine books, which attacked Christian heresies on the grounds that they were revivals of pagan philosophy. He is an important source for Presocratic philosophy through his quotations from thinkers like Heraclitus.

Historia Augusta (late fourth century AD).   Collection of biographies of Roman emperors from AD 117 to 285. They are presented as the work of six different authors, but scholars now believe that they were probably put together by a single (but unknown) author from various different sources. Some of the material is unreliable, but together the essays constitute an invaluable source of information about Roman imperial history of this period. Gibbon, for example, made great use of the work in his own history of the later Roman Empire.

Homer (eighth century BC).   The first and most celebrated figure in ancient Greek literature, who has remained an important inspiration throughout the Western tradition. Very little is known about his life for certain, and it has been variously speculated that he was blind, illiterate, two people, or a committee. If he was a single, literate person, he may have been the first to bring together and commit to a written text the oral materials from which the two mighty epics, the *Iliad* and the *Odyssey*, are certainly in part constructed. The poems seem at any rate to have been composed and constituted in their present form just at the time when the Greek alphabet was first introduced, though they continued to be recited orally to audiences by professional performers throughout the classical period. The *Iliad* tells the story of the capture of Troy by the Greeks, and the *Odyssey* the story of the adventures of Odysseus as he finds his way back home afterwards. Together they constituted for the Greeks a kind of bible of folk memories, heroic exploits, human insights, natural descriptions, and moral examples, all woven together in a supreme act of imaginative and artistic creation. Many of Homer's similes are drawn from the observed behaviour of birds, especially eagles and birds of prey, and there are several passages that indicate the importance in the contemporary culture of birds as omens, whose significance was interpreted by specialist priests or 'bird-watchers'.

Homeric Hymns.   Series of thirty-three hymns traditionally ascribed to Homer and composed in the hexameter verse of Homeric epic poetry, but which were in fact created later (perhaps in the seventh or sixth centuries BC) and were probably literary compositions not oral ones. They were written to honour the gods, explain the origins of certain cults, and retell various mythological stories. Number xxx is addressed to Gaia, the earth goddess.

Horace (65–8 BC).   Latin poet, born at Venusia in Apulia (southern Italy) to a well-off but not upper-class family and educated at Rome and Athens. Under the patronage of the rich aristocrat Maecenas, he was adopted into the circle of writers that included Virgil, was afforded a comfortable lifestyle, and effectively became the poet laureate at Rome. His works include his early (and often fierce) books of *Satires* and *Epodes* and his later literary *Epistles*, but he is best remembered for the lyrical poetry in his four books of *Odes*. These consist of personal poetry—dealing with themes of love, politics, friendship, and everyday life—and the mood is generally one of gentle irony, civilized contentment, and *carpe diem* (a phrase from one of these odes).

Hyginus (*c*.64 BC–AD 17).   Librarian of the Palatine Library founded by Augustus. He is the probable author of a Latin work entitled *Astronomy*, which is a compilation of 'constellation myths', deriving from Eratosthenes and other Hellenistic authors, and which was an important source for the canonical collection of these by Ptolemy of Alexandria in the second century AD.

Juvenal (early second century AD).   Latin satirist. We know almost nothing about his life, but he produced sixteen satirical poems (published in five books), which are the most famous examples of this genre in Roman literature and have provided a wealth of 'quotations' for later anthologists. His early satires in particular are notable for their *saeva indignatio* ('savage indignation'), being very aggressive and often highly vulgar attacks on the decadence, corruption, and hypocrisy of the Roman elite of the day. The longest and most notorious is the Sixth Satire (on Roman wives), after which his later work becomes somewhat more ironic and detached. The poems are an excellent source for the mores of the time, especially its extravagances in eating habits and social behaviour. He was a great influence on later satirical writing by authors like Johnson, Pope, and Molière.

Libanius (AD 314–*c*.393).   Greek man of letters. A native of Antioch, educated at Athens, he went on to become a renowned teacher of rhetoric (at Nicomedia, Constantinople, and Antioch) and a respected social historian and cultural critic. His surviving works include over sixty public speeches and some 1,600 letters, which together constitute a rich source of information on the political, cultural, and social life in the Eastern Empire in the fourth century AD. He wrote as a committed pagan but with a wide range of intellectual sympathies and social concerns.

Livy (59 BC–AD 17).   Roman historian, born at Patavium (Padua) in northern Italy, who gravitated to Rome, where he became on good terms with the Emperor Augustus. His major work was a gigantic history of Rome from its origins to 9 BC. This consisted of no fewer than 142 books, of which numbers 1–10 and 21–45 survive substantially intact and are the basis of most later histories of Rome. He was particularly admired for his easy, fluent style, described by the critic and scholar Quintilian as having a *lactea ubertas* ('milky richness').

Longus (second / third century AD).   Greek author of *Daphnis and Chloe*, a 'pastoral story' or novel in four books, which is the romantic tale of the adventures, sexual experimentations, and eventual marriage of two rustic innocents. It has proved a popular story, inspiring several distinguished artists and illustrators and Ravel's ballet of the same name. Goethe recommended reading the book once a year.

Lucan (AD 39–65). Latin epic poet, born in Corduba (now Córdoba, in southern Spain) and given an upper-class education in rhetoric and philosophy at Rome and Athens. He was initially taken up by the Emperor Nero, but then fell out with him, joined a conspiracy, and when that was exposed was forced eventually to commit suicide (supposedly reciting some of his own lines on the death of a soldier). His major, and only surviving, work is his poetic epic in ten books on the Civil War of 49–48 BC between Caesar and Pompey (*De bello civili*, also known as the *Pharsalia*). The story is one of unrelieved horror and violence, in which Caesar's crossing of the Rubicon unleashes the darkest human instincts and leads directly to the destruction of the Roman Republic.

Lucian (*c*.AD 120–80). Greek writer, born in Syria, whose first language was probably Aramaic. He was trained in rhetoric and philosophy and travelled widely as an itinerant teacher and lecturer. He wrote in a bewildering variety of styles and (mainly) prose genres, including essays, satires, dialogues, dramas, science fiction and adventure stories, all characterized by wit and a cultivated cynicism.

Lucretius (*c*.94–*c*.55 BC). Latin poet who was a great influence on Virgil, Horace, and other Roman poets and an important figure for Renaissance humanism and the Enlightenment. Almost nothing certain is known of his life, however. His only published work was the monumental didactic poem, *De rerum natura* ('On the nature of things'), written in hexameter verse and conventionally divided into six books. It is a popularization of the work of the Greek philosopher Epicurus (whose chief work was entitled *Peri phuseos*, 'On nature') and has the specific purpose of releasing people from the fears of death inspired by religion and superstition. To this end, Lucretius sets out a wholly materialistic account of the universe based on the theories of the Greek atomists, who posited an infinity of possible worlds, all constructed from elemental particles interacting according to the laws of nature that excluded any divine or supernatural intervention. His ethical conclusions recommend a simple life of gentle enjoyments, supportive friendships, and sociability. The *De rerum natura* offers an account of the evolution of our world and a description of all its natural phenomena, including a number of interesting comments on birds and bird behaviour; but it is also a work of vivid and passionate poetry that belies the sometimes technical subject matter.

Macrobius, also known as Theodosius (*fl. c*.AD 400). Roman scholar and philosopher, who wrote a grammatical treatise and a commentary on Cicero's *De republica*; but his best-known work is the *Saturnalia*, which purports to represent a series of conversations between eminent pagan Roman intellectuals on a wide range of both light-hearted and serious topics, rather in the manner of the Greek author Athenaeus (see above).

Martial (*c*.AD 40–104). Latin poet, born in Spain; he spent most of his writing career in Rome, supported by Seneca the Younger (who was also Spanish). His work spanned the reigns of four emperors: Titus, Domitian, Nerva, and Trajan, with each of whom he had to reach some accommodation. He published a series of fifteen books of *Epigrams*, most of them timed to coincide with the festival of Saturnalia in December, and these constitute an extended satirical commentary on the events of the day. They vary a good deal in tone and topic, including playful, flattering, bitter, abusive, and later on obscene poems. Most are technically very accomplished, pointed by wit and brevity.

Meleager (*fl. c.*100 BC). Poet from Gadara in Syria, who edited an anthology of Greek epigrams and lyric poetry. The anthology was known as *The Garland of Meleager*, each of the forty-six poets included being identified in the preface and assigned the name of a flower. The compilation itself is now lost, but its contents form part of the larger surviving *Greek Anthology*. His own poetry was largely erotic and was addressed to both boys and girls.

Moschus (*fl. c.*150 BC). Greek scholar and poet from Syracuse. His poetry was in the pastoral tradition of Theocritus and Bion, but the 'Lament for Bion' attributed to him (and quoted in this volume) must be by another author since Bion lived a generation or more after Moschus.

Nemesianus (late third century AD). Latin poet from Carthage, who wrote some very derivative pastoral poetry and is also named as the author of two didactic poems—on hunting and on bird-catching (*De aucipio*), of which only small fragments survive. The latter may have been wrongly ascribed to him.

Nicostratus (fourth century BC). Greek comic poet from the period of Middle Comedy (404–321 BC) whose work is known only through fragments, one of which is quoted by Athenaeus.

Oppian (late second century AD). Greek poet. He wrote a long didactic poem entitled *Halieutica* ('On fishing'), divided into five books and composed in hexameter verse. It contains a good deal of mythological material as well as practical advice for fishermen, and plays at times with the relationships between the hunter and the hunted. A companion work entitled *Cynegetica* ('On hunting') has sometimes been ascribed to Oppian but is probably by a later imitator.

Ovid (43 BC–AD 17). Latin poet, educated at Rome, who had a brief political career before devoting himself to writing. He became the leading Roman poet of his time but was banished by the emperor Augustus in AD 8 for 'a poem and a mistake' (the poem was the erotic *Ars amatoria*, 'The art of love', but the indiscretion remains a mystery). He spent the rest of his life at Tomis on the Black Sea and died there, still in exile. His prolific output can be roughly divided into love poetry (*Amores, Ars amatoria, Remedia amoris*), mythological poetry (*Metamorphoses, Heroides, Fasti*), and the poetry of exile (*Tristia, Epistolae ex Ponto*). The *Metamorphoses* ('Transformations') is an epic verse composition of fifteen books, retelling the tales and legends from classical and Near Eastern myths. It has proved to be one of the most popular works of all Latin literature, a beautiful and sustained feat of storytelling, whose influence can be traced through many different strands in Western art, literature, and culture.

Pausanias (*fl. c.*AD 150). Greek author from Magnesia (Lydia) who wrote a *Periegesis Hellados* ('Description of Greece'), which is a long travelogue and tour guide to the antiquities of mainland Greece, a sort of cultural Baedeker of its day (and still usable). Its ten books contain a great deal of useful and accurate information on the topography, history, monuments, art, and sanctuaries of the places he visited, but he has relatively little to say about the countryside he passes through or its wildlife, except for occasional comments on reported 'wonders'.

Pervigilium Veneris ('Vigil of Venus').   Famous romantic Latin poem in twenty-two verses, whose authorship and date, however, remain unknown. It has been variously dated as second century AD (possibly composed by Florus, a contemporary of Hadrian) or fourth century AD (possibly by Tiberianus, see below). The poem is a passionate invocation of Venus and the procreative power of love, apparently set in Sicily on the eve of the spring festival of Venus. It has sometimes been read as a kind of link between classical and medieval poetry, and it has attracted the attention of several modern poets and composers.

Petronius (died AD 66).   Roman satirical author, possibly identifiable with the politician of this name involved in intrigues at the court of Nero who was eventually forced to commit suicide in AD 66. He is the author of the *Satyricon* (more properly, the *Satyrica*), a huge picaresque novel composed as a medley of prose and poetry. Only small parts of the work survive, but these include the *Cena Trimalchionis* ('Feast of Trimalchio'), the story of a riotous and over-lavish feast at which Trimalchio and his hedonistic friends indulge in various culinary excesses and entertain one another with dubious stories. The work was an influence on Scott Fitzgerald's *The Great Gatsby* and there was a famous film version of it by Fellini.

Phaedrus.   See under Aesop.

Pherecrates (fifth century BC).   Athenian comic poet contemporary with Aristophanes. He produced at least nineteen plays, apparently of a very inventive kind; but only fragments of his work survive, in the form of quotations by other authors like Athenaeus.

Philip of Thessalonica (first century AD).   Greek poet and epigrammatist who put together an anthology of *Greek Epigrams*, including eighty of his own, published as *The Garland of Philip* during the first century AD. See also *Greek Anthology*.

Philo (first century AD).   Jewish philosopher who lived in Alexandria in Egypt during the early Roman Empire. He wrote a voluminous series of works, including commentaries on the Greek texts of the Bible, which sought to harmonize Greek and Jewish philosophical traditions. Among his Greek predecessors, he was strongly sympathetic to Plato and the Stoics in particular, and was himself a great influence on Neoplatonism and on later Christian theology and scholarship.

Pindar (*c*.518–*c*.446 BC).   Greek lyric poet, born near Thebes in Boeotia. He wrote in a wide range of poetic forms but only the four books of his choral 'victory odes' now survive, written in honour of the victors in the four great Panhellenic games (at Olympia, Delos, Nemea, and Isthmia). The poems skilfully weave into their celebratory narrative a great deal of mythical and didactic material and were hailed as models of eloquence and originality by later poets like Horace.

Plato (1) (fifth century BC).   Athenian comic poet contemporary with Aristophanes. We know thirty of his play titles, but his work has not survived, except in short quotations by others.

Plato (2) (*c*.428–*c*.348 BC).   The famous Greek philosopher—of such originality and importance that the subsequent history of Western philosophy has been dubbed 'a series of footnotes to Plato'. He wrote some thirty semi-fictionalized dialogues in which his teacher, Socrates, is usually the principal figure, many of which are outstanding works of literary as well as philosophical merit. References to birds or the natural world, however, are limited to figurative examples and incidental comments, though the short work *Menexenus* does contain an interesting metaphor about the earth as a nurturing 'mother', and the *Critias* has a very vivid description of environmental degradation.

Plautus (*fl.* late third / early second century BC).   Roman comic playwright, twenty-one of whose plays survive, though he probably wrote very many more. These are the earliest surviving works of Latin literature. They are generally quite close adaptations of models from Menander and the Greek 'New Comedy', with stock characters and plots based on love affairs, mistaken identities, and family quarrels. They were played as farce but throw an incidental light on the culture and everyday life of the time. His plots were in turn an influential source for some of Molière's and Shakespeare's comedies.

Pliny the Elder (AD 23–79).   Latin author, who was born to a wealthy north Italian family, studied at Rome and then had an active military and administrative career before retiring to devote himself fully to his writing. His productivity was extraordinary, as was the range of his output, spanning biography, history, rhetoric, military tactics, and science—a testament to his prodigious energies, curiosity, and application ('vita vigilia est': 'life is being awake'). From this great output 'only' the thirty-seven books of his *Natural History* survive; but this is itself an encyclopedic work that includes in its purview astronomy, geography, zoology, medicine, metallurgy, technology, and the arts. In the Preface he claims that it includes '20,000 facts worthy of note', derived from his tireless research in reading other published work. The 'facts' are actually a mish-mash of genuine information, secondhand reports, half-truths, and outright fallacies, but no less interesting for showing what some people did in fact believe at the time. Book x of this *Natural History* is devoted to birds. In it he attempts a classification of birds on the basis of the form of their feet and brings together a huge amount of valuable material, though he neither analyses it critically nor presents it in a clearly ordered way. His inexhaustible curiosity led in the end to his death. He was so eager to observe the eruption of Vesuvius at first hand that he went in too close and died from inhaling the fumes. His *Natural History* went on to achieve great celebrity, however, and was one of the first books to be printed in the vernacular in Europe (Nicholas Jenson's 1476 edition).

Pliny the Younger (*c*.AD 61–112).   Politician and letter-writer, nephew of Pliny the Elder, who adopted him and launched him on his legal and political career. He held various public offices at Rome and finally became governor of Bithynia (in the north-west of Asia Minor), but he is best known for his ten books of *Letters*, which are a rich source for the social and political history of his day and are also of considerable literary merit. They include the famous letter to Tacitus, describing the eruption of Vesuvius and his uncle's death at the scene, and an exchange with Trajan about the treatment of Christians.

Plutarch (*c.*AD 46–120).   Prolific Greek author, ranging across biography, history, popular science, and philosophy. He was from Chaeronea in Boeotia (central Greece), where he was happy to spend most of his adult life. He did, however, travel widely in Greece, Italy, Asia Minor, and Egypt, and had citizen rights at both Athens and Rome, so enjoyed a broadly cosmopolitan outlook. His best-known work is his compilation of *Lives* of famous Greek and Roman figures, presented as portraits of character, which were an important source for Shakespeare, Montaigne, and other literary figures from the Renaissance onwards and have remained continuously popular. He also wrote sixty or more short treatises and essays on diverse topics, collected as his *Moralia* or 'Moral essays', and these well indicate his general cast of mind, which was cultivated, urbane, genial, inquisitive, and erudite without being profound. An essay of particular interest for the present volume is 'The cleverness of animals', which makes some surprisingly modern points about animal (including avian) intelligence.

Porphyry (AD 224–*c.*305).   Neoplatonist philosopher, originally from Tyre (under the Syrian name 'Malchus'), but studied philosophy at Athens and at Rome (under Plotinus, whose works he edited). Most of his own writings have not survived, but we do have his treatise (in Greek) on vegetarianism entitled *On Abstinence from Animal Food*, which makes some interesting points about animal rationality (and, by implication, animal rights).

Propertius (*c.*50–*c.*10 BC).   Latin poet from Umbria, who settled in Rome and became part of the literary circle around the patron Maecenas. He wrote four books of *Elegies*, of which the first three are mostly love poems addressed to his mistress, Cynthia, to whom he was 'enslaved by love' in a long and difficult relationship (which ended badly). The fourth book is more varied and experimental.

Rhianus (born *c.*275 BC).   Cretan poet, who is known to have written several historical epics and a number of short epigrams in the Hellenistic style. Little of his work survives but we do have ten of the epigrams, which are artful in construction and on erotic themes, preserved in the *Greek Anthology*.

Rufinus (perhaps fourth or fifth century AD).   Greek poet, author of some thirty-eight short amatory epigrams in the *Greek Anthology*. The poet may have lived in the early Byzantine period, but we have no certain information about him.

Sappho (late seventh / early sixth century BC).   Famous Greek lyric poet from Lesbos, who was hailed in antiquity as 'the tenth Muse'. Most of her poetry survives only in fragments or in the form of quotations by others. It includes wedding songs and hymns to deities, as well as the love poetry addressed to other women and girls for which she is now best known. She herself seems to have had attachments to both men and women. Whatever the nature of these, it was quite normal in Greek society for adult 'mentors' to have physical relationships with maturing adolescents of the same gender.

Seneca the Younger (*c.*4 BC–AD 65).   Roman philosopher and tragedian, born at Córdoba in Spain and educated at Rome, where he enjoyed a successful political career and became first tutor and later political adviser to Nero, though he was eventually forced to commit suicide following accusations of conspiracy. He wrote voluminously and his output includes philosophical dialogues, moral essays, treatises on natural history, and a series of verse tragedies that were a great influence on Renaissance and Jacobean drama.

Sextus Empiricus (second century AD).   Greek philosopher. Nothing is known of his life, but the tag 'Empiricus' suggests a medical background. His surviving works are expositions (in Greek) of the philosophical school of Scepticism and sharply criticize the other 'dogmatic' schools of antiquity (Stoicism, Epicureanism, and the Peripatetics). Sextus' theories have proved more influential within the history of philosophy since their rediscovery in the sixteenth century than they ever were in the ancient world itself.

Silius Italicus (*c.*AD 26–102).   Latin poet of the generation after Virgil. His epic *Punica*, on the Second Punic War is (at over 12,000 lines) the longest surviving poem in Latin. He was hailed as Virgil's worthy successor by some, but the remark of Pliny the Younger that his work was marked 'more by diligence than inspiration' is the judgement that has remained.

Simmias (early third century BC).   Scholar–poet from Rhodes, who published some lexicographical studies and various kinds of poetry, but is best known for his three 'pattern poems' (*technopaignia*) respectively on wings, the axe, and the egg (see **5.12**, p. 300).

Simonides (*c.*556–*c.*468 BC).   Greek lyric poet from the island of Ceos (Kea) in the northwest Cyclades. He worked as an itinerant professional poet, accepting commissions and patronage where he could find them. He demonstrated great versatility across a range of genres, including epigrams, elegies, drinking-songs, choral laments, and paeans; but most of what survives from his prolific output is in quotations from others and in only fragmentary form. His most famous lines are the tomb epigraph composed in honour of the Spartan dead at Thermopylae.

Sophocles (496–405 BC).   Greek tragic poet, born at Colonus (a suburb of Athens), who enjoyed an active and respected role in Athenian public life as well as an exceptionally long dramatic career, in which he competed successfully against Aeschylus with his first play in 468 and produced his last in 406 just after the death of Euripides. He wrote some 120 plays over his lifetime but only seven of these survive complete: *Ajax*, *Women of Trachis*, *Antigone*, *Oedipus the King*, *Electra*, *Philoctetes*, and *Oedipus at Colonus*. Nonetheless, between them they exhibit a great variety of theatrical devices, stagecraft, and language, and a deep sense of the ambiguities and uncertainties of human existence. He won a reputation in the ancient world for his formal perfection and his realistic portrayal of character; and his work has remained the most consistently admired and influential of all Greek tragedy, even though later interpretations of it have differed widely.

Statius (*c.*AD 45–96).   Latin poet from Naples who became associated with the court of the Emperor Domitian in Rome. He wrote the *Silvae* (literally 'Forests', which by extension came to mean 'raw material' and hence 'Impromptus'), which are five books of largely honorific poems celebrating various public events and individual rites of passage, commissioned by Domitian and other rich patrons. The collection also includes one famous short poem of a quite different kind, addressed to 'Sleep' (v 4). His major surviving work, however, is the

Thebaid, a large-scale epic poem in twelve books that achieved great popularity in the Middle Ages and was said to have been a favourite work of Dante.

Stesichorus (*c*.632–*c*.556 BC).   Greek lyric poet from Himera (Sicily), roughly contemporary with Sappho and Alcaeus. Only fragments of and quotations from his very extensive output survive, but he seems to have produced large-scale, epic poems, mainly on mythological themes, which were probably choral works, to be sung and recited in performance. He had a reputation for technical metrical innovations of various kinds and for vivid imagery.

Strabo (*c*.64 BC–*c*.AD 21).   Greek geographer from Amaseia (in Pontus, Asia Minor) who completed his education in Rome. He travelled very widely through the Roman Empire ('from Armenia to Etruria, and from the Black Sea to the borders of Ethiopia') and composed a *Geography* in seventeen volumes, describing the physical geography of the Roman world, with frequent digressions on the history and customs of its peoples and on its plant and animal life. The work was intended to be a guide for statesmen and generals, but it existed for many years in just a single copy and only later became a standard reference work when its importance was recognized in the second century AD.

Suetonius (*c*.AD 70–130).   Latin biographer, probably born in Numidia, who went to Rome and attracted early attention there as an author and scholar. He had a successful political career holding various posts in the imperial administration, but was much better known as the author of two sets of biographies: *De viris illustribus* ('On famous men'), which dealt with Roman men of letters but has survived only in part; and the more important *De vita caesarum* ('On the lives of the emperors'), which is a largely complete set of imperial biographies from Caesar to Domitian, dealing with both their personal and their political lives. They are written more in the manner of a biographer than a historian, but remain an important source for the social life and culture of the times.

Tacitus (*c*.AD 56–118).   Major Roman historian, who held various political appointments in Rome. His first work was a biography of his father-in-law, Agricola, who was governor of Britain for seven years, which has interesting information on that Roman province. But his most important historical work comes in the *Histories* and the *Annals*, a series of accounts of the reigns of the Roman emperors from Tiberius in AD 14 to Domitian in his own day. His work is famous for its penetrating insights into character and for his compressed and incisive prose.

Teleclides (fifth century BC).   Athenian comic poet contemporary with Aristophanes. We know of eight of his play titles, but his work has not survived and is known only through quotations by others.

Terence (?184–?159 BC).   Roman comic playwright, who by tradition came to Rome as a slave from Carthage and gained his freedom and the patronage of the rich through his literary talents. His six plays, first produced between 166 and 160 BC, all survive. As with his Roman predecessor Plautus, his plays were based on Greek originals from Menander and the 'New Comedy', but were admired for their more elaborate plotting and their use of naturalistic language. They also give incidental insights into the daily life and culture of the time.

Tertullian (*c.*AD 155–240). Prolific early Christian Latin author, who came from Carthage in the Roman province of Africa. He defended Christianity against both paganism and what he considered various forms of doctrinal heresy, and is regarded as 'the father of Latin Christianity'.

Thales (*fl. c.*600 BC). Traditionally described as the first Greek philosopher and the earliest of a small group of 'natural philosophers' from Miletus in Ionia. He is credited with predicting an eclipse of the sun in 585 BC and with innovations in geometry and land measurement, but his importance derives more from his pronouncements on the importance of water as the original and underlying element in the world.

Theocritus (third century BC). Greek poet of the Hellenistic period, from Syracuse, who was effectively the creator of the genre of 'bucolic' or pastoral poetry. His thirty *Idylls* ('Little pictures') are presented as exchanges between shepherds and extol the simple country life, but are actually sophisticated and highly worked poems intended for a nostalgic urbanized readership. They were a great influence on Virgil and on Spenser.

Theognis (sixth century BC). Greek elegiac poet, a somewhat shadowy figure. A corpus of some 1,400 verses survives under his name but some are certainly misattributed. His own poetry seems to have been composed mainly for recitation at banquets and drinking parties and is 'elegiac' in terms of metre though not mood. The themes are the everyday preoccupations with life and living, politics, friendship, and death; the tone reflective and often witty; the attitude generally reactionary and pessimistic.

Theophrastus (*c.*372–*c.*286 BC). He succeeded Aristotle as head of the Lyceum (the famous school at Athens) and continued the tradition of research and the publication of treatises of an encyclopedic kind. He was himself an outstanding botanist and effectively founded that subject in the West. He wrote widely on zoological topics too, though these works are largely lost to us. He is best known now for his book *Characters*, a perceptive and amusing account of the main human personality types. Another work now attributed to him is *Peri semeion* ('On signs'), meaning 'weather signs', which may have been a source for Aratus (see above).

Thucydides (*c.*460–*c.*400 BC). Greek historian, born into an aristocratic Athenian family with political and commercial interests in Thrace (north-east Greece), to which he retreated in exile to write his pioneering study about the great war between Athens and Sparta from 432 to 404 BC, *The War of the Peloponnesians and the Athenians*. This was a new kind of history, with a strong emphasis on scientific accuracy and the detailed portrayal of the realities of political power, but it also contains a wealth of incidental information about the physical and cultural environment of the whole Greek world of the time. One striking reference to birds comes in his vivid description of the great plague that struck Athens in 430 BC, when even the carrion eaters avoided the many corpses.

Tiberianus (fourth century AD). Latin poet about whom little is known, except that he wrote a very lyrical 'nature poem' in the same unusual metre that is employed in the *Pervigilium Veneris* (see above), leading to the supposition that he might have been the author of that too.

Varro (116–27 BC). Latin author, who after a brief public career in Rome devoted himself to writing and became possibly the most prolific writer in the whole of Latin literature, completing over 600 books and covering a huge range of topics. Of these, the only substantial parts we have extant are several books from his etymological study, *De lingua Latina* ('On the Latin language') and all three books of his *De re rustica* ('On agriculture'), which is set in the form of a dialogue to try and make it more readable (not a wholly successful ambition). The latter work deals with the husbandry of 'the smaller animals' of the country villa, including both the common farmyard fowl (hens, ducks, and geese) and the more up-market specialities in which Varro is particularly interested (thrushes, peacocks, and doves). He also wrote a large encyclopedic work entitled *Pratum de variis rebus* (literally, 'Meadow of various things' or 'Miscellaneous delights'), which included a book 'On nature', of which only fragments survive.

Virgil (70–20 BC). The most important Latin poet of his age. Under the generous patronage of the statesman Maecenas he wrote a series of ten pastoral poems, the *Eclogues* (published 35 BC), in the style of Theocritus. He then produced the four books of *Georgics* (30 BC) about the farming year, which were ostensibly in the didactic genre pioneered by the Greek poet, Hesiod, but were in fact of much deeper literary and political significance; the work commends the traditional virtues of industry and frugality that were seen as the source of Rome's greatness, and sets out the rewards of a life lived in conformity with nature. Virgil is said to have read the *Georgics* aloud to Octavian (shortly to become the first emperor, Augustus) in 29 BC. His final and greatest work was the *Aeneid*, a national epic commissioned by Augustus to celebrate the growth and success of Rome and her empire. The story goes that the *Aeneid* was unfinished on Virgil's death, but Augustus ordered his executors to ignore Virgil's instruction that it be burned, so rescuing what went on to become the most influential work of all Latin literature. Dante regarded Virgil as a prophet of Christianity, who guided him to the Gates of Paradise in *The Divine Comedy*, and was 'il nostro maggior poeta', 'our greatest poet'.

Xenophanes (c.570–475 BC). Greek philosopher and poet from Ionia, who led 'a wandering life', as he tells us, and was an influential figure in the early Greek intellectual 'Enlightenment'. His work survives only in fragments of poetry, but includes some striking thoughts on such topics as anthropomorphism in religion and the geological inferences to be drawn from fossils. Karl Popper hailed his pronouncements on epistemology as an importance influence on his own philosophy of science.

Xenophon (c.430–c.350 BC). Greek historian, writer, and professional soldier. He was born in Athens and was a student of Socrates in the turbulent political period at the end of the great war between Athens and Sparta. He then served as a mercenary soldier, first for the Persian prince Cyrus and later for the Spartans. He wrote a range of books: histories of the period, philosophical memoirs of Socrates, biographies, and practical handbooks on subjects such as hunting and horsemanship. His best-known work is the *Anabasis* ('Ascent'), the story of the 10,000 Greek mercenaries who fought for Cyrus and who, after his defeat at Cunaxa in 401 BC, made a hazardous journey (under Xenophon's leadership) back to the Greek world by way of the Black Sea, which they famously greeted with cries of relief 'Thalatta, thalatta' ('The sea, the sea!').

ENDNOTES

In these notes I have used the following standard abbreviations for a few frequently cited ancient texts:

Aelian, *NA* (*De natura animalium / On Animals*), *VH* (*Varia historia / Miscellany*)
Aristotle, *HA* (*Historia animalium / History of Animals*), *GA* (*De generatione animalium / Generation of Animals*), *PA* (*De partibus animalium / Parts of Animals*)
Pliny, *NH* (*Naturalis historia / Natural History*)

I have made great use throughout of the following secondary works:

On birds in the ancient world:
Arnott, W. G. (2007) *Birds in the Ancient World: from A to Z*
Campbell, Gordon Lindsay (2014) (ed.) *The Oxford Handbook of Animals in Classical Thought and Life*
Martin, E. N. (1914) *The Birds and Animals of the Latin Poets*, Leland Stanford Junior University Publications: University Series, no. 13
Pollard, John (1977) *Birds in Greek Life and Myth*
Thompson, D'Arcy Wentworth (1895) *A Glossary of Greek Birds* (second edition 1936)
Toynbee, J. M. C. (1973) *Animals in Roman Life and Art*

On the status and distribution of birds in modern Greece and Italy:
Cramp, Stanley, Simmons, K., and Perrins, C. (1977–94) (eds) *Handbook of the Birds of Europe, the Middle East, and North Africa: birds of the Western Palearctic*, 9 vols
Handrinos, G. and Akriotis, T. (1997) *The Birds of Greece*
Mullarney, K., Svensson, L., Zetterstrom, D., and Grant, P. (2009) (eds) *The Collins Bird Guide* (second edition)

On birds in cultural history more generally:
Armstrong, E. A. (1958) *The Folklore of Birds*
Birkhead, Tim (2008) *The Wisdom of Birds: an illustrated history of ornithology*
Cocker, Mark (2005) *Birds Britannica*
Cocker, Mark (2013) *Birds and People*
Elphick, Jonathan (2014) *The World of Birds*
Ferber, Michael (2007) *A Dictionary of Literary Symbols* (second edition)
Mynott, Jeremy (2009) *Birdscapes: birds in our imagination and experience*

Tate, Peter (2007) *Flights of Fancy*

Thomas, Keith (1983) *Man and the Natural World: changing attitudes in England 1500–1800*

PART 1 BIRDS IN THE NATURAL WORLD

Epigraphs

p. 1 *Hirundo domestica* was Gilbert White's preferred designation for the barn swallow, which had been given its accepted scientific name, *Hirundo rustica*, by Carl Linnaeus ten years earlier in 1758. A few other early authorities like Blumenbach (1782) and Pallas (1811) also adopted White's version. White was especially fascinated by hirundines and swifts and always eagerly noted their arrival dates in his classic work *The Natural History and Antiquities of Selborne* (1789).

Introduction

p. 4 On the history of *phusis* as a concept, see Lloyd (1991) 417–34; Lloyd (2007) 131–50.

p. 4 On the history of the English word 'nature', see Lewis (1967) 24–74; Raymond Williams (1976) 184–89; Coates (1998).

p. 5 On birds as markers of time and place, see Mynott (2009) esp. ch. 7. On the decline of familiar migrants in Britain, see McCarthy (2009); Balmer et al. (2013) (eds); McCarthy (2015) esp. ch. 4; Maclean (2015); RSPB et al. *State of Nature* report (2016).

1 The Seasons

p. 8 On climate and the seasons in the ancient world generally, see Jeskins (1998); Sallares (2007). On the number of seasons, see the progression from Homer, *Iliad* v 749–51, Hesiod, *Theogony* 901, *Homeric Hymn* (to Demeter) 11 398–400, and Alcman fr. 20, through to Lucretius, *De rerum natura* v 737–47 and Horace, *Odes* iv 7.1–12. For a survey of related English folklore, see Groom (2013).

p. 9 On classical literary references to the autumn migration and possible differences in the perceptions of autumn then and now, see Martin (1914) 227–31.

p. 11 n.1 Simonides fr. 508 in D. A. Campbell (1991) (ed.). Aristotle, surprisingly, endorsed this fallacy (*HA* 542b4–24), and later writers like Dionysus (*On Birds* 11 8) embroidered it further, suggesting that kingfishers actually nested on the sea.

p. 11 n.2 For Latin references to 'cuckoldry', see Plautus, *Asinaria* 923, *Pseudolus* 96, and *Trinummus* 425. For the Greek sense of 'cuckoo' as stupid, see Aristophanes, *Acharnians* 598; Plato (comic poet) fr. 64; Dunbar (1995) (ed.) 491.

p. 12 caption to **1.3** Aristotle's remark about kingfishers 'hovering around boats' is at *HA* 542b22–25.

p. 14 The proverb is first recorded in a fragment (no. 33) from the fifth-century comic poet Cratinus, in Edmonds (1957) (ed.) and is repeated by Aristotle (*Nicomachean Ethics* I 7.16) and others. The Sappho fragment is no. 136 in D. A. Campbell (1982) (ed.); see also, on the nightingale as the bird of spring, Simonides fr. 586 in D. A. Campbell (1991) (ed.).

p. 14 This is a (free) combination and reconstruction of three fragments from Stesichorus' *Oresteia* nos. 210–12 in D. A. Campbell (1991) (ed.). These fragments all come to us through a scholiast's commentary on Aristophanes, *Peace* 797–81.

p. 15 caption to **1.5** For discussion of other interpretations of the St Petersburg swallow vase, see Immerwahr (2010); Steiner (2013). These authors draw particular attention to the *other* side of the vase as well as to an implied pederasty on the more familiar side.

p. 16 Democritus' weather calendar is reported by the astronomer Claudius Ptolemy (writing in Alexandria in the second century AD), in *Phaseis* ('Risings of the stars') II 66.23. See Graham (2010) (ed.) 600–03.

p. 16 n.2 On the 'bird winds', see Hippocrates, *Epidemics* VII 105 and [Aristotle], *Meteorologica* II 5–6, though [Aristotle], *De caelo* 395a4 seems to suggest that this is a northerly wind and Pliny, *NH* II 122 that it is a westerly one. For a discussion of these inconsistencies, see Morton (2001) 302–09. See also caption to **1.1**, p. 2 on the *chelidonia* ('swallow wind'). For a full discussion of the wind directions recognized in Aristotle, see Thompson (1918).

p. 18 On the subtleties of this passage in Virgil's *Georgics*, see Richard F. Thomas (1988) (ed.); there are also several borrowings from Lucretius worked into this (in particular *De rerum natura* I 250–64, II 992–1022, V 783–820).

2 Weather

p. 21 On the folklore of birds and weather forecasting, see Inwards (1898) 186–97; Armstrong (1958) 62–70, 84–88, 95–97; Marriott (1981) 129–65; Moss (1995) 22–28; Cocker (2013) index *s.v.* 'weather lore'.

p. 22 Marriott (1981). A surprising, if sceptical, source for several of them is Francis Bacon, in his *History of Winds* (1622). Alexandra Harris (2015) charts the history of creative responses to weather phenomena, real and imagined, in English culture.

p. 22 Edith Hall (2014) identifies seafaring as one of the defining characteristics of Greek character; see esp. pp. 1–6, 29–49, 75–99. Plato, at *Phaedo* 109b, refers to 'ants and frogs round a pond'. See also Beaulieu (2016).

p. 27 See Armstrong (1958) ch. 5, 'Bird of doom and deluge'; Tate (2007) 111–18.

p. 29 On the various Greek names for corvids, see Arnott (2007) 109–16. On similar confusions between rooks and crows in modern culture, see Cocker (2005) 411–13.

p. 30 On references to *liquidus* as a technical phonetic term, see the ancient grammarian Priscus I 2.11, II 2.13. See also the references to the *liquidae voces* of birds at Lucretius, *De rerum natura* II 146, V 1379. The C. Day Lewis translation of Virgil's *Georgics* was first published in 1940 and was reissued as an Oxford World's Classic in 1983. The H. R. Fairclough translation of the *Georgics* in volume 1 of his Loeb edition of Virgil was published in a revised edition in 1960. See also the commentary on this passage in Royds (1918) 40–44.

p. 30 See Theophrastus, *Weather Signs* 15–19, 28, 38–40, 52–53.

p. 32 Democritus fr. 276 in Graham, 2010; also cited in Theophrastus, *Weather Signs* 49.

3 Time

p. 33 See Lloyd (1991) 315: Landels (1979).

p. 33 n.1 On ancient conceptions of time, see Nilsson (1920); Onians (1951) 411–15; West (1978) (ed.) excursus II, 376–81; Whitrow (1988) chs 3–4; Bradley (2002); and, more generally, Lucas (2005). On the Greek historians 'inventing' historical time, see, for example Bernard Williams (2002) 149–71; Mynott (2013b) (ed.) lviii–lix.

p. 35 See, for example, 262–66, 322, and 359–61.

p. 36 n.1 See Cocker (2013) 63–68.

p. 36 For possible references to the cock as the generic 'bird', see Green (1985) 111, citing Euripides, *Iphigeneia in Aulis* 9f; Theocritus, *Idylls* xxiv 64; Aristophanes, *Birds* 481ff.; and other sources.

p. 39 n.1 On the longevity of the ravens in the Tower of London, see Cocker (2005) 428. But the record is held by a Swedish raven shot in 1839, which was claimed to be 69 years old: see Dresser (1891–96) vol. 4, 569; Dunbar (1995) (ed.) 404; see Ratcliffe (1997) 214 for a more conservative estimate. Other classical references to the longevity of corvids include Horace, *Odes* III 17.12–13; Ovid, *Metamorphoses* VII 274; Pliny, *NH* VII 153.

4 Soundscapes

p. 44 On literacy levels in an oral society, see Rosalind Thomas (1992). See also Havelock (1963); W. V. Harris (1989), who cites various census figures demonstrating the high illiteracy rates in various modern rural societies too (pp. 22–24). On ancient soundscapes generally, see D'Agnour (2007); Payne (2013); Hendy (2014) 51–102; Toner (2014) (ed.).

p. 44 The classic text, long quoted as the first instance of silent reading, is Augustine, *Confessions* VI 3. But this assumption has been challenged—for example, by Gavrilov (1997) and Burnyeat (1997). For an entertaining general discussion, see <http://kiwihellenist. blogspot.co.uk/2016/02/reading-silently-and-reading-out-loud.html>.

p. 44 On the sounds of spoken Greek and Latin, see Allen (1987); Allen (1989). For a (reconstructed) reading of a Sappho poem to illustrate the unfamiliar tonal effects, see and listen to <http://www.newyorker.com/books/page-turner/hearing-sappho>.

p. 45 On the sounds of ancient music, see Page (2000) 134; on ancient music more generally, see the selections of translated readings in Barker (1984) (ed.); Barker (1989) (ed.); West (1992); Murray and Wilson (2004) (eds).

p. 46 On noise in the city, see also Juvenal, *Satires* III 235–38; Martial, *Epigrams* XII 57; and (much later) Augustine, *Confessions* VI 8. But it did at least develop one's powers of concentration, according to Dio Chrysostom, *Discourses* XX 9–10.

p. 48 n.1 On the identity of the *ololugon*, Aristotle, *HA* 536a11–14 is clearly referring to a frog, and that is also the interpretation of Aratus, *Phaenomena* 948 (see p. 24) adopted in Kidd (1977); but see also Arnott (2007) 156–57 and the commentaries on this passage from Theocritus in Gow (1952) (ed.); Hunter (1999).

p. 49 The literature on nightingale mythology is vast, but see, in particular: Thompson (1895/1936) 16–22; Armstrong (1958) 186–92; Jeni Williams (1997); Ferber (2007) 136–40; Tate (2007) 81–87.

p. 51 For other nightingale references in poetry and drama, see, for example: Hesiod, *Works and Days* 208; Sappho fr. 136; Bacchylides 3.98; Simonides fr. 586; Aeschylus, *Agamemnon* 1142–48, *Supplices* 57–72; Sophocles, *Electra* 148–49, 1076–77 and *Ajax* 624–34; Euripides, *Hecuba* 337–38, *Helen* 1107–16, *Rhesus* 546–50 and *Phaethon* 63–67; Longus, *Daphnis and Chloe* III 12; Catullus 65.14; Ovid, *Heroides* XV 152–55; Seneca, *Hercules furens* 146–49; and the further discussion and references in Easterling (ed.), forthcoming commentary on Sophocles, *Oedipus at Colonus* lines 671–73.

p. 51 For the conventions of female lament, see Alexiou (1974); Barker (1984) (ed.) 63–71.

p. 51 For an anthology of nightingale poetry in English and thoughtful discussion, see Mabey (1993).

p. 52 On nightingales as social constructs, see Barker (2004); Cocker (2005) 340–43; Ferber (2007) 136–40.

p. 53 For other mentions of the kingfisher's 'song' in poetry, see Homer, *Iliad* IX 562; Meleager, 'Spring song', *Greek Anthology* IX 363 (see p. 17); [Lucian], *Halcyon* 1–2; further references in Thompson (1895) 29–32.

p. 53 The myth of the dying swan's song seems to occur first in Aeschylus, *Agamemnon* 1444–46 and then very regularly in both Greek and Latin imaginative literature: for example, in Euripides, *Heracles* 691–95; Aesop, *Fables* 233 in Perry (1952) (ed.); Ovid, *Metamorphoses* XIV 429–30. See further references in Thompson (1895) 106–07; Arnott (2007) 123; Ferber (2007) 214–15; and discussion in Cocker (2013) 90–92.

p. 53 Peter Pallas (1741–1811) was a German scientist who became professor of natural history at the Academy of Sciences in St Petersburg and travelled widely in Siberia and the Eastern Palearctic, identifying many new species that still bear his name (including six species of birds, various mammals and flowers, and a meteorite). His references to the whooper swan's physiology come in his two-volume *Zoographia Rosso-Asiatica* (1811) 210–15. There is anecdotal evidence of a similar experience with a dying whooper in Tomkies (1987) 26, and I am told that the phenomenon of apparent 'cries' from recently expired birds, if the air is squeezed out of them, is not uncommon (Tim Birkhead, personal communication).

p. 53 No more than 'possible' because these passages could also be translated to imply that the songs were *accompanied* by wing-beats. See Dunbar (1995) (ed.) 476–77.

p. 56 References to the cock's crow as 'cuckoo' include Aristotle, *HA* 631b28; Theocritus, *Idylls* VII 48, 123–24. See also Arnott (2007) 10.

p. 56 The crested and short-toed larks are presumably the species Aristotle is distinguishing at *HA* 617b20–23. Skylark, woodlark, and calandra lark are also found in the Mediterranean countries and are more musical but less common. See also the negative reference in the *Greek Anthology* IX 380, which Dioscorides may be quoting here.

p. 56 Blackbirds are referred to as 'songsters' (though no extended description is given of their songs) in epigrams in the *Greek Anthology* IX 76 (Antipater), IX 87 (Argentarius), IX 343 (Archias). See also the commentary in Gow and Page (1968) (eds) 82, 177, 466.

p. 57 n.1 For the 'kingfisher' names in Moschus, see Arnott (2007) 86–87, 93–94.

p. 58 On Isidore of Seville, see the edition and translation by Barney et al. (2006) in particular XII 7, pp. 263–69. On Latin folk etymologies more generally, see Maltby (1991).

p. 58 Varro's etymologies of bird names are at *De lingua Latina* V 75–76, VI 76. Suetonius' list of verbs representing animal calls are in the surviving fragments from Book X ('On nature') of his lost encyclopedic work *Pratum de variis rebus* (the 'Meadow of various things', that is 'Miscellaneous delights'). The Emperor Geta's word quizzes are reported in the *Historia Augusta*, 'Geta' V 4–8; there is a fuller list of the Latin verbs for various animal calls in McKeown (2010) 123. See also Aelian, *NA* V 51.

p. 58 There are examples of such transcriptions in Aristophanes, *Birds* 505, 507; Horace, *Satires* I 7.31 (cuckoo); Plautus, *Menaechmi* 654 (owl); Petronius, *Satyricon* 59 (cockerel).

p. 59 These suggested identifications occur in commentaries on Aristophanes in translations by W. Green (1879), W. W. Merry (1896), and B. B. Rogers (1930); and in Sommerstein (1987) and Dunbar (1995) (ed.).

p. 59 n.1 For modern research on the learning of bird song, see Thorpe (1961) 71–92; Armstrong (1963) 44–57; Catchpole and Slater (2008) 49–84; and (for a very technical survey) Zeigler and Marler (2008) (eds) 199–300.

p. 60 On the Beatrice Harrison story and other dubious cases, see Mynott (2009) 178–80, 312–17.

p. 61 Darwin (1871/2004) 108–09. See also Mithen (2005) 160–75, 283–86. Current research on this is referred to in <http://www.bbc.com/earth/story/20150512-birds-hold-the-key-to-language>.

p. 63 On references in tragedy to the impoverishment of a life without music, see, for example, Euripides, *Madness of Heracles* 676; Aeschylus, *Supplices* 681; Sophocles, *Oedipus at Colonus* 1221–23.

p. 63 On musical education, the key discussions are in Plato, *Republic* 397c–402a, 410a–412b, 423d–425a and *Laws* 653c–660c, 664b–671a, 700a–701b, 798d–799b, 799e–802e, 812b–e; in Aristotle, *Politics* 1337b23–36, 1338a9–37, 1339a11–1342b34. All these passages and many from other authors are translated with a helpful commentary in Barker (1984) (ed.); Barker (1989) (ed.). See also Galen's 'Character traits' in Singer (2013) (ed.) 163.

PART 2 BIRDS AS A RESOURCE

Introduction

p. 67 See Garnsey (1988) in particular Parts I and II and Conclusion.

p. 67 On conditions in the modern chicken industry, see Keith Thomas (1983) 143–50; Ellis (2007) 34–45; D. S. Murray (2008) 94; Cocker (2013) 64–5.

p. 68 Keith Thomas (1983) 17–50; G. H. Toulmin, *The Antiquity and Duration of the World* (1780; 1824 edition) 51–2; Henry More, *An Antidote against Atheism* (second edition 1655).

p. 69 On the ideal of self-sufficiency for both individuals and cities, see Thucydides I 37.3, II 36.3, 41.1, 51.3. On food supply generally, see Garnsey (1988).

5 Hunting and Fowling

p. 71 On Heracles and the Nemean lion (his first 'labour'), see Hesiod, *Theogony* 327–32; on the great Calydonian boar-hunt, see Ovid, *Metamorphoses* VIII 281–424; on Odysseus killing the boar of Parnassus, see Homer, *Odyssey* XIX 428–66.

p. 71 On these homosexual gift exchanges, see Dover (1989) 91–92; Lane Fox (1996) 131–32.

p. 71 n.1 The Greek term translated here as 'gallinule' is *porphurion* (*Birds*, line 707). There is a question whether this and *porphuris*, mentioned elsewhere in the text (line 304), are the same species. See further Arnott (2007) 197–99; Dunbar (1995) (ed.) 253–54, 449. The other possibility is that *porphurion* was just a confusingly generic term for all 'swamp-hens', including the much commoner moorhen (which one would in any case have expected to crop up more often in the literature, but is referred to only in occasional etymological references as a *pitulos*).

p. 72 On Spartan hunting practices and the dangers of making easy analogies with present-day hunting techniques and culture, see Cartledge (2003) 255–63.

p. 73 On cuckoos, see the brief reference in Epicharmus fr. 122, line 7 (R. Kassel and C. Austin (eds) *Poetae comici Graeci* vol. I (2001)); Pliny, *NH* X 11.27; but note also the caution about 'anomalous birds' on pp. 88 and 396.

p. 74 n.1 On later recipes for bird-lime, see MacPherson (1897) xxxi–xxxiii.

p. 75 There is a remarkable work on the history of some specialist devices by Arentsen and Fenech (2004), which has many illustrations of such equipment in use in the field. See also MacPherson (1897); Bub (1978); Shrubb (2013).

p. 80 A very similar poem with the same moral is attributed to Archias (*Greek Anthology* IX 343). The blackbird is again called a 'holy bird' in another epigram, by Rhianus (*Greek Anthology* XII 142).

p. 82 See Cocker (2013) 55–57 for more details and examples. See also Leigh Fermor (1958) 121–22, 136.

p. 83 n.2 Gladstone (1922) 76–77. See Cocker (2013) 56–57 for a more conservative assessment of the likely numbers. On the annual slaughter of birds, particularly migratory birds, in

Italy, Greece, and Malta today, see, for example, Jonathan Franzen, 'Last song for migrating birds', *National Geographic* CCXXIV (July 2013) 60–89.

p. 88 Douglas (1966) 69. See also my comments on the translation of the relevant species names in Mynott (2009) 272, and in chapter 17. Possible exceptions to the avoidance of owls and raptors as food items in the ancient world are mentioned by Aristotle, *HA* IX 618a; Pliny, *NH* X 69; Athenaeus 65e. But see also Oppian, *Halieutica* V 416ff. on the judgement that hunting dolphins was *apotropos* ('abominable').

6 Cooking and Eating

p. 91 On food, food supply, and cooking in the ancient world, see D. and P. Brothwell (1969); Gowers (1993); Wilkins, Harvey, and Dobson (1995) (eds); Dalby (1996); Garnsey (1999); Dalby (2003); Wilkins and Hill (2006) (eds); and esp. Chandezon (2015) 135–46.

p. 92 See Athenaeus 138e. On Spartan meal customs more generally, see Plutarch, *Sayings of the Spartans* (Lycurgus 1, 6) in *Moralia* III, and *Life of Lycurgus* X, XII.

p. 92 On bird markets in Athens, see Wycherley (1957) 197–98.

p. 93 See, for example, Cocker (2005) 417–18.

p. 94 Other references to thrushes in Greek comedy include Aristophanes, *Clouds* 339, *Peace* 1149, 1195, 1197, and *Birds* 1080; and the fragments quoted from Teleclides, Pherecrates, Plato, and Ephippus. There are also many other references to eating 'thrushes' (which may include various different thrush species) in such authors as Athenaeus (who makes some of these distinctions, quoting Aristotle, and who also quotes most of the above fragments at 64f– 65f); Plautus (e.g. *Bacchides* 792); and the Roman satirists Horace, Juvenal, and esp. Martial (e.g. *Epigrams* II 40.1, III 47.10, 58.26, IV 66.6, XI 21.5, XIII 50).

p. 94 The sources of the quotations in Athenaeus, *The Intellectuals' Dinner Party* are as follows: Telecides (268c), Pherecrates (269b), Nicostratus (65d), Ephippus (65c), Plato (441f), and Homer (65b).

p. 96 Edward Gibbon, *The History of the Decline and Fall of the Roman Empire* (1776–88) ch. 6.

7 Farming

p. 110 Osborne (1987) 26.

p. 110 For a general anthology on rural life in the ancient world, see K. D. White (1977). On agriculture and farming in ancient Greece, see Osborne (1987); on ancient Italy, see K. D. White (1970). For comparison, on the history of farming and its effects on birdlife in Britain, see Shrubb (2003).

p. 111 On birds as agricultural pests, see Aratus, *Phaenomena* 1094ff. (quoted on pp. 9–10); Aesop, *Fables* 194 (cranes), 297 (cranes), 298 (jackdaws, starlings, crane, crow) in Perry (1952) (ed.); [Aristotle] *Mirabilia* 119 (jackdaws); Virgil, *Georgics* I 119–20 (geese and cranes); Cicero, *On Old Age* XV 51 ('small birds' attacking grain); Pliny, *NH* XVIII 160; Plutarch, *Life of Demetrius* 28 (birds on grain).

p. 112 For early references to domestic geese, see, for example: Homer, *Odyssey* xv 160f.; Sophocles fr. 68 (A. C. Pearson (ed.) *The Fragments of Sophocles* vol. 3 (1917)), 'the tame goose and the dove upon the hearth'; Plato, *Gorgias* 471c and *Politicus* 264c.

p. 113 Varro, *De re rustica* I 1.7−9; Columella, *De re rustica* I 1.7. The most important figures before Cato inaugurated the Roman tradition seem to have been Hesiod, Xenophon, Archytus, Theophrastus, Hieron, and Epicharmus (the last two from Sicily), all of whom wrote in Greek and all of whom, except Hesiod, wrote in prose; and also Mago, a Carthaginian, who wrote a long and celebrated work in Punic. Two much later sources for Roman agriculture are Palladius (late fourth century AD) and the *Geoponica* (a Byzantine work, probably first compiled in the sixth century AD). K. D. White gives a full introduction to all these sources (1970) 14−46.

p. 116 Darwin (1859) ch. 1.

p. 117 See, for example, Cocker (2013) 64−65, and pp. 67 and 395.

p. 119 Daniel Defoe, 'Suffolk', in *A Tour through the Whole Island of Great Britain* (1724−26); see also Batty (1979) 151, who tells us that geese could be expected to cover 8 miles a day on such a march.

p. 123 Pliny, *NH* x 23; see also Varro III 6.1−2.

p. 124 On countryside cults in Greece, see Buxton (1994) esp. ch. 6, 80−113; Larson (2010).

p. 124 On various rural portraits, see Homer, *Iliad* XVIII 541−606 and *Odyssey* VII 112−32; Longus, *Daphnis and Chloe* II 3, III 5; Virgil, *Georgics* IV 125−46 and *Moretum*. On attachments to the countryside, see Thucydides II 14, 16−17; Aristophanes, *Peace* 1127−206; Virgil, *Georgics* II 458−512; Horace, *Satires* 2.6, *Epistle* I 10.13−25 (quoted here), and *Epode* II; Cicero, *On Old Age* xv 51−4, xvi 51−8; Martial, *Epigrams* III 58 (quoted here). See also, K. D. White (1977) *passim*.

p. 125 n.1 See Alcock (2001) 45−46. This evidence seems to contradict the belief Caesar recorded in his *Gallic War* V 12 (see p. 120).

PART 3 LIVING WITH BIRDS

Introduction

p. 129 An example of the argument from 'natural services' is Juniper (2013). The arguments are powerful but those deploying them risk basing the whole discussion on the econometric assumptions of their opponents. Examples of the argument from the intrinsic importance of the natural world are Wilson (1984); Wilson (2006); McCarthy (2015).

8 Captivity and Domestication

p. 131 On the archaeology of Hierakonpolis, see Rose (2010), reporting on the discoveries of the 2009 expedition led by Renée Friedman. See also Houlihan (1996) 4−5.

p. 133 On the history of the Tower of London menagerie and other early menageries, see Blunt (1976) 15−21; Grigson (2016) 42−44, 78−83. The reference to the 'Swedish owls' is in

John Strype's *Survey of the Cities of London and Westminster* (1720) vol. 1, 119: the reference to 'the Royal Theriotrophium' is in John Ray's *The Ornithology of Francis Willughby* (1678) 59.

p. 134 The *Encyclopédie méthodique par ordre des matières* ('Methodical encyclopedia by order of subject matter') was published between 1782 and 1832, as a revised and much expanded version of the original *Encyclopédie*, ed. Denis Diderot and Jean Le Rond D'Alembert (1751–72).

p. 134 The prospectus of 1825 is quoted, along with many other key documents, in Vevers (1976) (ed.). On the evolution of the role of zoos and public attitudes to wildlife more generally, see Jennison (1937); Elliston Allen (1976); Keith Thomas (1983); Jardine et al. (1996); Zimmerman et al. (2007).

p. 135 The peacock's feathers were proverbial for their beauty: see also Aesop, *Fables* 101, 472, 621 in Perry (1952) (ed.) and 328 in Gibbs (2002) (ed.).

p. 138 They also appear in Aesop, *Fables* 2, 101, 123, 126,129, 219, 298, 472. References here are to the numbering in B. E. Perry's monumental scholarly edition of *Aesopica* (1952) and his Loeb edition of the collections by Babrius and Phaedrus (1965). There is also a good selection of the fables in English translation in Gibbs (2002) (ed.).

p. 140 On Lesbia's 'sparrow', see the judicious summary by Arnott (2007) 227–28. Birkhead (2008) 380–81 favours the bullfinch option; Cocker (2013) 486–87 the erotic one; and McCarthy (2008) offers a general *jeu d'esprit* on the topic. But see the disapproving scholarly comment about such speculations in Goold (1983) (ed.) 4.

p. 140 Sappho's poem is quoted in the essay 'On literary composition' (§24) by Dionysius of Halicarnassus, and is fr. 1 in the standard edition of Sappho by D. L. Page (1955). See also Athenaeus 391e–f, quoting the same passage in Sappho. Other references associating sparrows with sexual lust include Aristophanes, *Lysistrata* 723; Xenophon (the novelist), *Ephesus* I 8; Pliny, *NH* x 137.

p. 141 On *passer* as a generic term, see Matthew 10:29–31; Bede, *A History of the English Church and People* II 13. See also Cocker (2013) 486–87.

p. 142 References to birds as presents include Aristophanes, *Birds* 707 (quail, gallinule, goose, peacock); Plato, *Lysis* 211e (quail, cockerel); Theocritus, *Idylls* V 96–97, 132 (pigeon); Athenaeus 373d ('birds'); Aelian *NA* XIII 25 (many species given to Indian royalty); Ovid, *Ars amatoria* II 269 (thrush, pigeon); Ausonius, *Letters* XVIII (thrushes, ducks). Other references to pets include Aristophanes, *Wasps* 129–30 (jackdaw); Aristotle *GA* III 6, 756b22–23 (jackdaw); Pliny the Younger, *Letters* IV 2 (parrot, blackbird, nightingale); Petronius, *Satyricon* 46 (goldfinch); Aelian, *NA* I 6 (goose, jackdaw), II 40 (eagle), v 28 (gallinule, cockerel), VI 29 (eagle), and VII 41 (goose); Aesop, *Fables* 244 (parrot); Plautus, *Two Captives* 1002–04 (jackdaw, quail, duck); Caesar, *De bello gallico* v 12.6 (goose in Britain); Pliny, *NH* x 26 (goose); Martial, *Epigrams* I 7 (dove); and the late author Agathias Scholasticus VII 204, 205 (partridge).

p. 142 n.2 On the auction prices at Pompeii, see Beard (2008) 178–79.

p. 143 On ancient references to bird mimics, see also Aristotle, *HA* VIII 597b25; Aesop, *Fables* 551 (raven); Plutarch 'Cleverness of animals', *Moralia* 973a–e (starlings, crows, parrots, jays); Aelian, *NH* VI 19 (jay, raven, wryneck, and others); Aelian, *VH* 14.30 ('songbirds'); Pliny, *NH* X 117−24 (parrots, magpie, jay, thrush, nightingale, raven, crow); Martial, *Epigrams* XIV 73 (parrot), XIV 76 (magpie); *Greek Anthology* IX 562 (Crinagoras, parrot), IX 280 (Apollonides, jay), VII 191 (Archias, jay); Porphyry III 4 (ravens, 'redbreasts' − possibly rock thrushes, jays, parrots); Sextus Empiricus, *Outlines of Pyrrhonism* I 73−74 (jays and others); Hippolytus, *Refutation* I 6.7−8 (parrots); Maximus of Tyre, *Lectures* 29.4.

p. 144 Summaries of research on bird mimicry can be found in Thorpe (1961) 113−20; Armstrong (1963) 53−56, 70−87; Catchpole and Slater (2008) 72−76; Marler and Slabbekoom (2004) (eds) 128−31. There is a lot still to learn about the biological function of mimicry in birds and the reasons why the capacity for it varies between species.

p. 144 On Mozart's starling, see West and King (1990); Birkhead (2008) 259−60. Mabey (1993) 37−39 retells a celebrated sixteenth-century story of nightingales mimicking human conversation but warns us that this may be 'an early urban myth'.

p. 144 On Ctesias, see Bigwood (1993); Nichols (2011).

p. 144 The 'literary pets' genre could be said to have started with Homer's touching descriptions of Odysseus' old dog recognizing his master on the latter's return home after some twenty years' absence (*Odyssey* XVII 291ff.) and of Penelope's geese (*Odyssey* XIX 535ff.). It was also a commonplace in Hellenistic epigrams: see those in the *Greek Anthology* VII 189−216, which feature cicadas, locusts, hare, partridge, magpie, swallow, dog, and dolphin, as well as an unidentifiable *elaios* bird, conceivably a rufous bush-robin (Arnott (2007) 43).

p. 148 n.1 Anecdote reported in Armstrong (1975) 63. Much greater cognitive feats were claimed by the scientist Irene Pepperberg for her African grey parrot, who had a 'vocabulary' of more than a hundred words, which he was said to apply with a high degree of referential accuracy (Pepperberg (2008)).

p. 148 n.2 We have two other versions of this same story. In one of them the birds gratify the man's wish, teaching other birds as well to say the words (Maximus of Tyre, *Lectures* 29.4). In the other, more complicated one, the birds (now identified as parrots) first comply, but the man then has his trick turned against him when a crafty Greek recaptures the birds and teaches them to expose him (Hippolytus, *Refutation* I 6.8). These stories and their relationships and sources are discussed in Catherine Osborne (1987).

9 Sports and entertainments

p. 152 On falconry in ancient India, see Aelian, *NA* IV 26 and Aelian's source, Ctesias, in Nichols (2011) 50, 65, 110−12, 144−45. Aelian gives a convincing description of falconry in this passage but an unconvincing account of the birds of prey used ('eagles, ravens and kites', only the first of which has ever been trained to perform this specialized role). On the history of falconry generally, see Macdonald (2006) esp. ch. 3.

p. 153 n.1 On the identification and classification of raptors in the ancient world, see Arnott (2007) 66−68 under *hierax*; Pollard (1977) 76−82. On the number of species currently resident in or regularly migrating through Greece, see Handrinos and Akriotis (1997) 127−48.

p. 154 This possibility was suggested to me by an experienced falconer, Richard Hines (personal communication, 6 July 2016), who finds the reported anecdotes highly implausible on practical grounds. Glasier (1986) 11 wonders if the practice as described was more akin to 'daring larks', where small falcons like hobbies were said to be used to frighten larks to make them cower on the ground and be more easily caught, but for technical reasons Hines is sceptical about that too.

p. 155 For example, Butler (1930), who says that 'the evidence of Martial is quite definite' (193) and goes on to quote further support from the Greek treatise on falconry by Demetrius of Constantinople, despite the fact that he was a medieval author writing in the thirteenth century. Butler claims that Demetrius must have had earlier sources such that 'one may fairly regard the sport of falconry as well established by that date [the second century AD]'. He was probably thinking of Oppian, Cynegetica 1 64 as Martial's source, but that one line is an even more slender reed than the Martial quotation and just refers to the kirkos ('hawk') as the 'companion to the hunter on his way into the woods'. More hawks from straw. On the scholarly issues about the text itself, see Leary (1996) (ed.) 285–86.

p. 155 n.1 On the 'Horus falcon' in ancient Egypt, see Houlihan (1986) 46–48; and on the very thin evidence for falconry, see Capart (1930) and Keimer (1950), who reference Adolf Erman's 1923 work, Die Literatur der Aegypter (English translation by Aylward M. Blackman (1927) see 189–90); but that work just cites a fragment of a New Kingdom (second millennium BC) text that contains the example of a 'bound raptor' (maybe a kite or a falcon) in an injunction to schoolchildren about discipline and training.

p. 156 On Graeco-Roman technology and the wheelbarrow mystery, see Lloyd (2002) 79–86, where he makes the point that the existence of slavery as a labour-saving device could be only a very partial explanation of the failure to innovate.

p. 156 Archery did, however, have a lower social status in warfare, if not among leisure activities, presumably because it was seen as the province of those who could not afford the heavy-duty hoplite weaponry and bear the brunt of a close-quarters battle; see Cartledge (1998) (ed.) 174. Perhaps this was partly also because of its oriental associations and its unmanly engagement from long distance rather than in the agon of hand-to-hand combat.

p. 157 On the cockfight as a cultural practice, see Cocker (2013) 69–73; for an anthropologist's interpretation of its deeper social significance, see Geertz (1973) on the Balinese cockfight.

p. 159 On cockfights and gambling, see Aeschines, Against Timarchus 1.53; Plutarch 'On the fortune of the Romans', Moralia 319f; Columella, VIII 2.5. On the use of garlic, see Aristophanes, Acharnians 165; Xenophon, Symposium IV 9. On the use of spurs, see Aristophanes, Birds 759, 1364–65.

p. 160 Other references to competitions involving partridges and quails include Aristophanes, Birds 1298–99, and Wasps 789; Plato, Lysis 211e; Alcibiades 1.120a; Athenaeus (Chrysippus) 464d; Plutarch, Life of Antony 319f; Ovid, Amores II 6.27; Pliny, NH XI 112; Columella VIII 2.5; Marcus Aurelius I 6; Pollux, Onomasticon IX 102, 107–09.

p. 162 n.2 On Commodus and the other statistics of slaughter, see Toynbee (1973) 21–22, citing Cassius Dio LI 22.5, LIV 26.1, LV 10.77–78, LVI 27.4–5, LIX 7.3, LX 7.3, LXI 9.1, LXVI

25.1, LXVIII 15; and *Historia Augusta*, 'Probus' XIX 1–8; see also Herodian I 15. For more sociological accounts, see Hopkins (1983) 1–30; Kyle (2014).

p. 163 n.1 On the abolition of cockfighting and other 'cruel sports', see Keith Thomas (1983) 41–50, 185–86; Malcolmson (1973) 118, 122, 135, and, on the class bias in this, 152–57.

p. 164 Geertz (1973) 417.

p. 166 For the agonistic culture in the rise of science, see Lloyd (1987b) 85–91, 97–101; and in sport, see Poliakoff (1987); Sansone (1988); Golden (1998). On the etymology of *agon*, see Poliakoff (1987) 181 n. 78; and esp. Nagy (1990) 23, 136–37, 385–87, 401–03. For some examples of the different uses of the word *agon* and its cognates in Greek sources, see Homer, *Iliad* XV 428; *Homeric Hymn* III 149–50, VI 19–20; Pindar, *Pythians* X 30, and *Olympians* I 7; Herodotus I 76.4, II 160.3–4, V 67.1, IX 33.3; Hippocrates, *On Joints* 58, 70; Thucydides I 22.4, III 104.3–6; Aristophanes, *Frogs* 785, 867, 873, 882, and *Wasps* 1479; Euripides, *Bacchae* 964, 975.

p. 166 On shared metaphors in sport and war, see Scanlon (1988) 230–44. Scanlon give a wide range of ancient references.

10 Relationships and Responsibilities

p. 167 Aesop's *Fables* are a rich source of moralizing stories about relationships in and between the human and animal worlds, and birds feature in many of them. For the form of Aesop references, see note to p. 138.

p. 169 n.1 References to the mud nests of 'swallows' in the *Greek Anthology*, for example, include X 2 (Antipater of Sidon), X 4 (Argentarius), X 5 (Thyillus). The barn swallow (*Hirundo rustica*) isn't always clearly distinguished in such passages from the four other hirundines that occur in Greece in the summer (red-rumped swallow, and house, sand, and crag martins) or even from the swift, though sometimes a reference to plumage details or voice makes the identification clear in context. Pliny, *NH* 10.92–95 distinguishes barn swallow, house martin, and sand martin by the different kinds of nests they build.

p. 170 I have simply derived these statistics of occurrences from the very good indexes to Perry's Loeb edition of Aesop (Babrius and Phaedrus (1965)) and Alan Sommerstein's translations of Aristophanes (vol. 12 (2002)). In one or two cases I have lumped species together (e.g. pigeon and ring dove), and I have often used generic terms (e.g. 'hawk', 'eagle') rather than guessing at individual species where they are unlikely to have been distinguished.

p. 171 See the detailed catalogue in Jashemski and Meyer (2002) (eds) 359–400. A comparable list of bird species is given in Antero Tammisto's study of the mosaics of the preceding period, Tammisto (1997); Tammisto analyses about seventy mosaics, which have 346 depictions of birds in them, representing in his view twenty-seven 'safely identifiable' species and seventy-two different taxa (though some of the proposed identifications seem very brave ones).

p. 171 An Indian mynah is presumably the species referred to in Aelian, *NA* XVI 3; see also the references to mimic 'blackbirds' at Aelian, *NA* VIII 24 and 'starlings' at Pliny, *NH* X 20. See more generally on mimics, pp. 143–48.

p. 172 On the jackdaw's taste for gold items, see Cicero, *In Defence of Flaccus* 76; Pliny, *NH* x 77; Ovid, *Metamorphoses* VII 466–68; 'jackdaw' becomes a proverbial rebuke to thieves (Lucian, *Runaways* 30).

p. 173 On kites taking sacrifices, see Aristophanes, *Birds* 865, 891–92, and *Peace* 1099–100; Aesop, *Fables* 324 (Perry); Ovid, *Metamorphoses* II 716–19. Birds frequenting (and sometimes infesting) temples were clearly a common phenomenon: see Herodotus, I 159; Aesop (Babrius 118, Perry 227); Aelian, *VH* v 17; Euripides, *Ion* 107, 154–77, 177–78, 1196–98.

p. 173 Corvids scavenging corpses or pecking out the eyes of live victims are mentioned at Aeschylus, *Agamemnon* 1472–74; Aristophanes, *Birds* 582–84, and *Acharnians* 92–93; Aristotle, *HA* VIII 593b14, x 609b7; Aelian, *NA* II 51; Catullus 108.5; Horace, *Epistle* I 16.48; Petronius, *Satyricon* 58; Juvenal, *Satires* VIII 251. For the saying 'Go to the crows', see Theognis 833; Aristophanes, *Birds* 27; Menander, *Dyskolos* 112.

p. 174 The many references to vultures as scavengers include Homer, *Iliad* IV 237, XI 162, XVI 836, XXII 42; *Odyssey* XI 578–79, XXII 30; Herodotus, *Histories* I 140; Euripides, *Trojan Women* 599–600, and *Rhesus* 513–15; Aelian, *NA* II 46; Dionysius I 5; Aristotle, *HA* 563a5–12; *Greek Anthology* IX 77 (Antipater); Lucretius IV 678–80, VI 1215–21. And in ancient mythology vultures were said to feed unceasingly on the liver of the unfortunate Prometheus, bound to his rock (Hesiod, *Theogony* 506–25; Aeschylus, *Prometheus Bound* 1021–25), and on that of Tityus, son of Gaia, in Hades (Homer, *Odyssey* XI 576–81; Virgil, *Aeneid* VI 595–600; Lucretius III 984–94; Ovid, *Metamorphoses* IV 457–58).

p. 174 On the sense of smell in vultures, see Birkhead (2012) 129–36.

p. 174 For the example of vultures in India, see Juniper (2013) 1–2, 131–36. Herodotus may be referring to a similar Persian practice at I 140.

p. 175 n.1 On the plague at Athens, see further Mynott (2013b) (ed.) 118–23 and nn. See also the parallel account in Lucretius VI 1215–21.

p. 175 There are similar Aesop stories at Babrius 13, 33 (the latter identifying jackdaws and starlings as the main pests).

p. 176 n.1 On the identity of the flying snakes, see also Rawlinson (1880) vol. I, 124 n.; Rosalind Thomas (2000) 139–42.

p. 177 Other references to the line hung with feathers (Latin *formido*) are at Oppian, *Cynegetica* IV 383–92; Virgil, *Aeneid* XII 749, and *Georgics* III 371; Seneca, *Phaedra* 46, and *De ira* II 11.5; Lucan, *Pharsalia* IV 437–38.

p. 178 The proverb of the eagle shot with his own feathers is also found at Aristophanes, *Birds* 808. See further Aesop, *Fables* 437 (Perry); Hesiod, *Shield of Heracles* 130–34.

p. 179 Pherecrates, *Old Women* (fr. 38) quoted in Athenaeus 395b.

p. 179 On pigeon-fancying, see the charming poem in the tradition of Anacreon (*Anacreonta* fr. 15), ed. M. L. West, *Carmina Anacreonta* (1984); and from the Roman period Varro III 7; Columella VIII 8; Pliny, *NH* x 53; Martial, *Epigrams* VIII 32. See also **3.5** and pp. 325–27, and Jennison (1937) 12–13 (for Greek examples), 102–05 (for Roman ones).

p. 181 n.1 On personal names given to birds and other pets in Greece, see Athenaeus 606b–e; McKeown (2013) 50–52. On the naming of horses and dogs in Rome, see Columella VII 12.13; Toynbee (1973) 106–24, 177–83.

p. 181 Aelian records anecdotes about acts of devotion between humans and birds in *NA* I 6 (goose, jackdaw), II 40 (eagle), V 29 (goose), VI 29 (eagle), VII 41 (goose), and *VH* XIII 31 (sparrow). See also Athenaeus 606b–e (cockerel, goose, peacock).

p. 182 Dissenting voices from within the Aristotelian tradition were his successors Theophrastus and Strato, and from outside it the Pythagoreans and Platonists like Plutarch and Porphyry. For the general intellectual background to this debate, see Sorabji (1993). For some later parallels, see Keith Thomas (1983) pts III, IV.

p. 182 On the calls and distribution of rock partridges and chukars, see Aristotle, *HA* 536b13–14; Aelian, *NA* III 35; Pliny, *NH* X 78; for a discussion and other references, see Arnott (2007) 174.

p. 183 See Lorenz (1952) chs 8, 11, on his raven Roah; see also Sorabji (1993) 83–86. If correctly reported, this may have been an example of what ethologists call 'insight learning', see Birkhead, Wimpenny and Montgomerie (2014) 308–10; or perhaps it is more a result of the raven's 'mood' than any intended addressee (a suggestion by the raven expert, Bernd Heinrich, personal communication via Patrick Bateson). The capacity would be more unexpected in a partridge than a raven, but tame partridges crop up regularly in Aesop— for example at 23, 244, 361 (Perry) and 135 (Babrius)—and are described as 'musical' at 124 (Babrius). See also the sentimental epitaphs for pet partridges in the *Greek Anthology* VII 203–06.

PART 4 INVENTION AND DISCOVERY

11 Wonders

p. 191 On the later research by David Lack and others on 'Darwin's finches', see Birkhead, Wimpenny, and Montgomerie (2014) 43–54. On the myth surrounding Darwin's own discovery, see Sulloway (1982).

p. 192 A full account unravelling the urban myth about spinach is set out in Rekdal (2014). The myth of the origins is ironically perpetuated in Skabarek and McCormick (1998) 31.

p. 193 This example of misattributed kite folklore was spotted by Graham Huxstep, letter in *British Birds* 108 (March 2015) 178. The trail of references runs from Gurney (1921) 154 through David Lack (1943) 176 to Cocker (2005) 117, Carter (2007) 139, and Self (2014) 124. The original (misquoted) source is Aelian, *NA* II 43.

p. 193 Works in the genre of paradoxography include Aelian's *Varia historia* ('Miscellany'), [Aristotle], *Mirabilia* ('Wonders'), and other books of 'marvels' attributed to such shadowy authors as Palaephatus, Antigonus of Carystus, Apollonius paradoxographus, Phlegon of Tralles, and Heracleitus paradoxographus. See also Rosalind Thomas (2000) 135–67 on the ways in which Herodotus and the early natural philosophers and medical writers drew on and contributed to these reports of natural wonders.

p. 194 See Meinertzhagen (1959) 224–25 and the comments in Cocker (2013) 216–17. As an example of the fluidity of the Greek terms for birds, *trochilos* in other contexts also seems to refer to (1) a wren and (2) an edible wader of some kind, perhaps a smaller plover or a sandpiper. See further Arnott (2007) 247–48 for other ancient references. For the debunking of the story and a faked photo, see the blog by Adam Britton, dated 6 September 2009 <http://crocodilian.blogspot.co.uk/2009/09/crocodile-myths-1-curious-trochilus.html>.

p. 195 For variations of the story about the cinnamon bird, see also Aristotle, *HA* 616a6–13; Aelian, *NA* II 34. But the Roman authors tend to connect cinnamon with the phoenix and its funeral pyre: see Ovid, *Metamorphoses* XV 391–407; Pliny, *NH* X 4, 97, XII 85; Statius, *Silvae* II 6.87–88. See Arnott (2007) 97–98 for other references; see Detienne (1972, English translation 1977) 14–20 for some comparative anthropological background.

p. 195 On the phoenix, see references in Arnott (2007) 191–92 and discussions in Pollard (1977) 99–100 and Cocker (2013) 117–19.

p. 196 Meinertzhagen (1954) 362.

p. 201 On Herodotus and his speculations about natural population control, see Rosalind Thomas (2000) 139–53, which also gives references to parallel discussions in the medical literature, attempting to explain why some human peoples are more prolific than others.

p. 201 For the tradition of stories about the white blackbirds on Cyllene, see [Aristotle], *Mirabilia* 831b14–17; Aristotle, *HA* 617a12–15; Aelian (citing Sostratus), *NA* V 27; Pliny, *NH* X 80. D'Arcy Thompson (1895) 101 quotes the German ornithologist Dr A. Lindenmayer, who claims actually to have seen them there (*Die Vögel Greichenlands* (1860) 30). See also the discussions in Pollard (1977) 35–36 and Peter Levi's translation, *Pausanias: Guide to Greece* II (1971) 413 n.

p. 202 On the distribution of snowfinches in Greece, see Handrinos and Akriotis (1997) 288.

p. 202 n.1 The happy phrase 'history in disguise' occurs in Spence (1921) 42.

p. 203 On the absence of a statistical relationship between magpie numbers and those of songbirds, see Birkhead (1991) and subsequent work summarized in Newson, Rexstad, Baillie, Buckland, and Aebischer (2010). See more generally: <http://www.rspb.org.uk/discoverandenjoynature/discoverandlearn/birdguide/name/m/magpie/effect_on_songbirds.aspx and http://www.bto.org/news-events/press-releases/are-predators-blame-songbird-declines>.

p. 203 On cryptozoology, see Heuvelmans (1995). On the 'wish to believe', see also Monbiot (2013) 49–61.

p. 204 On 'wonder' as a concept, see more generally Hepburn (1984); Mynott (2015).

12 Medicine

p. 206 For the general background, see Lloyd (1979) 10–58.

p. 206 For a general introduction to Hippocrates and translations of selections from this corpus of work, see Lloyd (1978) (ed.).

p. 207 On Empedocles, see Lloyd (1979) 33–38. Moreover, the writings we have under the name 'Hippocrates' incorporate sharply differing views on the proper scientific methodology. Compare, for example, the discussion in *Tradition in Medicine* (20) with that in *Regimen* (1 2) and see Lloyd (1978) (ed.) 37–43.

p. 208 n.1 Galen's enormous output is published in twenty-two volumes in the edition of C. G. Kuhn (1821–33), but even these are not comprehensive and many of the texts remain to be translated into English. A good selection of the key texts in English translation is in Singer (2006) (ed.).

p. 212 n.1 On Pliny's 'Encyclopedia', see Lloyd (1983) 135–49; Doody (2010) esp. 1–39.

p. 215 On swallow-stones and other medicinal folk remedies involving swallows, see Turner (2015) 110–16.

p. 216 For the surviving fragments of Sophocles' play *The Root-Cutters* (*Rhizotomoi*), see the Loeb edition *Sophocles*, vol. 3: *Fragments*, ed. Hugh Lloyd-Jones (1996) 269–70, fr. 534. On the root-cutters and the drug-sellers themselves, see Lloyd (1983) 119–45.

p. 216 On fallacies of reasoning specifically in medicine, see Skabarek and McCormick (1998); see also the notorious spinach case, pp. 191–92.

p. 217 On oracles, see Mynott (2009) 266–67, 289–91, 342 n.

13 Observation and Enquiry

p. 221 n.1 On Anaximander's 'book', see Kirk, Raven, and Schofield (1983) 102–03; see also the cautions there about the known titles of these early books. For another large collection of Presocratic texts in translation, see Graham (2010) (ed.).

p. 222 See Karl Popper, 'Back to the Presocratics', an address given in 1958, repr. in Popper (1963) 153–65, and the critical response by Kirk (1960), mediated by Lloyd (1991) 100–20; see also Attfield (2013). For the other references, see Schrödinger (1954/1996); Sagan (1980) 194–210; Hawking and Mlodinow (2010) 26–36. See also the physicist Steven Weinberg (2015) 3–14.

p. 223 n.2 On the smooth dogfish example and some of Aristotle's other discoveries, see Lloyd (1968) 79–81; Leroi (2014) 66–74. On the example of the cuckoo, see p. 239 n.2.

p. 223 For a very positive assessment of Aristotle as an empirical scientist by a modern biologist, see Leroi (2014). See also Lloyd (1979) 200–25; Lloyd (1983) 7–57; Lloyd (1987a); Lloyd (1991) 100–20.

p. 227 n.1 The key texts on these (mainly vernacular) taxonomic terms are *HA* 490a13ff., 490b7ff.; *PA* 642b5ff., 643a7ff., 643b9ff., 644a28ff. In the case of the 'main kinds' Aristotle does go on to invent various other groupings to which he attaches more technical names like 'bloodless / blooded' (= invertebrate / vertebrate), 'hard-shelled / soft-shelled' (= testacea / crustacea), 'softies' (= cephalopods), 'egg-laying tetrapods' (= most reptiles and amphibians), and so on. The ambiguity and inconsistency in his use of these terms has led to a large secondary literature. See in particular the introduction to the Loeb edition of the *History of*

Animals, ed. A. L. Peck (1965) pp. lxiv–lxix; Pellegrin (1982); Balme (1987); Lennox (1987); J. J. Hall (1991); Lloyd (1991) 1–26; Leroi (2014) 101–19, 272–79.

p. 229 n.1 On the number of species of birds named in Aristotle, see J. J. Hall (1991) 146 n. 77, where the estimated range in the different references is between 126 and 160. For an early work enumerating these, see Evans (ed.) (1903), an edition and translation of William Turner's volume on the bird names in Aristotle and Pliny (1544). See also Leroi (2014) 384–95.

p. 230 n.4 For the identification of the *kinklos* and other references, see Pollard (1977) 71; Arnott (2007) 96–97. The verb in question is used by Theocritus (*Idylls* v 117) in a homosexual context, a passage that in A. S. F. Gow's edition of 1950 is tactfully translated into Latin rather than English.

p. 231 For other references to variations in bird songs and calls, according to season, gender, location, age, and behaviour, see Lucretius, *De rerum natura* II 144–47, v 1078–86; Pliny, *NH* x 80; Aelian, *NA* XII 28; Plutarch, 'Cleverness of animals', *Moralia* 973a–b.

p. 231 On 'dualizers', see in particular Aristotle, *PA* 697a15–697b26 and the discussion in Lloyd (1983) 44–53. On Aristotle's rejection of dichotomous division as a means of uniquely identifying species, see *PA* 639b4–7, 642b5–644b22, and the discussions referenced at p. 227 n.1.

p. 233 On the identity of *apodes*, another little twist here is that the sand martin *Riparia riparia* (which is otherwise very similar to the crag martin *Ptyonoprogne rupestris*) does have a tiny tuft of feathers on the legs, but nothing like the trousered look of the house martin *Delichon urbicum*. Pliny, *NH* x 114 seems to be distinguishing *apodes* from swallows and describing them as swifts 'that never rest, except on the nest'; but he also uses the term *cupselus* as an alternative name, mirroring the confusion in Aristotle.

p. 234 Female bird song is rare in the temperate regions, but less so in the tropics: for examples, see Elphick (2014) 160. See also Armstrong (1963) 175–87; Catchpole and Slater (2008) 123–28; for a survey of recent research, suggesting that female bird song is quite a widespread phenomenon, see Garamszegi et al. (2007).

p. 234 The sources of these and other such myths are set out in Ferber (2007); Tate (2007); Cocker (2013). On 'halcyon days', see also p. 11.

p. 234 On the distribution of the subspecies of scops owl, see Arnott (2007) 217–18; Cramp, Simmons, and Perrins (1977–94) (eds) vol. 4 (1985) 454–65; Handrinos and Akriotis (1997) 203–04. There is a good deal of uncertainty still about migratory movements and winter ranges.

p. 235 I am indebted for these two examples to Arnott (1977), though it seems to me that the 'shrill calls' described by Aristotle could also be part of the chukar's repertoire. The field guide cited here is *The Collins Bird Guide* (second edition 2009) 54–55. See also, on the different partridge calls made in different locations, Athenaeus 390a–c.

p. 236 n.2 For the history of this adage and the uses of it by Linnaeus, Darwin, Alfred Marshall, and others, see Fishburn (2004).

p. 239 n.2 On the history of the discoveries about this aspect of cuckoo behaviour, see Nick Davies (2015) 155–58. See also [Aristotle], *Reported Marvels* 830b11–18 for another ancient reference.

p. 239 On differences of kind and degree between animals and humans, see in particular Aristotle, *HA* 588a16–588b3; Lloyd (1983) 26–43; Lloyd (2013). For more general discussions of associated difficulties with anthropomorphism, see Kennedy (1992); Mynott (2009) 23–27, 289–96; Mynott (2013a).

p. 240, caption to **4.10** Other versions of the 'Crow and the Pebbles' story are found in Aelian, *NH* 2.48; Pliny, *NH* 10.125; Plutarch, 'Cleverness of animals', *Moralia* 967a.

p. 241 The key discussion of the 'main kinds' of birds is in Book VIII of the *History of Animals*, concentrated in §3 (592b–594a). On the later influence of Aristotle's categories, see esp. J. J. Hall (1991) 223–43. On the importance of the Ray–Willughby taxonomy, see Birkhead (2008) esp. ch. 1; Birkhead (forthcoming) ch. 8.

PART 5 THINKING WITH BIRDS

Introduction

p. 243 *Totemism*, English translation by Rodney Needham (1963) 89.

p. 244, caption to **5.1** See further details of the history of the engravings and publication of this image: <http://www.britishmuseum.org/research/collection_online/collection_object_details.aspx?objectId=3235714&partId=1>. The engraving, attributed to Bernard Picart (1673–1733), seems to be based on one of these.

p. 246 Such ideas are further explored in Mynott (2009) 262–96. See also Rowland (1978); Ferber (2007) *passim*.

14 Omens and Auguries

p. 250 For other references to these superstitions, see Sommerstein (1987) 244; Dunbar (1995) (ed.) 456–58; Dillon (1996) 100–01. For other examples of *ornis* (or *oionos*) as 'omen', see Homer, *Iliad* X 277, XII 243, XXIV 219; Herodotus IX 91; Pindar, *Pythians* IV 19, Aristophanes, *Wealth* 63; Euripides, *Orestes* 788; Thucydides VI 27. On the persistence of superstitions of this kind, see Keith Thomas (1983) 70–81; Groom (2013) 53–73.

p. 250 I have adapted some text here from Mynott (2009) 268–70. See also the discussions in Pollard (1977) 116–29; Dillon (1996) 99–121; Strunk (2014) 310–23.

p. 250 On other female augurs, see also Herodotus II 54–57 and the general discussions of divination in Price (1985) and Bowden (2005) 12–40.

p. 253 On left / right as a category of opposites in primitive thought, see Lloyd (1966) 38–41.

p. 254 On the Aeschylus legend, see Aelian, *NA* VII 16; Pollard (1948).

p. 254 Other raptor references in Homer include *Iliad* VII 58–60, VIII 247f., XII 200–08, 231–40, XIII 821–3, 831f., XXIV 315–21, and *Odyssey* II 146–60, XV 160–66. See also Aeschylus,

Seven against Thebes 24–29; Herodotus III 76; Xenophon, *Anabasis* VI 1. 23–24; Arrian, *Anabasis* II 3.3–6; and the many references in D'Arcy Thompson (1895) 1–10.

p. 255 The heron episode is at Homer, *Iliad* X 272–82. On the role of bird omens in founding new cities, see Pausanias IV 34.8; Callimachus, *Aetia* II 58–67; Pollard (1977) 122. The Alexander anecdote is recounted in Arrian, *Anabasis* I 25.

p. 256 On recent scientific investigations of the sense of smell in birds, see Birkhead (2012) 127–61. On raven myths more generally, see Armstrong (1958) 71–93; Tate (2007) 111–18; Cocker (2013) 383–90; and for an account by a modern author inclined to believe in some of this, see Nozedar (2006) 60–75.

p. 258 Other references in Latin literature include Ovid, *Metamorphoses* X 452–54; Seneca, *Hercules furens* 686–87; Propertius, *Elegies* IV 3.59–62. It is then a small step from superstition to magic, as in Horace, *Epodes* V 17–20; Columella X 348–50; Seneca, *Medea* 731–74; Lucan, *Pharsalia* VI 686–88; Propertius III 29; Ovid, *Fasti* VI 131–62. The secondary literature on owls in folklore is huge: more references from both classical and later Western literature are to be found particularly in Martin (1914) 44–45, 154, 200–03; Tate (2007) 91–99.

p. 260 See also the references in Aristophanes, *Birds* 480; Horace, *Odes* III 27.15–16; Virgil, *Aeneid* VII 187–91; Ovid, *Fasti* III 37; Strabo, *Geography* V 4.2. The fullest discussion of woodpeckers in world folklore is in Armstrong (1958) 94–112, but there is a more sceptical assessment of their role in classical cults in Pollard (1977) 172–77. See also Henig, Scarisbrick, and Whiting (1994) 78 (item 133).

p. 261 On the *collegium* of augurs and the invocation of Romulus, see Livy, *History of Rome* VI 41.4 (quoted here); Cicero, *On Divination* II 70, *On Duties* III 66, and *On Laws* II 19–21. See also the discussions in Beard, North, and Price (1998) vol. 1, 182–84, vol. 2, 166–72; Strunk (2014) 312–14.

p. 262 For these various procedures and the terminology, see Cicero, *On Divination* I 120 (*alites* and *oscines*), *On Laws* II 21 (observations *de caelo*), and *On Duties* III 65–66; Tacitus, *Annals* II 13, XV 30 (the *templum*); Livy, *History of Rome* X 40; Cicero, *On Divination* II 70–74 (the *pullarius* and the omens *ex tripudiis*).

p. 262 n.2 The story of Pulcher and the chickens is reported in Cicero, *On the Nature of the Gods* II 7; Suetonius, *On the Lives of the Emperors* (Tiberius) III 2.2. Cicero gives other cases of generals wilfully ignoring unwelcome warnings at *On Divination* I 74ff., in particular Flaminius, who also challenges the methodology (I 77).

p. 264 Similar criticisms of venality are directed at the famous seer Teiresias at Sophocles, *Antigone* 1055, and *Oedipus Tyrannus* 387–89; Euripides, *Bacchae* 255–57. For other references and a discussion of the quoted passage from Euripides, *Helen*, see Allan (2008) (ed.) 231–33.

p. 265 On the various expulsions of astrologers and others from Rome, see Beard, North, and Price (1998) vol. 1, 113, 161, 228–44.

p. 266 Evans-Pritchard (1937). I discuss this case at greater length in Mynott (2009) 289–91.

15 Magic and Metamorphosis

p. 267 Keith Thomas (1971) 800.

p. 268 On attempts to legislate against magical practices, see Beard, North, and Price (1998) vol. 1, 228–44; Ogden (2002) 275–99. For a classic literary defence against such a charge, see Apuleius, *Defence on a Charge of Magic* (*c.*AD 160), though the supposed charms used here were fish not birds. On definitions and interpretations of magic in the classical world more generally, see Gordon (2001).

p. 268 n.1 On ancient astronomers as astrologers, see for example Cicero, *On Divination* II 87; Pliny, *NH* II 95; and more generally Lloyd (1979) 4–8; Lloyd (1987b) 38–49.

p. 269 For classical references on Thessalian witches 'drawing down the moon', see Ogden (2002) 236–40.

p. 269 On erotic charms and the sources of these recipes, see Ogden (2002) 227–44.

p. 271 On the scarcity of wrynecks, see Hopkinson (1988) (ed.) 158; Handrinos and Andriotis (1997) 213. On wrynecks and the wheel, see Gow (1950) (ed.), second edition (1952) vol. 2, 41; Ogden (2002) 107–12, 240–42. For later interpretations of jinx magic, see Copenhaver (2015) 72–76.

p. 271 Crane dances are mentioned in Plutarch, *Lives* (Theseus) 21; owl dances by Aelian, *NA* 15. 28 and Athenaeus 391a.

p. 272 On the fidelity of crows, see also Aelian, *NA* III 9 (quoted on pp. 256–57).

p. 274 For Pliny's ambivalence on magical practices, see *NH* XXVIII 85, XXX 1–18, and other references given in Lloyd (1983) 140–41 n. 76.

p. 274 n.1 The various sources for the crow (raven) myth here include Eratosthenes, *Epitome* 41; Aratus, *Phaenomena* 448–49; Hyginus, *Astronomy* II 40; Ovid, *Fasti* II 243–66; Aelian, *NA* I 47. There is a helpful translation and discussion of the key sources for all these constellation myths in Hard (2015) (ed.) esp. 20, 56, 110–11.

p. 276 Aristotle's main discussions of metamorphosis come at *GA* 732a26–32, *HA* 551a13–552b26. The Greek word *metamorphosis* occurs first in a passage in the work of the geographer Strabo, first century AD (I 2.11), in a catalogue of 'wonders' in Homer's *Odyssey*. But although the actual word was not used until this late date there was a long Greek literary tradition on the topic itself: see Forbes Irving (1990); Buxton (2009). Two authors in particular produced reference works (now lost) on which Ovid will have drawn: Boios (date uncertain), *Ornithogonica* ('Bird origins') and Nicander (second century BC), *Heteroioumena* ('Transformations').

p. 277 The *OED* lists just a few earlier usages, which seem to occur in non-technical contexts: Osbern Bokenham (1447); Thomas More (1533); John Marston (1598); E.M. Bolton (1619).

p. 277 Ted Hughes, *Tales from Ovid* (1997) p. ix.

p. 278 For a comprehensive list of examples of metamorphosis into birds in classical myths, see Forbes Irving (1990) 223–60, and see his analysis of the defining characteristics of the bird stories (96–127). The similar story of the transformation of Lycaon (into a wolf) is an exception among the mammal stories.

p. 279 There are several other versions of the Tereus / Procne / Philomela myth. For a full analysis, see Forbes Irving (1990) 99–107. In an earlier Greek version the transformations of the sisters are reversed (see March (1988) 373–74 and Mynott (2009) 285–86).

p. 280 n.2 On the *meleagrides*, see Pliny, NH xxxvii 40–41 (citing a reference as early as Sophocles); Ovid, *Metamorphoses* vi 667–68; Aelian, *NA* iv 42; Strabo, *Geography* v 1.9, xvi 4.5; Varro iii 9.18–19; Athenaeus 654c, 655c–f. See also Pollard (1977) 94, 162–63; Arnott (2007) 138–40.

p. 280 Other escapist metamorphoses include Combe (Ovid, *Metamorphoses* vii 382–83); Ciris (viii 148–51); and Aesacus (xi 784–95), this last a more complicated case involving rescue from attempted suicide.

p. 280 On the 'war between the cranes and the pygmies', see Homer, *Iliad* iii 6–7; Aristotle, *HA* 597a4–9; Aelian, *NH* xii 59; Pliny, *NH* vi 70, vii 26, x 58. For a rationalization, see Graves (1955) vol. i, 56 n. 4, 194.

p. 283 On the 'birds of Memnon', see also Pausanias x 31.6; Aelian, *NA* v 1; Pliny, *NH* x 74; Arnott (2007) 140–41.

16 Signs and Symbols

p. 285 Ancient accounts of dreams include Homer, *Odyssey* xix 562–67 (matched by Virgil, *Aeneid* vi 893–96); Herodotus i 107–08, i 120–21, v 55–56, vii 12–18 (and many other cases of prophetic dreams); Theophrastus, *Characters* xvi 11; Lucian, *The Dream*. There are also more analytical discussions in Hippocrates, *Regimen* 4; Plato, *Timaeus* 71e–72b; two minor works attributed to Aristotle (*On Prophecy in Sleep* 462b–464b and *On Dreams* 458a–462b); Lucretius iv 757–822, 962–1036 (including an interesting discussion of animal dreams at 984–1010); Cicero, *On Divination* i 39–65, 119–48; Galen, *On Diagnosis in Dreams*. Lloyd (1987b) 30–37 summarizes the ancient medical contexts.

p. 286 The first vernacular translations of Artemidorus were: Italian (1540), French (1555), English (1563), German (1570). Freud seems to have read Artemidorus in the German edition of F. S. Krauss (1881). On the later history and use of Artemidorus' work, see more generally: Dodds (1951) 102–34; Foucault (1984) 4–36; Price (1986); Cox Miller (1994); Grafton, Most, and Settis (2010) (eds) 285–86. There is a modern edition of the *Oneirocritica* with text, translation, and commentary by Daniel E. Harris-McCoy (2012).

p. 287 n.2 For anecdotes about kites as rapacious scavengers, see Sophocles fr. 767; Aristophanes, *Birds* 891–92, 1622–25; Aelian, *NA* ii 47; and see pp. 172–73. For some modern parallels involving red kites in Britain, see Cocker (2005) 114–19.

p. 288 On the conflation of signification and causation, see Artemidorus ii 17 (the example of cormorants and seabirds), ii 20 (cranes and storks); there are similar confusions in other writers about weather phenomena (see chapter 2 and, for example, Aratus 918; Virgil, *Georgics* i 361).

p. 288 On ancient stork folklore, see Aristotle, *HN* 615b23–24; Aelian, *NA* iii 23, viii 20; Aristophanes, *Birds* 1353–57; Pliny, *NH* x 61. And for some modern parallels, see Cocker (2013) 120–25.

p. 289 On the cultural identity of the robin, see Mynott (2009) 33–4, 385 n. 34; Andrew Lack (2008).

p. 289 n.1 On Homeric similes, see Moulton (1977) 135–39; Edwards (1991) (ed.) 24–41. The number count of similes in Homer depends very much on how you define them; the statistics I quote refer only to the 'long similes' (there are another 240 'short' ones).

p. 290 On formal distinctions (or the lack of them) between similes and metaphors, see Buxton (2004).

p. 291 Examples of references to terms of endearment and abuse are (in sequence): Aristophanes, *Wealth* 1010–11; Plautus, *Asses* 666–67, 693–94; Aristophanes, *Knights* 1020; Athenaeus 99d; Euripides, *Andromache* 75; Plautus, *Persa* 409; Seneca, *De constantia* 17.1.

p. 291 n.1 On the explanation of these nicknames, the best guesses are in Dunbar (1995) (ed.) 639–44.

p. 291 Bats were sometimes thought of as a kind of 'night bird'. On the classification of bats, see Arnott (2007) 150–52 under *nykteris*. Aristotle placed them in a category intermediate between mammals and birds, see *Parts of Animals* 697b1–12; Aesop, *Fables* 172, 566 (Perry); and the riddle in Plato, *Republic* 479c.

p. 292 For the variant nightingale proverbs, see Theocritus, *Idylls* I 136, V 136; Lucian, *The Fisherman* 37.

p. 293 On the use of metaphors from flight, see Stanford (1936). On the topic generally Stanford remarks: 'of all stylistic devices metaphors are the most fugacious of interpretation in a foreign idiom' (1). On the various interpretations, both ancient and modern, of 'wingless words', see Stanford (1936) 136–37; Vivante (1975) 1–12.

p. 293 On cranes as the inspiration for Greek letter forms, see also Cicero, *On the Nature of the Gods* II 49.1–6; Lucan, *Pharsalia* V 711–16; Martial, *Epigrams* IX 12.7–8; Hyginus, *Fabulae* 277; Cassiodorus, *Variae*, 'Letter' 8.12; Isidore of Seville, *Etymologies* XII 7.14–15. Versions of this story are repeated in several later histories of folklore, often connected with other myths about the hero Palamedes or the god Mercury (Hermes), each of whom supposedly had a role in the invention of the Greek alphabet. See, for example, the Renaissance author Edward Topsell (1572–1625), *The Fowles of Heaven; or history of birdes*, originally unpublished but now available ed. Thomas Harrison and F. David Hoeniger (1972) 177–212.

p. 294 On 'winged boats', see Homer, *Odyssey* XI 125; Euripides, *Hippolytus* 752. These and other examples are discussed in Padel (1974).

p. 294 On the flight of souls, see for example Homer, *Odyssey* X 494–95, XI 219–23, XXIV 5–9; Plato, *Phaedrus* 246c–e; Virgil, *Aeneid* VI 292–94, 700–02. On the Pandora myth, see Hesiod, *Works and Days* 90–105. More generally, see Rowland (1978) pp. xii–xv; Padel (1992) 129–32.

p. 296 On the Battle of the Teutoburg Forest and the recovery of the Eagles, see Tacitus, *Annals* I 55–69; Cassius Dio, *History of Rome* LVI 18–24, LX 8; on the quasi-religious veneration of the standards, see Ovid, *Fasti* III 115–16, V 579–86; Ovid *Ex Ponto* II 8.69–70; Pliny, *NH* XIII 23; Silius Italicus, *Punica* VI 25–40; Tacitus, *Annals* I 39, II 17; Josephus, *The Jewish War* VI 316; Tertullian, *Apologeticus* XVI 8.

p. 296 On eagles as emblems, see Mynott (2009) 273–78, 342–44.

p. 298 For the Pindar legend about Delphi, see Strabo, *Geography* IX 3.6; Pindar fr. 54.

p. 298 On other erotic contexts, see, for example, the notes on homosexual gift exchanges (pp. 71–72) and on the swallow vase (p. 15); for examples involving herons, see Siron (2015).

p. 299 n.1 The Simmias poem and the metrical note are reproduced from the Loeb edition of *The Greek Anthology*, ed. W. R. Paton, vol, 3, XV 27.

p. 300 See Birkhead (2012) for a landmark study on how birds perceive the world; see Mynott (2013a) for some reflections on the language of metaphors. For the use made by some later authors of classical literary symbols and motifs, see Charpentier (2010).

p. 301 Carl Jung, *Wandlungen und Symbole der Libido* (1912); first English translation as *Psychology of the Unconscious* (1916).

PART 6   BIRDS AS INTERMEDIARIES

17 Fabulous Creatures

p. 306 Virgil's account of the 'Golden Bough' episode is at *Aeneid* VI 136–211. Curiously this is the only reference to the Golden Bough in classical literature. Its identity is obscure, though Virgil compares it to mistletoe at VI 205–09. The supposed effect of Avernus on birds is described at *Aeneid* VI 236–42 and Strabo, *Geography* V 4.5, and is disputed at [Aristotle], *Mirabilia* 839a12–26.

p. 307 On the school of thinkers most influenced by Frazer, see Ackerman (1991); for a summary of the criticisms later levelled at Frazer, see esp. 46–47.

p. 308 Aston (2014) 366. For twentieth-century examples of discussions of woodpecker cults, see Cook (1903); Cook (1904); Armstrong (1958) 94–112; Clare Lees (2002); and more generally Pollard (1977) 172–77.

p. 308 On the changing models of explanation, see Clifford Geertz, 'Religion as a cultural system', in Geertz (1973) 87–125; Gould (1985) 1–33; Lloyd (1987b) 1–49.

p. 310 There is a fuller listing of monsters and hybrids, with their genealogies, in Hesiod, *Theogony* 270–336. For entertaining literary accounts of these 'fabulous creatures', see Borges (1967); and T. H. White (1956), a translation of a twelfth-century Latin bestiary.

p. 311, caption to **6.3** For an alternative description of the Stymphalian birds, see Apollodorus, *Library of Greek Mythology* II 5.6. On their supposed identity, see Levi (1971) (ed. and trans.) 420–23; Benton (1972) 172–73; Pollard (1977) 98–99; Arnott (2007) 231–32.

p. 316 On birds as polluters of domestic buildings, see pp. 172–73. For birds in sacred sites and temples, see Herodotus I 159, II 64; Euripides, *Ion* 102–108, 154–160. The Harpies are described as 'obscene birds' at Virgil, *Aeneid* III 241, 262, as are the Furies (in the form of owls) at XII 876. A classic account of defilement, abomination, and exceptions to natural classifications is in

Douglas (1966) esp. ch. 3, 'The abominations of Leviticus', 51–71. See more specifically on 'unclean animals' in classical culture, Parker (1983) 357–65.

p. 316 On possible analogies from women's bodies and experiences, see Padel (1992) 99–113; Lowe (2015) 70–163.

p. 316 On the formation of the classical myths, see Kirk (1974) esp. 13–91; and for a judicious summary, see Buxton (1994) esp. 169–217.

p. 317 A modern bestiary of this kind is Henderson (2012), which takes its inspiration from both the medieval bestiaries and the witty tribute to them in Borges (1967).

p. 319 On butterfly numbers: for Britain, see Marren (2015) 10, 237–61; for Greece, see Pamperis (1997).

p. 319 On butterflies as 'little birds', see Beavis (1988) 121 n. 7.

p. 321 Thompson (1927) 153. On the symbolism of butterflies, see Davies and Kathirithamby (1986) 99–107; Marren (2015) 154–74.

p. 321 The original claim about the number of Eskimo words for snow was made by Franz Boas, in *The Handbook of American Indian Languages* (1911) 25–26; for the 'refutation', see Pullum (1991) 159–71. There have since been other claims and counterclaims. It seems to depend very much on what you count as a 'word' and which of the many Inuit languages you choose as your source.

p. 321 *Papilio* occurs at Ovid, *Metamorphoses* xv 374 in a funereal context. There are also several references in scientific treatises in the tradition of Aristotle, often with more reference to moths (Pliny, *NH* xi 65, 77, 112, xxi 81), though Pliny also mentions butterflies specifically as 'a sign of spring' at *NH* xviii 209.

18 Messengers and Mediators

p. 324 Aristotle, *Politics*, 1280b37.

p. 324 On the vocabulary and rituals of ancient sacrifice, see Faraone and Naiden (eds) (2012) esp. 1–10; Ekroth (2014). On the history of attitudes to animal sacrifice in the ancient world, see Sorabji (1993) 170–94; Beard, North, and Price (1998) vol. 2, 148–65; Villing (2017) 63–101.

p. 324 For some other references to birds as sacrifices, see Philip, *Greek Anthology* vi 231; Ovid, *Fasti* i 441–56; Pausanias, *Description of Greece* iv (Messenia) 31.9, vii (Achaea) 18.12; Suetonius, *Gaius* 22, 57; Macrobius, *Saturnalia* iii 8.4. On sacrifices of cockerels, see also Artemidorus V 9. 'Sacred birds' are mentioned in an Egyptian context by Herodotus at ii 65, 67.

p. 326 n.1 Pausanias mentions the guild of 'Doves' at Dodona in his *Description of Greece* x (Phocis) 12.3. Other references to doves as messengers or with divine connections include Euripides, *Ion* 1196–208; Virgil, *Aeneid* vi 190–204; Martial viii 32.

p. 328 On the 'Pythagorean' rules of abstinence, see Diogenes Laertius, *Lives of the Philosophers* viii 34–35; Kirk, Raven, and Schofield (1983) 230–31.

p. 329 n.2 The classic case is that of Melampus, described at Apollodorus, *Library of Greek Mythology* 1 9.11. For a sceptical reaction, see Pliny, *NH* x 137.

p. 330 For the comparison with Shelley, see Buck (1937) 138.

p. 333 The sources for Prodicus are all secondary and often much later. The key ones are translated and discussed in Guthrie (1969) 238–42.

19 Mother Earth

p. 335 See Lovelock (1979). Its subsequent scientific influence is briefly summarized in Lenton (2016).

p. 335 See Fairclough (1930); Glacken (1967). Schiller does go on to make some important distinctions between different classical authors, but Homer is his chief example of a 'naive' poet exhibiting a very different attitude to nature from that represented by later European sensibilities. The translation of the quotation from Schiller is based on the one used as an epigraph in Fairclough's book.

p. 337 Pericles delivered the famous 'Funeral Speech' in praise of Athenian democracy in the winter of 431–430 BC, at the beginning of the great war between Athens and Sparta (see Thucydides 11 34–37). Aspasia was reputed to have had a hand in drafting that and was hence a natural choice for Plato's literary invention in the *Menexenus*, which has various parallels of sentiment and phrasing.

p. 343 Andrew Marvell, 'The Garden', line 48.

p. 343 The idea of a *locus amoenus* became a literary trope in pastoral poetry. The earliest examples probably hark back beyond this Plato passage to Homer and his descriptions of the idyllic gardens of Alcinous (*Odyssey* vii 112ff.). See the discussions in the editions of the relevant titles in the series Cambridge Greek and Latin Classics: Coleman (1977) (ed.) 1–9, 22–23; Richard Thomas (1988) (ed.) vol. i, 244–63; Hunter (1999) (ed.) 12–17, 191–93; Younis (2011) (ed.) 95–97. For references to Ovid's *Metamorphoses* and a more general discussion, see Hinds (2002).

20 Epilogue

p. 350 On the decline of wildlife in modern Britain, see note to p. 5.

p. 351 On soil erosion and the *Critias* quotation, see Grove and Rackham (2003) 8–10, 288–89; on Mediterranean ecological history more generally, see Meiggs (1982); Jeskins (1998); Sallares (2007); Thommen (2009); Broodbank (2013).

p. 351 On hunting, see chapter 6, and on the exploitation of animals in circuses, see chapter 10. See also Hughes (2007) esp. 60–62, though I think he here exaggerates the likely effects on bird populations (as opposed to those on big mammals). On ancient attitudes to environmental questions more generally, see Hughes (1994) and its second edition (Hughes (2014)); Shipley and Salmon (1996) (eds); Westra and Robinson (1997) (eds); Eckerman (2017) 80–92. Hughes takes a very strong line on environmental degradation and argues that it was, in effect, responsible for 'the decline of classical civilisations'.

p. 352 n.1 On Respighi's recording of nightingales, see Mynott (2009) appendix 3, as a cautionary tale of what can go wrong on such occasions.

p. 352 On population sizes and urban birds, see pp. 50–52, 109–10, 168–72, 271, 288. See also Lamberton and Rotroff (1985).

p. 352 The Oxford survey was conducted in 2013 by Andy Gosler, lecturer in the Edward Grey Institute of Field Ornithology (Department of Zoology, University of Oxford) and director of the Ethno-Ornithology World Archive; the results will be published in a forthcoming article by Gosler and Tilling, 'Natural history knowledge in the UK: a formal measure of student competence'. For the statistics of the species in Aesop and Aristophanes and at Pompeii, see chapter 10 and appendix.

p. 353 On animal play-titles and costumes, see Green (1985); Rothwell (2007) 102–44, 187–211; Compton-Engle (2015) 110–24.

p. 353 n.1 See Arnott (2007) for the lexicon of ancient bird names. On onomatopoeic common names in English, see Mynott (2009) ch. 9, and esp. 61–2, 240, 260–61.

p. 355 The Herodotus references are at II 22 (dark skin) and III 12 (skull thicknesses). There is a good discussion of Herodotus' ethnographies and their relationship to larger fifth-century debates involving natural scientists and medical writers in Rosalind Thomas (2000) esp. chs 2–4.

p. 357 Quoted by Diogenes Laertius, *Lives of the Philosophers* VII 87.

p. 357 The key Stoic and Epicurean texts can be found in translation in Long and Sedley (1987) (eds) esp. vol. I, 57–65, 274–79, 323–32.

p. 358 n.1 On insects in ancient literature and myth, see Davies and Kathirithamby (1986); Egan (2014).

p. 358 For Plato's definition of man see *Politicus* 266e; and for the Diogenes anecdote, see Diogenes Laertius, *Lives of the Philosophers* VI 40.

p. 362 caption to **6.17** See also <www.cambridgegreekplay.com>; Easterling (1999).

Appendix

p. 363 Pollard (1977) 13 estimates that there are seventy-nine 'readily identifiable' species in *The Birds* alone but doesn't list them. My own Aristophanes lists are largely derived from Dunbar (1995) (ed.) and Sommerstein (2002), but tend to be more conservative. On some of Sommerstein's identifications, see Geoffrey Arnott's review in *Classical Review* 38 (1988) 21–13. See also chapter 10 and the note to p. 170.

p. 365 On a comparative study of bird images in mosaics, see note to p. 171.

p. 366 On the absence of the roller from classical literature, see Pollard (1977) 55; Arnott (2007) 27 under *Chalkis*.

BIBLIOGRAPHY

Ackerman, Robert (1991) *The Myth and Ritual School: J. G. Frazer and the Cambridge Ritualists*

Alcock, Joan P. (2001) *Food in Roman Britain*

Alexiou, M. (1974) *The Ritual Lament in Greek Tradition*

Allan, William (2008) (ed.) *Euripides: Helen*

Allen, W. S. (1987) *Vox Graeca* (third edition)

Allen, W. S. (1989) *Vox Latina* (second edition)

Arentsen, Herman and Fenech, Natalino (2004) *Lark Mirrors: folk art from the past*

Armstrong, E. A. (1958) *The Folklore of Birds*

Armstrong, E. A. (1963) *A Study of Bird Song*

Armstrong, E. A. (1975) *Discovering Bird Song*

Arnott, W. G. (1977) 'Some peripatetic birds: treecreepers, partridges, woodpeckers', *Classical Quarterly* 27: 335–37

Arnott, W. G. (2007) *Birds in the Ancient World: from A to Z*

Aston, Emma (2014) 'Part-animal gods', in Campbell, Gordon Lindsay (2014) (ed.) 366–83

Attfield, Robin (2013) 'Popper and Xenophanes', *Philosophy* 89: 13–33

Balme, D. M. (1987) 'Aristotle's use of division and differentiae', in Gotthelf and Lennox (1987) (eds) 69–89

Balmer, Dawn, et al. (2013) (eds) *BTO Bird Atlas, 2007–11*

Barker, Andrew (1984) (ed.) *Greek Musical Writings*, vol. 1

Barker, Andrew (1989) (ed.) *Greek Musical Writings*, vol. 2

Barker, Andrew (2004) 'Transforming the nightingale', in Murray and Wilson (2004) (eds) 185–204

Barney, Stephen, et al. (2006) *The Etymologies of Isidore of Seville*

Batty, J. (1979) *Domesticated Ducks and Geese*

Beard, Mary (2008) *Pompeii: the life of a Roman town*

Beard, Mary, North, John, and Price, Simon (1998) *Religions of Rome*, 2 vols

Beaulieu, Marie-Claire (2016) *The Sea in the Greek Imagination*

Beavis, Ian C. (1988) *Insects and Other Invertebrates in Classical Antiquity*

Benton, Sylvia (1972) 'Note on sea birds', *Journal of Hellenic Studies* 92: 172–73

Bigwood, J. M. (1993) 'Ctesias's parrot', *Classical Quarterly* 43: 321–27

Birkhead, T. R. (1991) *The Magpies*

Birkhead, T. R. (2008) *The Wisdom of Birds: an illustrated history of ornithology*

Birkhead, T. R. (2012) *Bird Sense: what it's like to be bird*

Birkhead, T. R. (forthcoming) *The Wonderful Mr Willughby*

Birkhead, Tim, Wimpenny, Jo, and Montgomerie, Bob (2014) *Ten Thousand Birds: ornithology since Darwin*

Blunt, W. (1976) *The Ark in the Park*

Borges, Jorge Luis (1967) *The Book of Imaginary Beings*

Bowden, Hugh (2005) *Classical Athens and the Delphic Oracle*

Bradley, Richard (2002) *The Past in Prehistoric Societies*

Broodbank, Cyprian (2013) *The Making of the Middle Sea: a history of the Mediterranean from the beginning to the emergence of the classical period*

Brothwell, D. and P. (1969) *Food in Antiquity*

Bub, Hans (1978) *Bird Trapping and Bird Banding* (English translation 1991)

Buck, D. (1937) *Mythology and the Romantic Tradition*

Burnyeat, M. F. (1997) 'Postscript on silent reading', *Classical Quarterly* 47: 74–76

Butler, A. J. (1930) *Sport in Classic Times*

Buxton, Richard (1994) *Imaginary Greece*

Buxton, Richard (2004) 'Similes and other likenesses', in Robert Fowler (ed.), *The Cambridge Companion to Homer*, 139–55

Buxton, Richard (2009) *Forms of Astonishment: Greek myths of metamorphosis*

Campbell, D. A. (1982) (ed.) *Greek Lyric Poetry*, vol. 1, Loeb Library

Campbell, D. A. (1991) (ed.) *Greek Lyric Poetry*, vol. 3, Loeb Library

Campbell, Gordon Lindsay (2014) (ed.) *The Oxford Handbook of Animals in Classical Thought and Life*

Capart, J. (1930) 'Falconry in ancient Egypt', *Isis* 14: 222

Carter, Ian (2007) *The Red Kite*

Cartledge, Paul (1998) (ed.) *The Cambridge Illustrated History of Greece*

Cartledge, Paul (2003) *The Spartans* (second edition)

Catchpole, C. P. and Slater, P. J. B. (2008) *Bird Song: biological themes and variations* (second edition)

Chandezon, Christophe (2015) 'Animals, meat and alimentary by-products', in John Wilkins and Robin Nadeau (eds) *A Companion to Food in the Ancient World*, 135–46

Charpentier, Isabelle (2010) 'Emblematics in ornithology in the sixteenth and seventeenth centuries', *Emblematica* 18: 79–109

Clare Lees, Anthony (2002) *The Cult of the Green Bird*

Coates, P. (1998) *Nature: Western attitudes since ancient times*

Cocker, Mark (2005) *Birds Britannica*

Cocker, Mark (2013) *Birds and People*

Coleman, Robert (1977) (ed.) *Virgil: Eclogues*

Compton-Engle, Gwendolyn (2015) *Costume in the Comedies of Aristophanes*

Cook, A. B. (1903) 'Zeus, Jupiter and the oak', *Classical Review* 17: 174–86, 268–78, 403–21

Cook, A. B. (1904) 'Zeus, Jupiter and the oak', *Classical Review* 18: 75–89

Copenhaver, Brian P. (2015) *Magic in Western Culture: from antiquity to the Enlightenment*

Cox Miller, Patricia (1994) *Dreams in Late Antiquity: studies in the imagination of a culture*

Cramp, Stanley, Simmons, K., and Perrins, C. (1977–94) (eds) *Handbook of the Birds of Europe, the Middle East, and North Africa: birds of the Western Palearctic*, 9 vols

D'Agnour, Armand (2007) 'The Sound of *Mousike*: reflections on aural change in ancient Greece', in Robin Osborne (ed.) *Debating the Athenian Cultural Revolution*, 288–300

Dalby, Andrew (1996) *Siren Feasts: a history of food and gastronomy in Greece*

Dalby, Andrew (2003) *Food in the Ancient World, from A to Z*

Darwin, Charles (1859) *The Origin of Species by Means of Natural Selection*

Darwin, Charles (1871/2004) *The Descent of Man, and Selection in Relation to Sex*, ed. James Moore and Adrian Desmond (Penguin Classics, 2004)

Davies, Malcolm and Kathirithamby, Jeyaraney (1986) *Greek Insects*

Davies, Nick (2015) *Cuckoo: cheating by nature*

Detienne, M. (1972) *The Gardens of Adonis* (English translation 1977)

Dillon, Matthew (1996) 'The importance of *oionomanteia* in Greek divination', in Matthew Dillon (ed.) *Religion in the Ancient World*, 99–121

Dodds, E. R. (1951) *The Greeks and the Irrational*

Doody, A. (2010) *Pliny's Encyclopedia*

Douglas, Mary (1966) *Purity and Danger*

Dover, Kenneth (1989) *Greek Homosexuality* (second edition)

Dresser, H. E. (1891–6) *History of the Birds of Europe*

Dunbar, Nan (1995) (ed.) *Aristophanes: Birds*

Easterling, P. E. (forthcoming) (ed.) *Sophocles: Oedipus at Colonus*

Easterling, Pat and Muir, John (1985) (eds) *Greek Religion and Society*

Easterling, Pat (1999) 'The early history of the Cambridge Greek play: 1882–1912', in Christopher Stray (ed.) *Cambridge Philological Society*, supplementary vol. 24, 27–47

Eckerman, Chris (2017) 'Ancient Greek literature and the environment: a case study with Pindar's *Olympian 7*', in John Parham and Louise Westling (eds) A Global History of Literature and the Environment, 80–92

Edmonds, J. M. (1957) (ed.) *The Fragments of Attic Comedy*, vol. 1

Edwards, Mark W. (1991) (ed.) *The Iliad: a commentary*, vol. 5: books xvii–xx

Egan, Rory (2014) 'Insects', in Campbell, Gordon Lindsay (2014) (ed.) 180–91

Ekroth, G. (2014) 'Animal sacrifice in antiquity', in Campbell, Gordon Lindsay (2014) (ed.) 324–54

Ellis, Hattie (2007) *Planet Chicken*

Elliston Allen, David (1976) *The Naturalist in Britain; a social history*

Elphick, Jonathan (2014) *The World of Birds*

Evans, A. H. (1903) (ed.) *Turner on Birds*

Evans-Pritchard, E. E. (1937) *Witchcraft, Oracles and Magic among the Azande*, ed. Eva Gillies (1976) (abridged edition)

Fairclough, H. R. (1930) *Love of Nature among the Greeks and Romans*

Faraone, C. A. and Naiden, F. S. (2012) (eds) *Greek and Roman Sacrifice: ancient victims, modern observers*

Ferber, Michael (2007) *A Dictionary of Literary Symbols* (second edition)

Fishburn, Geoffrey (2004) 'Natura non fecit saltum in Alfred Marshall (and Charles Darwin)', *History of Economics Review* 40: 59–68

Forbes Irving, P. M. C. (1990) *Metamorphosis in Greek Myths*

Foucault, Michel (1984) *The History of Sexuality*, vol. 3

Garamszegi. L. Z., et al. (2007) 'The evolution of song in female birds in Europe', *Behavioural Ecology* 18: 86–96

Garnsey, Peter (1988) *Famine and Food Supply in the Graeco-Roman World*

Garnsey, Peter (1999) *Food and Society in Classical Antiquity*

Gavrilov, A. K. (1997) 'Techniques of reading in classical antiquity', *Classical Quarterly* 47: 56–73

Geertz, Clifford (1973) *The Interpretation of Cultures*

Gibbs, Laura (2002) (ed.) *Aesop's Fables*, Oxford World's Classics

Glacken, C. J. (1967) *Traces on the Rhodian Shore*

Gladstone, Hugh (1922) *Record Bags and Shooting Records*

Glasier, Phillip (1986) *Falconry and Hawking*

Golden, Mark (1998) *Sport and Society in Ancient Greece*

Goold, G. P. (1983) (ed.) *Catullus*

Gordon, Richard (2001) 'Imagining Greek and Roman magic', in Valerie Flint et al. (eds) *Witchcraft and Magic in Europe*, vol. 2: *Ancient Greece and Rome*, 159–275

Gosler, A. G. and Tilling, S. M. (forthcoming) 'Natural history knowledge in the UK: a formal measure of student competence'

Gotthelf, A. and Lennox, J. G. (1987) (eds) *Philosophical Issues in Aristotle's Biology*

Gould, John (1985) 'On making sense of Greek religion', in Easterling and Muir (1985) (eds) 1–33

Gow, A. S. F. (1950) (ed.) *Theocritus* (second edition 1952)

Gow, A. S. F. and Page, D. L. (eds) (1968) *The Greek Anthology: The Garland of Philip*, 2 vols

Gowers, Emily (1993) *The Loaded Table: representations of food in Roman literature*

Grafton, Anthony, Most, Glenn, and Settis, Salvatore (2010) (eds) *The Classical Tradition*

Graham, Daniel W. (2010) (ed.) *The Texts of Early Greek Philosophy*

Graves, Robert (1955) *The Greek Myths*, 2 vols

Green, J. R. (1985) 'A representation of the *Birds* of Aristophanes', in *Greek Vases in the J. Paul Getty Museum*, 95–118

Grigson, Caroline (2016) *Menagerie: the history of exotic animals in England*

Groom, Nick (2013) *The Seasons: an elegy for the passing of the year*

Grove, A. T. and Rackham, Oliver (2003) *The Nature of Mediterranean Europe: an ecological history*

Gurney, J. H. (1921) *Early Annals of Ornithology*

Guthrie, W. K. C. (1969) *A History of Greek Philosophy*, vol. 3: *The Fifth-Century Enlightenment*

Hall, Edith (2014) *Introducing the Ancient Greeks*

Hall, J. J. (1991) *The Classification of Birds in Aristotle and Early Modern Naturalists*

Handrinos, G. and Akriotis, T. (1997) *The Birds of Greece*

Hard, Robin (2015) (ed.) *Eratosthenes and Hyginus: Constellation Myths*

Harris, Alexandra (2015) *Weatherlands: writers and artists under English skies*

Harris, W. V. (1989) *Ancient Literacy*

Havelock, Eric A. (1963) *Preface to Plato*

Hawking, Stephen and Mlodinow, Leonard (2010) *The Grand Design*

Henderson, Caspar (2012) *The Book of Barely Imagined Beings*

Hendy, David (2014) *Noise: a human history of sound and listening*

Henig, Martin, Scarisbrick, Diana, and Whiting, Mary (1994) *Classical Gems: ancient and modern intaglios and cameos in the Fitzwilliam Museum*

Hepburn, Ronald (1984) *Wonder and Other Essays*

Heuvelmans, Bernard (1995) *On the Track of Unknown Animals* (third edition)

Hinds, Stephen (2002) 'Landscape with figures: aesthetics of place in the *Metamorphoses* and its tradition', in Philip Hardie (ed.) *The Cambridge Companion to Ovid*, 122–49

Hopkins, Keith (1983) *Death and Renewal: sociological studies in Roman history*

Hopkinson, Neil (1988) (ed.) *A Hellenistic Anthology*

Houlihan, P. F. (1986) *The Birds of Ancient Egypt*

Houlihan, P. F. (1996) *The Animal World of the Pharaohs*

Hughes, J. Donald (1994) *Pan's Travail: environmental problems of the ancient Greeks and Romans*

Hughes, J. Donald (2007) 'Hunting in the ancient world', in Linda Kalof (ed.) *A Cultural History of Antiquity*, 47–50

Hughes, J. Donald (2014) *Environmental Problems of the Greeks and Romans* (second edition of Hughes (1994))

Hunter, Richard (1999) (ed.) *Theocritus*

Immerwahr, Henry R. (2010) 'Hipponax and the swallow vase', *American Journal of Philology* 131: 573–87

Inwards, Richard (1898) *Weather Lore*

Jardine, Nicholas, et al. (1996) *Cultures of Natural History*

Jashemski, W. F. and Meyer, F. G. (2002) (eds) *The Natural History of Pompeii*

Jennison, George (1937) *Animals for Show and Pleasure in Ancient Rome*

Jeskins, Patricia (1998) *The Environment and the Classical World*

Juniper, Tony (2013) *What has Nature Ever Done for Us?*

Keimer, L. (1950) 'Falconry in ancient Egypt', *Isis* 41: 52

Kennedy, J. S. (1992) *The New Anthropomorphism*

Kidd, D. (1977) (ed.) *Aratus*

Kirk, G. S. (1960) 'Popper on science and the Presocratics', *Mind* 69: 318–39

Kirk, G. S. (1974) *The Nature of Greek Myths*

Kirk, G. S., Raven, J. E., and Schofield, M. (1983) *The Presocratic Philosophers* (second edition)

Kyle, D. G. (2014) 'Animal spectacles in the ancient world: meat and meaning', in T. F. Scanlon (ed.) *Sport in the Greek and Roman World*, vol. 2, 269–95

Lack, Andrew (2008) *Redbreast: the robin in life and literature*

Lack, David (1943) *The Life of the Robin*

Lamberton, Robert D. and Rotroff, Susan I. (1985) *Birds of the Athenian Agora*, Publications of the American School of Classical Studies at Athens

Landels, John G. (1979) 'Water-clocks and time measurement in classical antiquity', *Endeavour* 3: 32–37

Lane Fox, Robin (1996) 'Ancient hunting: from Homer to Polybius', in Shipley and Salmon (eds) *Human Landscapes in Classical Antiquity*, 119–53

Larson, Jennifer (2010) 'A land full of gods', in Donald Ogden (ed.) *A Companion to Greek Religion*, 56–70

Leary, T. J. (1996) (ed.) *Martial Book XIV: the Apophoreta*

Leigh Fermor, Patrick (1958) *Mani*

Lennox, J. G. (1987) 'Kinds, forms of kinds and the more and the less in Aristotle's biology', in Gotthelf and Lennox (1987) (eds) 339–59

Lenton, Tim (2016) *Earth System Science: a very short introduction*

Leroi, A. M. (2014) *The Lagoon: how Aristotle invented science*

Levi, Peter (1971) (ed. and trans.) *Pausanias: Guide to Greece*, vol. 2

Lewis, C. S. (1967) *Studies in Words*

Lloyd, G. E. R. (1966) *Polarity and Analogy: two types of argumentation in early Greek thought*

Lloyd, G. E. R. (1968) *Aristotle: the growth and structure of his thought*

Lloyd, G. E. R. (1978) (ed.) *Hippocratic Writings*

Lloyd, G. E. R. (1979) *Magic, Reason and Experience*

Lloyd, G. E. R. (1983) *Science, Folklore and Ideology*

Lloyd, G. E. R. (1987a) 'Empirical research in Aristotle's biology', in Gotthelf and Lennox (1987) (eds) 53–63

Lloyd, G. E. R. (1987b) *The Revolutions of Wisdom*

Lloyd, G. E. R. (1991) *Methods and Problems in Greek Science*

Lloyd, G. E. R. (2002) *The Ambitions of Curiosity*

Lloyd, G. E. R. (2007) *Cognitive Variations*

Lloyd, G. E. R. (2013) 'Aristotle on the natural sociability of animals', in Verity Harte and Melissa Lane (eds), *Politeia in Greek and Roman Philosophy*, 277–93

Long, A. A. and Sedley, D. N. (1987) (eds) *The Hellenistic Philosophers*, 2 vols

Lorenz, Konrad (1952) *King Solomon's Ring*

Lovelock, James (1979) *Gaia: a new look at life on earth*

Lowe, Dunstan (2015) *Monsters and Monstrosity in Augustan Poetry*

Lucas, Gavin (2005) *The Archaeology of Time*

Mabey, Richard (1993) *Whistling in the Dark*, reissued as *The Book of Nightingales* (1997)

McCarthy, M. (2008) 'When is a sparrow not a sparrow?', *The Independent* (29 August)

McCarthy, M. (2009) *Say Goodbye to the Cuckoo*

McCarthy, M. (2015) *The Moth Snowstorm: nature and joy*

Macdonald, H. (2006) *Falcon*

McKeown, J. C. (2010) *A Cabinet of Roman Curiosities*

McKeown, J. C. (2013) *A Cabinet of Greek Curiosities*

Maclean, Norman (2015) *A Less than Green and Pleasant Land: our threatened wildlife*

MacPherson, H. A. (1897) *A History of Fowling*

Malcolmson, Robert W. (1973) *Popular Recreations in English Society, 1700–1850*

Maltby, Robert (1991) *Lexicon of Ancient Latin Etymologies*

March, Jenny (1988) *Dictionary of Classical Mythology*

Marler, P. R. and Slabbekoom, H. (2004) (eds) *Nature's Music: the science of bird song*

Marren, Peter (2015) *Rainbow Dust*

Marriott, Paul. J. (1981) *Red Sky at Night, Shepherd's Delight? Weather lore of the English countryside*

Martin, E. N. (1914) *The Birds and Animals of the Latin Poets*, Leland Stanford Junior University Publications, University Series, no. 13

Meiggs, Russell (1982) *Trees and Timber in the Ancient Mediterranean World*

Meinertzhagen, Richard (1954) *Birds of Arabia*

Meinertzhagen, Richard (1959) *Pirates and Predators*

Mithen, Steven (2005) *The Singing Neanderthals: the origins of music, language, mind and body*

Monbiot, George (2013) *Feral: searching for enchantment on the frontiers of rewilding*

Morton, Jamie (2001) *The Role of the Physical Environment in Ancient Greek Seafaring*

Moss, Stephen (1995) *Birds and Weather*

Moulton, Carroll (1977) *Similes in the Homeric Poems*

Mullarney, K., Svensson, L., Zetterstrom, D., and Grant, P. (2009) (eds) *The Collins Bird Guide* (second edition)

Murray, D. S. (2008) *The Guga Hunters*

Murray, Penelope and Wilson, Peter (2004) (eds) *Music and the Muses: the culture of 'mousike' in the classical Athenian city*

Mynott, Jeremy (2009) *Birdscapes: birds in our imagination and experience*

Mynott, Jeremy (2013a) 'Between science and sentimentality', in Andrea Row and Jane Warrilow (eds) *Things Unspoken* 1–9

Mynott, Jeremy (2013b) (ed.) *Thucydides*

Mynott, Jeremy (2015) 'Wonder: some reflections on Clare and Thoreau', *John Clare Society Journal* 34: 75–86

Nagy, Gregory (1990) *Pindar's Homer: the lyric possession of an epic past*

Newson, S. E., Rexstad, E. A., Baillie, S. R., Buckland, S. T., and Aebischer, N. J. (2010) 'Population changes of avian predators and grey squirrels in England: is there evidence for an impact on avian prey populations?', *Journal of Applied Ecology* 47: 244–52

Nichols, Andrew G. (2011) *Ctesias: On India. Translation and commentary*

Nilsson, M. P. (1920) *Primitive Time Reckoning*

Nozedar, Adele (2006) *The Secret Language of Birds*

Ogden, Daniel (2002) *Magic, Witchcraft and Ghosts in the Greek and Roman Worlds: a sourcebook*

Onians, R. B. (1951) *The Origins of European Thought*

Osborne, Catherine (1987) *Rethinking Early Greek Philosophy*

Osborne, Robin (1987) *Classical Landscape with Figures*

Padel, Ruth (1974) 'Imagery of the Elsewhere: two choral odes of Euripides', *Classical Quarterly* 24: 227–41

Padel, Ruth (1992) *In and Out of the Mind: Greek images of the tragic self*

Page, Christopher (2000) 'Ancestral voices', in Patricia Kruth and Henry Stobbart (eds) *Sound*, 133–50

Pamperis, L. N. *Butterflies of Greece* (1997)

Parker, Robert (1983) *Miasma: pollution and purification in early Greek religion*

Payne, Mark (2013) 'The understanding ear: synaesthesia, paresthesia and talking animals', in Shane Butler and Alex Purves (eds), *Synaesthesia and the Ancient Senses*, 43–52

Pellegrin, P. (1982) *Aristotle's Classification of Animals* (English translation 1986)

Pepperberg, Irene (2008) *Alex and Me*

Perry, B. E. (1952) (ed.) *Aesopica*

Perry, B. E. (1965) (ed.) *Babrius and Phaedrus*, Loeb Library

Poliakoff, M. B. (1987) *Combat Sports in the Ancient World: competition, violence and culture*

Pollard, John (1948) 'Birds in Aeschylus', *Greece & Rome* 17: 116–27

Pollard, John (1977) *Birds in Greek Life and Myth*

Popper, Karl (1963) *Conjectures and Refutations*

Price, Simon (1985) 'Delphi and divination', in Easterling and Muir (1985) (eds) 128–54

Price, Simon (1986) 'The future of dreams: from Freud to Artemidorus', *Past and Present* 113: 3–37 (reprinted with minor changes in Robin Osborne (2004) (ed.) *Studies in Ancient Greek and Roman Society*, 226–59)

Pullum, Geoff (1991) *The Great Eskimo Vocabulary Hoax and Other Irreverent Essays in the Study of Language*

Ratcliffe, Derek (1997) *The Raven*

Rawlinson, G. (1880) *The History of Herodotus*

Rekdal, Ole Bjorn (2014) 'Academic urban myths', *Social Studies in Science* 44: 638

Rose, Mark (2010) 'World's first zoo', *Archaeology: a Publication of the Archaeological Institute of America* 63 (1)

Rothwell, Kenneth S. (2007) *Nature, Culture and the Origins of Greek Comedy: a study of animal choruses*

Rowland, Beryl (1978) *Birds with Human Souls: a guide to bird symbolism*

Royds, T. F. (1918) *The Beasts, Birds and Bees of Virgil*

Ruggieri, Luciano and Festari, Igor (2005) *A Birdwatcher's Guide to Italy*

Sagan, Carl (1980) *Cosmos*

Sallares, Robert (2007) 'Ecology', in Walter Scheidel, Ian Morris, and Richard P. Saller (eds) *The Cambridge Economic History of the Greco-Roman World*, ch. 2

Sansone, D. (1988) *Greek Athletics and the Genesis of Sport*

Scanlon, T. F. (1988) 'Combat and contest: athletic metaphors for warfare in Greek literature', in S. J. Bandy (ed.) *Coroebus Triumphs*, 230–44

Schrödinger, Erwin (1954/1996) *Nature and the Greeks* (reprinted with new introduction 1996)

Self, Andrew (2014) *Birds of London*

Shipley, Graham and Salmon, John (1996) (eds) *Human Landscapes in Classical Antiquity*

Shrubb, Michael (2003) *Birds, Scythes and Combines*

Shrubb, Michael (2013) *Feasting, Fowling and Feathers; a history of the exploitation of wild birds*

Singer, P. N. (2006) (ed.) *Galen: Selected Works*

Singer, P. N. (2013) (ed.) *Galen: Psychological Writings*

Siron, Nicolas (2015) 'La jeune fille au héron: genre et érotique dans l'iconographie grecque (VIe–IVe siècle avant J.-C.)', *Clio: Femmes, Genre, Histoire* 42: 217–42

Skabarek, P. and McCormick, J. (1998) *Follies and Fallacies in Medicine* (third edition)

Sommerstein, Alan H. (1987) *The Comedies of Aristophanes*, vol. 6: *Birds*

Sommerstein, Alan H. (2002) *The Comedies of Aristophanes*, vol. 12: *Index*

Sorabji, Richard (1993) *Animal Minds and Human Morals: the origins of the Western debate*

Spence, Lewis (1921) *An Introduction to Mythology*

Stanford, W. D. (1936) *Greek Metaphor: studies in theory and practice*

Steiner, Deborah (2013) 'Swallow this: a pelike within late archaic song and visual culture', *Helios* 40: 41–70

Strunk, Peter (2014) 'Animals and divination', in Campbell, Gordon Lindsay (2014) (ed.) 310–23

Sulloway, Frank J. (1982) 'Darwin and his finches: the evolution of a legend', *Journal of the History of Biology* 15: 1–53

Tammisto, Antero (1997) *Birds in Mosaics: a study on the representation of birds in Hellenistic and Romano-Campanian tessellated mosaics to the early Augustinian age*

Tate, Peter (2007) *Flights of Fancy*

Thomas, Keith (1971) *Religion and the Decline of Magic: studies in popular beliefs in sixteenth- and seventeenth-century England*

Thomas, Keith (1983) *Man and the Natural World: changing attitudes in England, 1500–1800*

Thomas, Richard F. (1988) (ed.) *Virgil: Georgics*, 2 vols

Thomas, Rosalind (1992) *Literacy and Orality in Ancient Greece*

Thomas, Rosalind (2000) *Herodotus in Context*

Thommen, Lukas (2009) *An Environmental History of Ancient Greece and Rome* (English translation 2012)

Thompson, D'Arcy Wentworth (1895) *A Glossary of Greek Birds* (second edition 1936)

Thompson, D'Arcy Wentworth (1918) 'The Greek winds', *Classical Review* 32: 49–56

Thompson, D'Arcy Wentworth (1927) 'Natural science', in R. W. Livingstone (ed.) *The Legacy of Greece*, 137–62

Thorpe, W. H. (1961) *Bird-Song*

Tomkies, Mike (1987) *On Wing and Wild Water*

Toner, Jerry (2014) (ed.) *A Cultural History of the Senses in Antiquity*

Toynbee, J. M. C. (1973) *Animals in Roman Life and Art*

Turner, Angela (2015) *Swallow*

Vevers, Gwynne (1976) (ed.) *London's Zoo*

Vivante, Paolo (1975) 'On Homer's winged words', *Classical Quarterly* 25: 1–12

Villing, Alexandra (2017) 'Don't kill the goose that lays the golden egg? Some thoughts on bird sacrifices in ancient Greece' in Sarah Hitch and Ian Rutherford (eds)*Animal Sacrifice in the Ancient World*, ch. 3

Weinberg, Steven (2015) *To Explain the World: the discovery of modern science*

West, M. L. (1978) (ed.) *Hesiod: Works and Days*

West, M. L. (1992) *Ancient Greek Music*

West, M. J. and King, A. P. (1990) 'Mozart's starling', *American Scientist* 78: 106–14

Westra, Laura and Robinson, Thomas M. (1997) (eds) *The Greeks and the Environment*

White, K. D. (1970) *Roman Farming*

White, K. D. (1977) *Country Life in Classical Times*

White, T. H. (1956) *The Book of Beasts*

Whitrow, G. J. (1988) *Time in History*

Wilkins, John, Harvey, David, and Dobson, Mike (1995) (eds) *Food in Antiquity*

Wilkins, John and Hill, Shaun (2006) *Food in the Ancient World*

Williams, Bernard (2002) *Truth and Truthfulness: an essay in genealogy*

Williams, Jeni (1997) *Interpreting Nightingales*

Williams, Raymond (1976) *Keywords: a vocabulary of culture and society*

Wilson, E. O. (1984) *Biophilia*

Wilson, E. O. (2006) *Creation*

Wycherley, R. E. (1957) *The Athenian Agora*, vol. 3

Younis, Harvey (2011) (ed.) *Plato: Phaedrus*

Zeigler, H. P. and Marler, P. (2008) (eds) *The Neuroscience of Birdsong*

Zimmerman, Alexandra, et al. (2007) *Zoos in the 21st Century: catalysts for conservation*

PICTURE CREDITS

PUBLISHER'S ACKNOWLEDGEMENTS

We are grateful for permission to reprint extracts from the following copyright material as epigraphs.

The Authorized Version of the Bible (The King James Bible), the rights in which are vested in the Crown, reproduced by permission of the Crown's Patentee, Cambridge University Press.

Jorge Luis Borges with Margarita Guerrero: Foreword to the first edition of *The Book of Imaginary Beings* translated by Andrew Hurley (Jonathan Cape, 1970/ Penguin 1974, 1987), copyright © 1967 by Editorial Kier, S A, copyright © 1995 by Maria Kodama, translation copyright © 2005 by Penguin Group (USA) Inc, reproduced by permission of The Wylie Agency (UK) Ltd and Viking Books, an imprint of Penguin Publishing Group, a division of Penguin Random House LLC. All rights reserved.

C P Cavafy: 'Ithaka' translated by Evangelos Sachperogolou, from *The Collected Poems* (Oxford World Classics, 2007), reproduced by permission of Oxford University Press.

F H Hinsley: *British Intelligence in the Second World War* (abridged edition, Cambridge University Press, 1993), Crown © copyright, used under the terms of the Open Government Licence v 3.0.

Claude Lévi-Strauss: *Le totémisme aujourd'hui* (PUF, 1962), copyright © Presses Universitaires de France 1962, reproduced by permission of Presses Universitaires de France.

Keith Thomas: *Man and the Natural World: Changing attitudes in England 1500–1800* (Allen Lane, 1983), copyright © Keith Thomas 1983, reproduced by permission of Sir Keith Thomas.

Oxford English Dictionary (OED, 2e) Definition of 'winged words' reproduced by permission of Oxford University Press.

We have made every effort to trace and contact all copyright holders before publication. If notified, the publisher will be pleased to rectify any errors or omissions at the earliest opportunity.

INDEX OF BIRDS

Species are listed under the common English names and the italicized ancient Greek and Latin names, as referred to in the text. Many of these are generic rather than specific names (e.g. 'buzzard' rather than 'common buzzard') where the distinction was not made or is not relevant. Names in inverted commas (like 'figbird') refer to ancient descriptions of species whose identity is unclear.

Illustrations are indicated by an italic 'i' following the page number.

An italic 'n' indicates a footnote and the number after 'n' refers to the footnote number if there is more than one footnote on the page.

GENERAL INDEX

Entries in **bold** refer to passages quoted from ancient authors.
Illustrations are indicated by an italic '*i*' following the page number.
'*n*' indicates a footnote, the number after '*n*' refers to the footnote number if there is more than one footnote on the page.